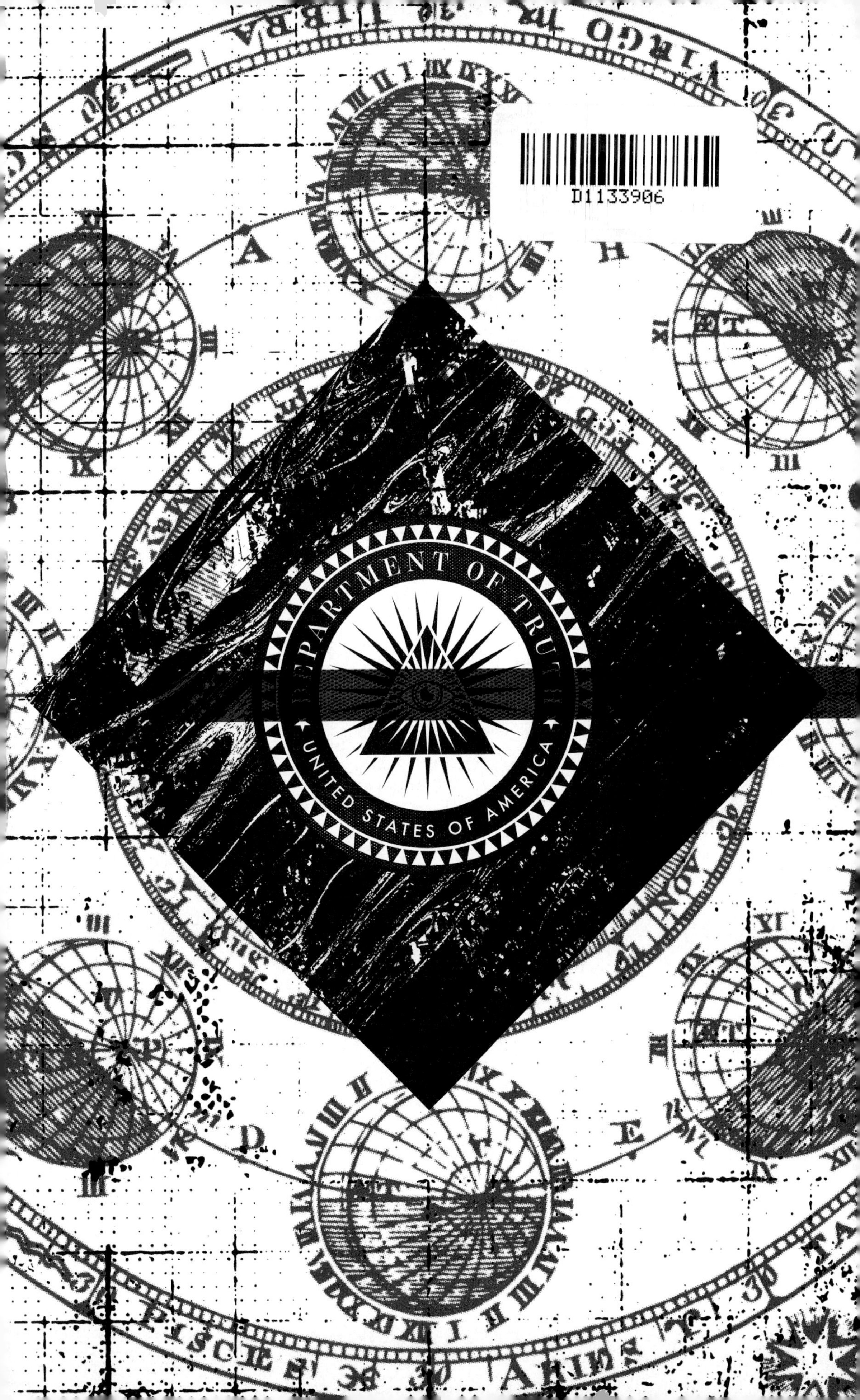
DEPARTMENT OF TRUTH
UNITED STATES OF AMERICA

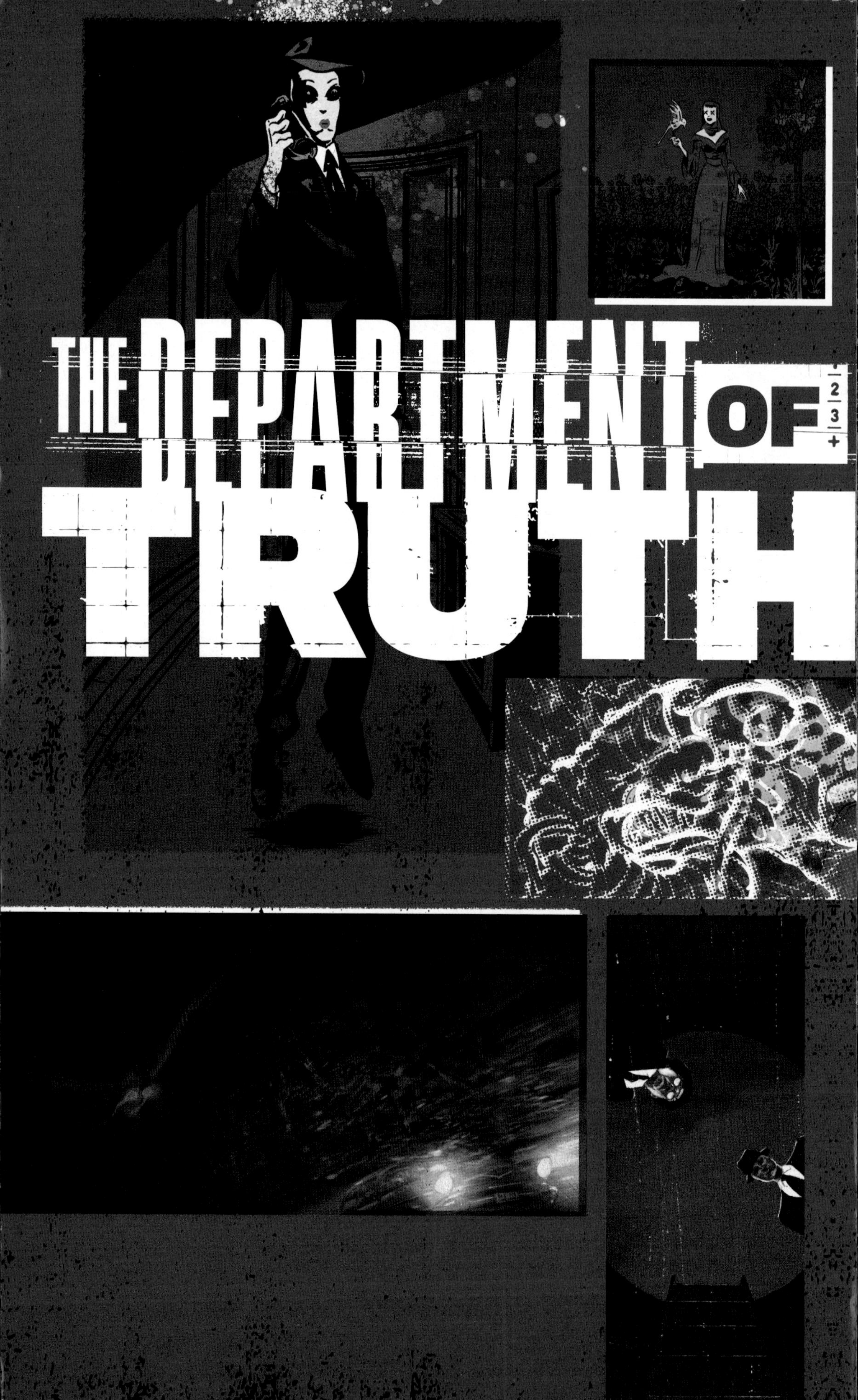
THE DEPARTMENT OF
TRUTH

VOLUME 03:

FREE COUNTRY

WRITER: >>>>>>
JAMES TYNION IV

ISSUE 6: >>>>>>
ART BY ELSA CHARRETIER
COLORS BY MATT HOLLINGSWORTH

ISSUE 7: >>>>>>
ART BY TYLER BOSS
COLORS BY ROMAN TITOV

ISSUE 14: >>>>>>
ART BY JOHN J. PEARSON

ISSUE 15: >>>>>>
ART BY DAVID ROMERO

ISSUE 16: >>>>>>
ART BY ALISON SAMPSON
COLORS BY JORDIE BELLAIRE

ISSUE 17: >>>>>>
ART BY JORGE FORNES
COLORS BY JORDIE BELLAIRE

LETTERER: >>>>>>
ADITYA BIDIKAR

DESIGNER: >>>>>>
DYLAN TODD

EDITOR: >>>>>>
STEVE FOXE

THE DEPARTMENT OF TRUTH CREATED BY
JAMES TYNION IV & MARTIN SIMMONDS

THE DEPARTMENT OF TRUTH, VOL. 3. First printing. April 2022. Published by Image Comics, Inc. Office of publication: PO BOX 14457, Portland, OR 97293.
ISBN: 978-1-5343-2119-9.

TINYONION TINYONIONSTUDIOS.COM

Saucer-type 1965

DEPARTMEN
UNITED STATE

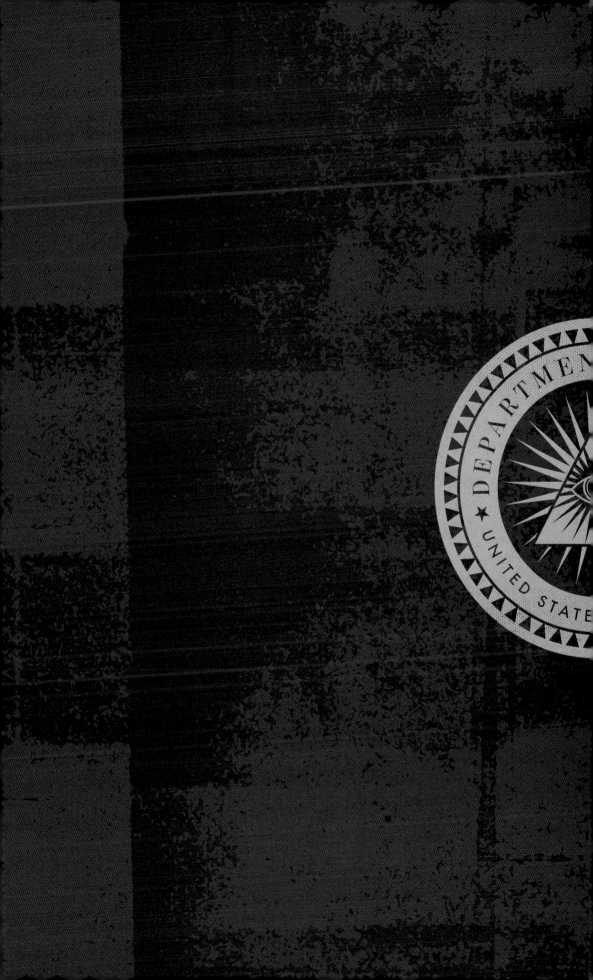

DEVIATION 1 /

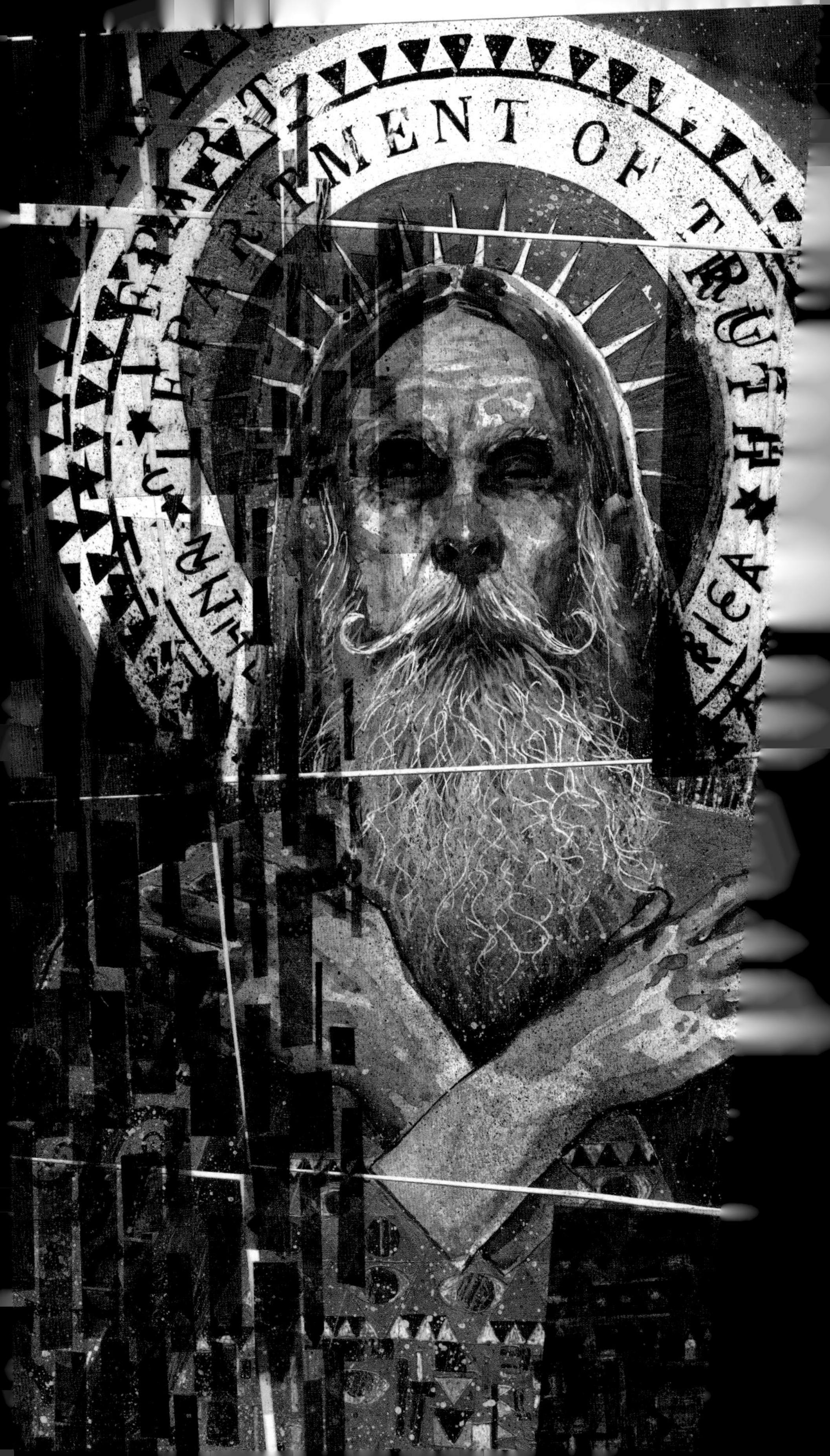
DEPARTMENT OF TRUTH

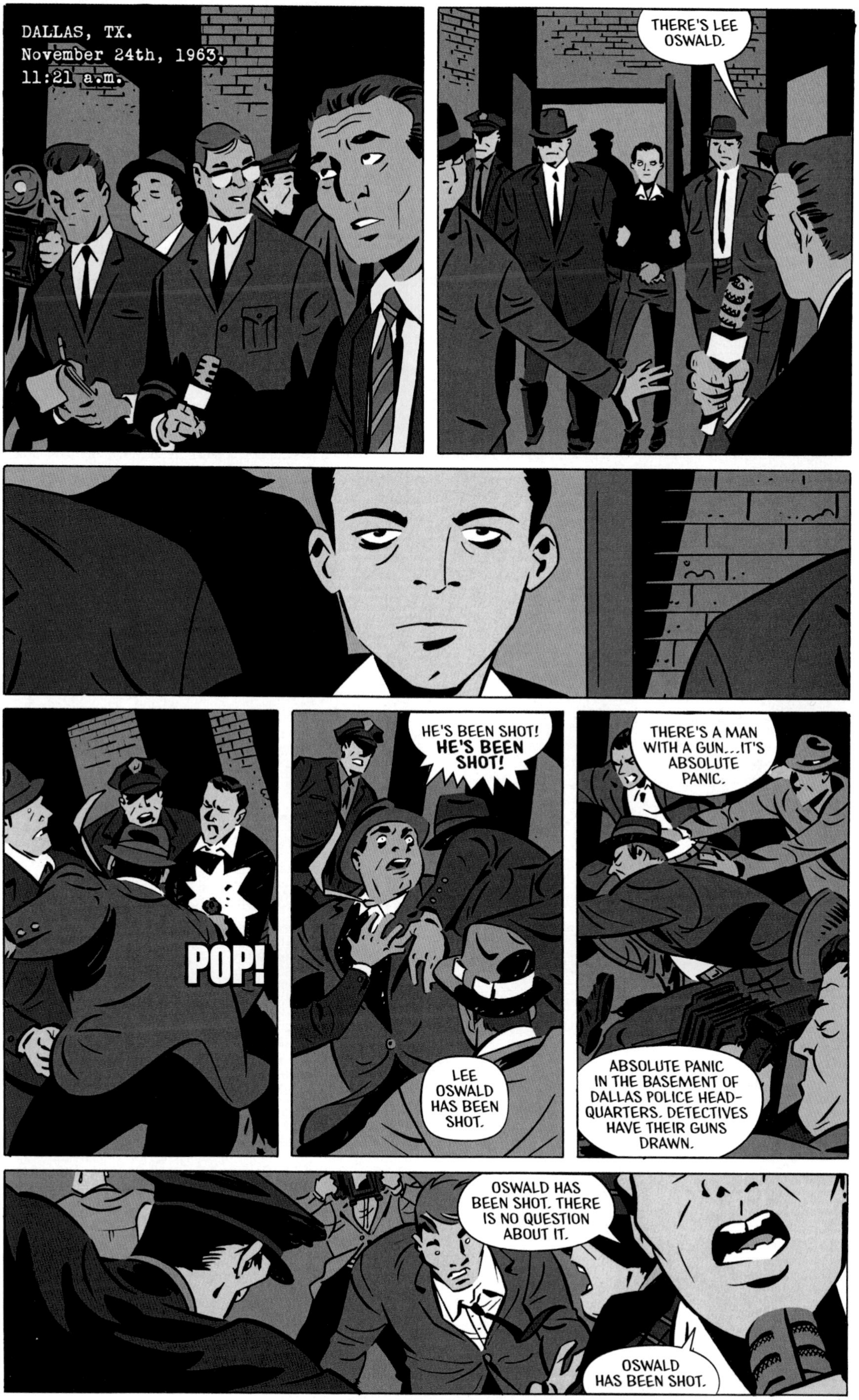
DALLAS, TX.
November 24th, 1963.
11:21 a.m.
THERE'S LEE OSWALD.
POP!
HE'S BEEN SHOT! HE'S BEEN SHOT!
LEE OSWALD HAS BEEN SHOT.
THERE'S A MAN WITH A GUN...IT'S ABSOLUTE PANIC.
ABSOLUTE PANIC IN THE BASEMENT OF DALLAS POLICE HEAD-QUARTERS. DETECTIVES HAVE THEIR GUNS DRAWN.
OSWALD HAS BEEN SHOT. THERE IS NO QUESTION ABOUT IT.
OSWALD HAS BEEN SHOT.

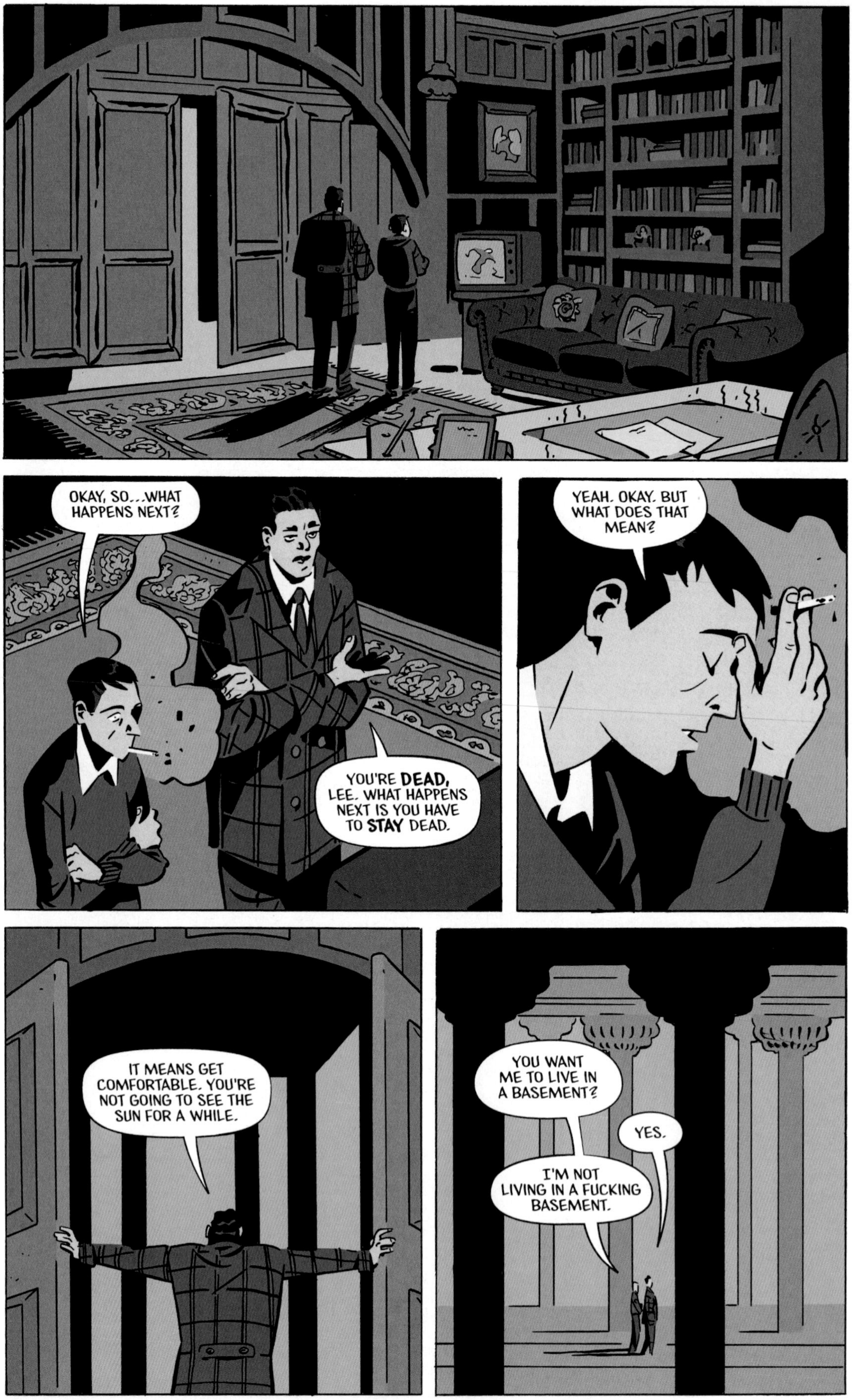
OKAY, SO...WHAT HAPPENS NEXT?
YOU'RE **DEAD,** LEE. WHAT HAPPENS NEXT IS YOU HAVE TO **STAY** DEAD.
YEAH. OKAY. BUT WHAT DOES THAT MEAN?
IT MEANS GET COMFORTABLE. YOU'RE NOT GOING TO SEE THE SUN FOR A WHILE.
YOU WANT ME TO LIVE IN A BASEMENT?
YES.
I'M NOT LIVING IN A FUCKING BASEMENT.

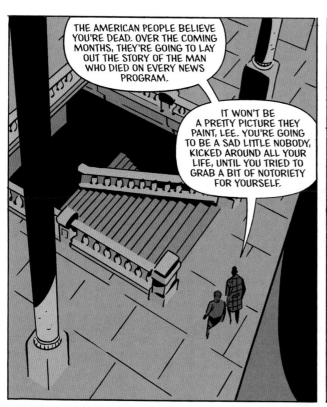

THE AMERICAN PEOPLE BELIEVE YOU'RE DEAD. OVER THE COMING MONTHS, THEY'RE GOING TO LAY OUT THE STORY OF THE MAN WHO DIED ON EVERY NEWS PROGRAM.

IT WON'T BE A PRETTY PICTURE THEY PAINT, LEE. YOU'RE GOING TO BE A SAD LITTLE NOBODY, KICKED AROUND ALL YOUR LIFE, UNTIL YOU TRIED TO GRAB A BIT OF NOTORIETY FOR YOURSELF.

BUT IT'S CRUCIAL THAT THAT STORY END WITH A VERIFIABLE DEATH. THAT'S WHY IT HAD TO HAPPEN OUT IN THE OPEN, ON LIVE TELEVISION, IN FRONT OF MILLIONS.

YOU ARE, AT PRESENT, ONE OF THE MOST RECOGNIZABLE PEOPLE IN THE COUNTRY. WE DO NOT WANT PEOPLE TO SEE YOU WALKING AROUND WASHINGTON DC.

THEN PUT ME IN A FUCKING CABIN IN THE WOODS, FAR AWAY FROM HERE.

THAT WOULDN'T SERVE MY PURPOSES.

IT'S TIME FOR YOU TO GO TO SCHOOL, LEE.

WHAT THE FUCK IS THIS PLACE, EVEN?

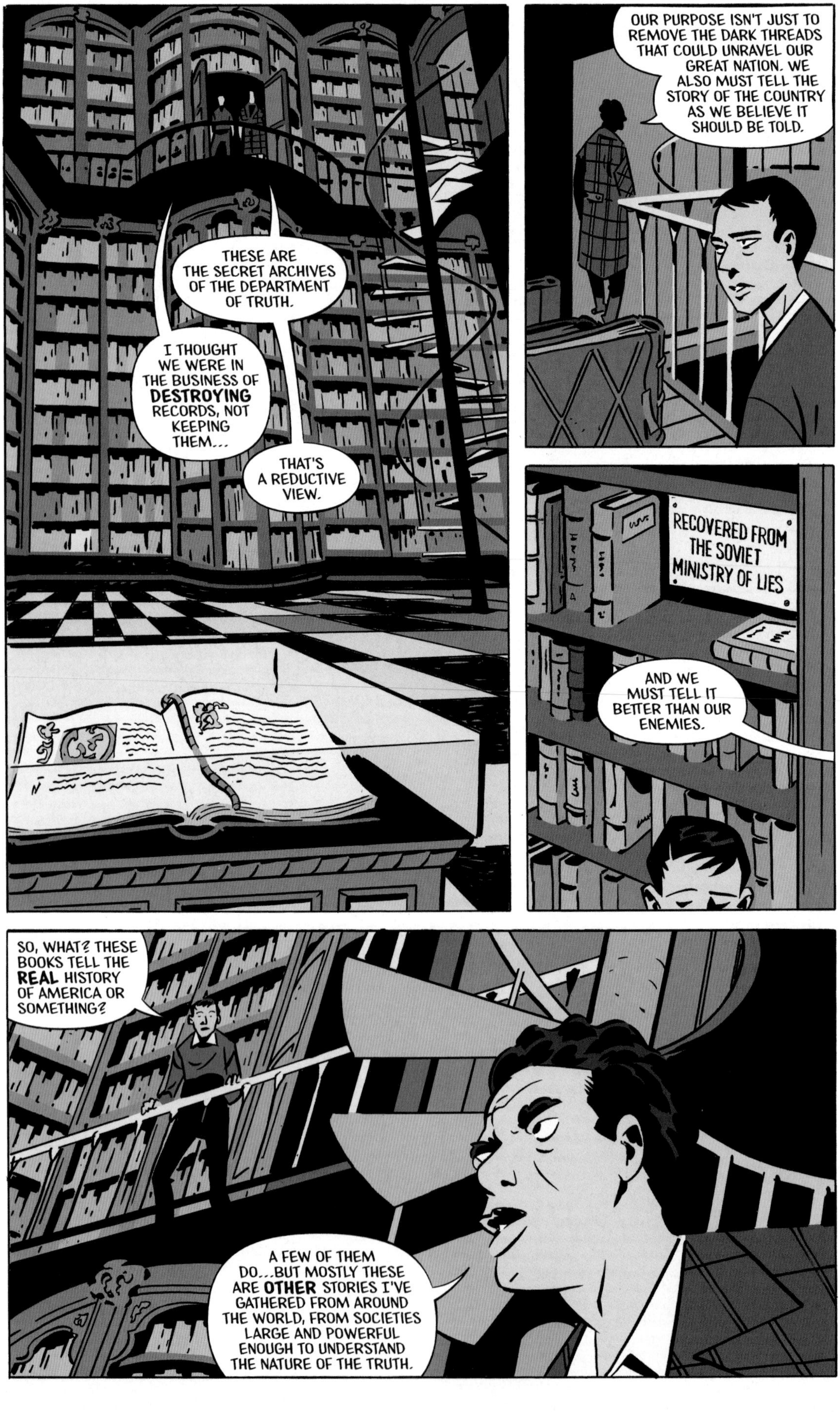
THESE ARE THE SECRET ARCHIVES OF THE DEPARTMENT OF TRUTH.
I THOUGHT WE WERE IN THE BUSINESS OF **DESTROYING** RECORDS, NOT KEEPING THEM...
THAT'S A REDUCTIVE VIEW.
OUR PURPOSE ISN'T JUST TO REMOVE THE DARK THREADS THAT COULD UNRAVEL OUR GREAT NATION. WE ALSO MUST TELL THE STORY OF THE COUNTRY AS WE BELIEVE IT SHOULD BE TOLD.
RECOVERED FROM THE SOVIET MINISTRY OF LIES
AND WE MUST TELL IT BETTER THAN OUR ENEMIES.
SO, WHAT? THESE BOOKS TELL THE **REAL** HISTORY OF AMERICA OR SOMETHING?
A FEW OF THEM DO...BUT MOSTLY THESE ARE **OTHER** STORIES I'VE GATHERED FROM AROUND THE WORLD, FROM SOCIETIES LARGE AND POWERFUL ENOUGH TO UNDERSTAND THE NATURE OF THE TRUTH.

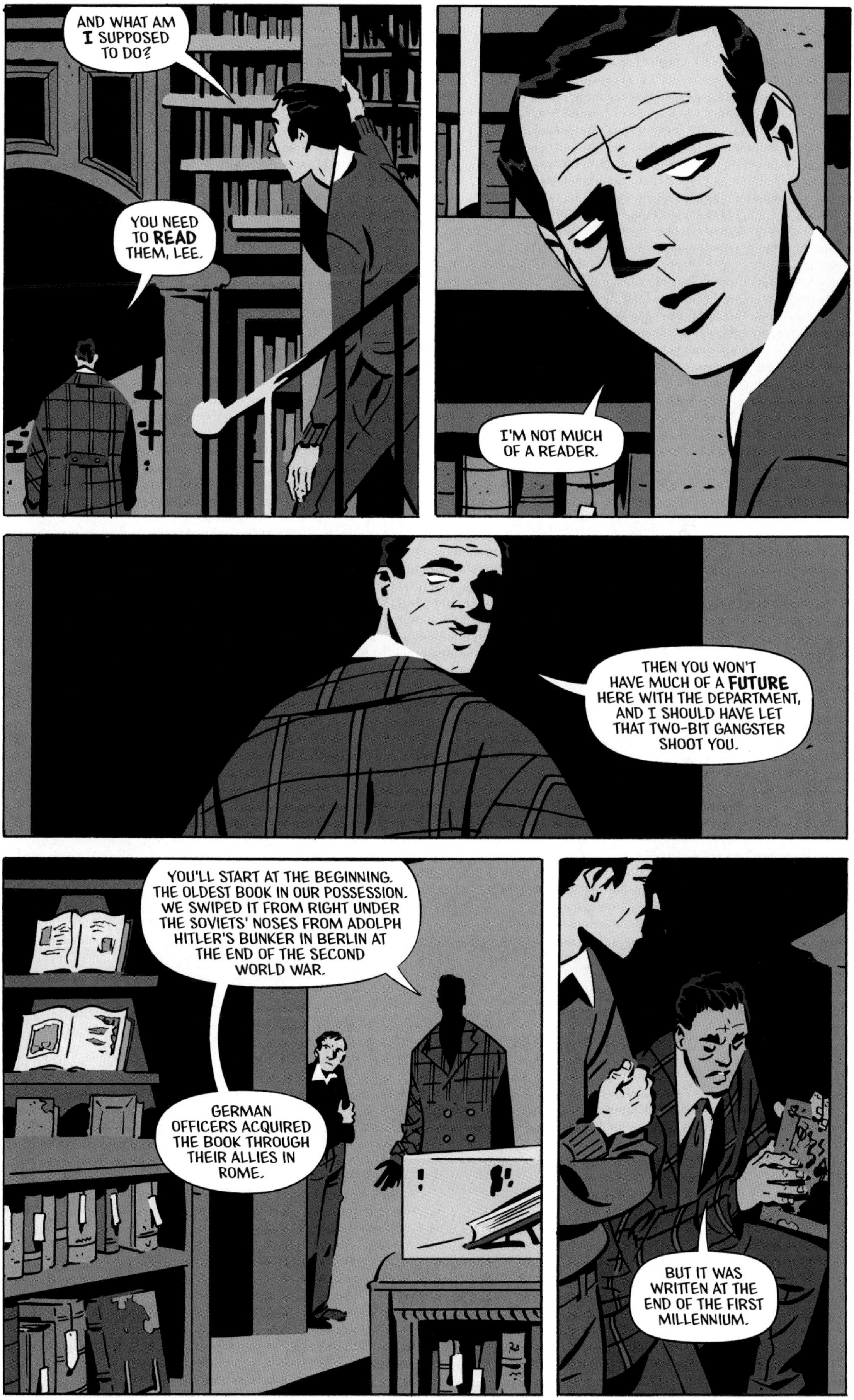
AND WHAT AM I SUPPOSED TO DO?
YOU NEED TO READ THEM, LEE.
I'M NOT MUCH OF A READER.
THEN YOU WON'T HAVE MUCH OF A FUTURE HERE WITH THE DEPARTMENT, AND I SHOULD HAVE LET THAT TWO-BIT GANGSTER SHOOT YOU.
YOU'LL START AT THE BEGINNING. THE OLDEST BOOK IN OUR POSSESSION. WE SWIPED IT FROM RIGHT UNDER THE SOVIETS' NOSES FROM ADOLPH HITLER'S BUNKER IN BERLIN AT THE END OF THE SECOND WORLD WAR.
GERMAN OFFICERS ACQUIRED THE BOOK THROUGH THEIR ALLIES IN ROME.
BUT IT WAS WRITTEN AT THE END OF THE FIRST MILLENNIUM.

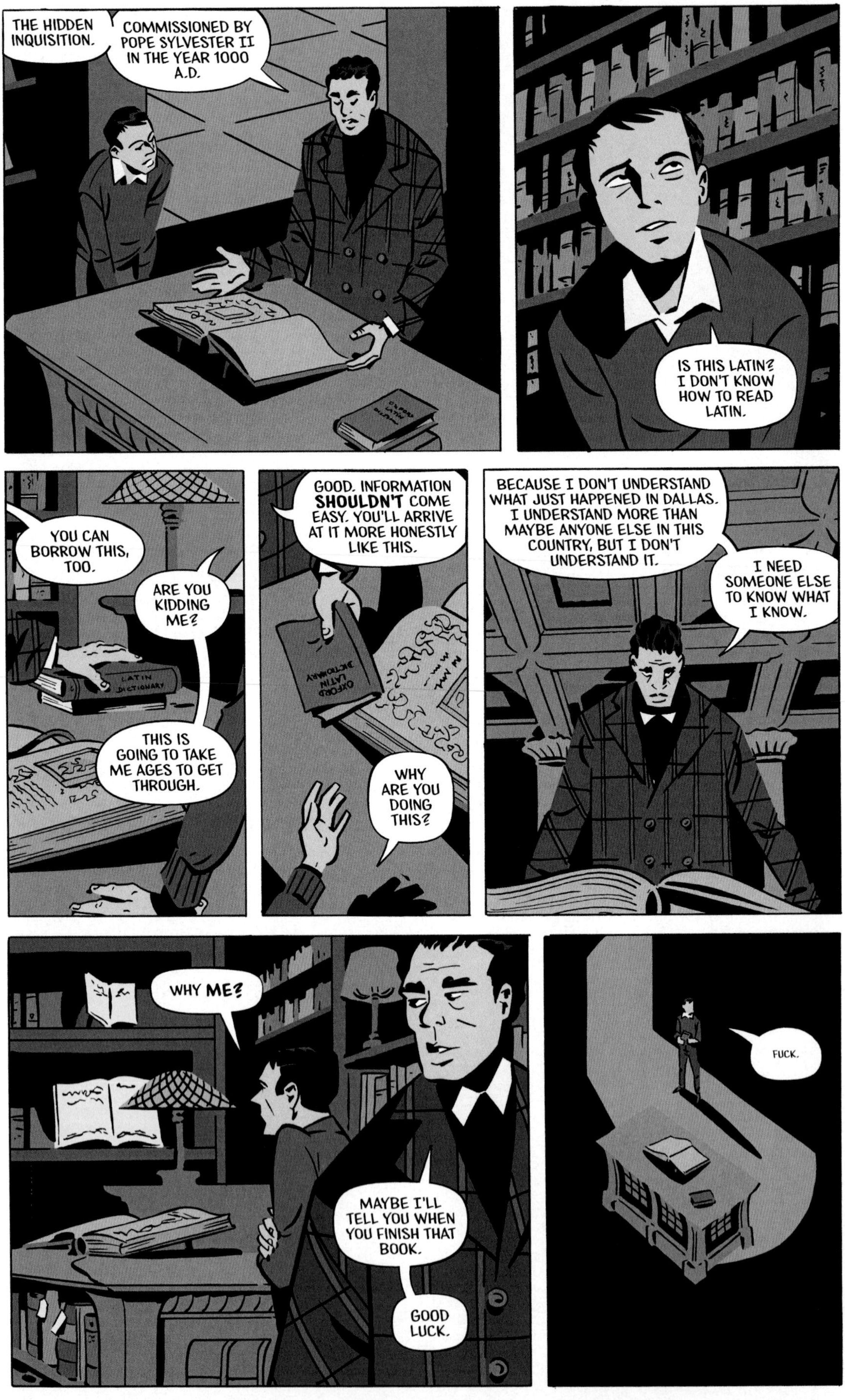
THE HIDDEN INQUISITION.
COMMISSIONED BY POPE SYLVESTER II IN THE YEAR 1000 A.D.
OXFORD LATIN DICTIONARY
IS THIS LATIN? I DON'T KNOW HOW TO READ LATIN.
YOU CAN BORROW THIS, TOO.
ARE YOU KIDDING ME?
LATIN DICTIONARY
THIS IS GOING TO TAKE ME AGES TO GET THROUGH.
GOOD. INFORMATION **SHOULDN'T** COME EASY. YOU'LL ARRIVE AT IT MORE HONESTLY LIKE THIS.
OXFORD LATIN DICTIONARY
WHY ARE YOU DOING THIS?
BECAUSE I DON'T UNDERSTAND WHAT JUST HAPPENED IN DALLAS. I UNDERSTAND MORE THAN MAYBE ANYONE ELSE IN THIS COUNTRY, BUT I DON'T UNDERSTAND IT.
I NEED SOMEONE ELSE TO KNOW WHAT I KNOW.
WHY **ME**?
MAYBE I'LL TELL YOU WHEN YOU FINISH THAT BOOK.
GOOD LUCK.
FUCK.

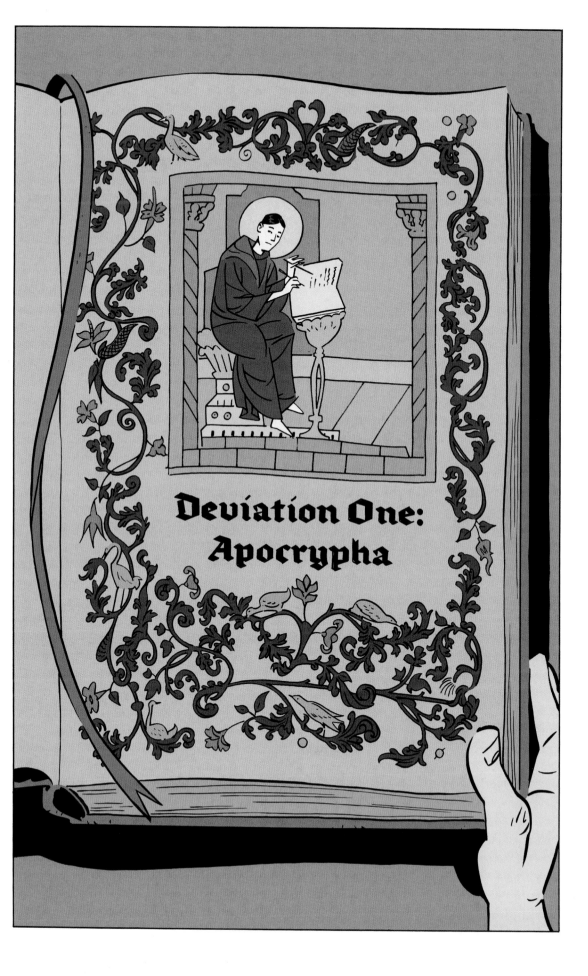

Deviation One: Apocrypha

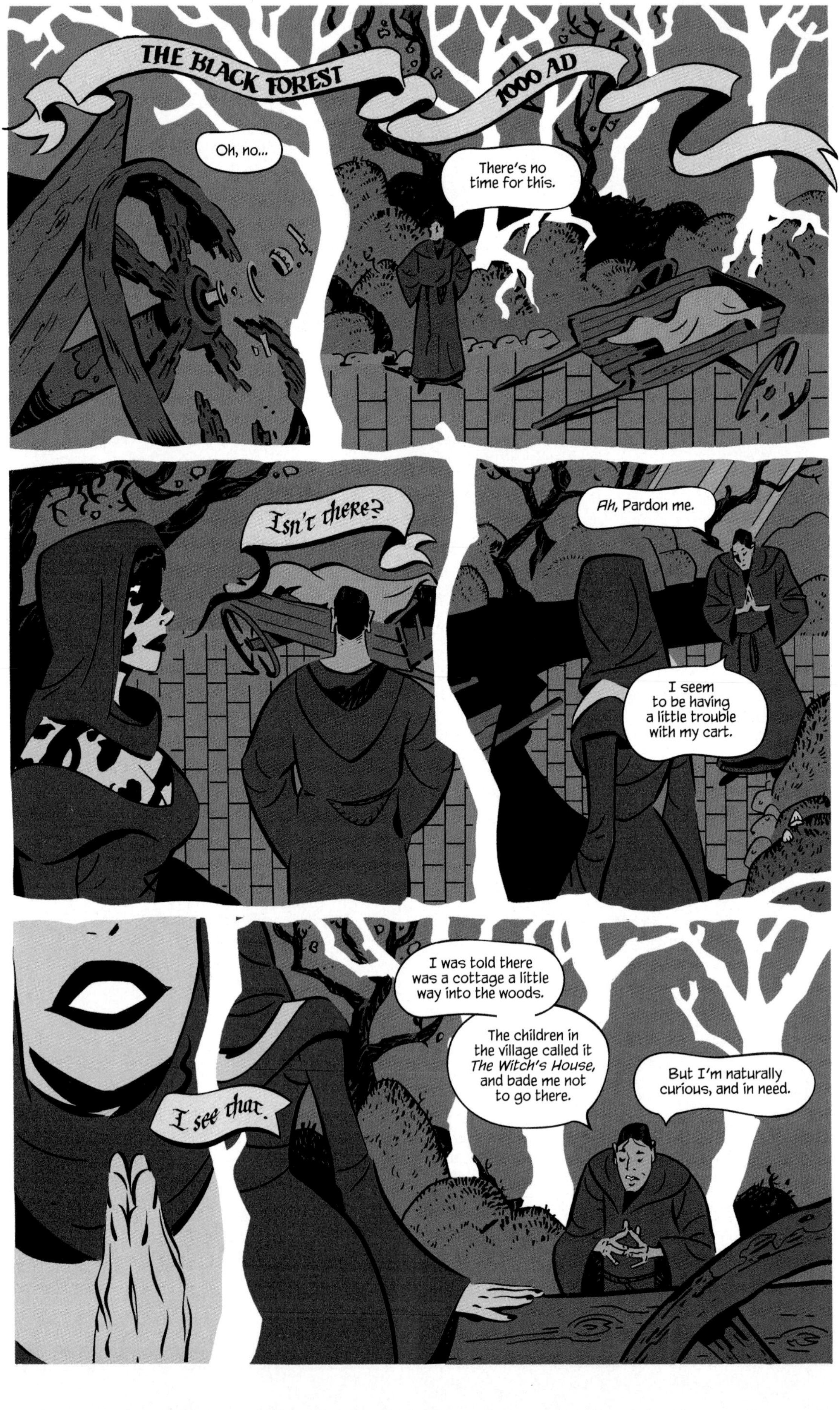
THE BLACK FOREST
1000 AD
Oh, no...
There's no time for this.
Isn't there?
Ah, Pardon me.
I seem to be having a little trouble with my cart.
I see that.
I was told there was a cottage a little way into the woods.
The children in the village called it *The Witch's House,* and bade me not to go there.
But I'm naturally curious, and in need.

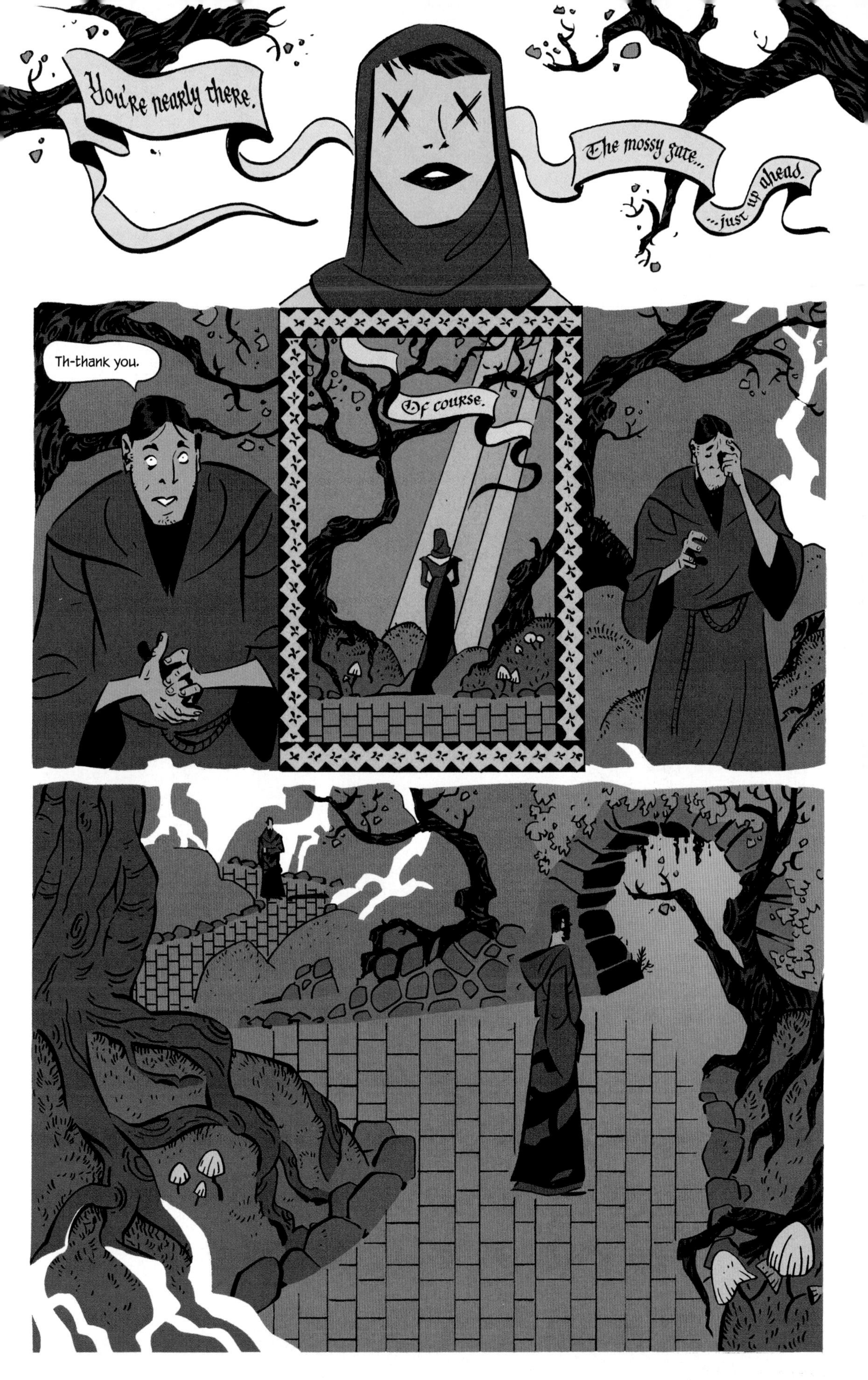
You're nearly there.
The mossy gate...
...just up ahead.
Th-thank you.
Of course.

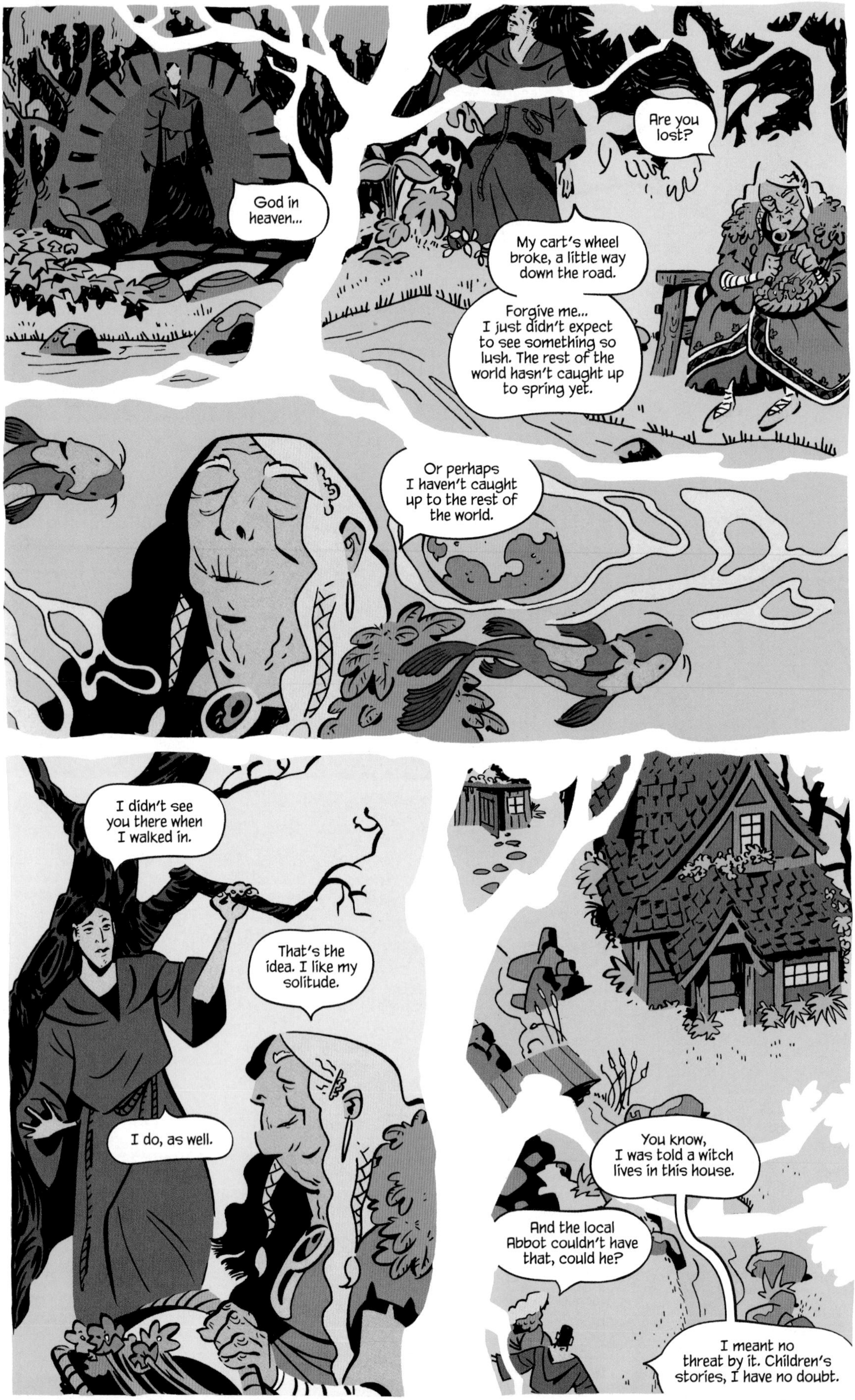
God in heaven...
Are you lost?
My cart's wheel broke, a little way down the road.
Forgive me... I just didn't expect to see something so lush. The rest of the world hasn't caught up to spring yet.
Or perhaps I haven't caught up to the rest of the world.
I didn't see you there when I walked in.
That's the idea. I like my solitude.
I do, as well.
You know, I was told a witch lives in this house.
And the local Abbot couldn't have that, could he?
I meant no threat by it. Children's stories, I have no doubt.

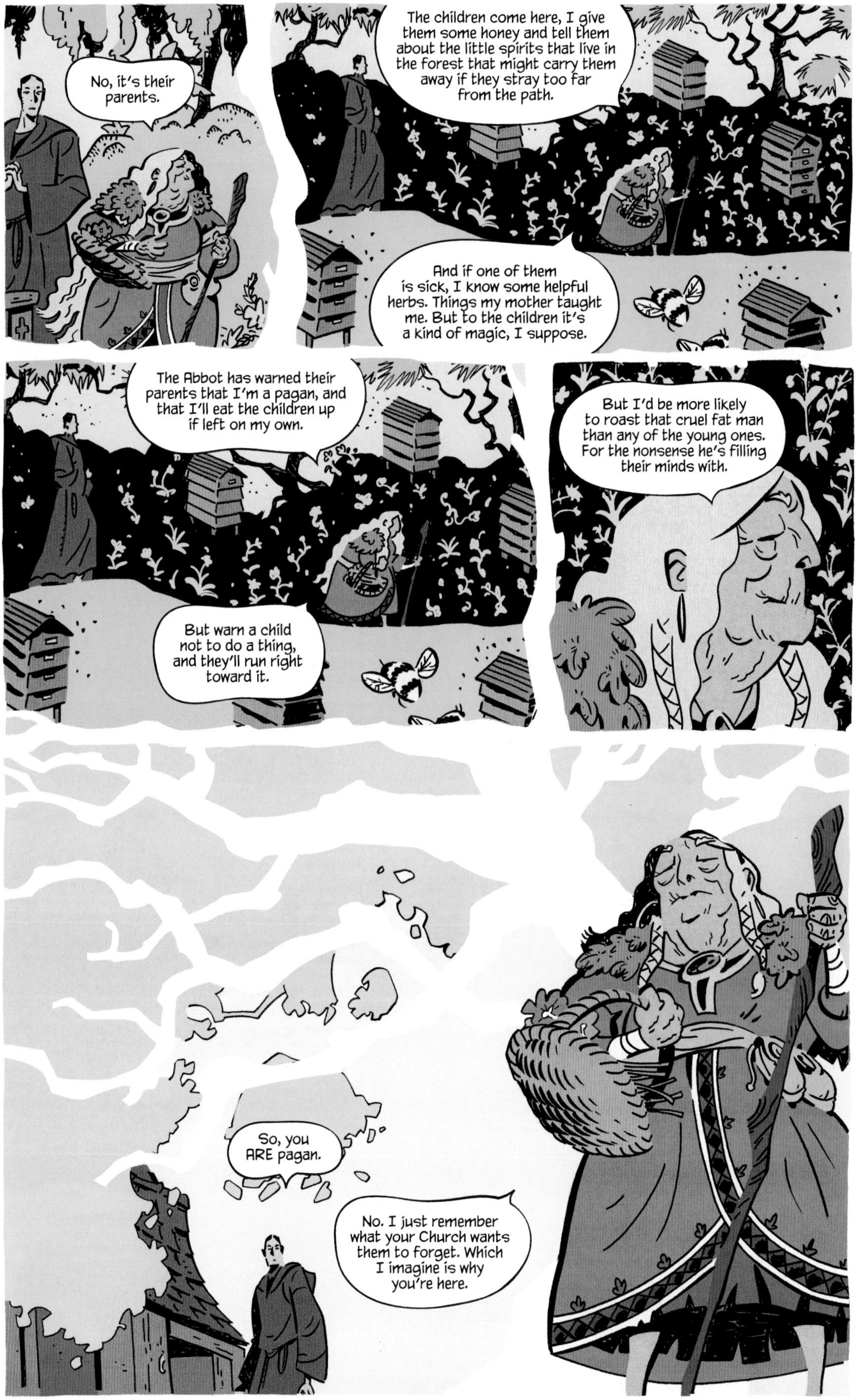
No, it's their parents.
The children come here, I give them some honey and tell them about the little spirits that live in the forest that might carry them away if they stray too far from the path.
And if one of them is sick, I know some helpful herbs. Things my mother taught me. But to the children it's a kind of magic, I suppose.
The Abbot has warned their parents that I'm a pagan, and that I'll eat the children up if left on my own.
But warn a child not to do a thing, and they'll run right toward it.
But I'd be more likely to roast that cruel fat man than any of the young ones. For the nonsense he's filling their minds with.
So, you ARE pagan.
No. I just remember what your Church wants them to forget. Which I imagine is why you're here.

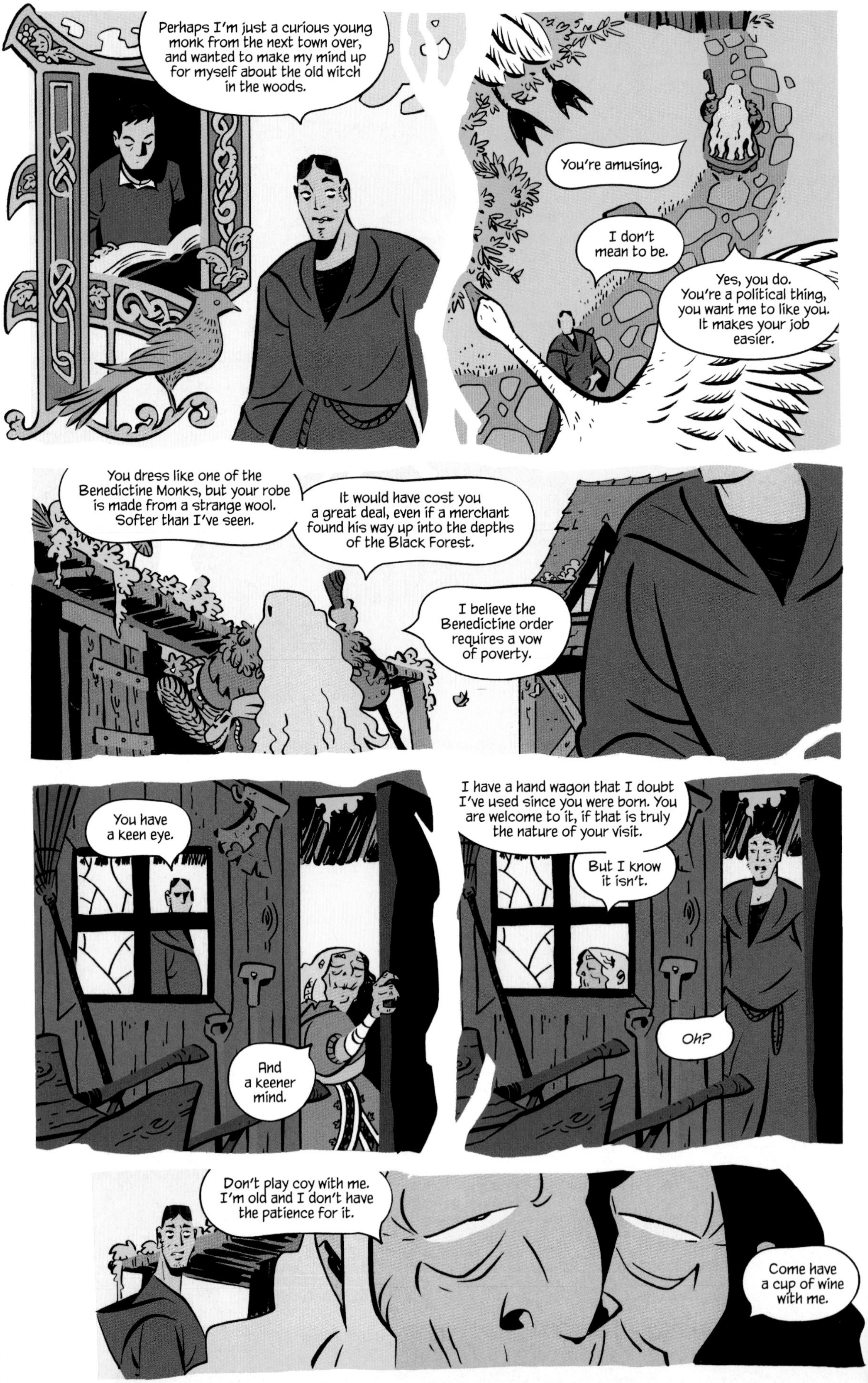
Perhaps I'm just a curious young monk from the next town over, and wanted to make my mind up for myself about the old witch in the woods.
You're amusing.
I don't mean to be.
Yes, you do. You're a political thing, you want me to like you. It makes your job easier.
You dress like one of the Benedictine Monks, but your robe is made from a strange wool. Softer than I've seen.
It would have cost you a great deal, even if a merchant found his way up into the depths of the Black Forest.
I believe the Benedictine order requires a vow of poverty.
You have a keen eye.
And a keener mind.
I have a hand wagon that I doubt I've used since you were born. You are welcome to it, if that is truly the nature of your visit.
But I know it isn't.
Oh?
Don't play coy with me. I'm old and I don't have the patience for it.
Come have a cup of wine with me.

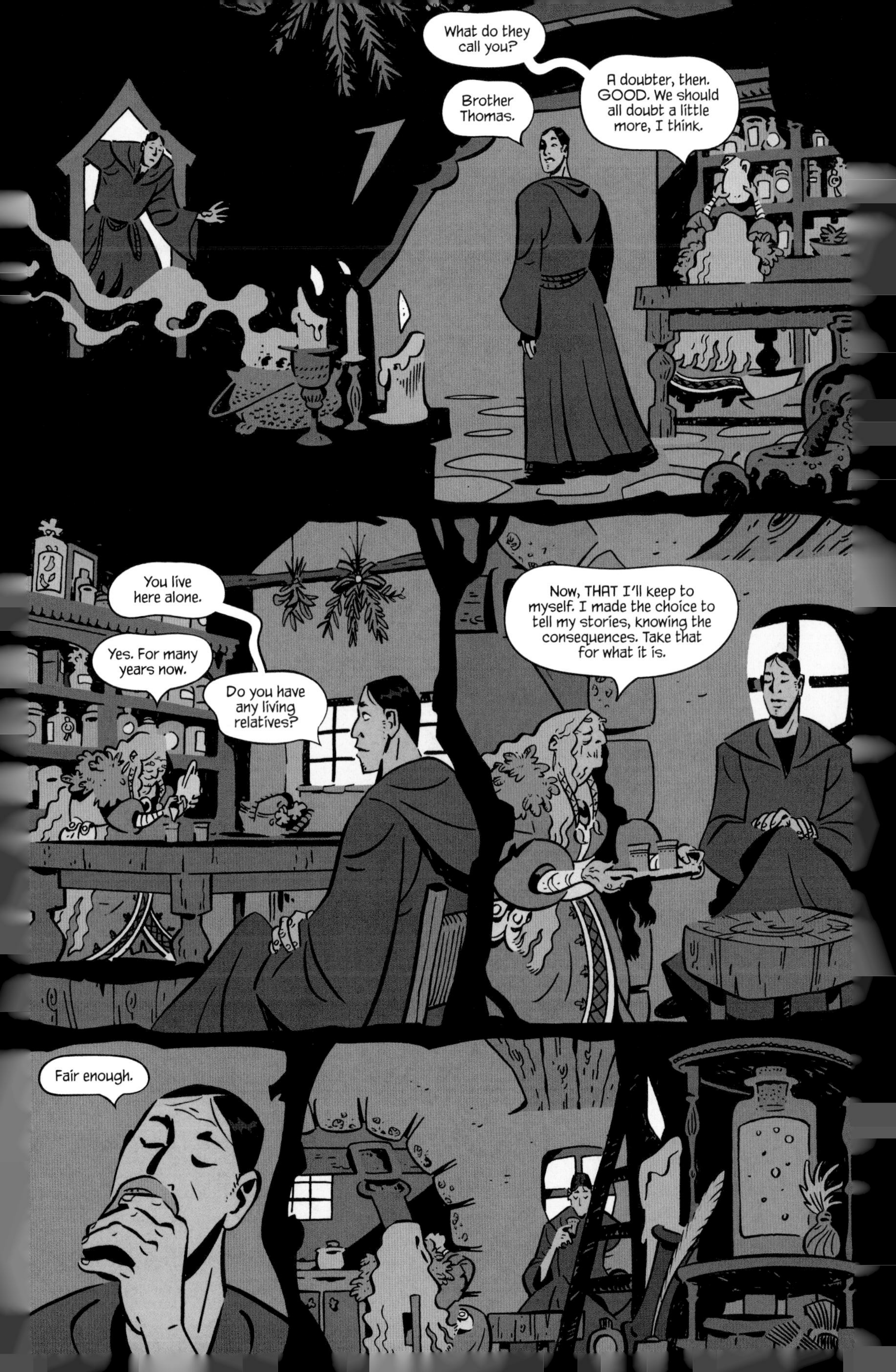
What do they call you?
Brother Thomas.
A doubter, then. GOOD. We should all doubt a little more, I think.
You live here alone.
Yes. For many years now.
Do you have any living relatives?
Now, THAT I'll keep to myself. I made the choice to tell my stories, knowing the consequences. Take that for what it is.
Fair enough.

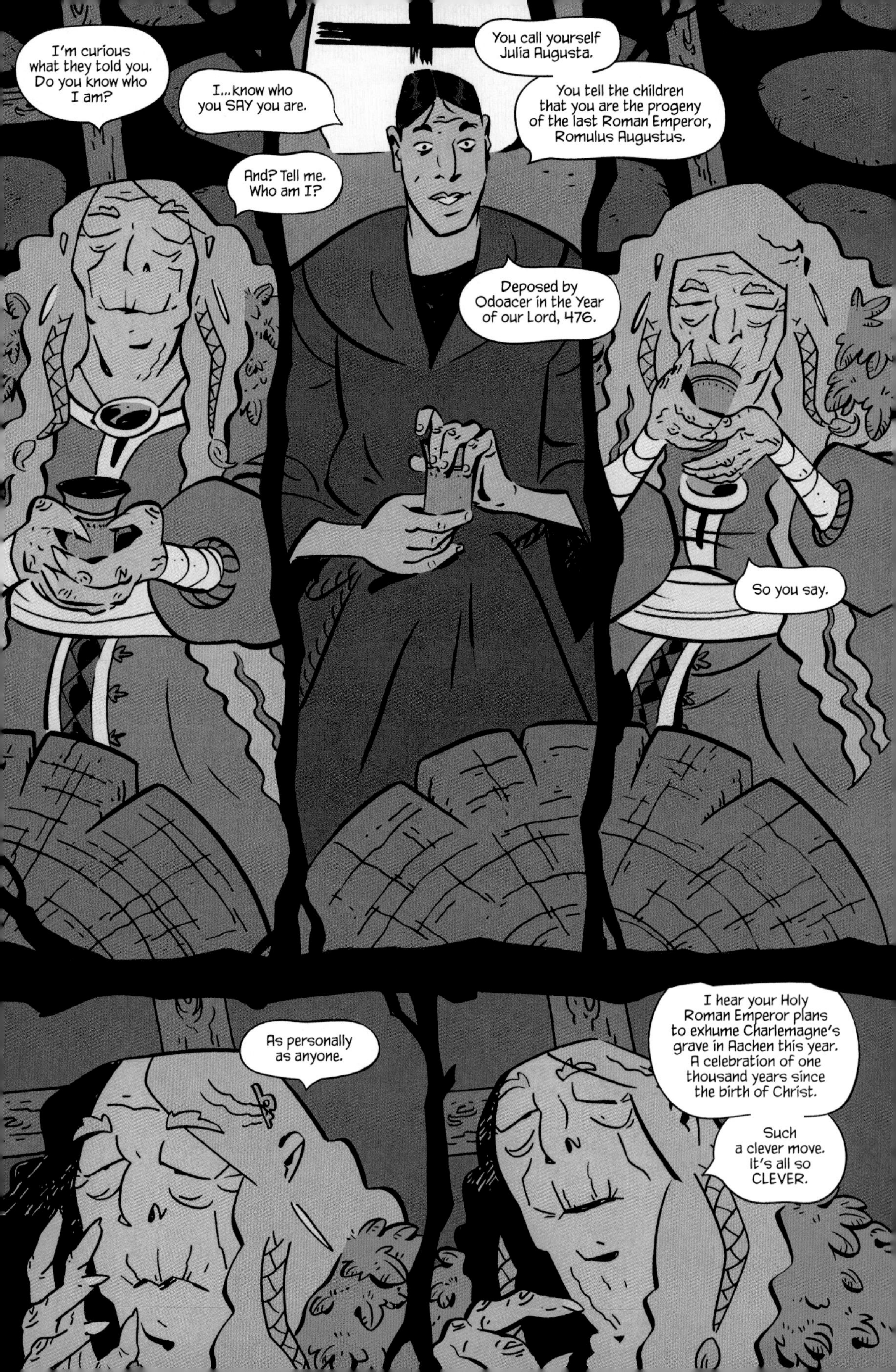

I'm curious what they told you. Do you know who I am?
I...know who you SAY you are.
You call yourself Julia Augusta.
You tell the children that you are the progeny of the last Roman Emperor, Romulus Augustus.
And? Tell me. Who am I?
Deposed by Odoacer in the Year of our Lord, 476.
So you say.
As personally as anyone.
I hear your Holy Roman Emperor plans to exhume Charlemagne's grave in Aachen this year. A celebration of one thousand years since the birth of Christ.
Such a clever move. It's all so CLEVER.

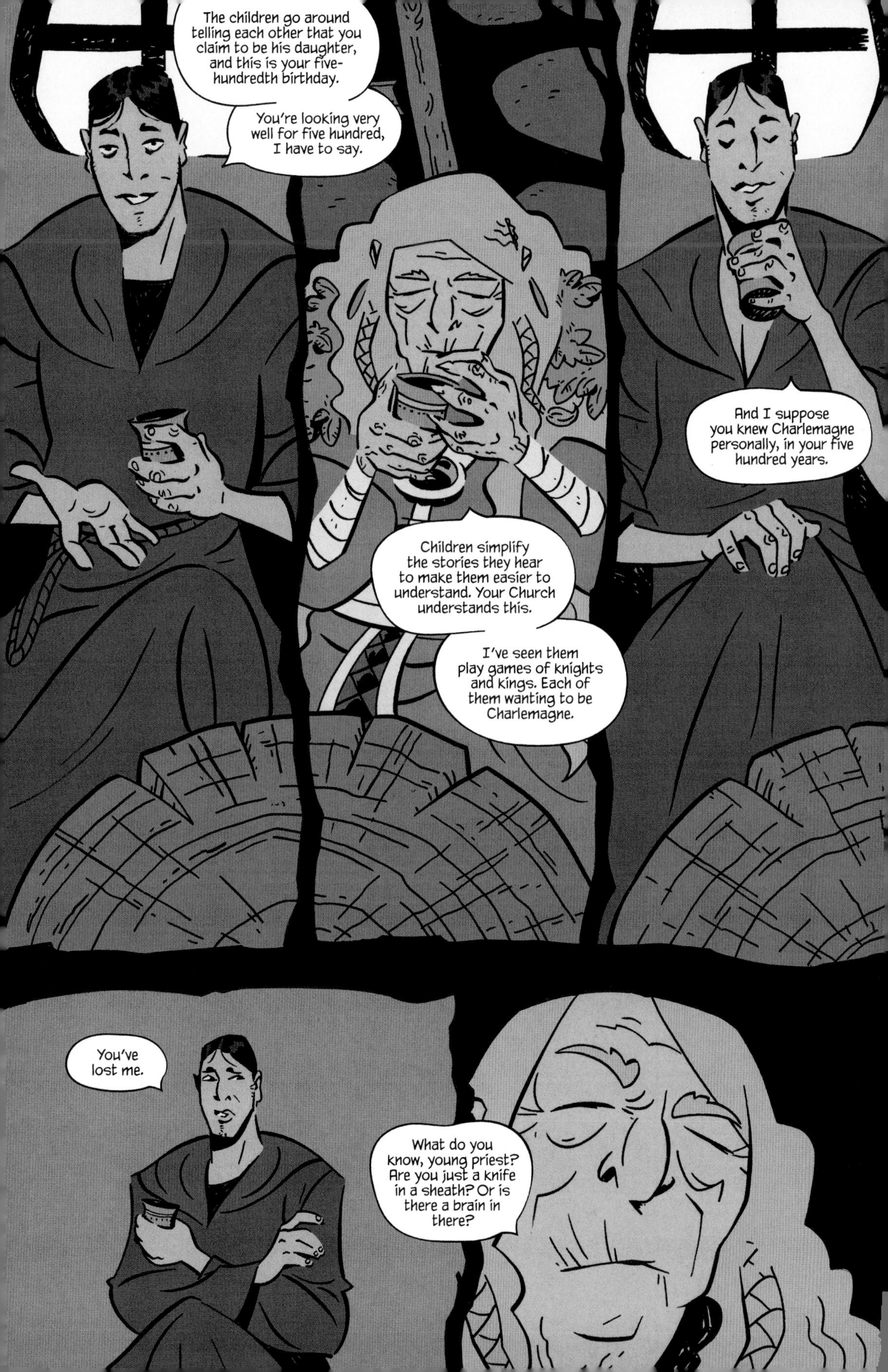
The children go around telling each other that you claim to be his daughter, and this is your five-hundredth birthday.
You're looking very well for five hundred, I have to say.
And I suppose you knew Charlemagne personally, in your five hundred years.
Children simplify the stories they hear to make them easier to understand. Your Church understands this.
I've seen them play games of knights and kings. Each of them wanting to be Charlemagne.
You've lost me.
What do you know, young priest? Are you just a knife in a sheath? Or is there a brain in there?

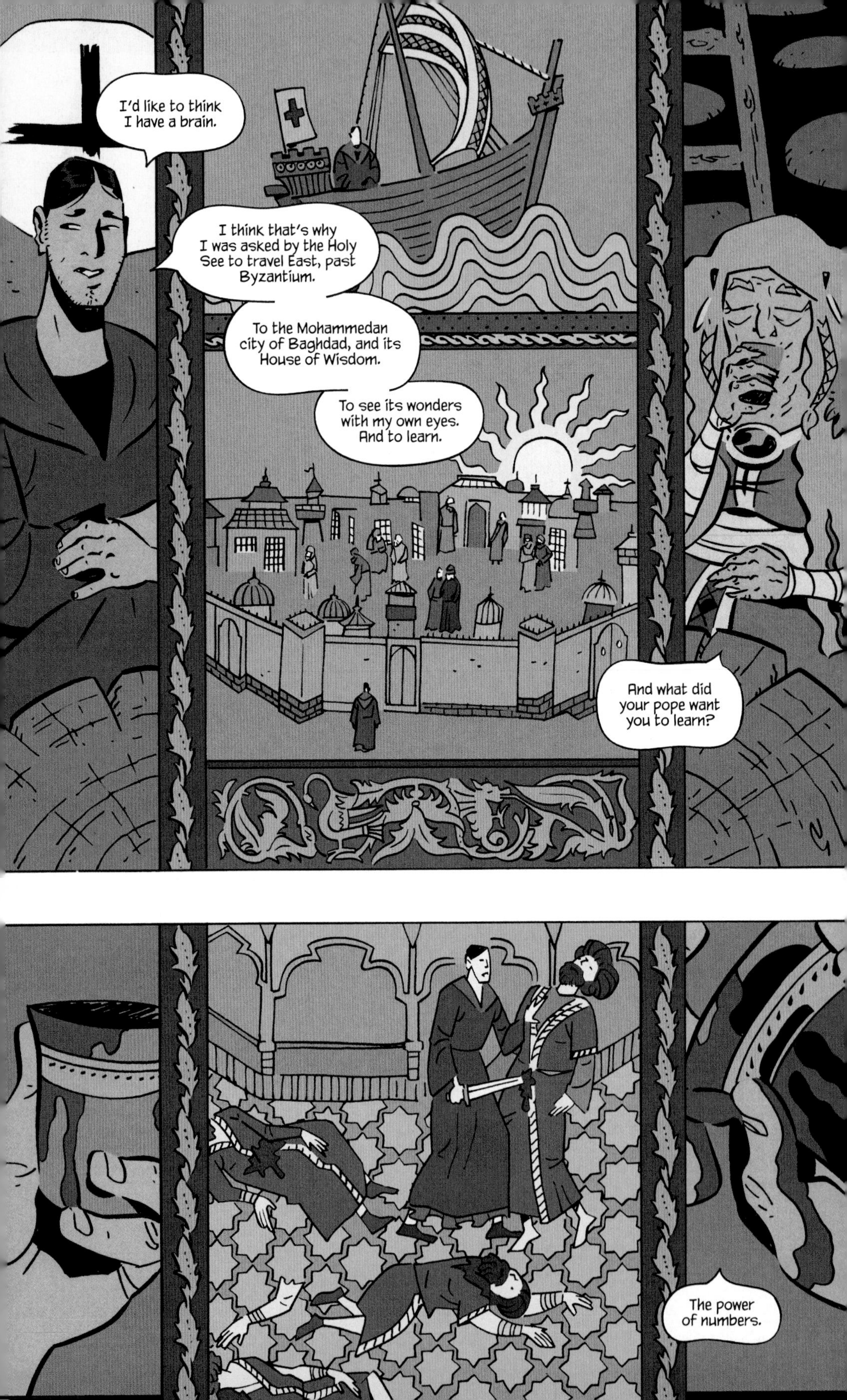
I'd like to think I have a brain.
I think that's why I was asked by the Holy See to travel East, past Byzantium.
To the Mohammedan city of Baghdad, and its House of Wisdom.
To see its wonders with my own eyes. And to learn.
And what did your pope want you to learn?
The power of numbers.

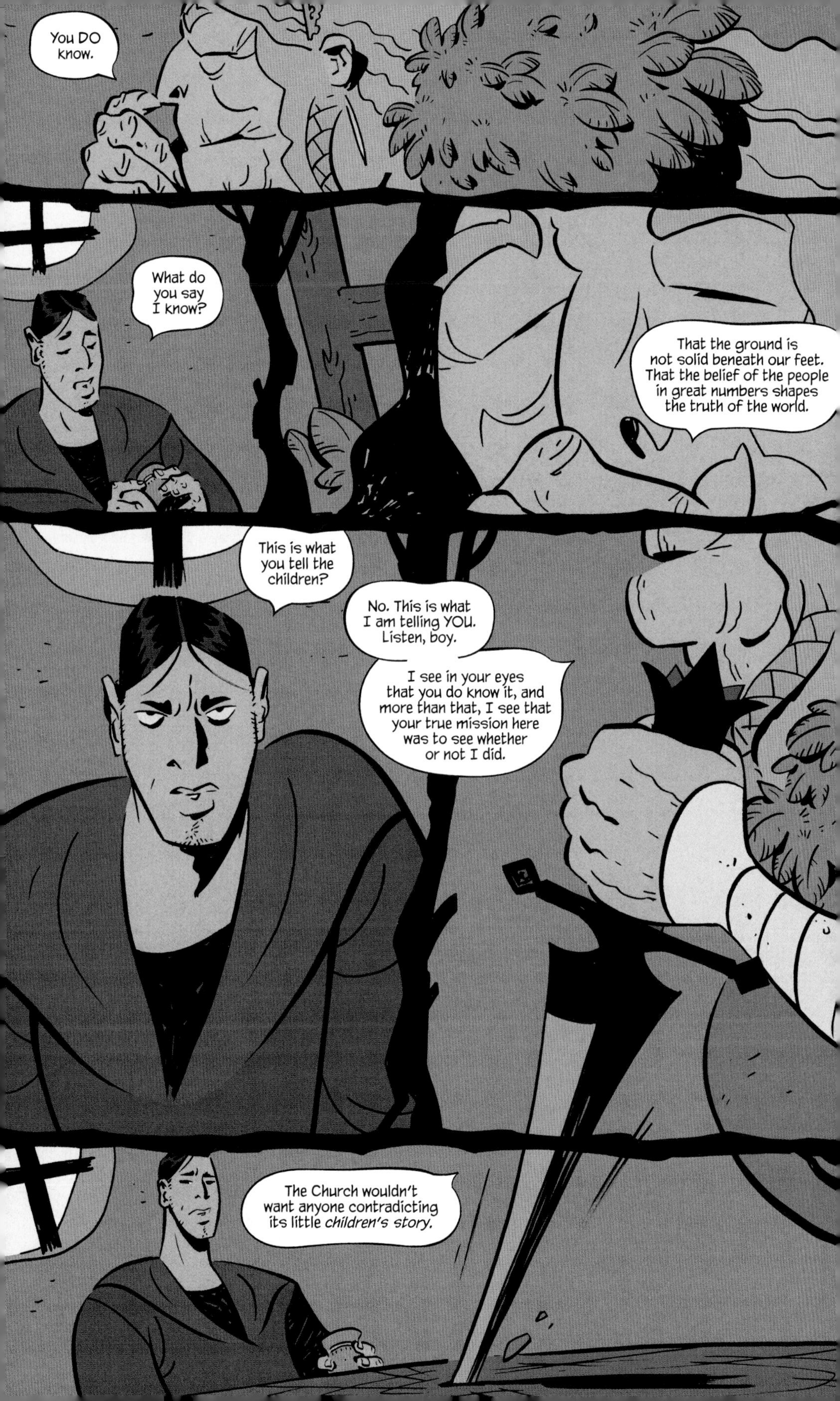
You DO know.
What do you say I know?
That the ground is not solid beneath our feet. That the belief of the people in great numbers shapes the truth of the world.
This is what you tell the children?
No. This is what I am telling YOU. Listen, boy.
I see in your eyes that you do know it, and more than that, I see that your true mission here was to see whether or not I did.
The Church wouldn't want anyone contradicting its little *children's story.*

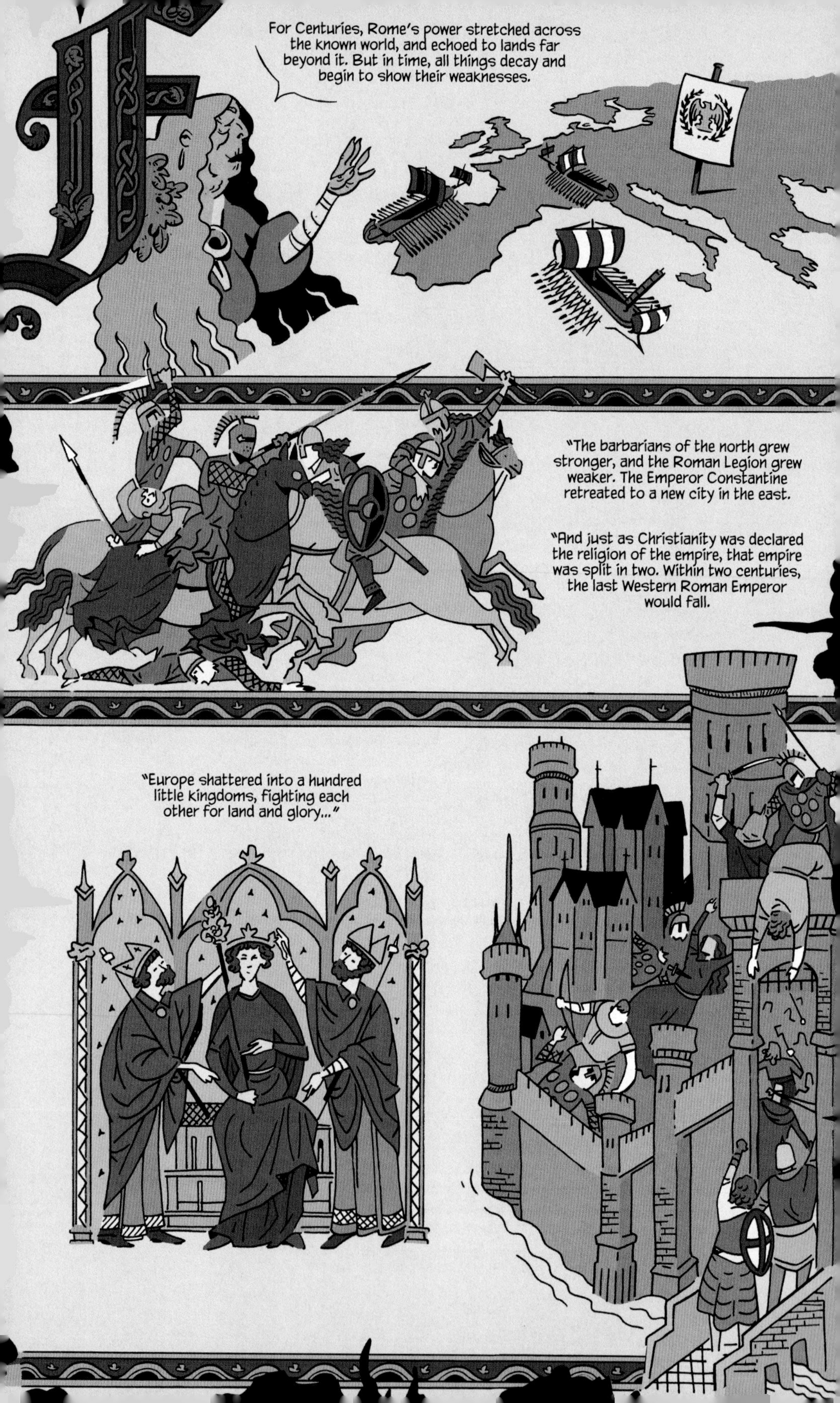
For Centuries, Rome's power stretched across the known world, and echoed to lands far beyond it. But in time, all things decay and begin to show their weaknesses.
"The barbarians of the north grew stronger, and the Roman Legion grew weaker. The Emperor Constantine retreated to a new city in the east.
"And just as Christianity was declared the religion of the empire, that empire was split in two. Within two centuries, the last Western Roman Emperor would fall.
"Europe shattered into a hundred little kingdoms, fighting each other for land and glory..."

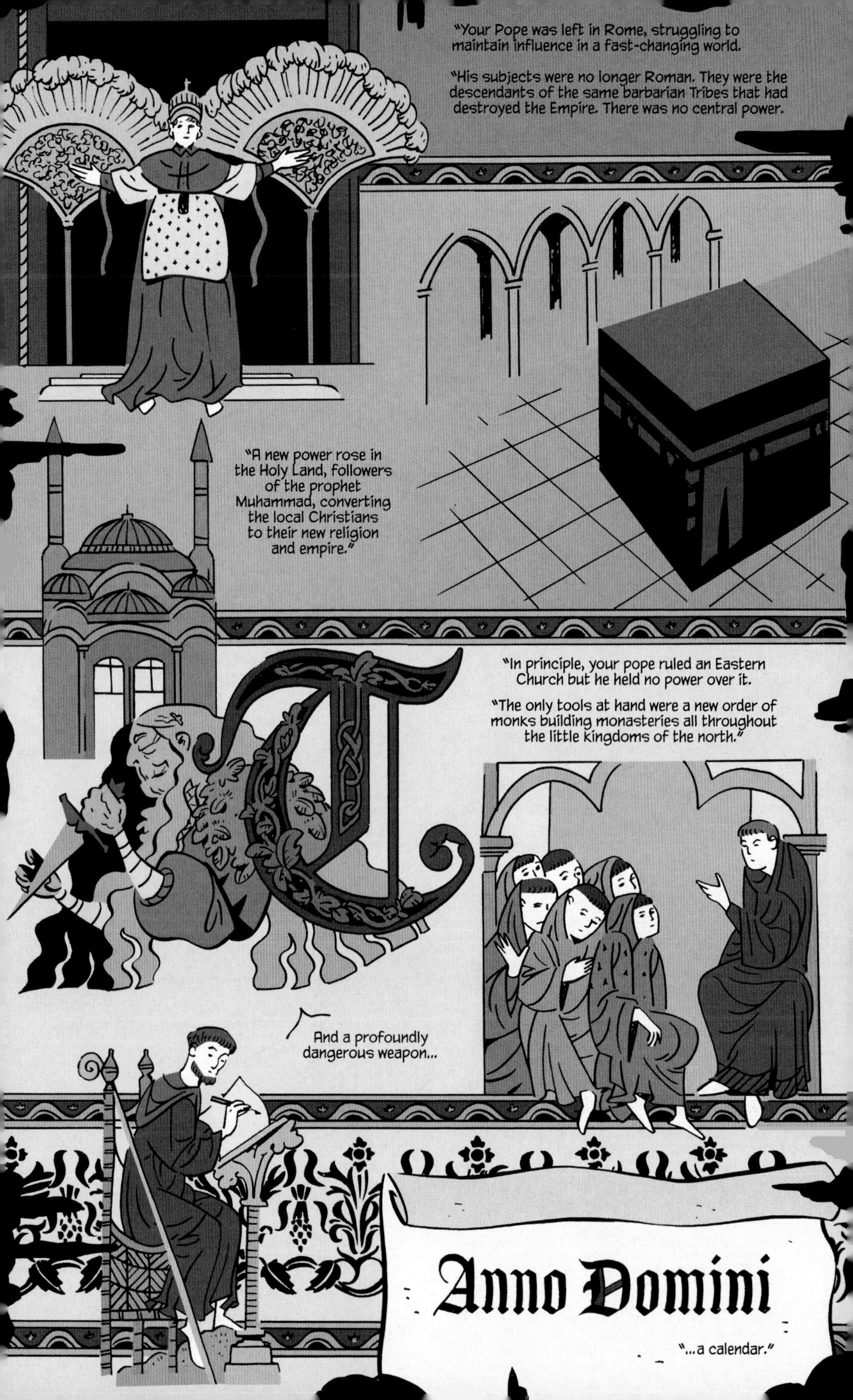
"Your Pope was left in Rome, struggling to maintain influence in a fast-changing world.
"His subjects were no longer Roman. They were the descendants of the same barbarian Tribes that had destroyed the Empire. There was no central power.
"A new power rose in the Holy Land, followers of the prophet Muhammad, converting the local Christians to their new religion and empire."
"In principle, your pope ruled an Eastern Church but he held no power over it.
"The only tools at hand were a new order of monks building monasteries all throughout the little kingdoms of the north."
And a profoundly dangerous weapon...
Anno Domini
"...a calendar."

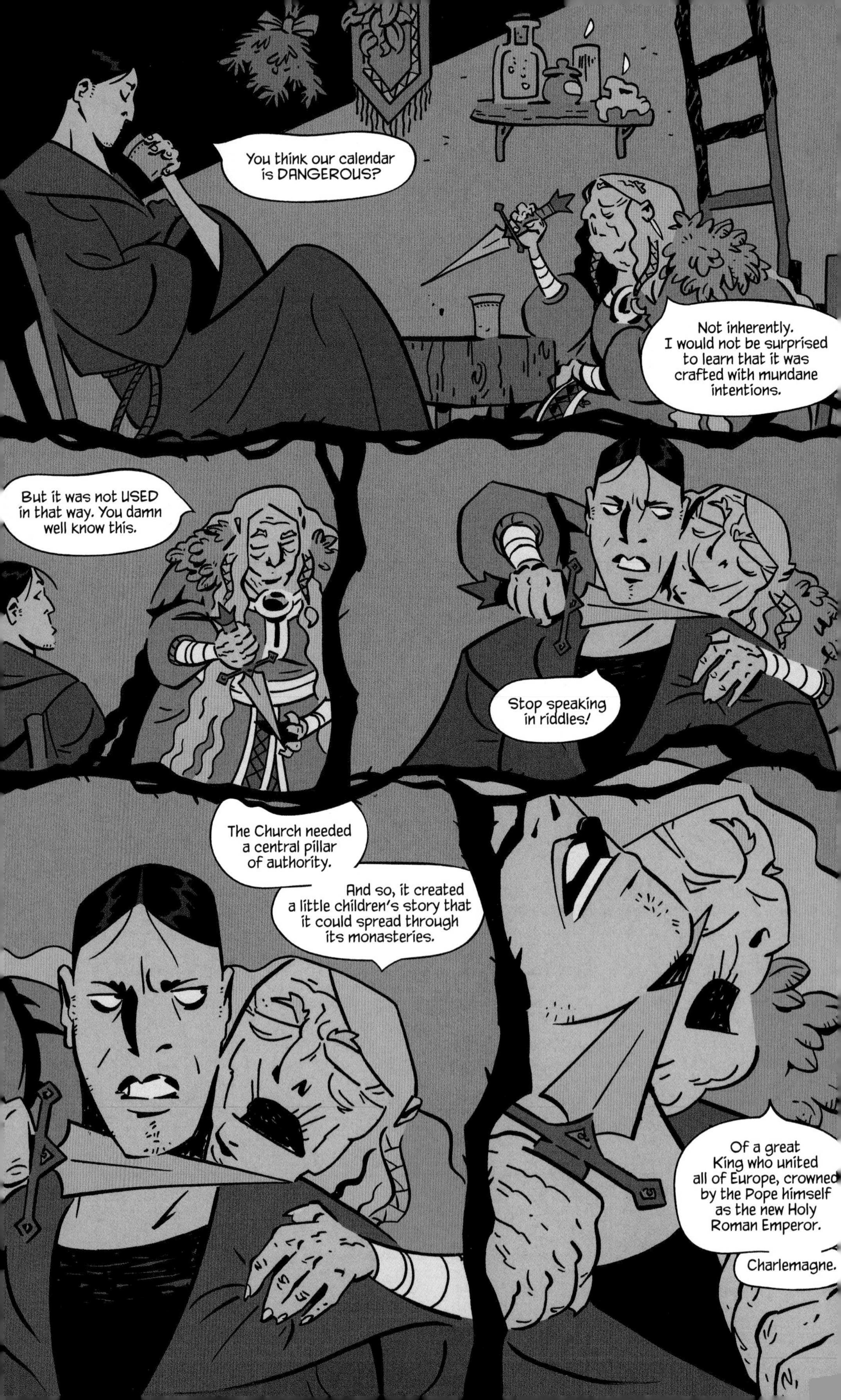
You think our calendar is DANGEROUS?
Not inherently. I would not be surprised to learn that it was crafted with mundane intentions.
But it was not USED in that way. You damn well know this.
Stop speaking in riddles!
The Church needed a central pillar of authority.
And so, it created a little children's story that it could spread through its monasteries.
Of a great King who united all of Europe, crowned by the Pope himself as the new Holy Roman Emperor.
Charlemagne.

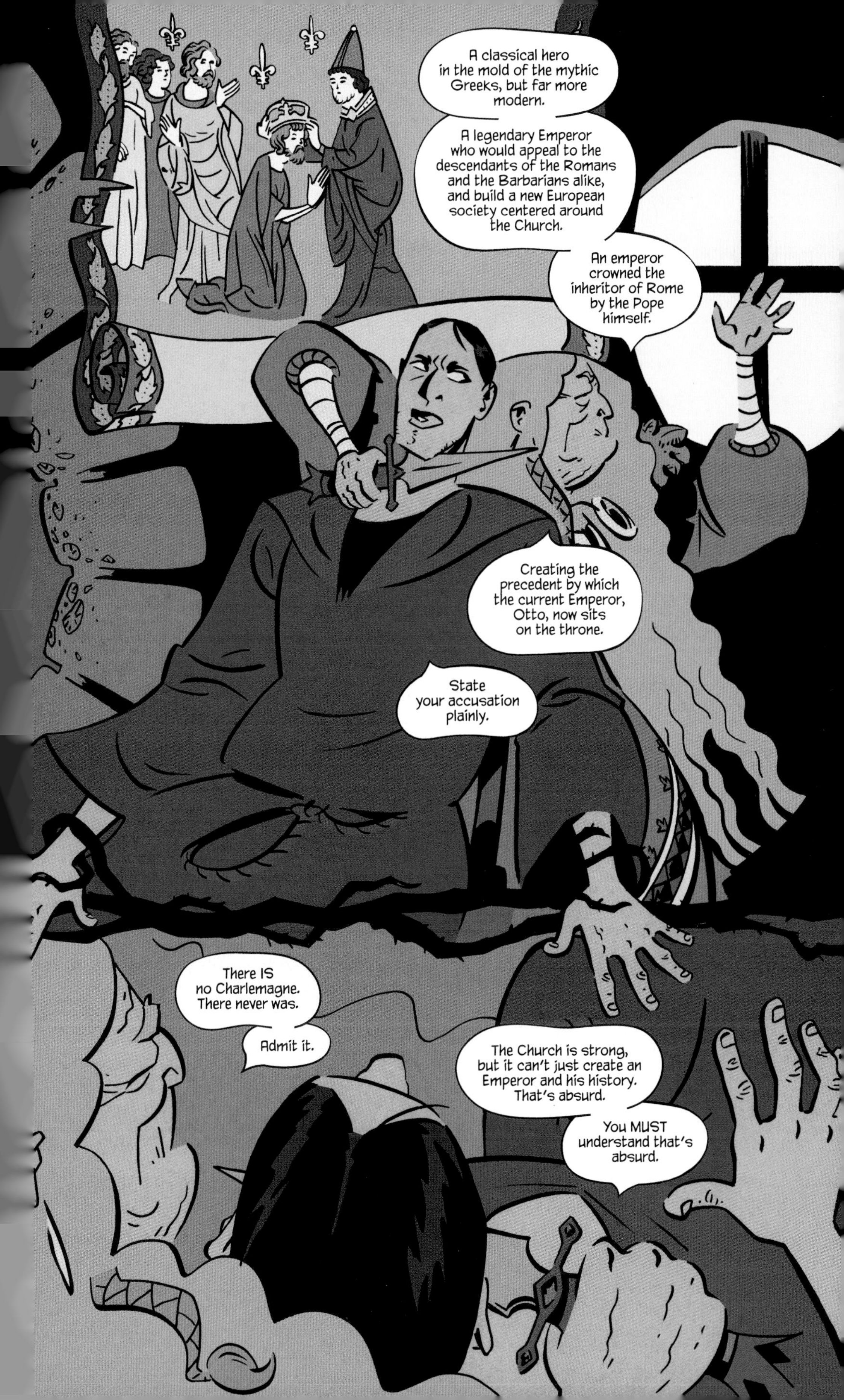
A classical hero in the mold of the mythic Greeks, but far more modern.
A legendary Emperor who would appeal to the descendants of the Romans and the Barbarians alike, and build a new European society centered around the Church.
An emperor crowned the inheritor of Rome by the Pope himself.
Creating the precedent by which the current Emperor, Otto, now sits on the throne.
State your accusation plainly.
There IS no Charlemagne. There never was.
Admit it.
The Church is strong, but it can't just create an Emperor and his history. That's absurd.
You MUST understand that's absurd.

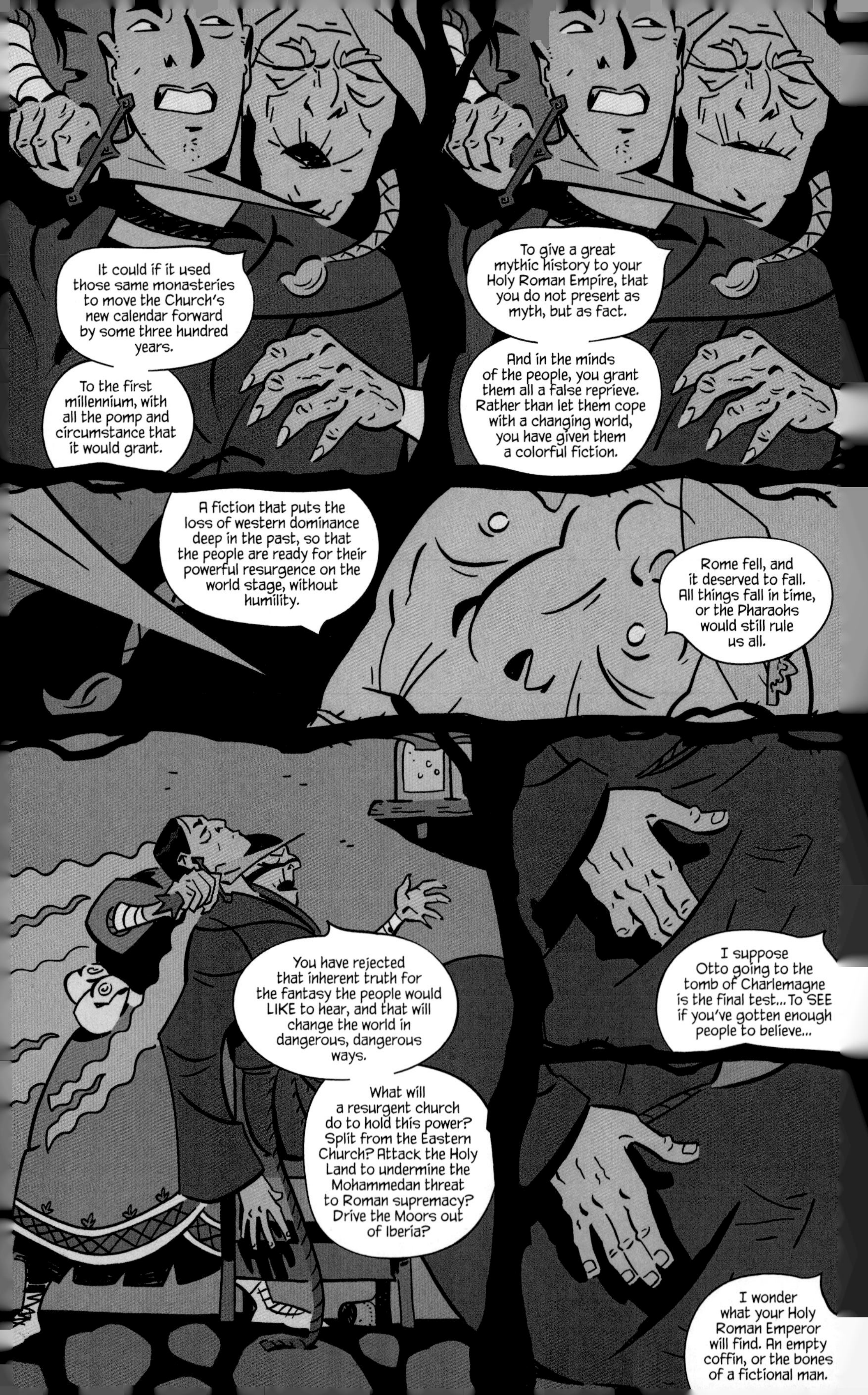
It could if it used those same monasteries to move the Church's new calendar forward by some three hundred years.
To the first millennium, with all the pomp and circumstance that it would grant.
To give a great mythic history to your Holy Roman Empire, that you do not present as myth, but as fact.
And in the minds of the people, you grant them all a false reprieve. Rather than let them cope with a changing world, you have given them a colorful fiction.
A fiction that puts the loss of western dominance deep in the past, so that the people are ready for their powerful resurgence on the world stage, without humility.
Rome fell, and it deserved to fall. All things fall in time, or the Pharaohs would still rule us all.
You have rejected that inherent truth for the fantasy the people would LIKE to hear, and that will change the world in dangerous, dangerous ways.
What will a resurgent church do to hold this power? Split from the Eastern Church? Attack the Holy Land to undermine the Mohammedan threat to Roman supremacy? Drive the Moors out of Iberia?
I suppose Otto going to the tomb of Charlemagne is the final test... To SEE if you've gotten enough people to believe...
I wonder what your Holy Roman Emperor will find. An empty coffin, or the bones of a fictional man.

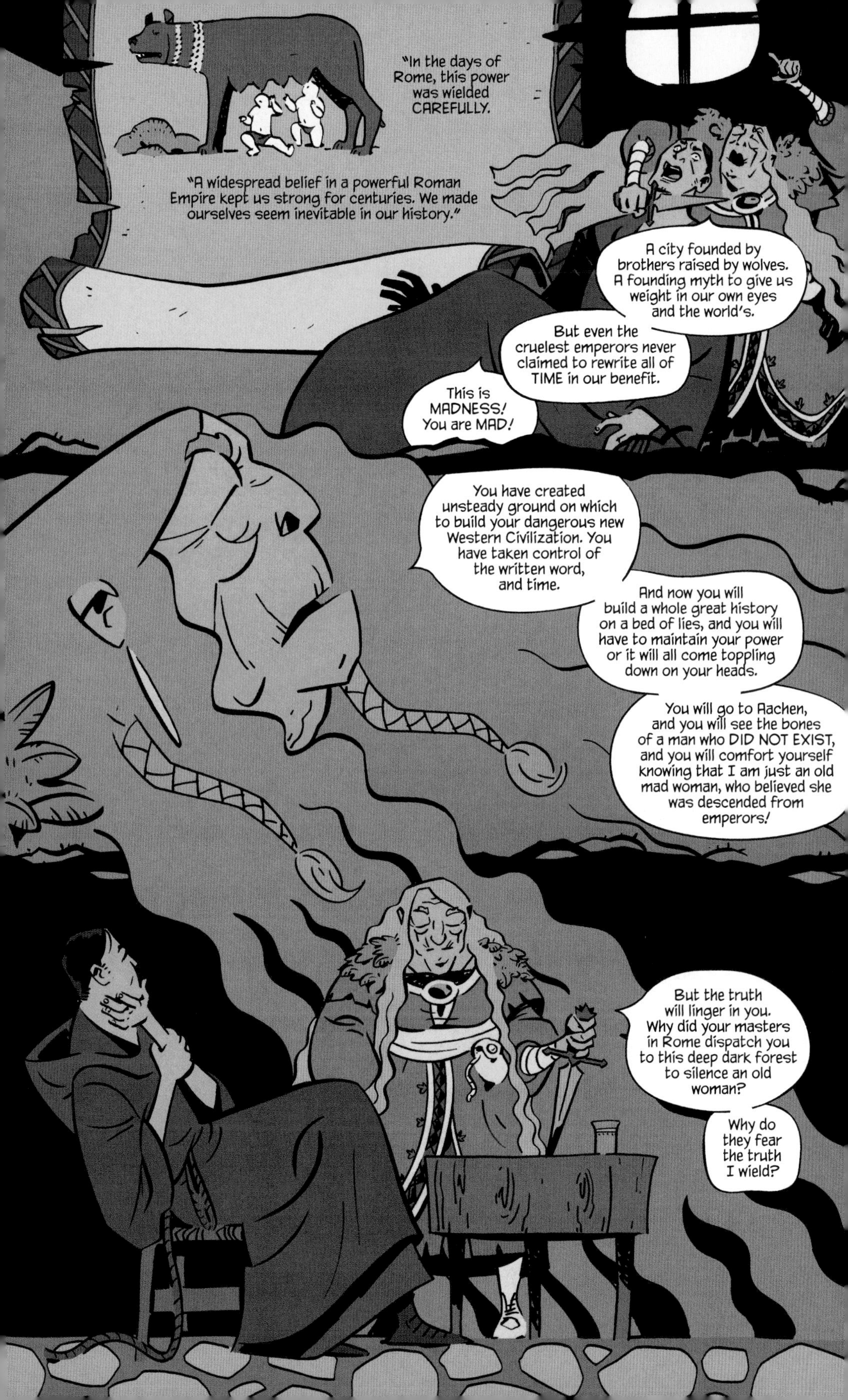
"In the days of Rome, this power was wielded CAREFULLY.
"A widespread belief in a powerful Roman Empire kept us strong for centuries. We made ourselves seem inevitable in our history."
A city founded by brothers raised by wolves. A founding myth to give us weight in our own eyes and the world's.
But even the cruelest emperors never claimed to rewrite all of TIME in our benefit.
This is MADNESS! You are MAD!
You have created unsteady ground on which to build your dangerous new Western Civilization. You have taken control of the written word, and time.
And now you will build a whole great history on a bed of lies, and you will have to maintain your power or it will all come toppling down on your heads.
You will go to Aachen, and you will see the bones of a man who DID NOT EXIST, and you will comfort yourself knowing that I am just an old mad woman, who believed she was descended from emperors!
But the truth will linger in you. Why did your masters in Rome dispatch you to this deep dark forest to silence an old woman?
Why do they fear the truth I wield?

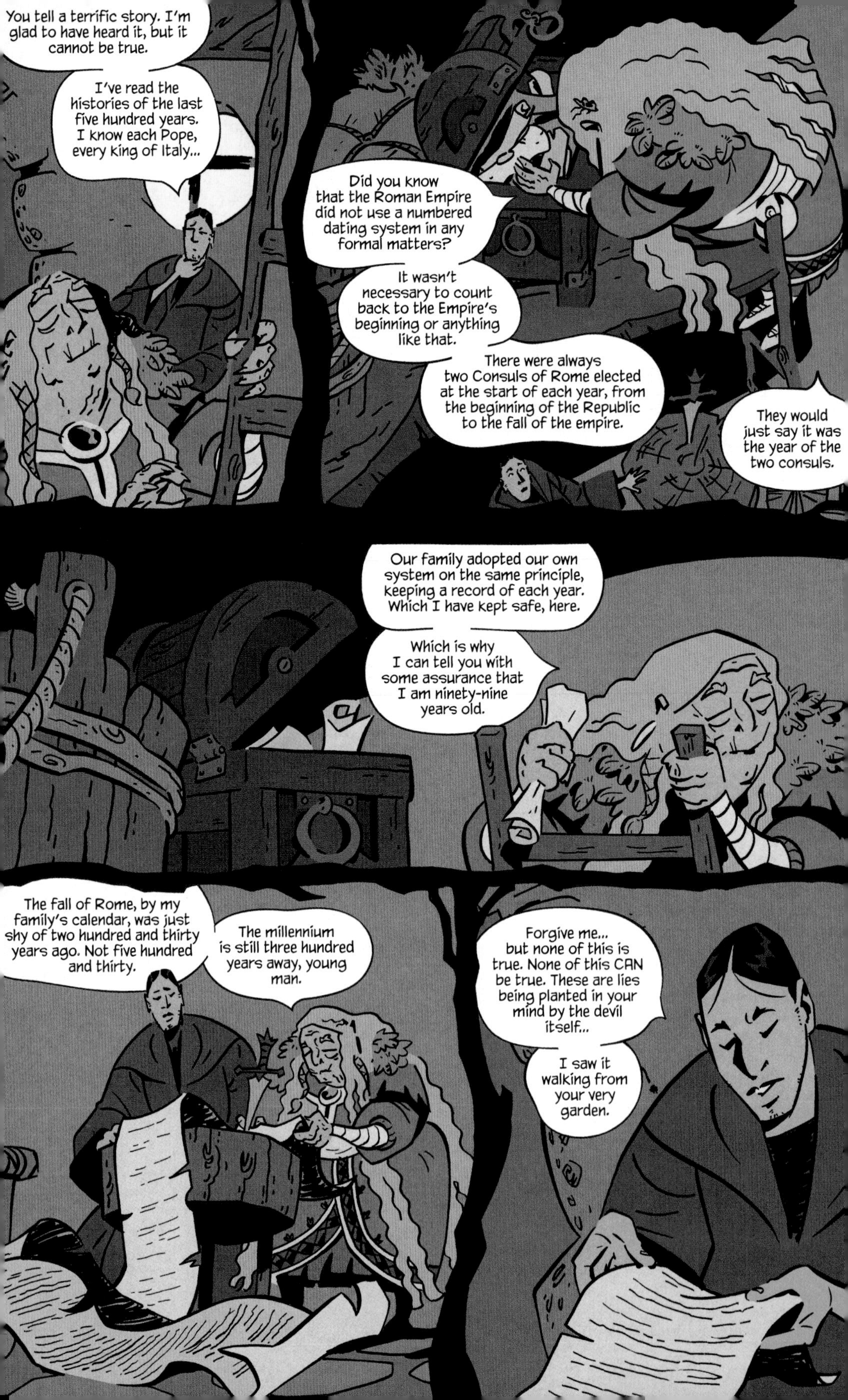
You tell a terrific story. I'm glad to have heard it, but it cannot be true.
I've read the histories of the last five hundred years. I know each Pope, every king of Italy...
Did you know that the Roman Empire did not use a numbered dating system in any formal matters?
It wasn't necessary to count back to the Empire's beginning or anything like that.
There were always two Consuls of Rome elected at the start of each year, from the beginning of the Republic to the fall of the empire.
They would just say it was the year of the two consuls.
Our family adopted our own system on the same principle, keeping a record of each year. Which I have kept safe, here.
Which is why I can tell you with some assurance that I am ninety-nine years old.
The fall of Rome, by my family's calendar, was just shy of two hundred and thirty years ago. Not five hundred and thirty.
The millennium is still three hundred years away, young man.
Forgive me... but none of this is true. None of this CAN be true. These are lies being planted in your mind by the devil itself...
I saw it walking from your very garden.

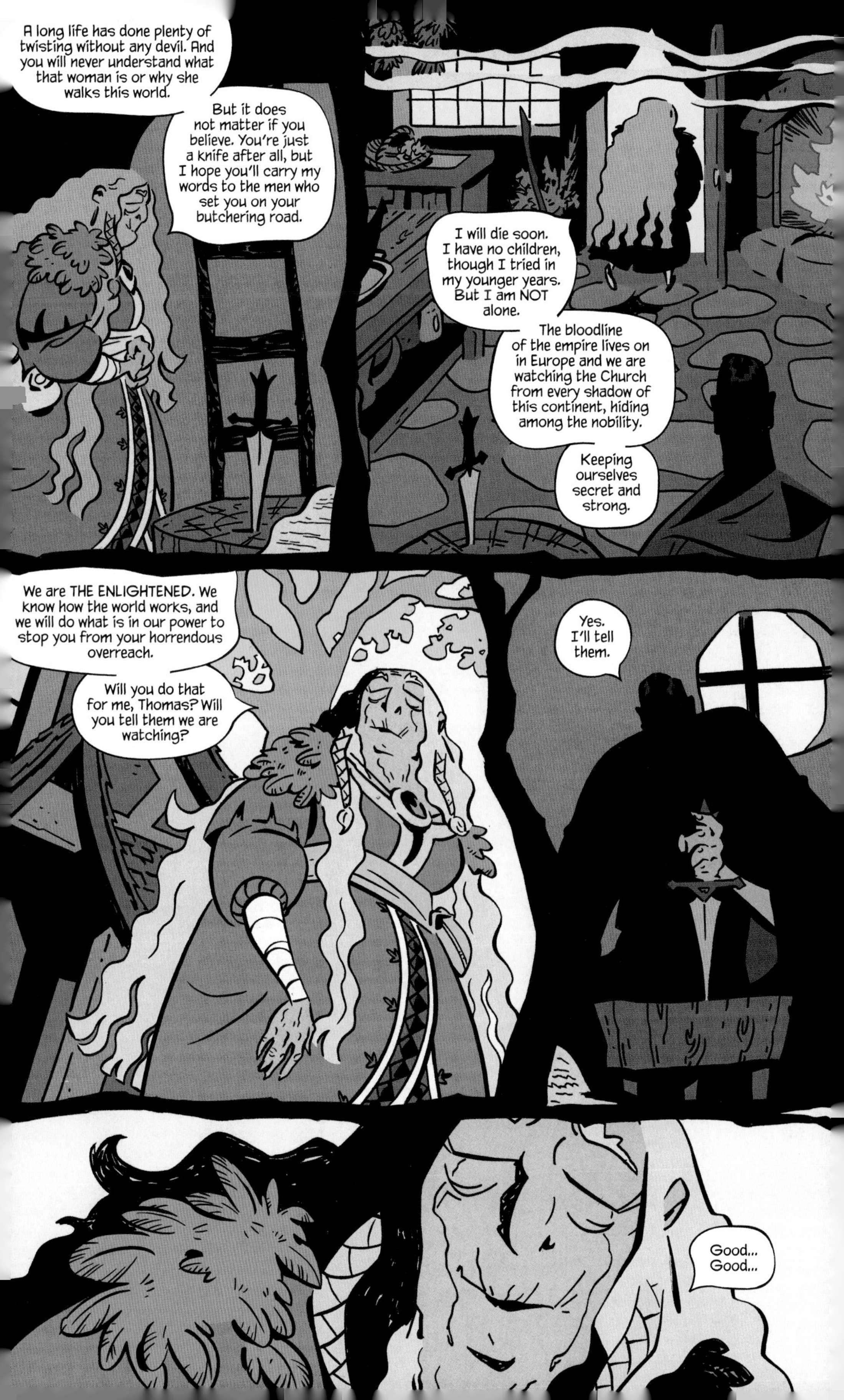
A long life has done plenty of twisting without any devil. And you will never understand what that woman is or why she walks this world.
But it does not matter if you believe. You're just a knife after all, but I hope you'll carry my words to the men who set you on your butchering road.
I will die soon. I have no children, though I tried in my younger years. But I am NOT alone.
The bloodline of the empire lives on in Europe and we are watching the Church from every shadow of this continent, hiding among the nobility.
Keeping ourselves secret and strong.
We are THE ENLIGHTENED. We know how the world works, and we will do what is in our power to stop you from your horrendous overreach.
Will you do that for me, Thomas? Will you tell them we are watching?
Yes. I'll tell them.
Good... Good...

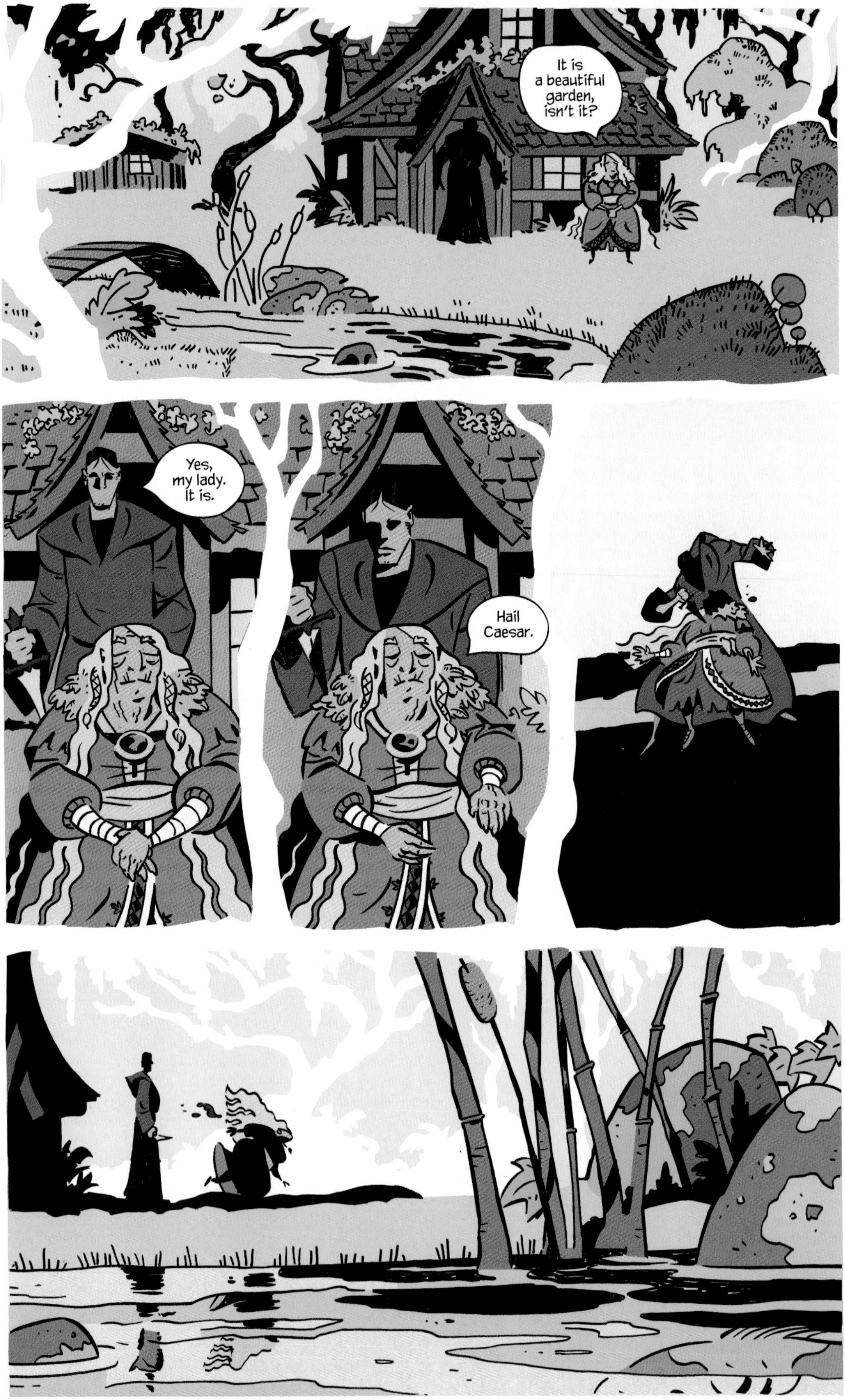
It is a beautiful garden, isn't it?
Yes, my lady. It is.
Hail Caesar.

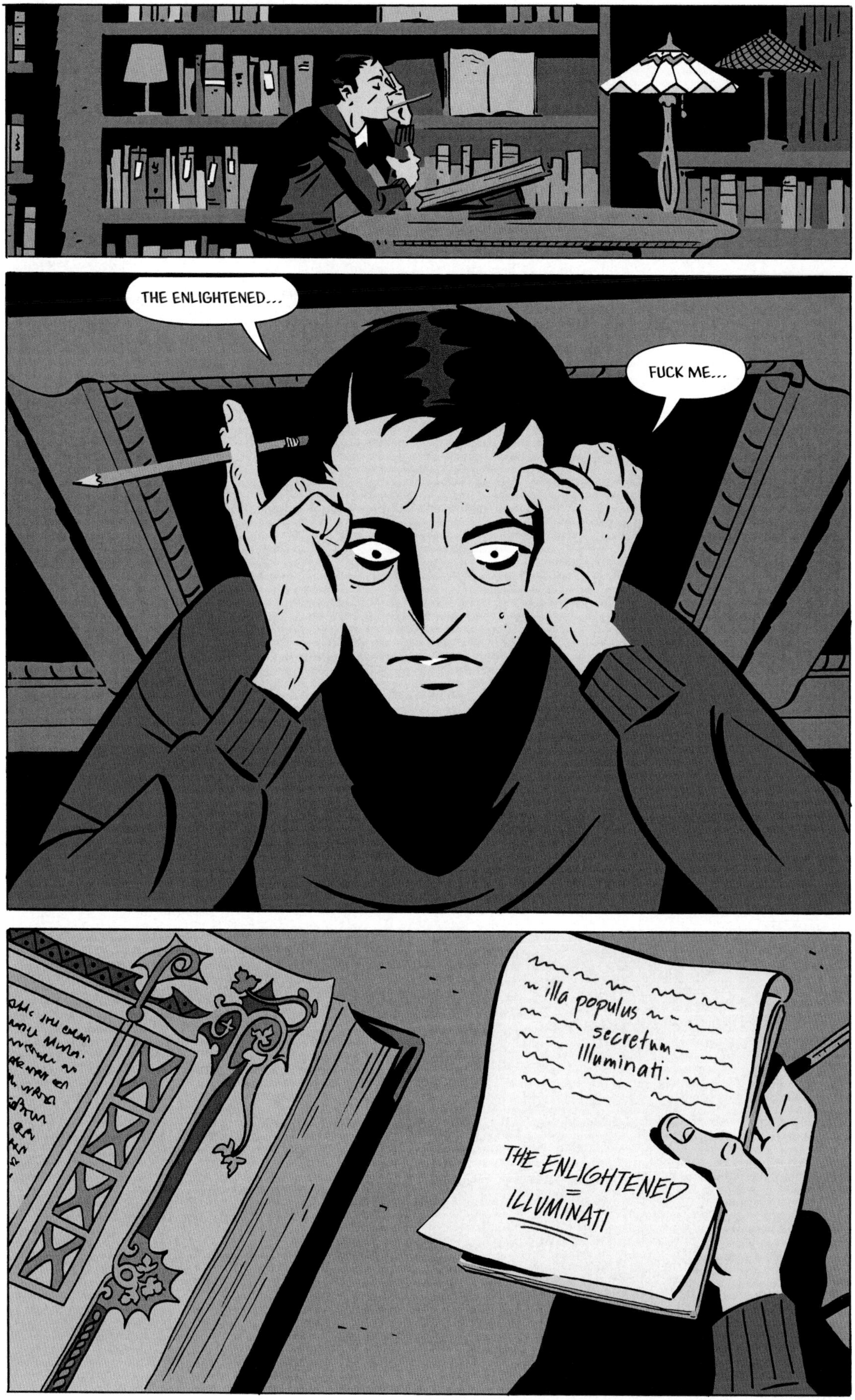
THE ENLIGHTENED...
FUCK ME...
illa populus
secretum
Illuminati.
THE ENLIGHTENED
=
ILLUMINATI

DEVIATION 2

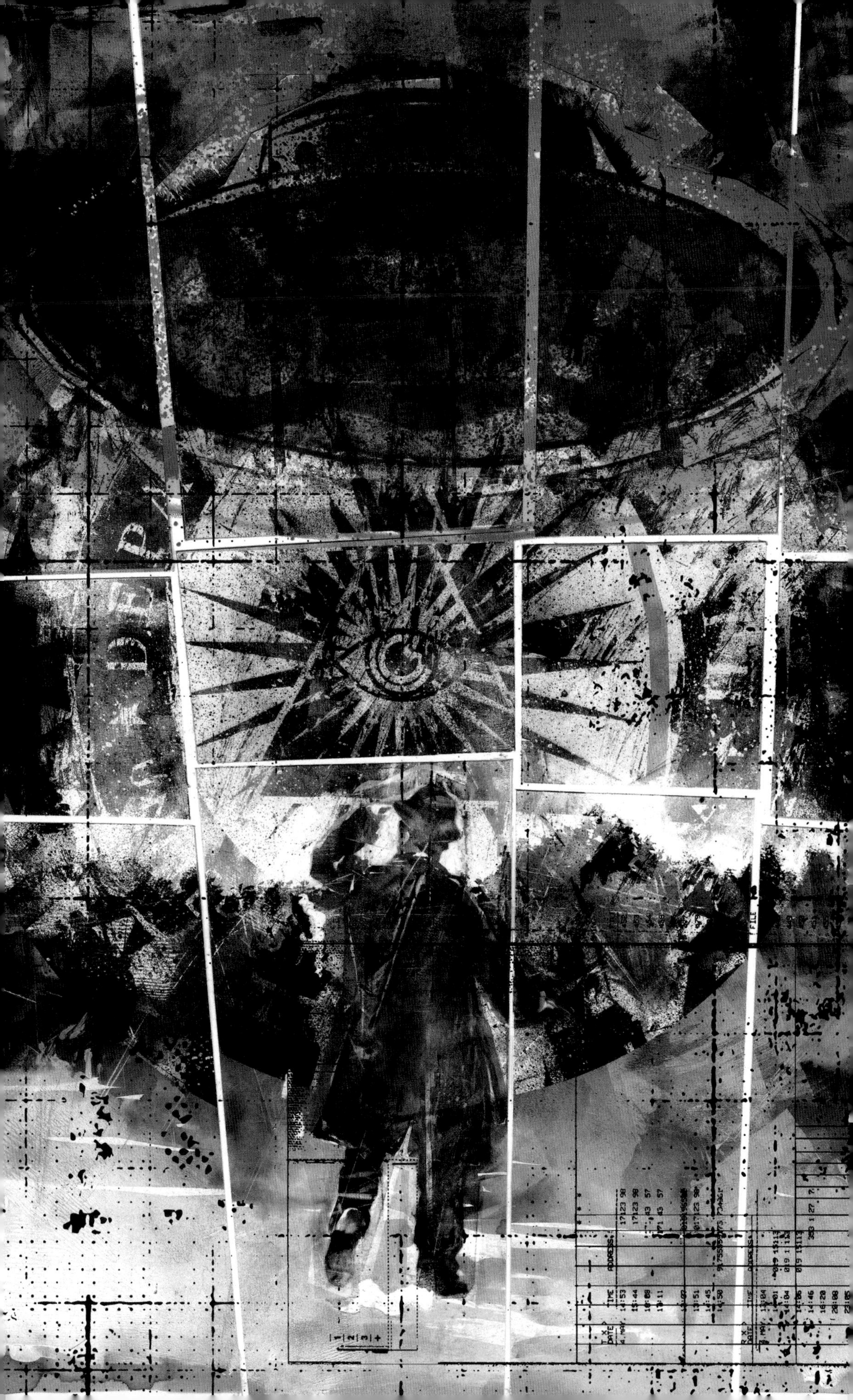

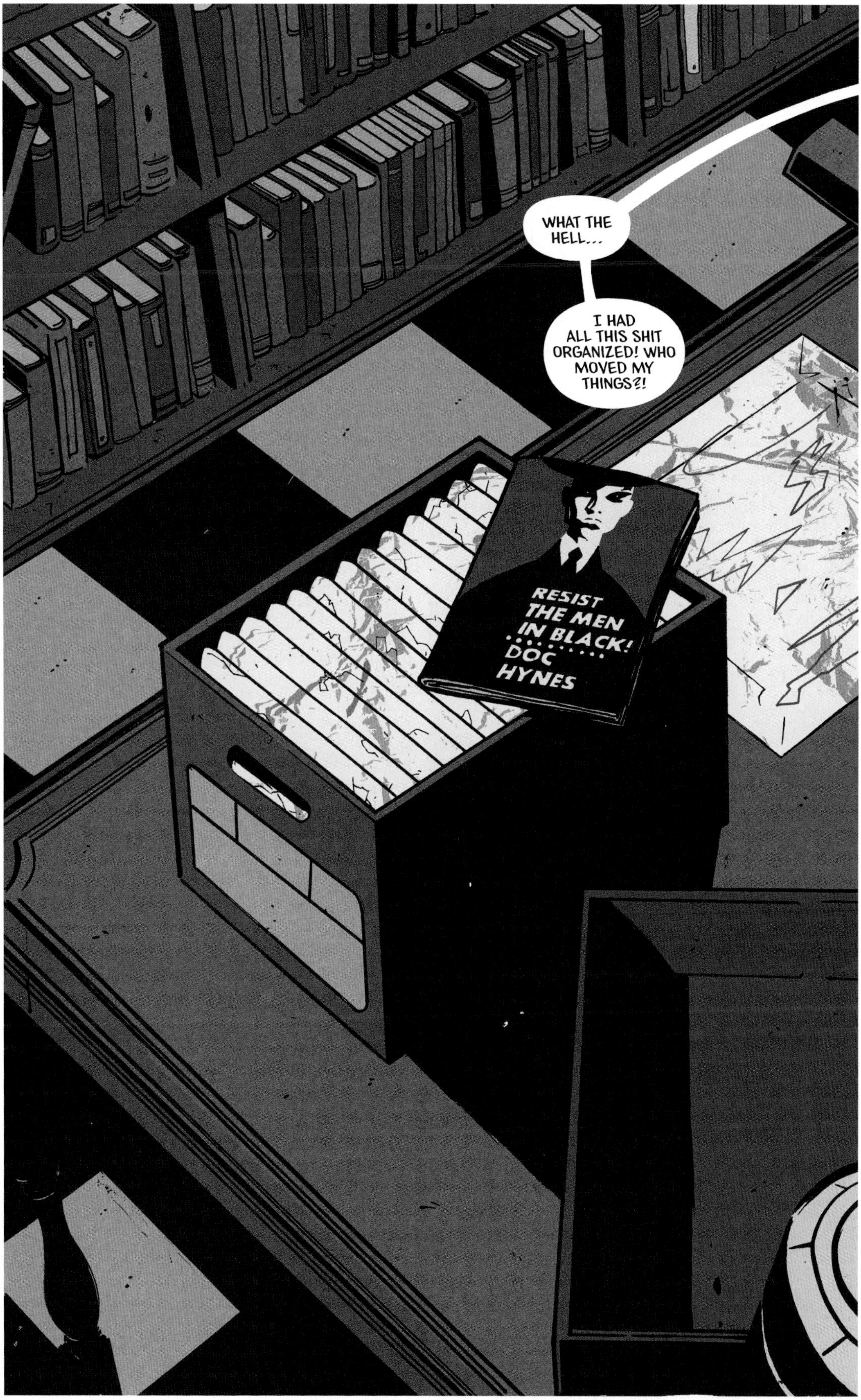
WHAT THE HELL...
I HAD ALL THIS SHIT ORGANIZED! WHO MOVED MY THINGS?!
RESIST THE MEN IN BLACK!
DOC HYNES

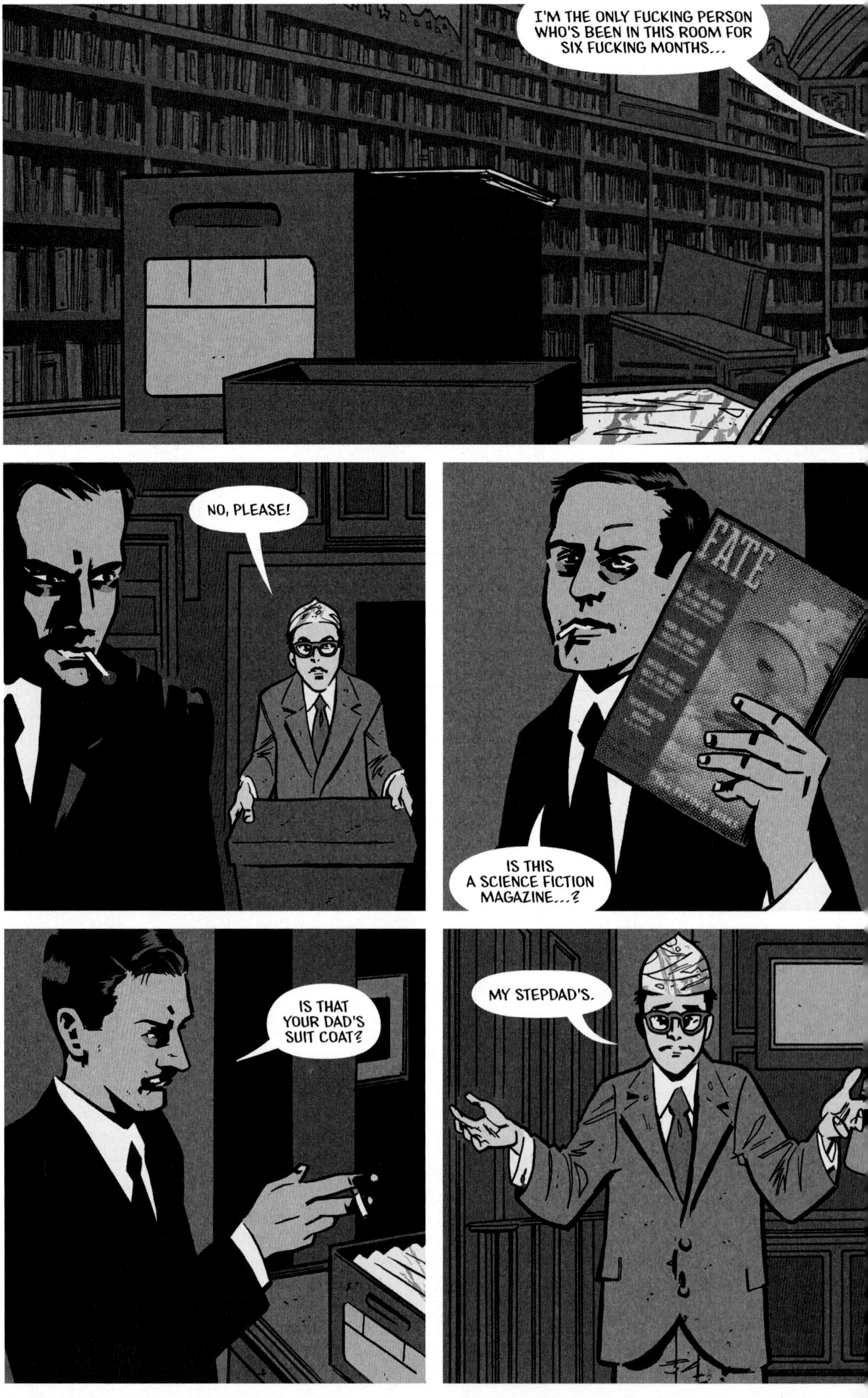
I'M THE ONLY FUCKING PERSON WHO'S BEEN IN THIS ROOM FOR SIX FUCKING MONTHS...
NO, PLEASE!
FATE
IS THIS A SCIENCE FICTION MAGAZINE...?
IS THAT YOUR DAD'S SUIT COAT?
MY STEPDAD'S.

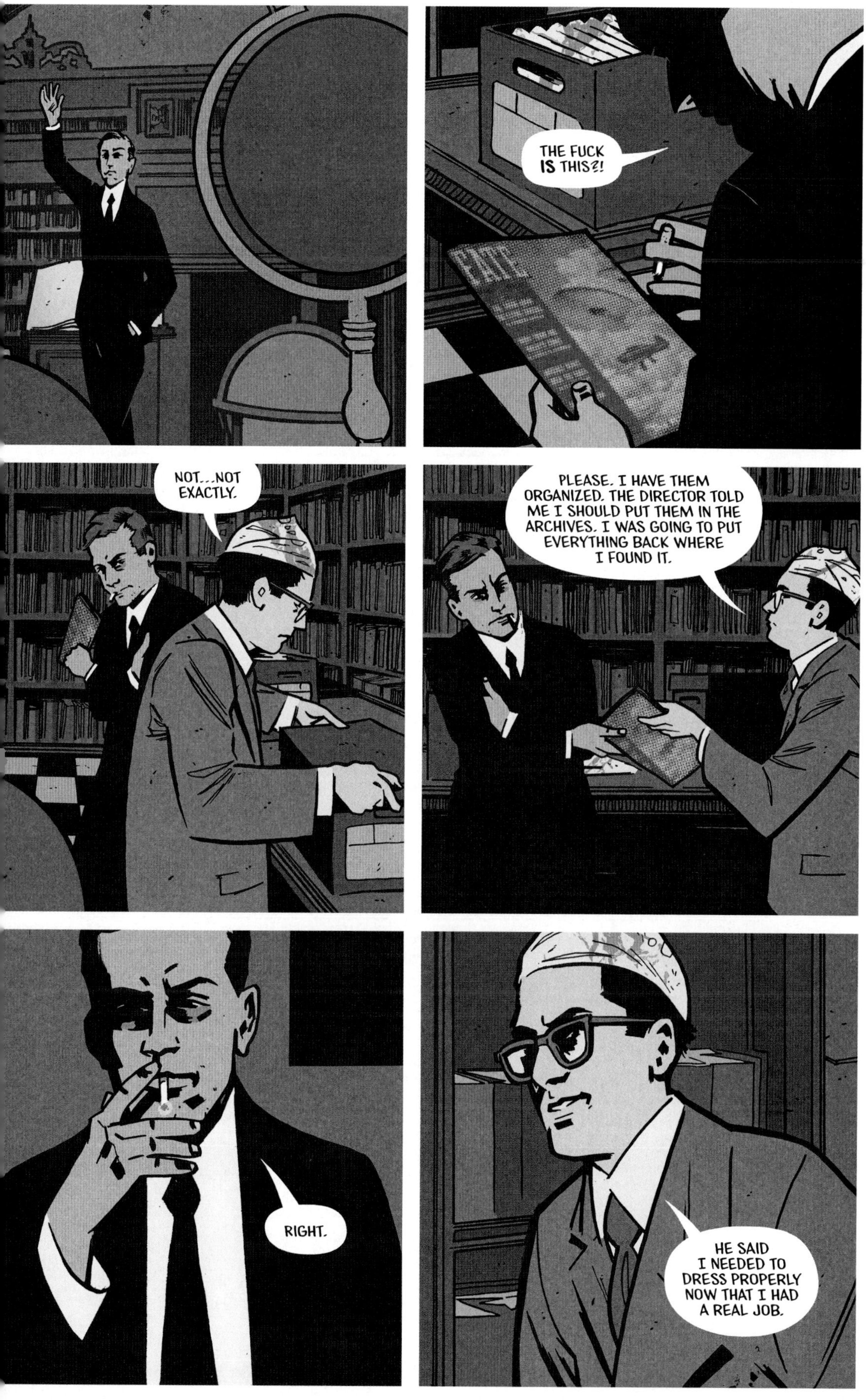
THE FUCK IS THIS?!
NOT...NOT EXACTLY.
PLEASE. I HAVE THEM ORGANIZED. THE DIRECTOR TOLD ME I SHOULD PUT THEM IN THE ARCHIVES. I WAS GOING TO PUT EVERYTHING BACK WHERE I FOUND IT.
RIGHT.
HE SAID I NEEDED TO DRESS PROPERLY NOW THAT I HAD A REAL JOB.

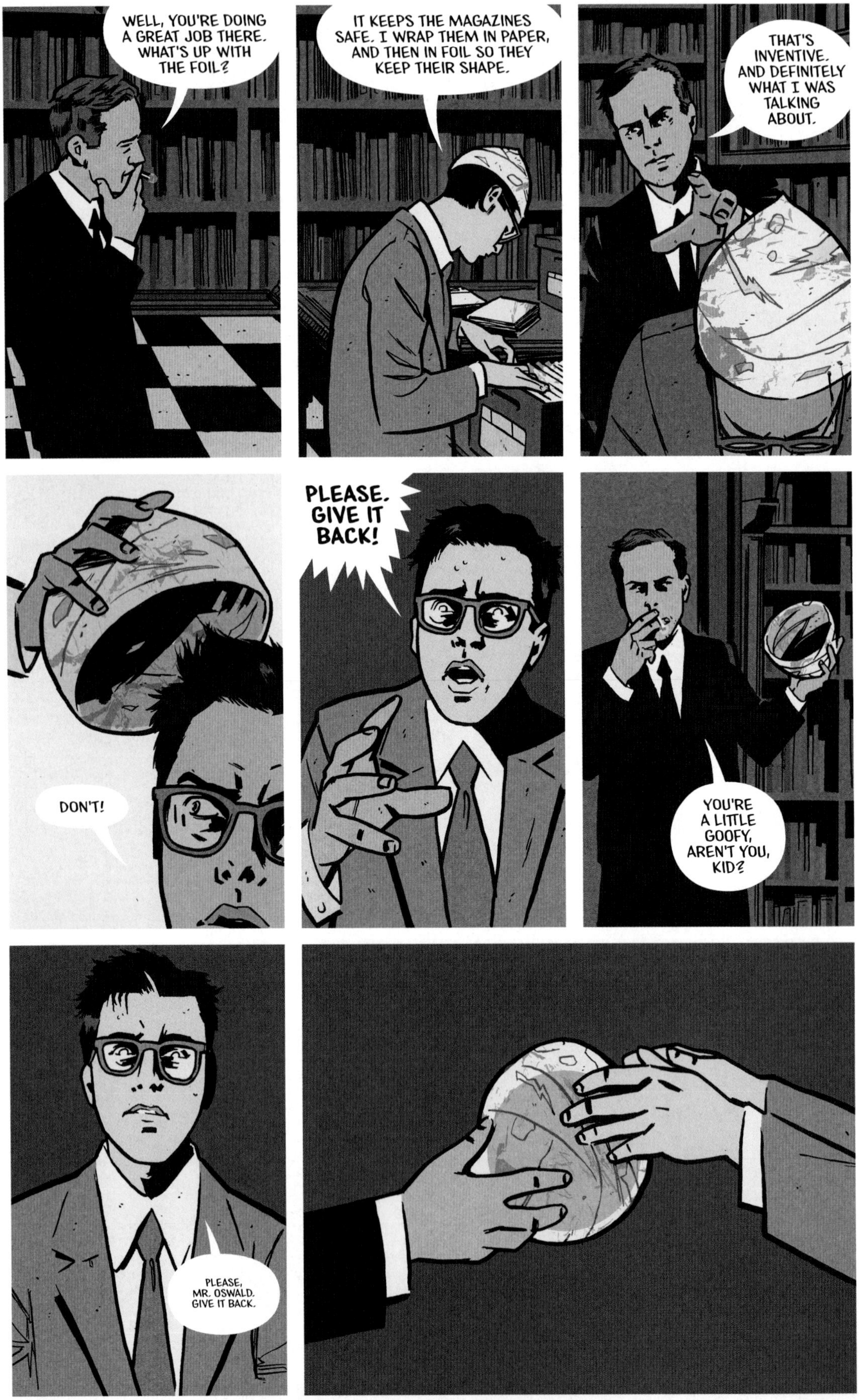
WELL, YOU'RE DOING A GREAT JOB THERE. WHAT'S UP WITH THE FOIL?
IT KEEPS THE MAGAZINES SAFE. I WRAP THEM IN PAPER, AND THEN IN FOIL SO THEY KEEP THEIR SHAPE.
THAT'S INVENTIVE. AND DEFINITELY WHAT I WAS TALKING ABOUT.
DON'T!
PLEASE. GIVE IT BACK!
YOU'RE A LITTLE GOOFY, AREN'T YOU, KID?
PLEASE, MR. OSWALD. GIVE IT BACK.

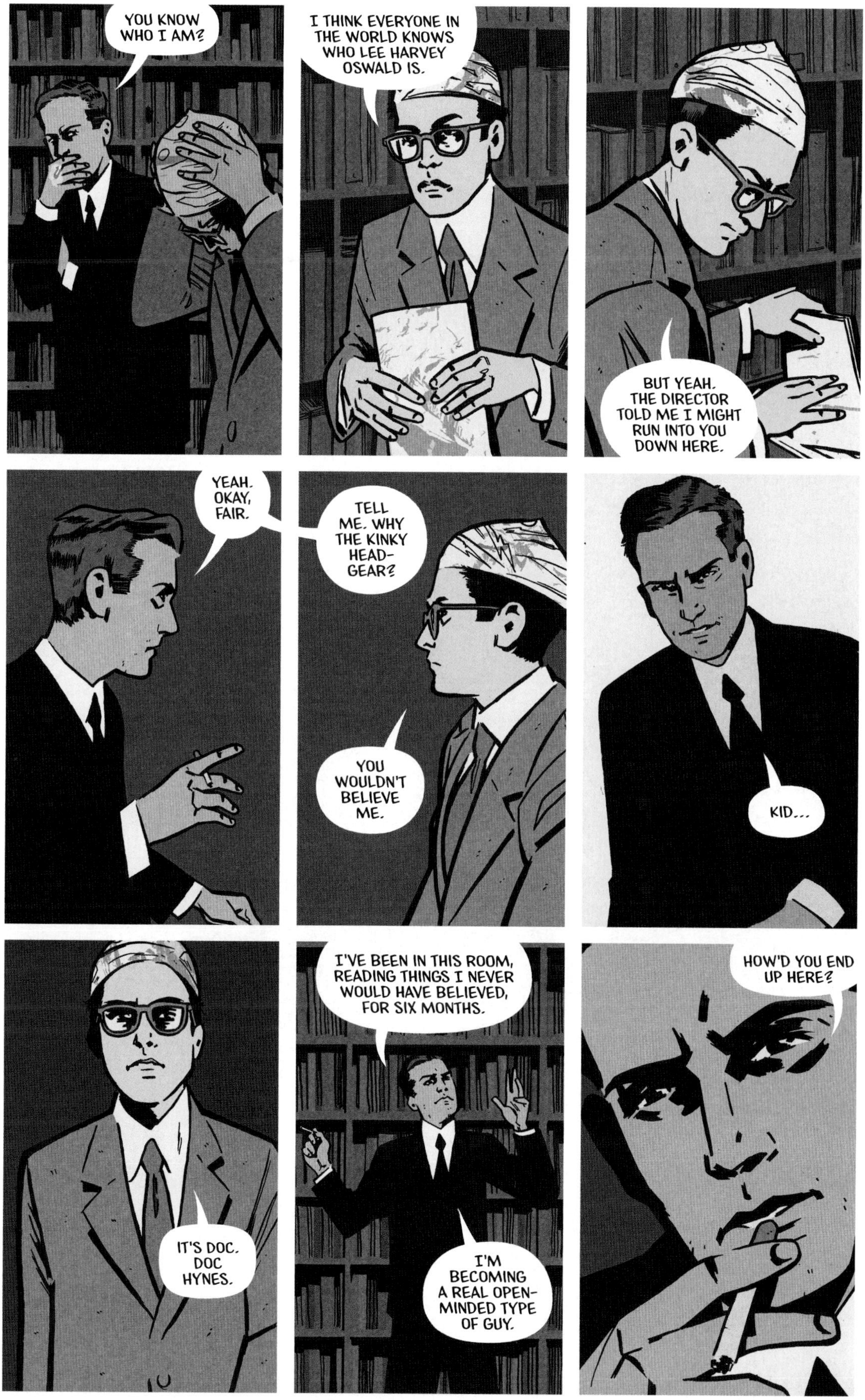
YOU KNOW WHO I AM?
I THINK EVERYONE IN THE WORLD KNOWS WHO LEE HARVEY OSWALD IS.
BUT YEAH. THE DIRECTOR TOLD ME I MIGHT RUN INTO YOU DOWN HERE.
YEAH. OKAY, FAIR.
TELL ME. WHY THE KINKY HEAD-GEAR?
YOU WOULDN'T BELIEVE ME.
KID...
IT'S DOC. DOC HYNES.
I'VE BEEN IN THIS ROOM, READING THINGS I NEVER WOULD HAVE BELIEVED, FOR SIX MONTHS.
I'M BECOMING A REAL OPEN-MINDED TYPE OF GUY.
HOW'D YOU END UP HERE?

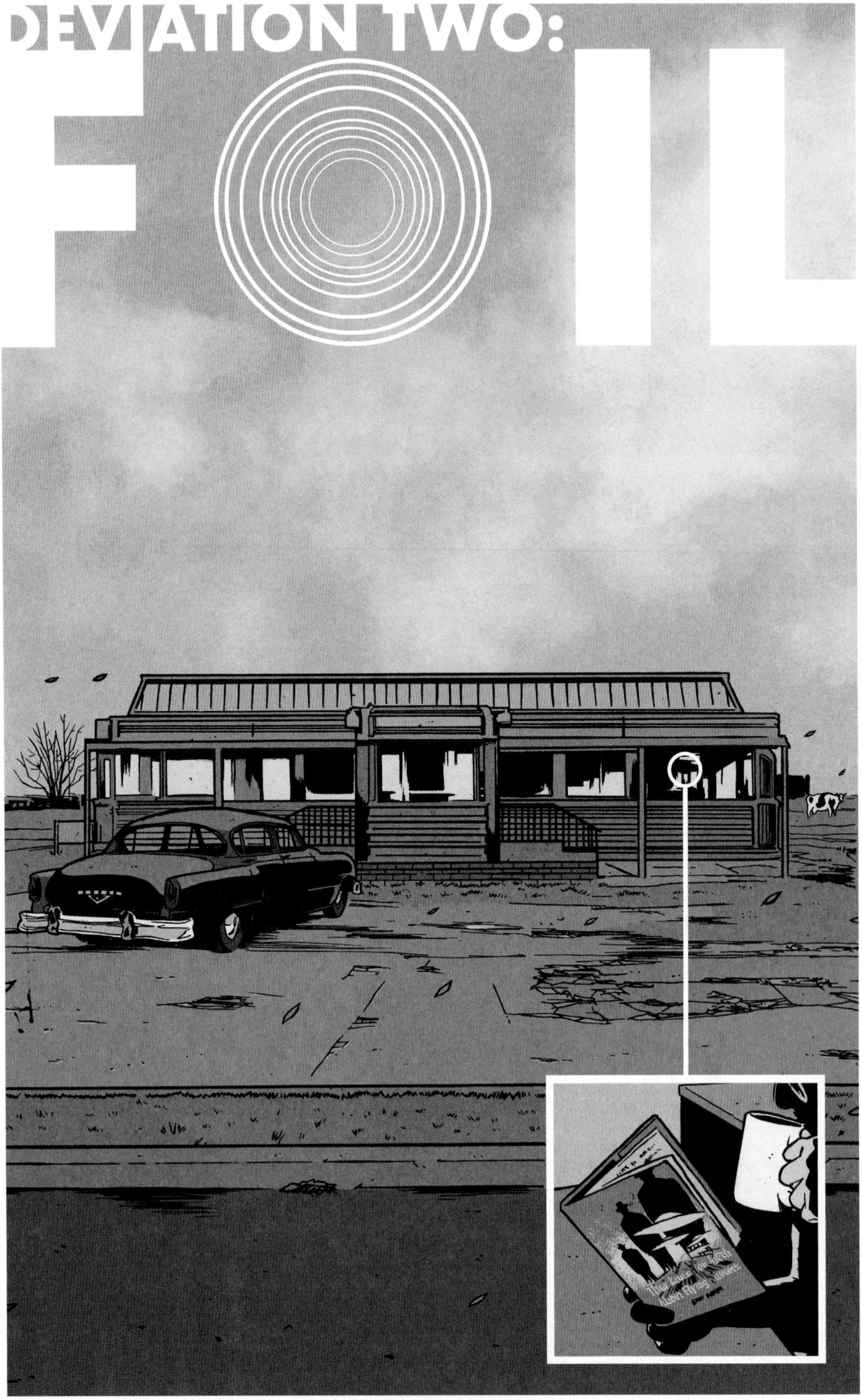
DEVIATION TWO:
FOIL

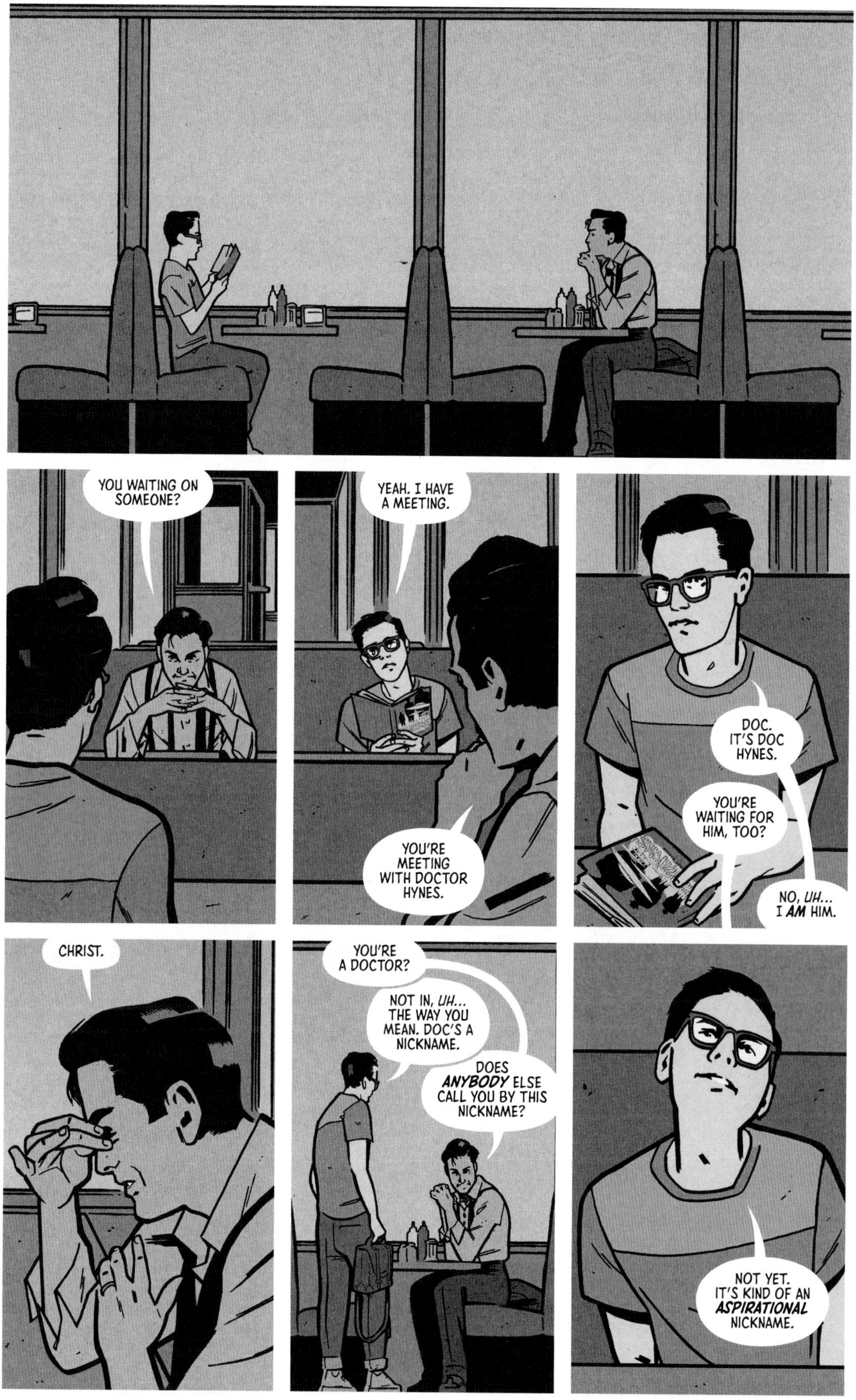

YOU WAITING ON SOMEONE?
YEAH. I HAVE A MEETING.
YOU'RE MEETING WITH DOCTOR HYNES.
DOC. IT'S DOC HYNES.
YOU'RE WAITING FOR HIM, TOO?
NO, *UH*... I ***AM*** HIM.
CHRIST.
YOU'RE A DOCTOR?
NOT IN, *UH*... THE WAY YOU MEAN. DOC'S A NICKNAME.
DOES ***ANYBODY*** ELSE CALL YOU BY THIS NICKNAME?
NOT YET. IT'S KIND OF AN ***ASPIRATIONAL*** NICKNAME.

THIS WAS A BAD IDEA. I DROVE SIX HOURS FOR THIS BAD IDEA.

YOU'RE FROM THE GOVERNMENT.

YEAH, KID. I'M FROM THE GOVERNMENT.

YOU SHOULD GET SOME PIE. THEY DO GOOD PIE HERE.

I DON'T WANT ANY--

YOU WANT ANYTHING?

JUST A COFFEE.

AND A SLICE OF PEACH PIE.

NO. JUST THE COFFEE.

I MEANT FOR ME.

FINE.

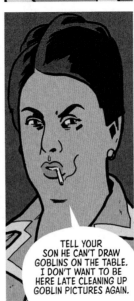
TELL YOUR SON HE CAN'T DRAW GOBLINS ON THE TABLE. I DON'T WANT TO BE HERE LATE CLEANING UP GOBLIN PICTURES AGAIN.

YES, MA'AM.

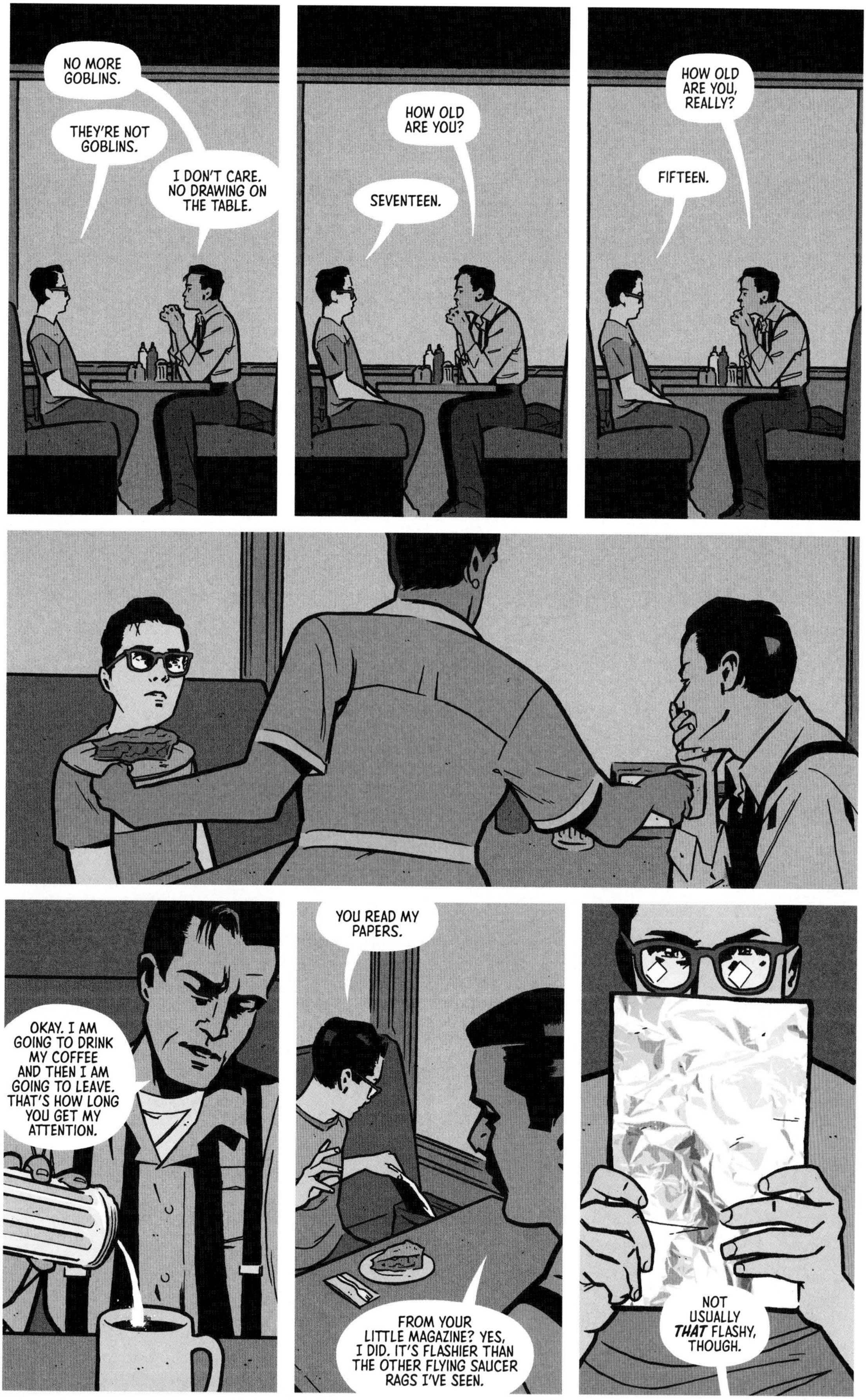
NO MORE GOBLINS.
THEY'RE NOT GOBLINS.
I DON'T CARE. NO DRAWING ON THE TABLE.
HOW OLD ARE YOU?
SEVENTEEN.
HOW OLD ARE YOU, REALLY?
FIFTEEN.
OKAY. I AM GOING TO DRINK MY COFFEE AND THEN I AM GOING TO LEAVE. THAT'S HOW LONG YOU GET MY ATTENTION.
YOU READ MY PAPERS.
FROM YOUR LITTLE MAGAZINE? YES, I DID. IT'S FLASHIER THAN THE OTHER FLYING SAUCER RAGS I'VE SEEN.
NOT USUALLY *THAT* FLASHY, THOUGH.

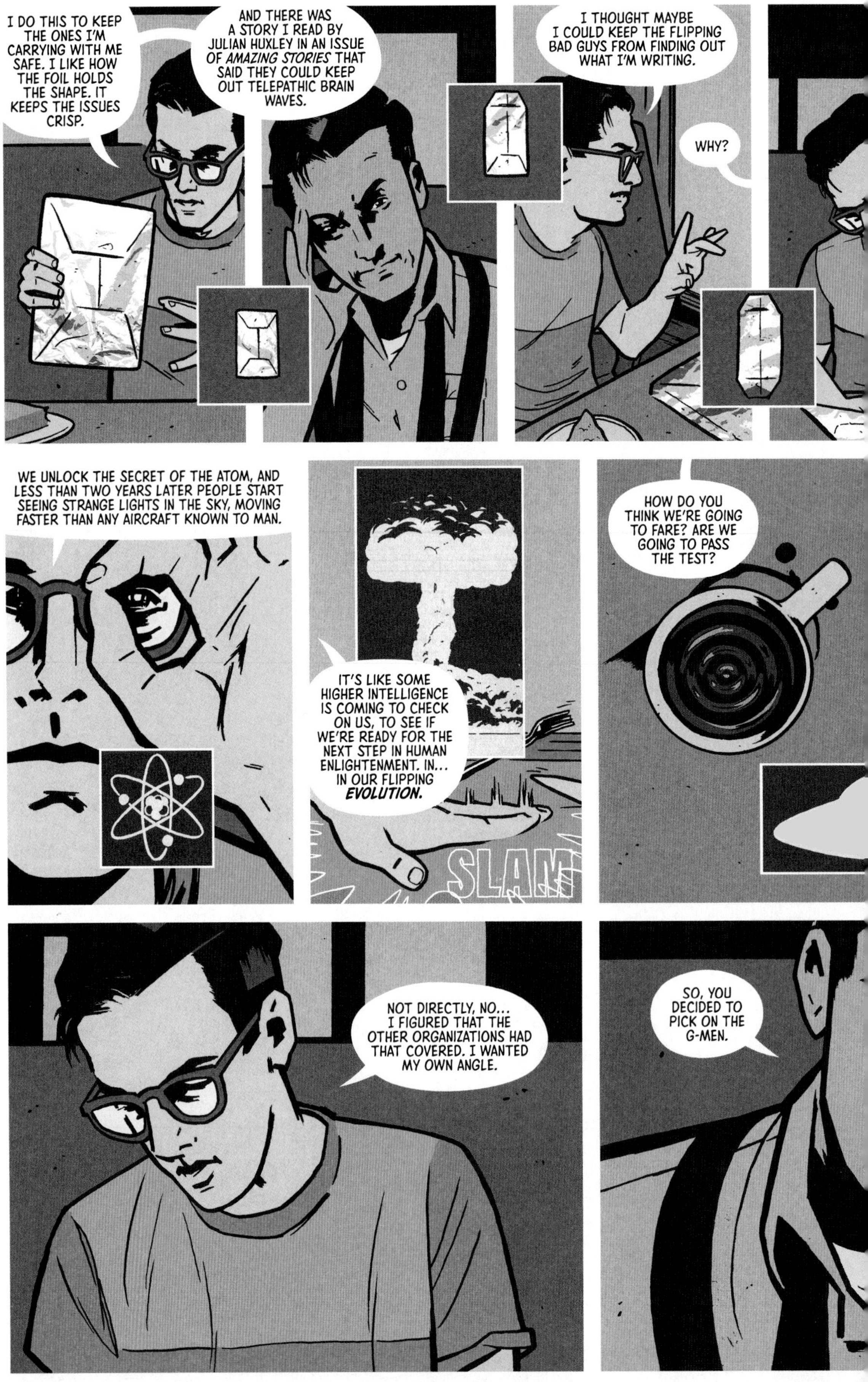
I DO THIS TO KEEP THE ONES I'M CARRYING WITH ME SAFE. I LIKE HOW THE FOIL HOLDS THE SHAPE. IT KEEPS THE ISSUES CRISP.
AND THERE WAS A STORY I READ BY JULIAN HUXLEY IN AN ISSUE OF *AMAZING STORIES* THAT SAID THEY COULD KEEP OUT TELEPATHIC BRAIN WAVES.
I THOUGHT MAYBE I COULD KEEP THE FLIPPING BAD GUYS FROM FINDING OUT WHAT I'M WRITING.
WHY?
WE UNLOCK THE SECRET OF THE ATOM, AND LESS THAN TWO YEARS LATER PEOPLE START SEEING STRANGE LIGHTS IN THE SKY, MOVING FASTER THAN ANY AIRCRAFT KNOWN TO MAN.
IT'S LIKE SOME HIGHER INTELLIGENCE IS COMING TO CHECK ON US, TO SEE IF WE'RE READY FOR THE NEXT STEP IN HUMAN ENLIGHTENMENT. IN... IN OUR FLIPPING ***EVOLUTION.***
SLAM
HOW DO YOU THINK WE'RE GOING TO FARE? ARE WE GOING TO PASS THE TEST?
NOT DIRECTLY, NO... I FIGURED THAT THE OTHER ORGANIZATIONS HAD THAT COVERED. I WANTED MY OWN ANGLE.
SO, YOU DECIDED TO PICK ON THE G-MEN.

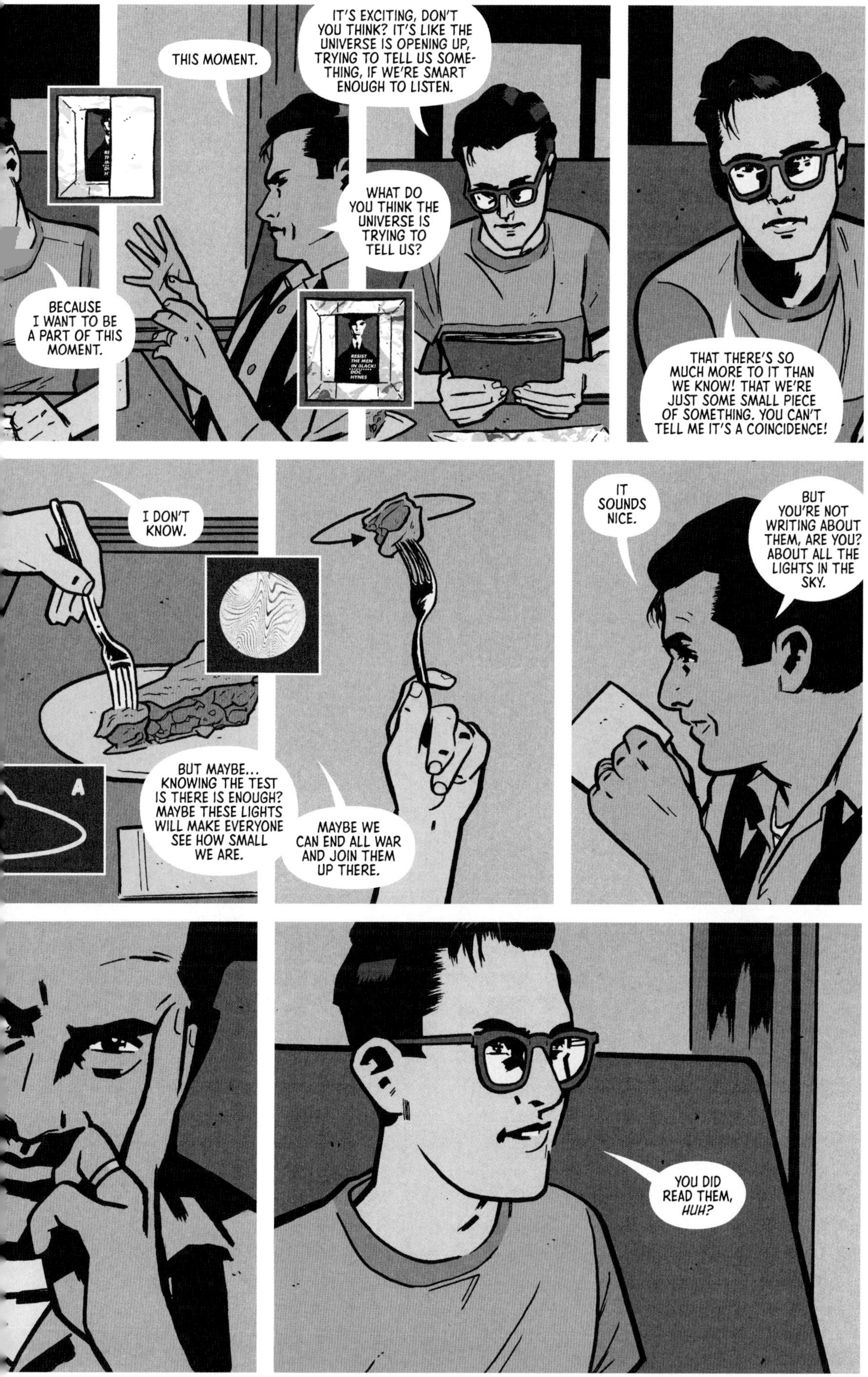
BECAUSE I WANT TO BE A PART OF THIS MOMENT.
THIS MOMENT.
IT'S EXCITING, DON'T YOU THINK? IT'S LIKE THE UNIVERSE IS OPENING UP, TRYING TO TELL US SOME-THING, IF WE'RE SMART ENOUGH TO LISTEN.
WHAT DO YOU THINK THE UNIVERSE IS TRYING TO TELL US?
RESIST THE MEN IN BLACK! DOC HYNES
THAT THERE'S SO MUCH MORE TO IT THAN WE KNOW! THAT WE'RE JUST SOME SMALL PIECE OF SOMETHING. YOU CAN'T TELL ME IT'S A COINCIDENCE!
I DON'T KNOW.
BUT MAYBE... KNOWING THE TEST IS THERE IS ENOUGH? MAYBE THESE LIGHTS WILL MAKE EVERYONE SEE HOW SMALL WE ARE.
MAYBE WE CAN END ALL WAR AND JOIN THEM UP THERE.
IT SOUNDS NICE.
BUT YOU'RE NOT WRITING ABOUT THEM, ARE YOU? ABOUT ALL THE LIGHTS IN THE SKY.
YOU DID READ THEM, *HUH?*

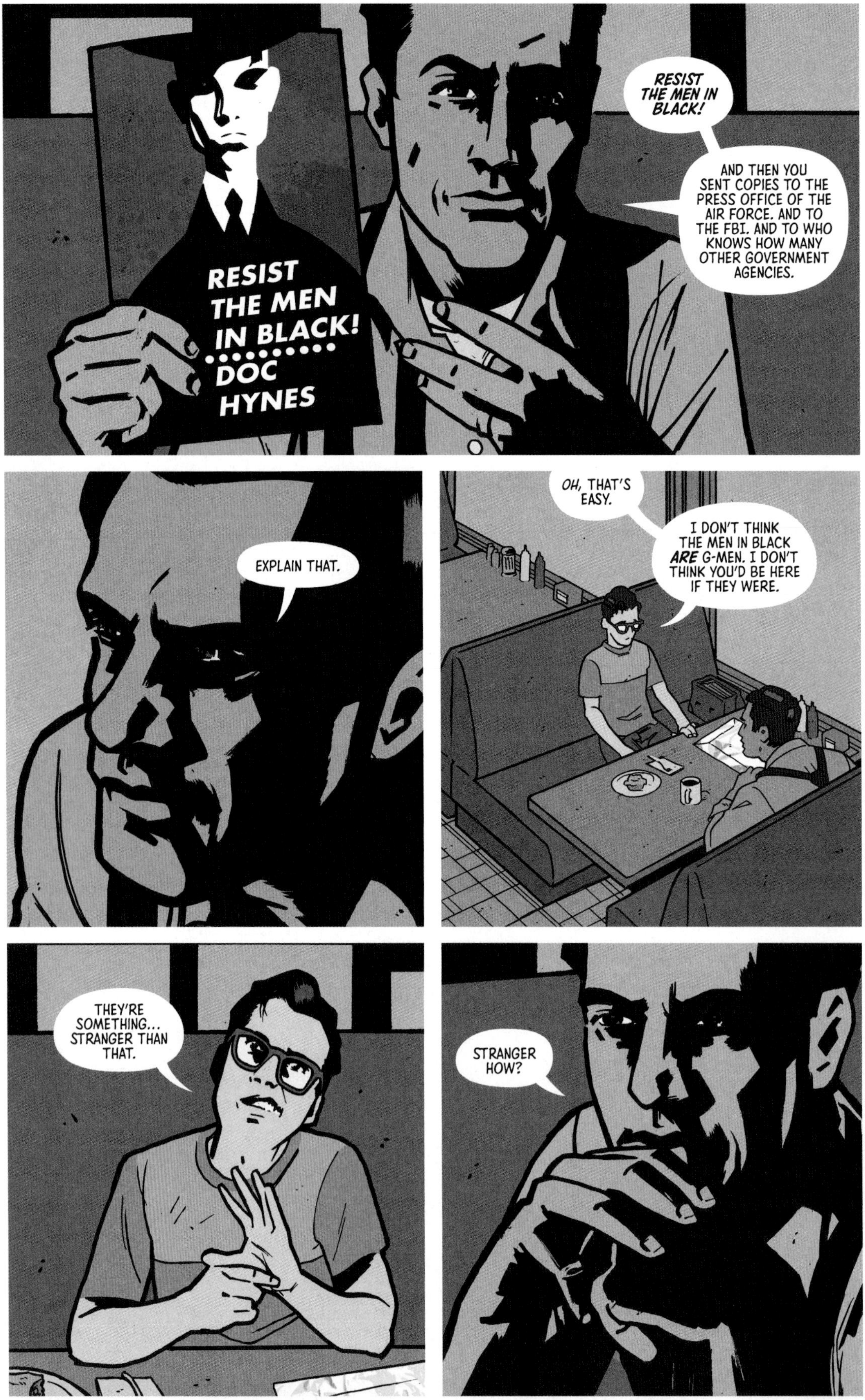

RESIST THE MEN IN BLACK! DOC HYNES
RESIST THE MEN IN BLACK!
AND THEN YOU SENT COPIES TO THE PRESS OFFICE OF THE AIR FORCE. AND TO THE FBI. AND TO WHO KNOWS HOW MANY OTHER GOVERNMENT AGENCIES.
EXPLAIN THAT.
OH, THAT'S EASY.
I DON'T THINK THE MEN IN BLACK ARE G-MEN. I DON'T THINK YOU'D BE HERE IF THEY WERE.
THEY'RE SOMETHING... STRANGER THAN THAT.
STRANGER HOW?

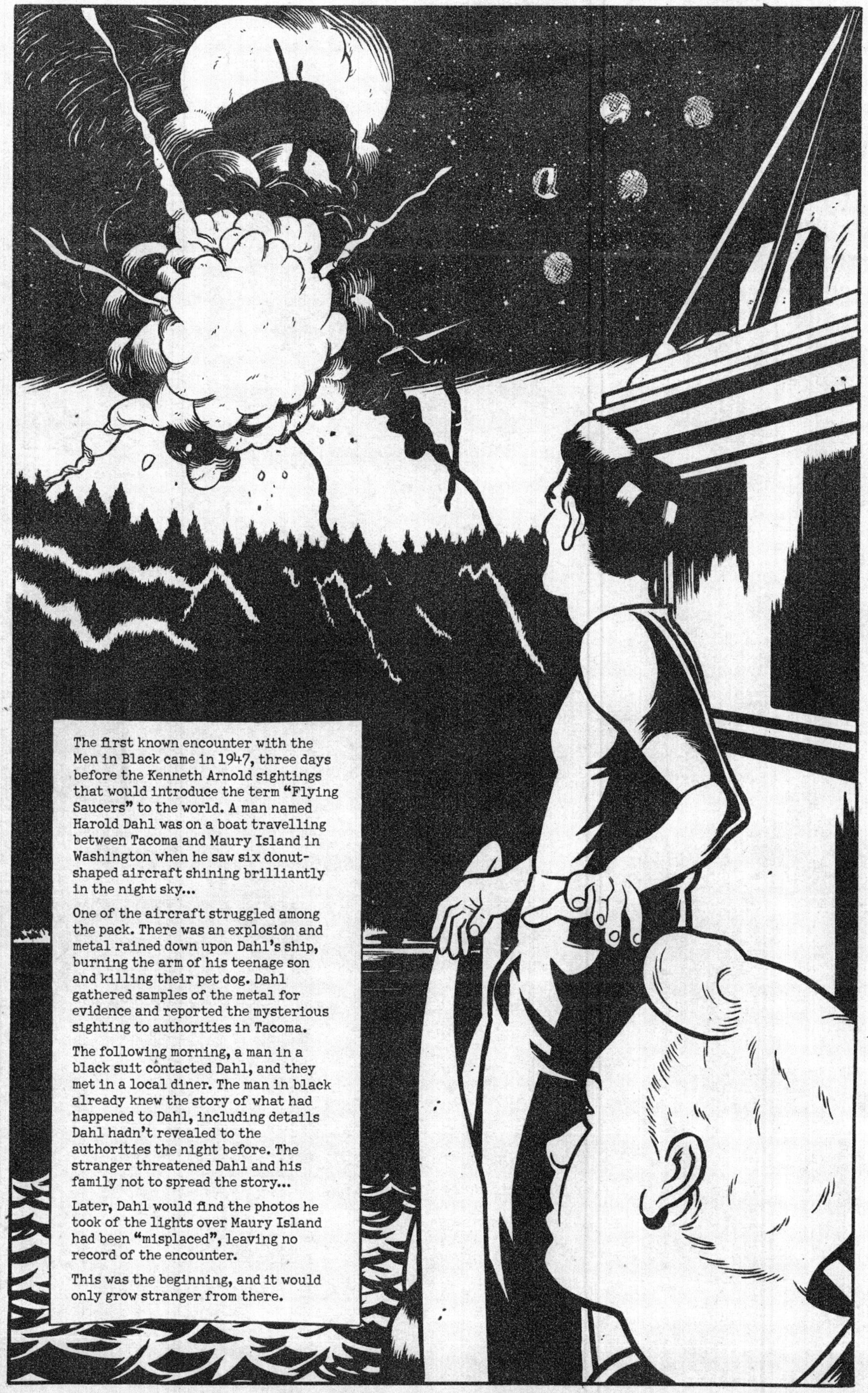
The first known encounter with the Men in Black came in 1947, three days before the Kenneth Arnold sightings that would introduce the term "Flying Saucers" to the world. A man named Harold Dahl was on a boat travelling between Tacoma and Maury Island in Washington when he saw six donut-shaped aircraft shining brilliantly in the night sky...
One of the aircraft struggled among the pack. There was an explosion and metal rained down upon Dahl's ship, burning the arm of his teenage son and killing their pet dog. Dahl gathered samples of the metal for evidence and reported the mysterious sighting to authorities in Tacoma.
The following morning, a man in a black suit contacted Dahl, and they met in a local diner. The man in black already knew the story of what had happened to Dahl, including details Dahl hadn't revealed to the authorities the night before. The stranger threatened Dahl and his family not to spread the story...
Later, Dahl would find the photos he took of the lights over Maury Island had been "misplaced", leaving no record of the encounter.
This was the beginning, and it would only grow stranger from there.

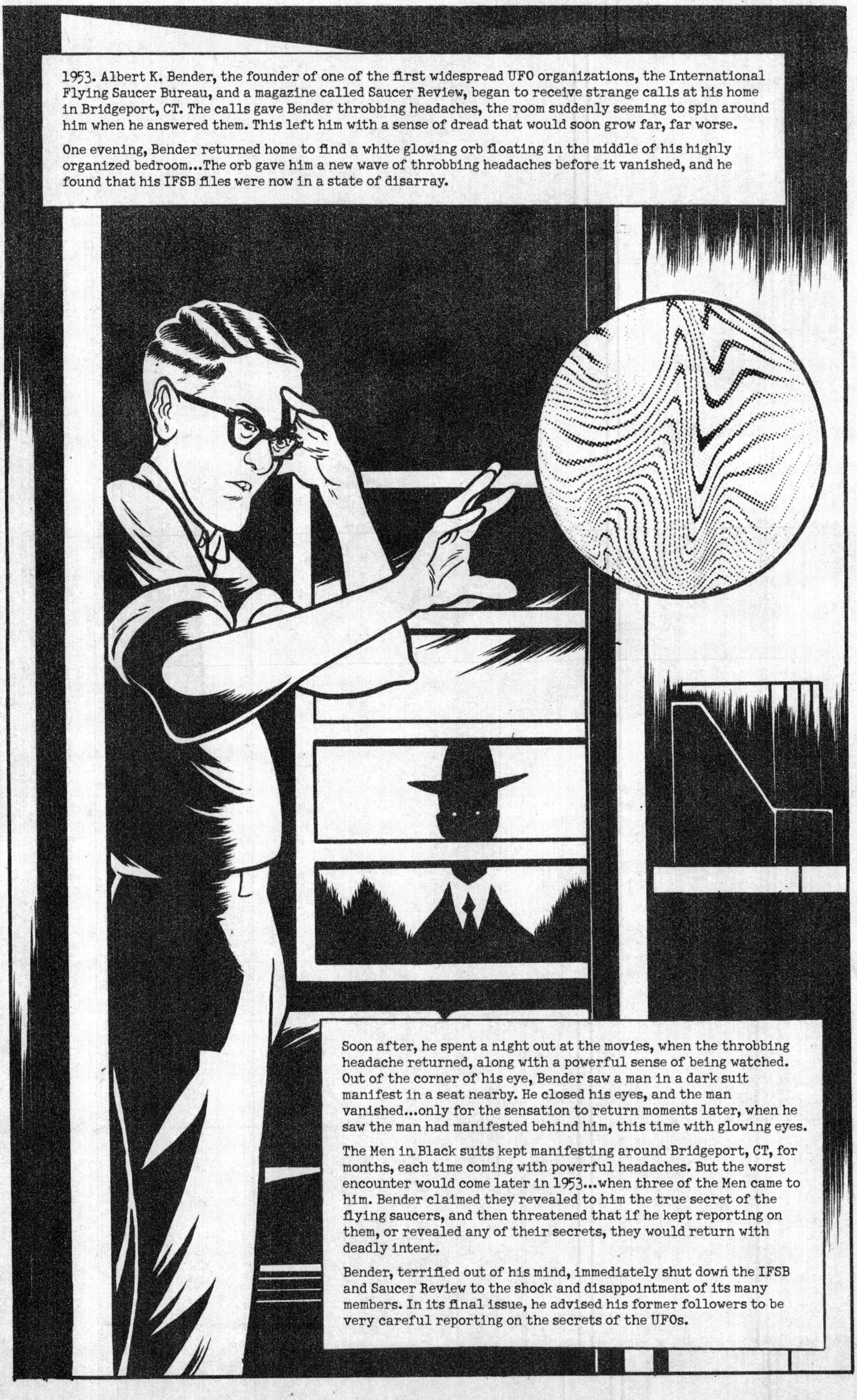
1953. Albert K. Bender, the founder of one of the first widespread UFO organizations, the International Flying Saucer Bureau, and a magazine called Saucer Review, began to receive strange calls at his home in Bridgeport, CT. The calls gave Bender throbbing headaches, the room suddenly seeming to spin around him when he answered them. This left him with a sense of dread that would soon grow far, far worse.
One evening, Bender returned home to find a white glowing orb floating in the middle of his highly organized bedroom...The orb gave him a new wave of throbbing headaches before it vanished, and he found that his IFSB files were now in a state of disarray.
Soon after, he spent a night out at the movies, when the throbbing headache returned, along with a powerful sense of being watched. Out of the corner of his eye, Bender saw a man in a dark suit manifest in a seat nearby. He closed his eyes, and the man vanished...only for the sensation to return moments later, when he saw the man had manifested behind him, this time with glowing eyes.
The Men in Black suits kept manifesting around Bridgeport, CT, for months, each time coming with powerful headaches. But the worst encounter would come later in 1953...when three of the Men came to him. Bender claimed they revealed to him the true secret of the flying saucers, and then threatened that if he kept reporting on them, or revealed any of their secrets, they would return with deadly intent.
Bender, terrified out of his mind, immediately shut down the IFSB and Saucer Review to the shock and disappointment of its many members. In its final issue, he advised his former followers to be very careful reporting on the secrets of the UFOs.

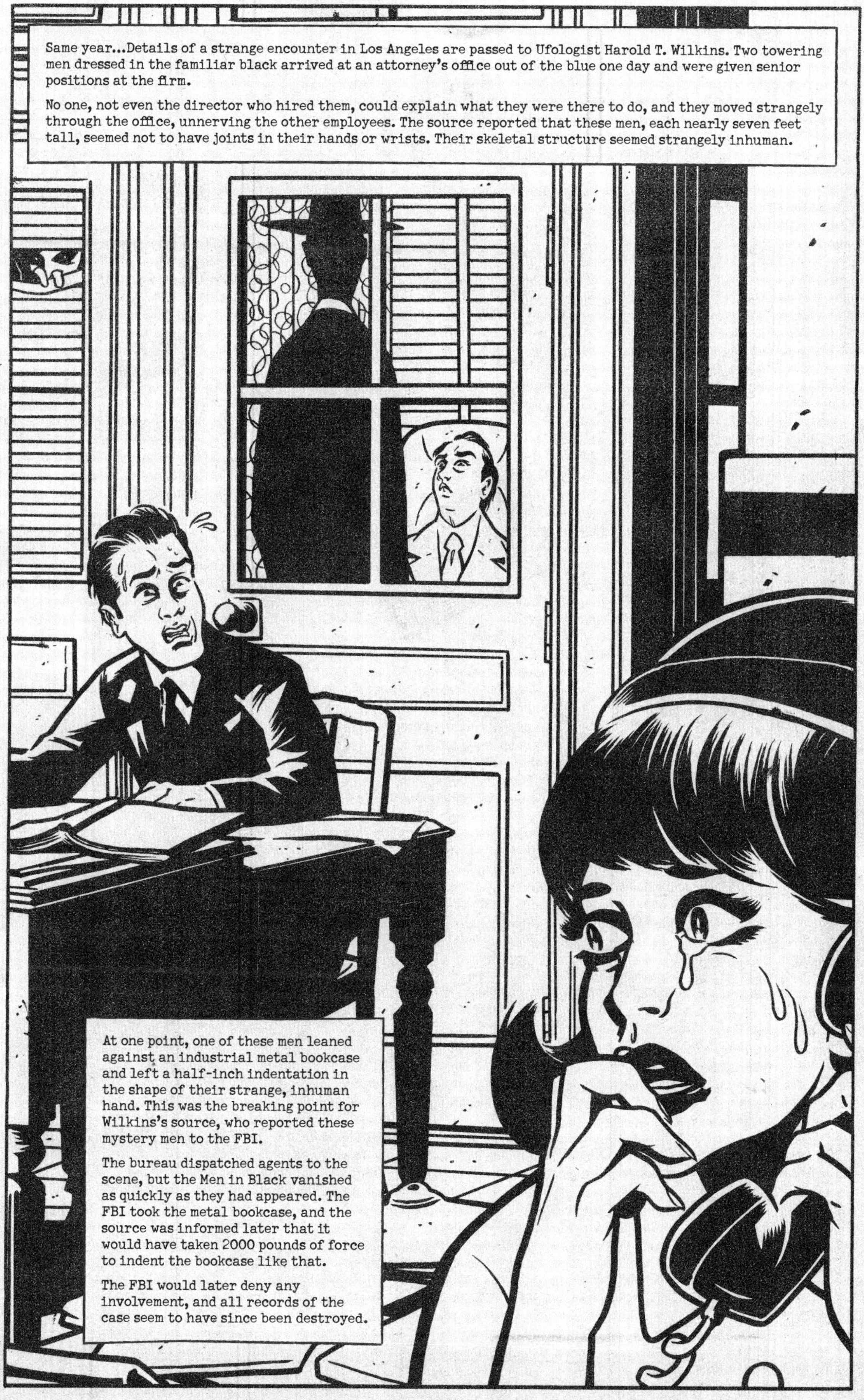
Same year...Details of a strange encounter in Los Angeles are passed to Ufologist Harold T. Wilkins. Two towering men dressed in the familiar black arrived at an attorney's office out of the blue one day and were given senior positions at the firm.
No one, not even the director who hired them, could explain what they were there to do, and they moved strangely through the office, unnerving the other employees. The source reported that these men, each nearly seven feet tall, seemed not to have joints in their hands or wrists. Their skeletal structure seemed strangely inhuman.
At one point, one of these men leaned against an industrial metal bookcase and left a half-inch indentation in the shape of their strange, inhuman hand. This was the breaking point for Wilkins's source, who reported these mystery men to the FBI.
The bureau dispatched agents to the scene, but the Men in Black vanished as quickly as they had appeared. The FBI took the metal bookcase, and the source was informed later that it would have taken 2000 pounds of force to indent the bookcase like that.
The FBI would later deny any involvement, and all records of the case seem to have since been destroyed.

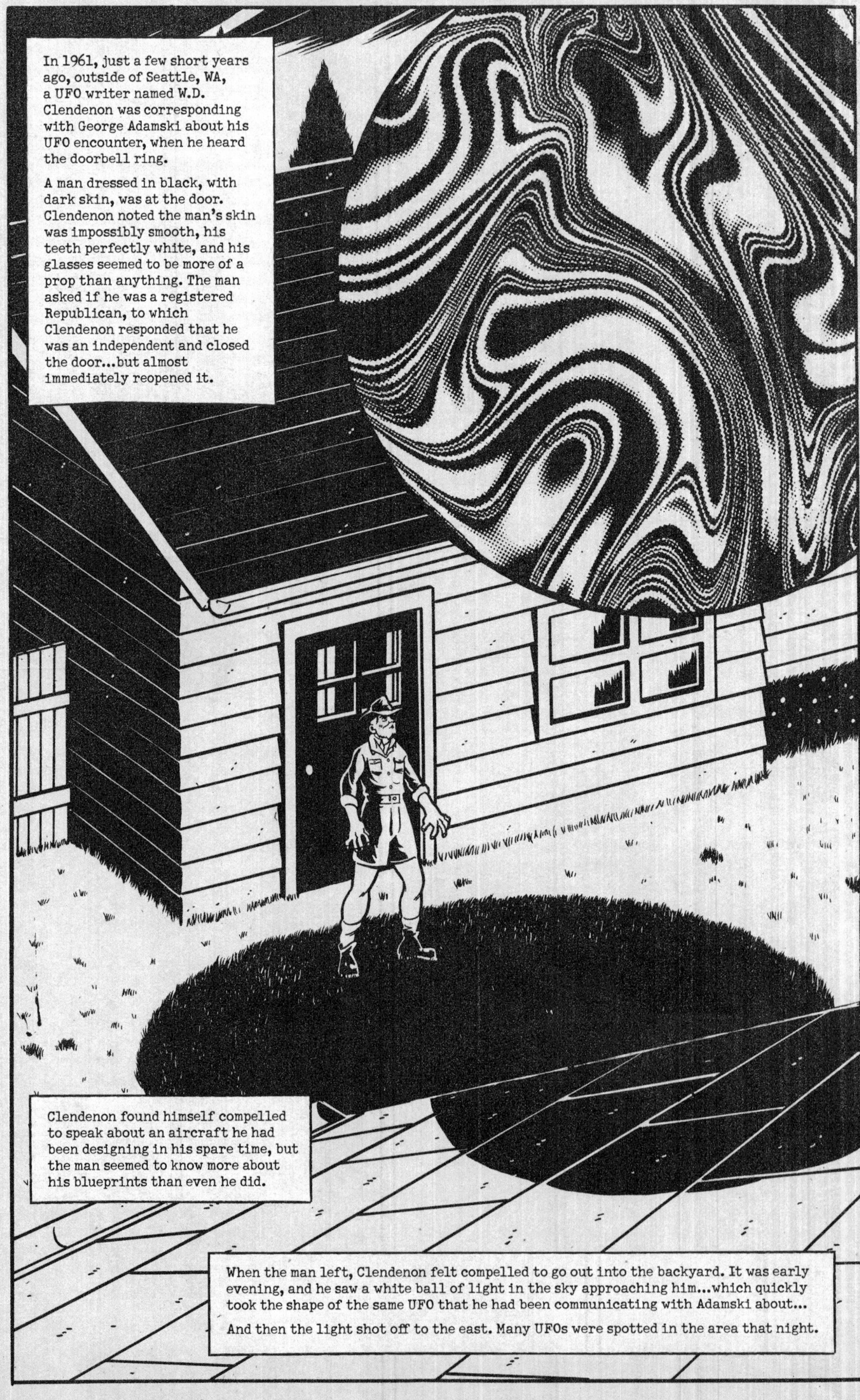
In 1961, just a few short years ago, outside of Seattle, WA, a UFO writer named W.D. Clendenon was corresponding with George Adamski about his UFO encounter, when he heard the doorbell ring.
A man dressed in black, with dark skin, was at the door. Clendenon noted the man's skin was impossibly smooth, his teeth perfectly white, and his glasses seemed to be more of a prop than anything. The man asked if he was a registered Republican, to which Clendenon responded that he was an independent and closed the door...but almost immediately reopened it.
Clendenon found himself compelled to speak about an aircraft he had been designing in his spare time, but the man seemed to know more about his blueprints than even he did.
When the man left, Clendenon felt compelled to go out into the backyard. It was early evening, and he saw a white ball of light in the sky approaching him...which quickly took the shape of the same UFO that he had been communicating with Adamski about...
And then the light shot off to the east. Many UFOs were spotted in the area that night.

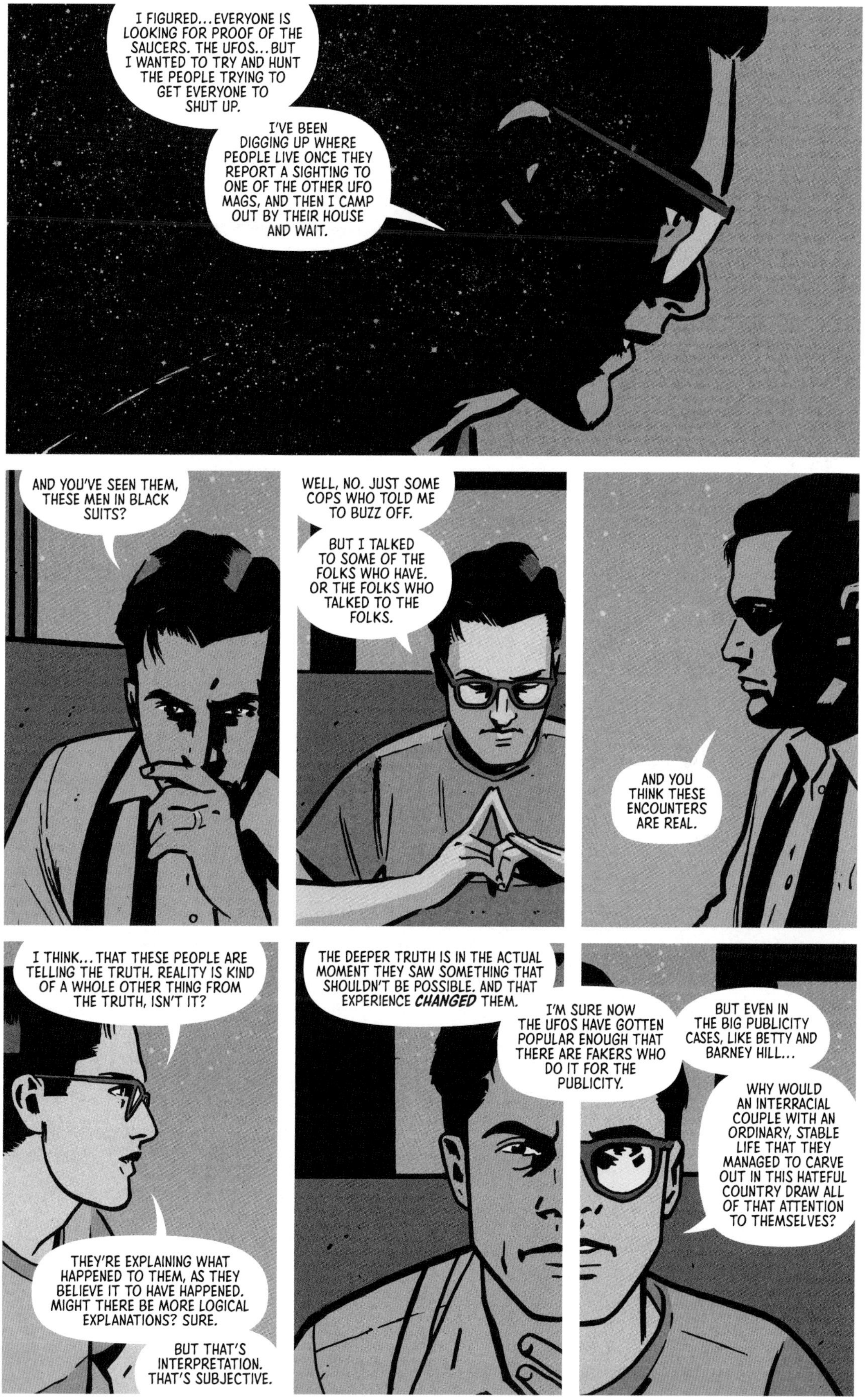
I FIGURED...EVERYONE IS LOOKING FOR PROOF OF THE SAUCERS. THE UFOS...BUT I WANTED TO TRY AND HUNT THE PEOPLE TRYING TO GET EVERYONE TO SHUT UP.
I'VE BEEN DIGGING UP WHERE PEOPLE LIVE ONCE THEY REPORT A SIGHTING TO ONE OF THE OTHER UFO MAGS, AND THEN I CAMP OUT BY THEIR HOUSE AND WAIT.
AND YOU'VE SEEN THEM, THESE MEN IN BLACK SUITS?
WELL, NO. JUST SOME COPS WHO TOLD ME TO BUZZ OFF.
BUT I TALKED TO SOME OF THE FOLKS WHO HAVE. OR THE FOLKS WHO TALKED TO THE FOLKS.
AND YOU THINK THESE ENCOUNTERS ARE REAL.
I THINK...THAT THESE PEOPLE ARE TELLING THE TRUTH. REALITY IS KIND OF A WHOLE OTHER THING FROM THE TRUTH, ISN'T IT?
THEY'RE EXPLAINING WHAT HAPPENED TO THEM, AS THEY BELIEVE IT TO HAVE HAPPENED. MIGHT THERE BE MORE LOGICAL EXPLANATIONS? SURE.
BUT THAT'S INTERPRETATION. THAT'S SUBJECTIVE.
THE DEEPER TRUTH IS IN THE ACTUAL MOMENT THEY SAW SOMETHING THAT SHOULDN'T BE POSSIBLE. AND THAT EXPERIENCE *CHANGED* THEM.
I'M SURE NOW THE UFOS HAVE GOTTEN POPULAR ENOUGH THAT THERE ARE FAKERS WHO DO IT FOR THE PUBLICITY.
BUT EVEN IN THE BIG PUBLICITY CASES, LIKE BETTY AND BARNEY HILL...
WHY WOULD AN INTERRACIAL COUPLE WITH AN ORDINARY, STABLE LIFE THAT THEY MANAGED TO CARVE OUT IN THIS HATEFUL COUNTRY DRAW ALL OF THAT ATTENTION TO THEMSELVES?

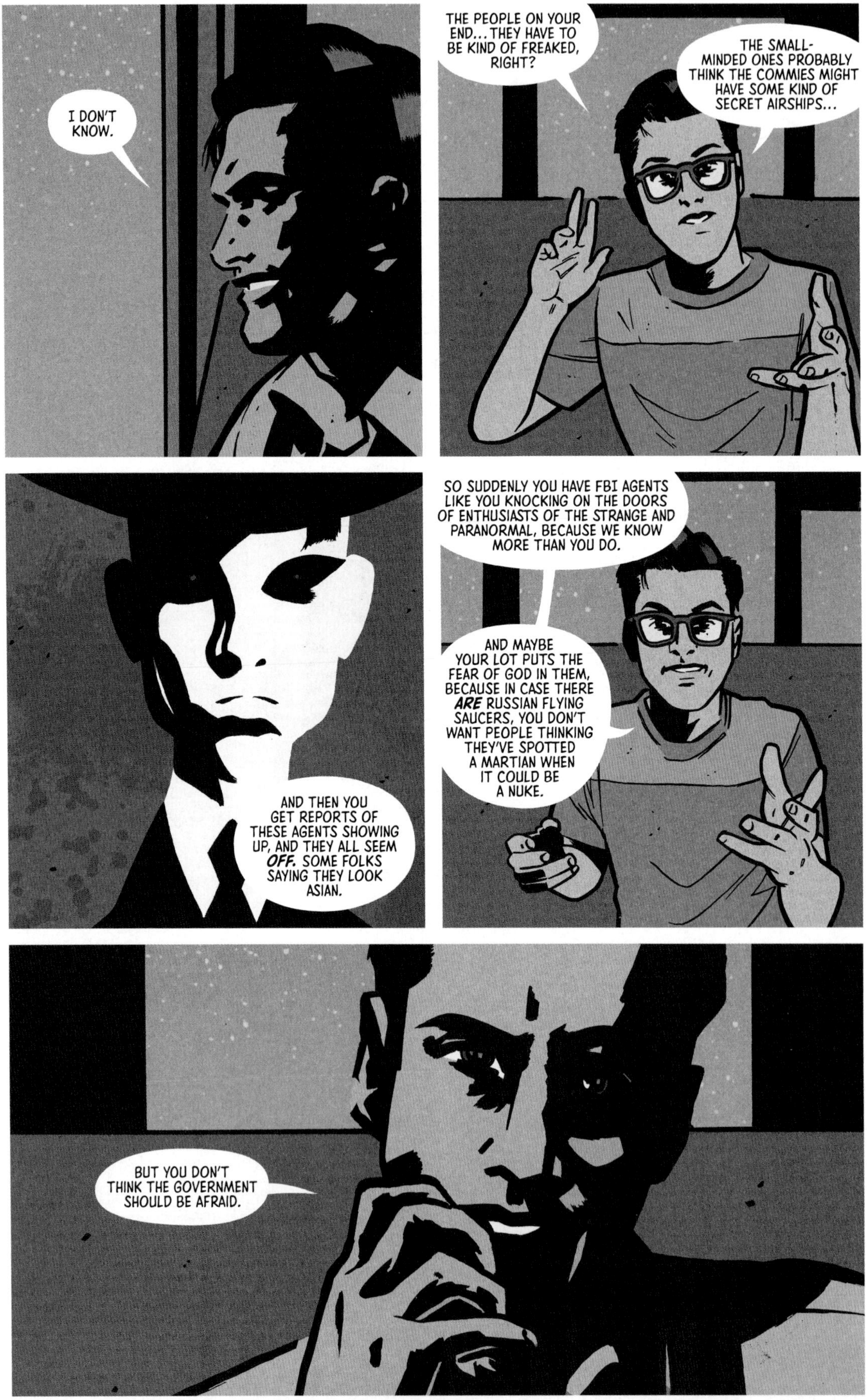
I DON'T KNOW.
THE PEOPLE ON YOUR END... THEY HAVE TO BE KIND OF FREAKED, RIGHT?
THE SMALL-MINDED ONES PROBABLY THINK THE COMMIES MIGHT HAVE SOME KIND OF SECRET AIRSHIPS...
AND THEN YOU GET REPORTS OF THESE AGENTS SHOWING UP, AND THEY ALL SEEM *OFF.* SOME FOLKS SAYING THEY LOOK ASIAN.
SO SUDDENLY YOU HAVE FBI AGENTS LIKE YOU KNOCKING ON THE DOORS OF ENTHUSIASTS OF THE STRANGE AND PARANORMAL, BECAUSE WE KNOW MORE THAN YOU DO.
AND MAYBE YOUR LOT PUTS THE FEAR OF GOD IN THEM, BECAUSE IN CASE THERE *ARE* RUSSIAN FLYING SAUCERS, YOU DON'T WANT PEOPLE THINKING THEY'VE SPOTTED A MARTIAN WHEN IT COULD BE A NUKE.
BUT YOU DON'T THINK THE GOVERNMENT SHOULD BE AFRAID.

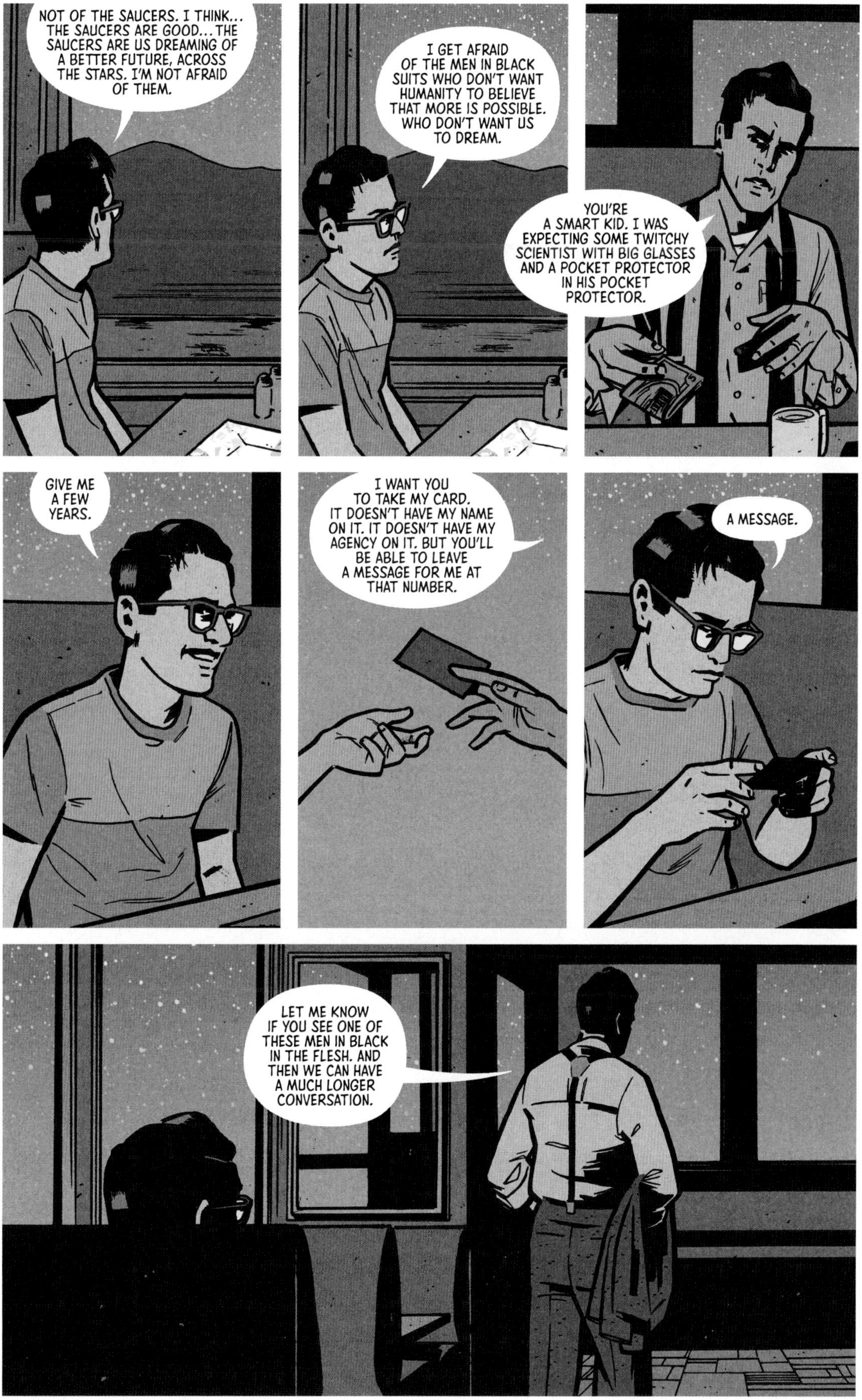
NOT OF THE SAUCERS. I THINK... THE SAUCERS ARE GOOD... THE SAUCERS ARE US DREAMING OF A BETTER FUTURE, ACROSS THE STARS. I'M NOT AFRAID OF THEM.
I GET AFRAID OF THE MEN IN BLACK SUITS WHO DON'T WANT HUMANITY TO BELIEVE THAT MORE IS POSSIBLE. WHO DON'T WANT US TO DREAM.
YOU'RE A SMART KID. I WAS EXPECTING SOME TWITCHY SCIENTIST WITH BIG GLASSES AND A POCKET PROTECTOR IN HIS POCKET PROTECTOR.
GIVE ME A FEW YEARS.
I WANT YOU TO TAKE MY CARD. IT DOESN'T HAVE MY NAME ON IT. IT DOESN'T HAVE MY AGENCY ON IT. BUT YOU'LL BE ABLE TO LEAVE A MESSAGE FOR ME AT THAT NUMBER.
A MESSAGE.
LET ME KNOW IF YOU SEE ONE OF THESE MEN IN BLACK IN THE FLESH. AND THEN WE CAN HAVE A MUCH LONGER CONVERSATION.

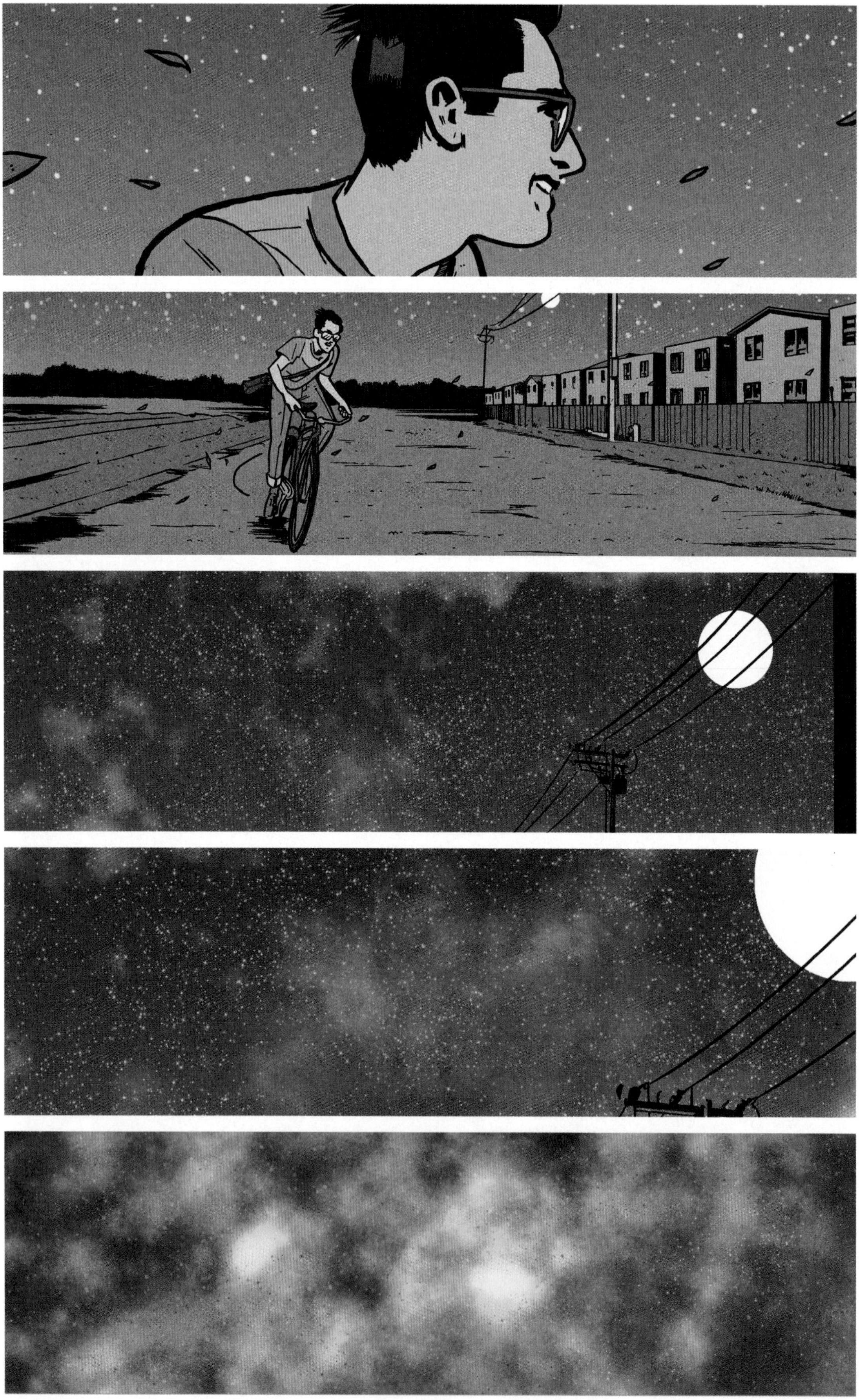

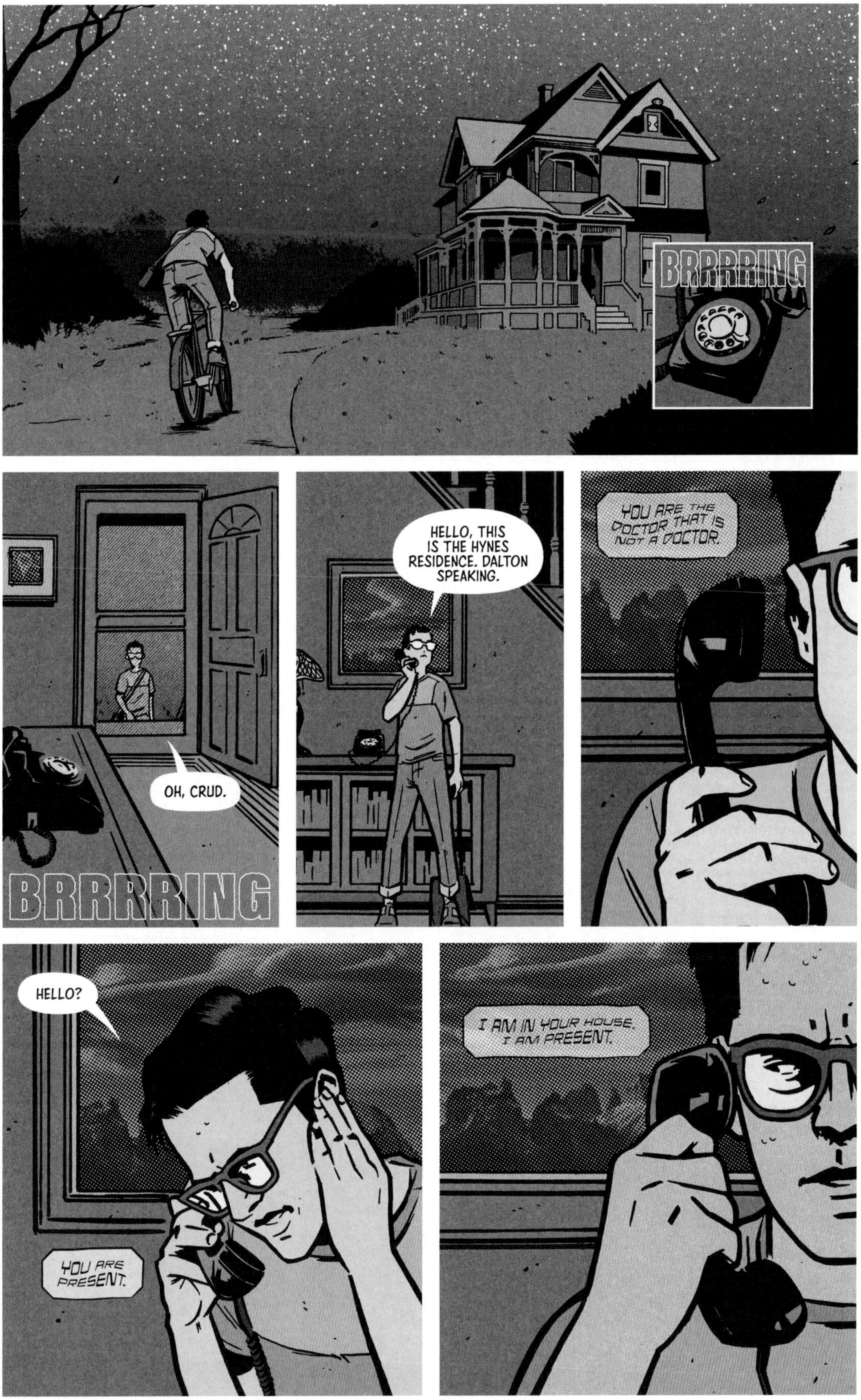
BRRRRING
OH, CRUD.
BRRRRING
HELLO, THIS IS THE HYNES RESIDENCE. DALTON SPEAKING.
YOU ARE THE DOCTOR THAT IS NOT A DOCTOR.
HELLO?
YOU ARE PRESENT.
I AM IN YOUR HOUSE. I AM PRESENT.

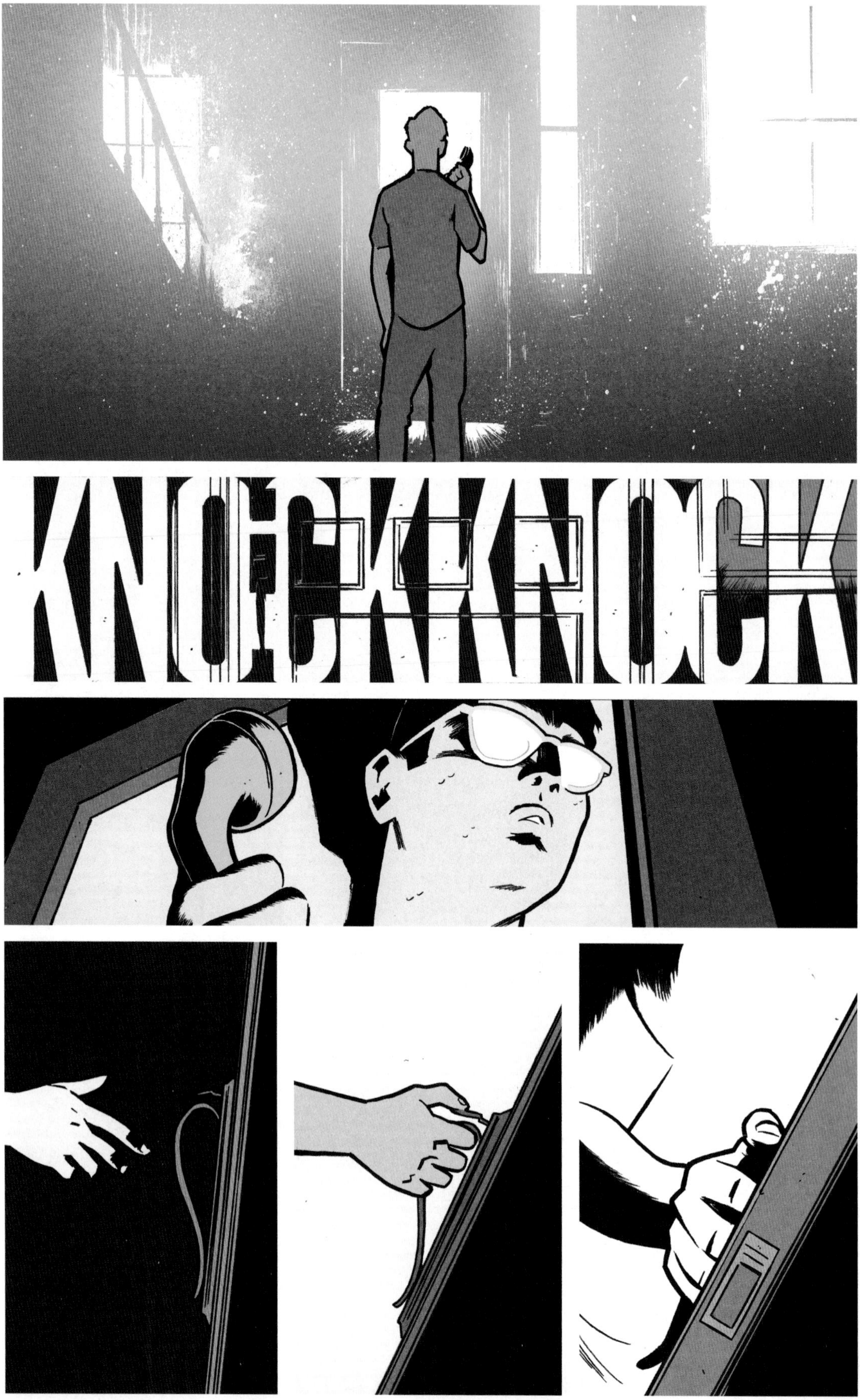
KNOCK KNOCK

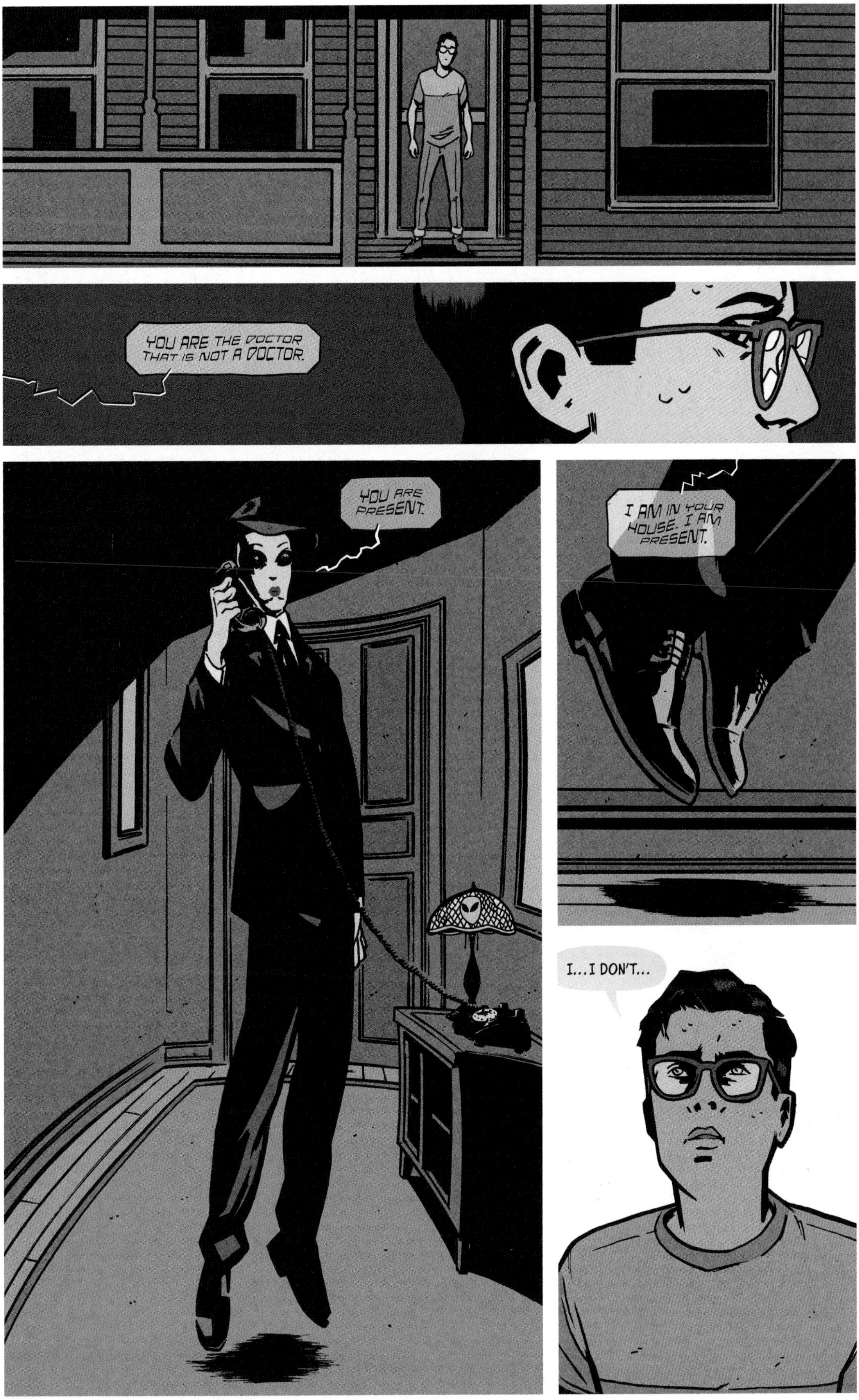
YOU ARE THE DOCTOR THAT IS NOT A DOCTOR.
YOU ARE PRESENT.
I AM IN YOUR HOUSE. I AM PRESENT.
I...I DON'T...

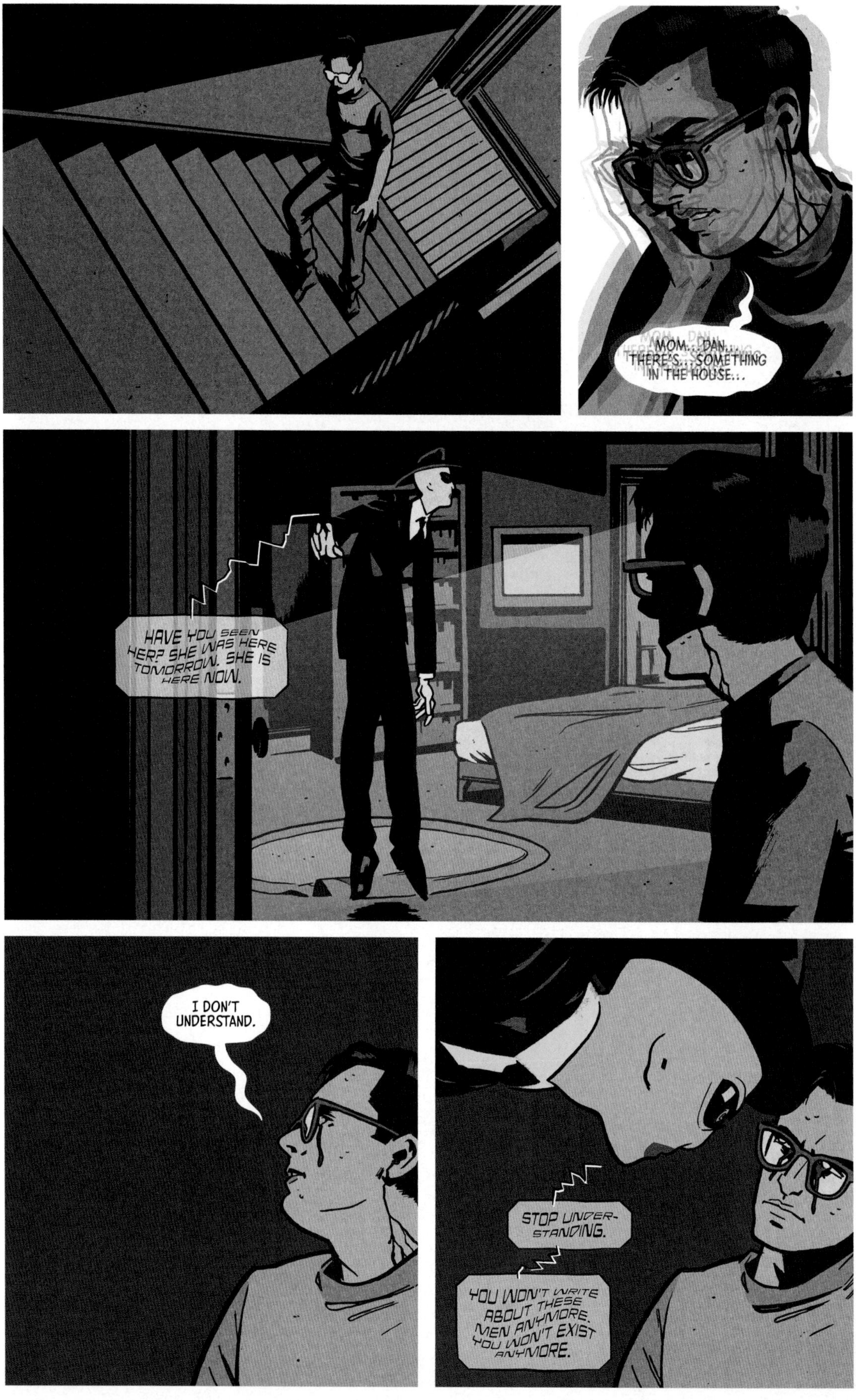
MOM... DAN... THERE'S... SOMETHING IN THE HOUSE...
HAVE YOU SEEN HER? SHE WAS HERE TOMORROW. SHE IS HERE NOW.
I DON'T UNDERSTAND.
STOP UNDER-STANDING.
YOU WON'T WRITE ABOUT THESE MEN ANYMORE. YOU WON'T EXIST ANYMORE.

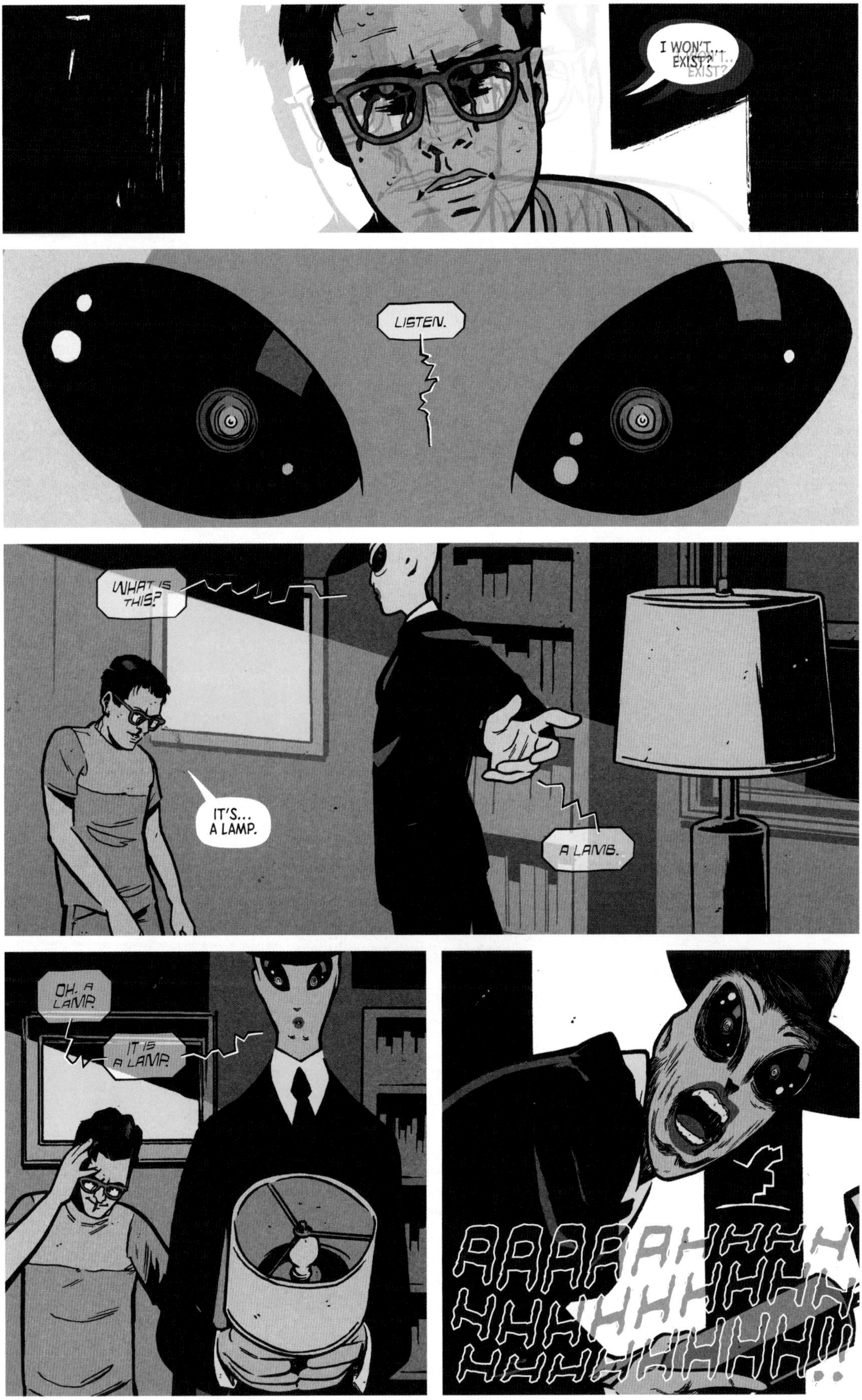
I WON'T... EXIST?
LISTEN.
WHAT IS THIS?
IT'S... A LAMP.
A LAMB.
OH. A LAMP.
IT IS A LAMP.
AAAAHHHHHHHHHHHHHHHHHHHHHH!!

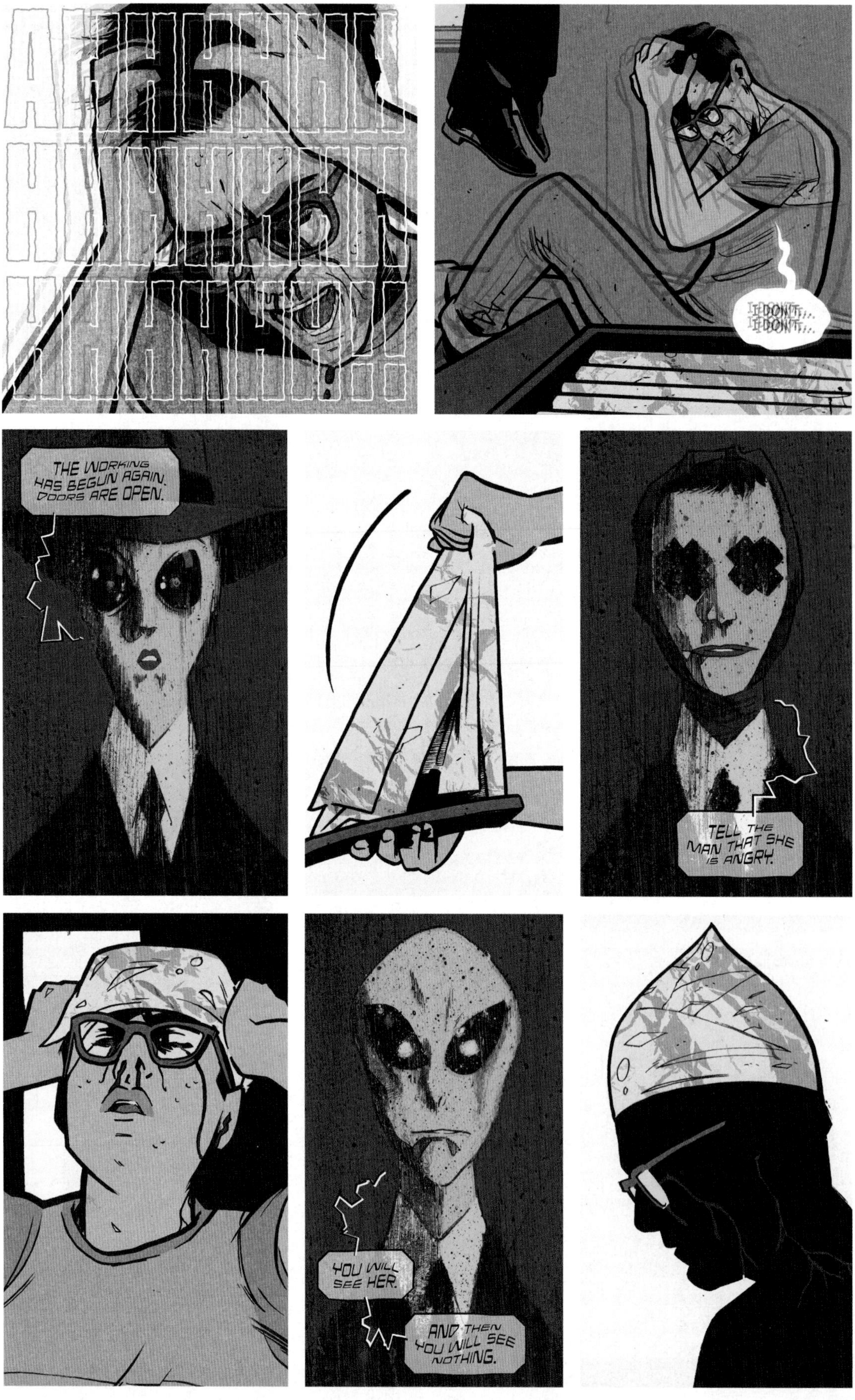
AHHHHHH
HHHHHHH
HHHHHH!!
I DON'T...
I DON'T...
THE WORKING HAS BEGUN AGAIN. DOORS ARE OPEN.
TELL THE MAN THAT SHE IS ANGRY.
YOU WILL SEE HER.
AND THEN YOU WILL SEE NOTHING.

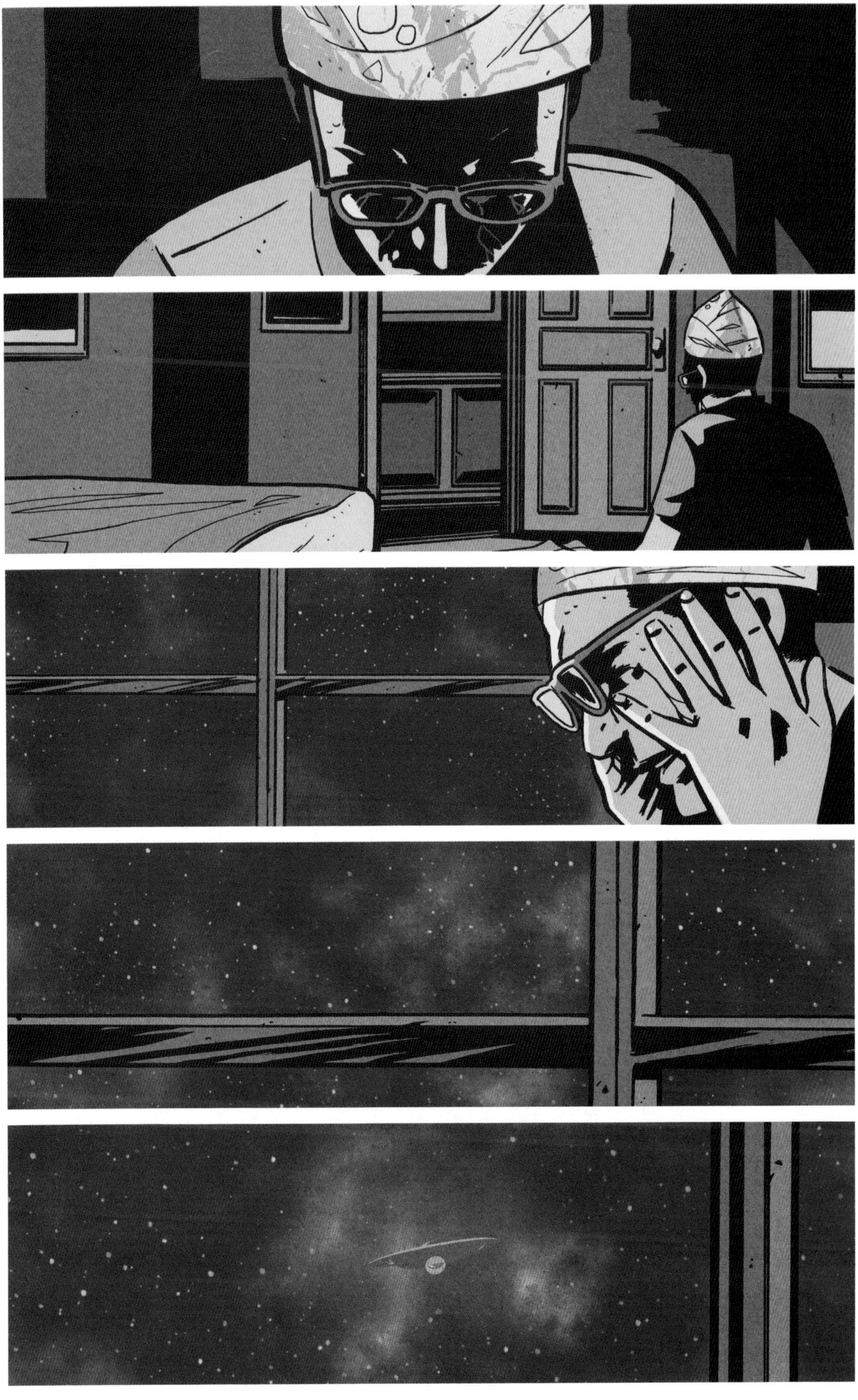

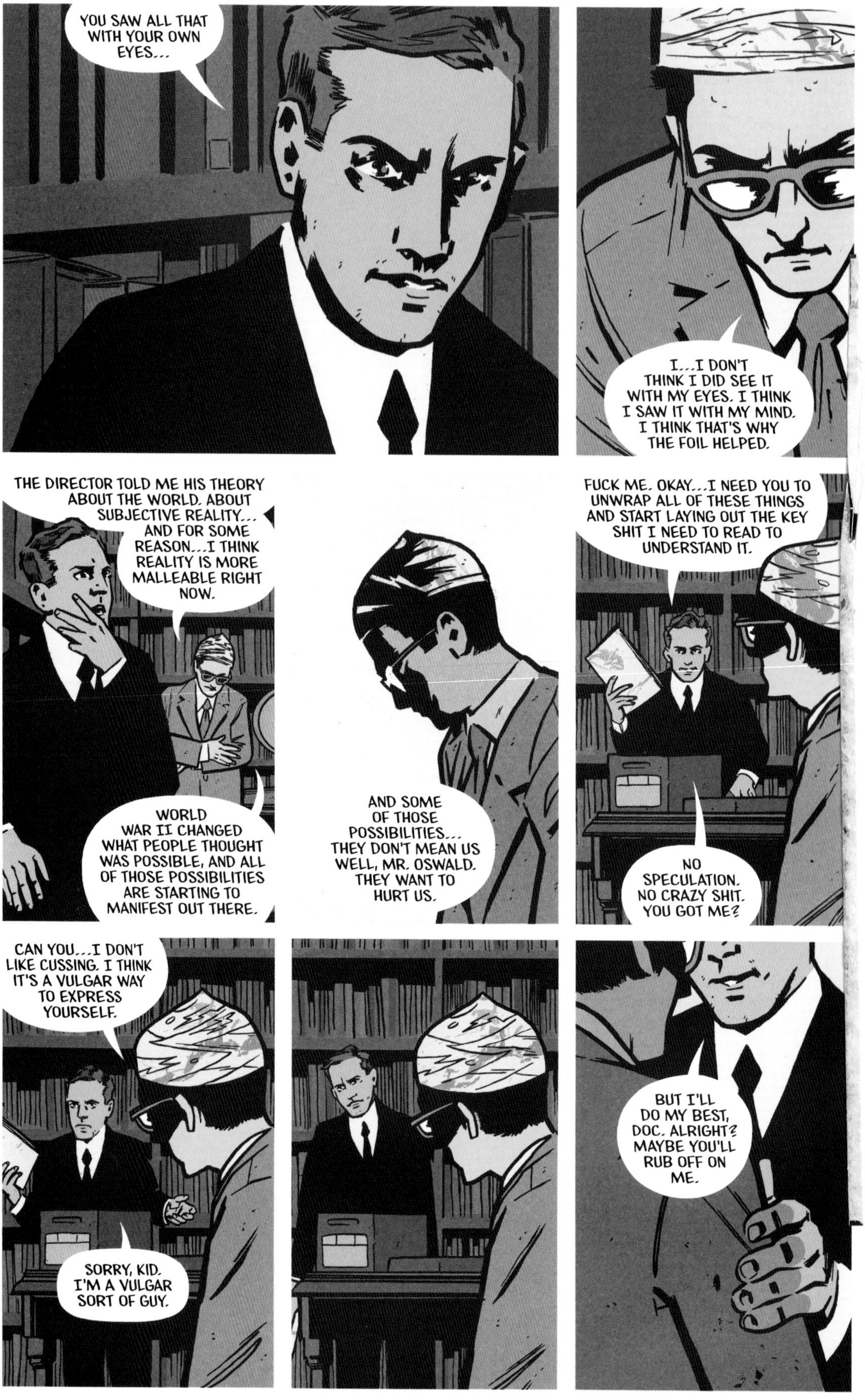
YOU SAW ALL THAT WITH YOUR OWN EYES...
I...I DON'T THINK I DID SEE IT WITH MY EYES. I THINK I SAW IT WITH MY MIND. I THINK THAT'S WHY THE FOIL HELPED.
THE DIRECTOR TOLD ME HIS THEORY ABOUT THE WORLD. ABOUT SUBJECTIVE REALITY...
AND FOR SOME REASON...I THINK REALITY IS MORE MALLEABLE RIGHT NOW.
WORLD WAR II CHANGED WHAT PEOPLE THOUGHT WAS POSSIBLE, AND ALL OF THOSE POSSIBILITIES ARE STARTING TO MANIFEST OUT THERE.
AND SOME OF THOSE POSSIBILITIES... THEY DON'T MEAN US WELL, MR. OSWALD. THEY WANT TO HURT US.
FUCK ME. OKAY...I NEED YOU TO UNWRAP ALL OF THESE THINGS AND START LAYING OUT THE KEY SHIT I NEED TO READ TO UNDERSTAND IT.
NO SPECULATION. NO CRAZY SHIT. YOU GOT ME?
CAN YOU...I DON'T LIKE CUSSING. I THINK IT'S A VULGAR WAY TO EXPRESS YOURSELF.
SORRY, KID. I'M A VULGAR SORT OF GUY.
BUT I'LL DO MY BEST, DOC. ALRIGHT? MAYBE YOU'LL RUB OFF ON ME.

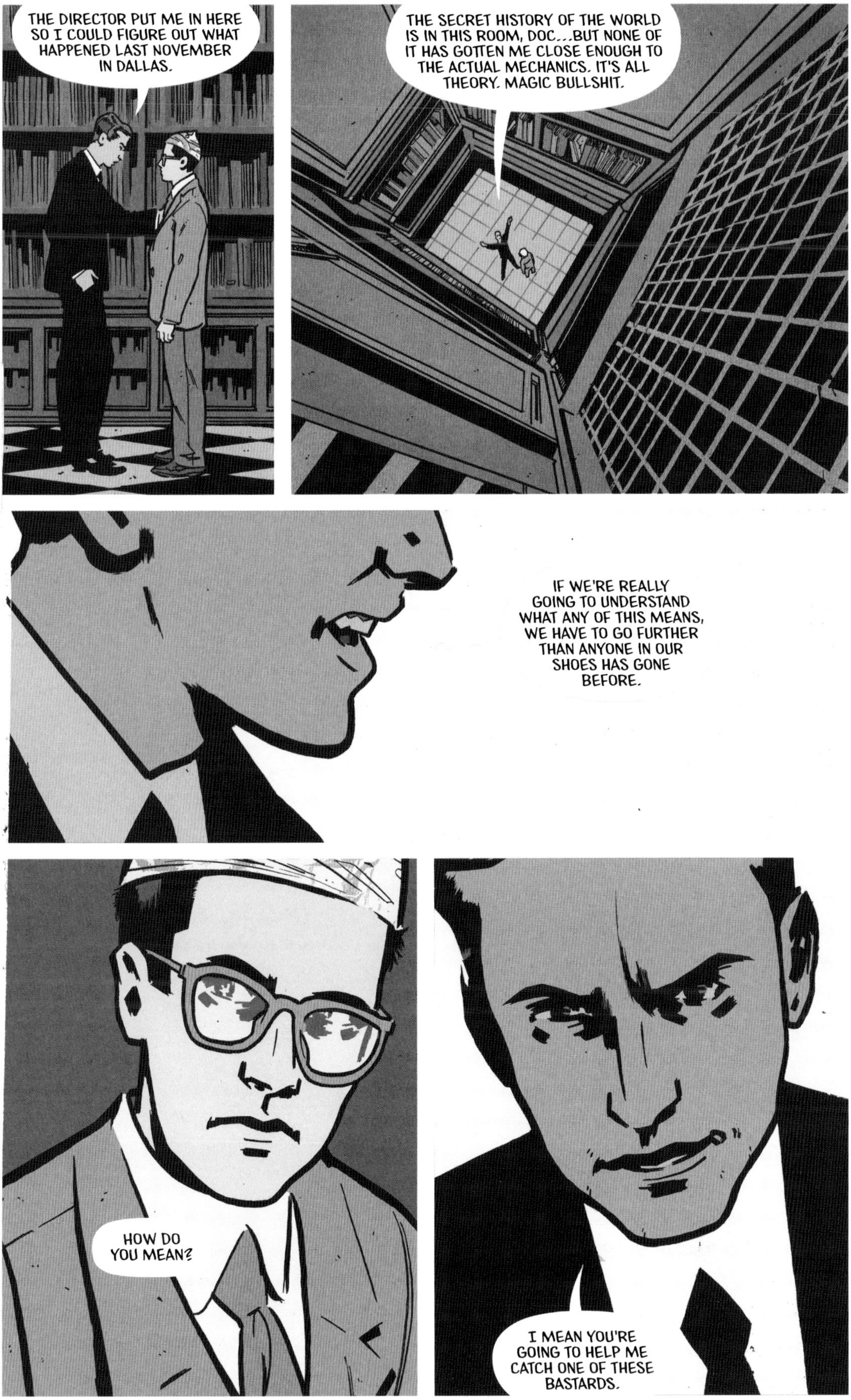
THE DIRECTOR PUT ME IN HERE SO I COULD FIGURE OUT WHAT HAPPENED LAST NOVEMBER IN DALLAS.
THE SECRET HISTORY OF THE WORLD IS IN THIS ROOM, DOC...BUT NONE OF IT HAS GOTTEN ME CLOSE ENOUGH TO THE ACTUAL MECHANICS. IT'S ALL THEORY. MAGIC BULLSHIT.
IF WE'RE REALLY GOING TO UNDERSTAND WHAT ANY OF THIS MEANS, WE HAVE TO GO FURTHER THAN ANYONE IN OUR SHOES HAS GONE BEFORE.
HOW DO YOU MEAN?
I MEAN YOU'RE GOING TO HELP ME CATCH ONE OF THESE BASTARDS.

DEVIATION 3 /

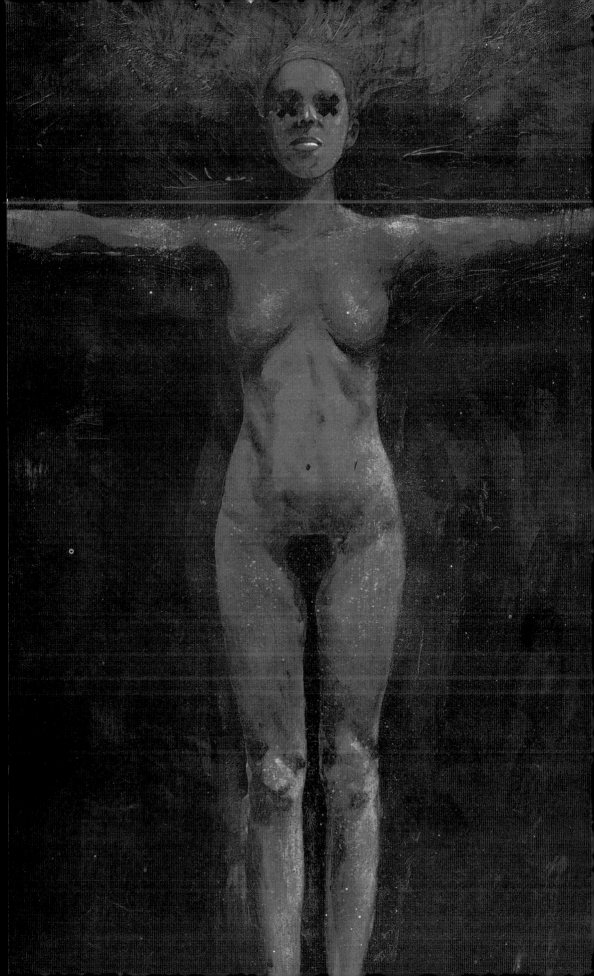

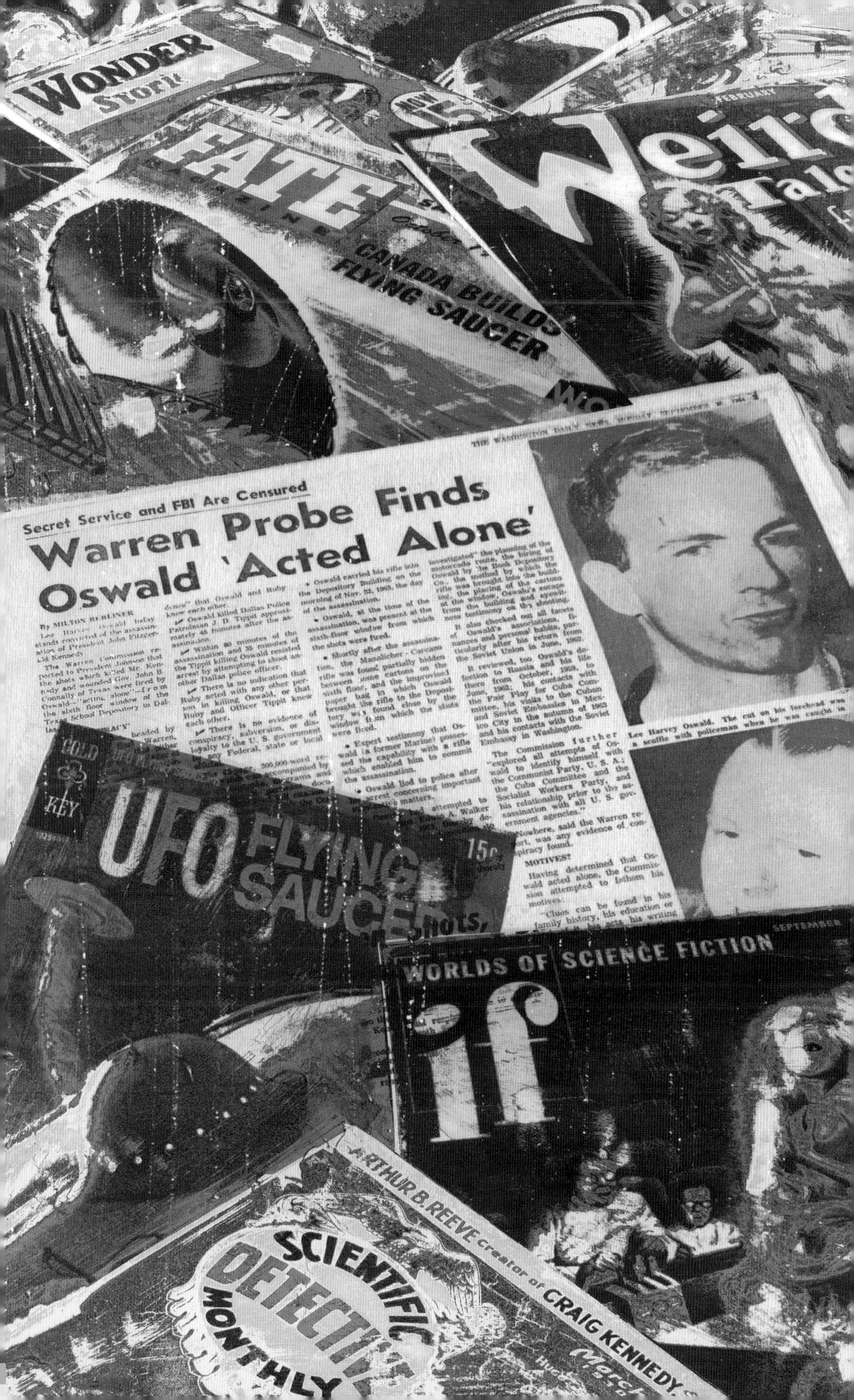
WONDER STORIES
FATE
CANADA BUILDS FLYING SAUCER
Weird Tales
FEBRUARY
Secret Service and FBI Are Censured
Warren Probe Finds Oswald 'Acted Alone'
By MILTON BERLINER
Lee Harvey Oswald. The cut on his forehead was a scuffle with policeman when he was caught in
MOTIVES?
GOLD KEY
UFO FLYING SAUCERS
15c
WORLDS OF SCIENCE FICTION
SEPTEMBER
if
ARTHUR B. REEVE Creator of CRAIG KENNEDY
SCIENTIFIC DETECTIVE MONTHLY

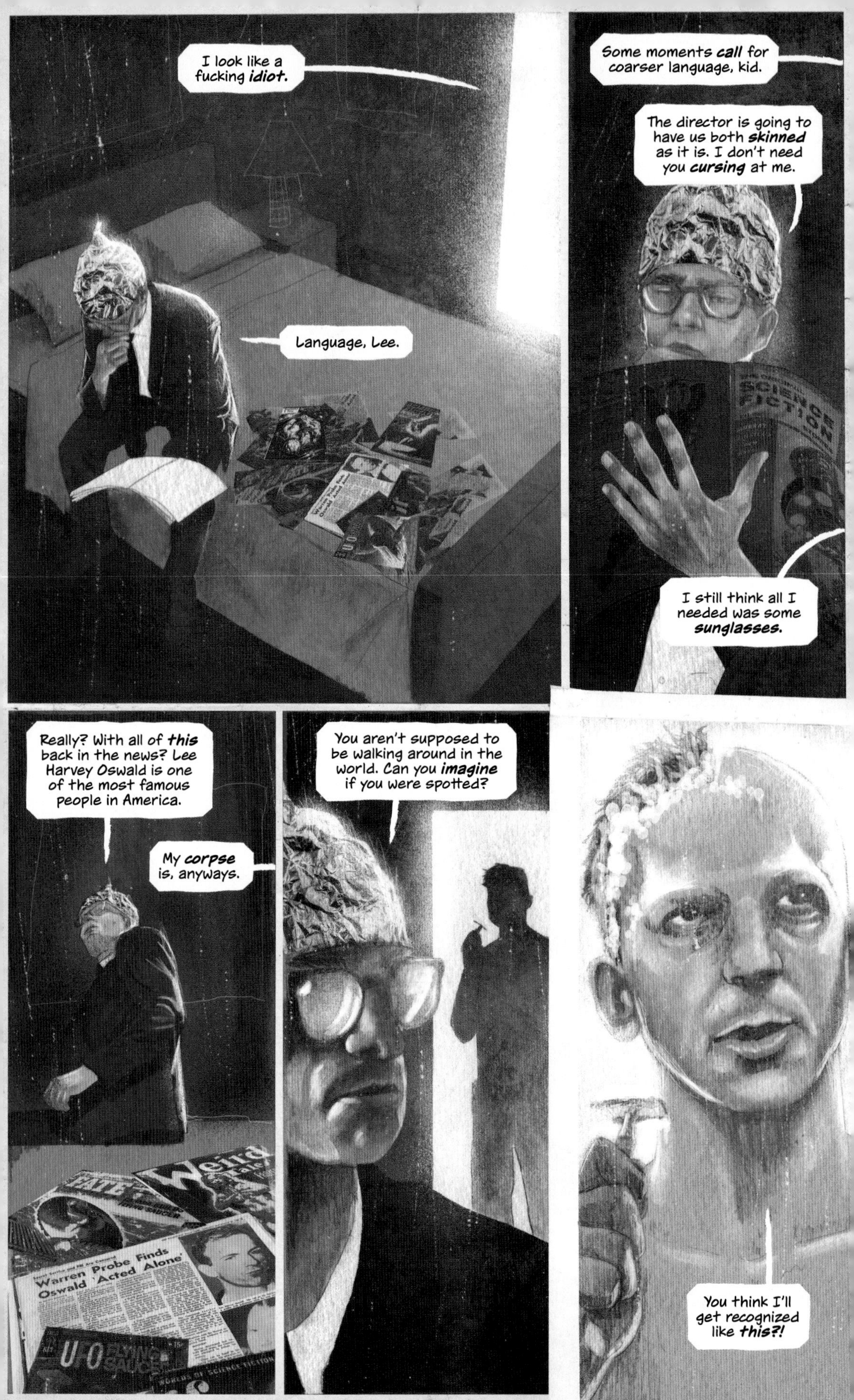
I look like a fucking idiot.
Language, Lee.
Some moments call for coarser language, kid.
The director is going to have us both skinned as it is. I don't need you cursing at me.
I still think all I needed was some sunglasses.
Really? With all of this back in the news? Lee Harvey Oswald is one of the most famous people in America.
My corpse is, anyways.
Warren Probe Finds Oswald 'Acted Alone'
You aren't supposed to be walking around in the world. Can you imagine if you were spotted?
You think I'll get recognized like this?!

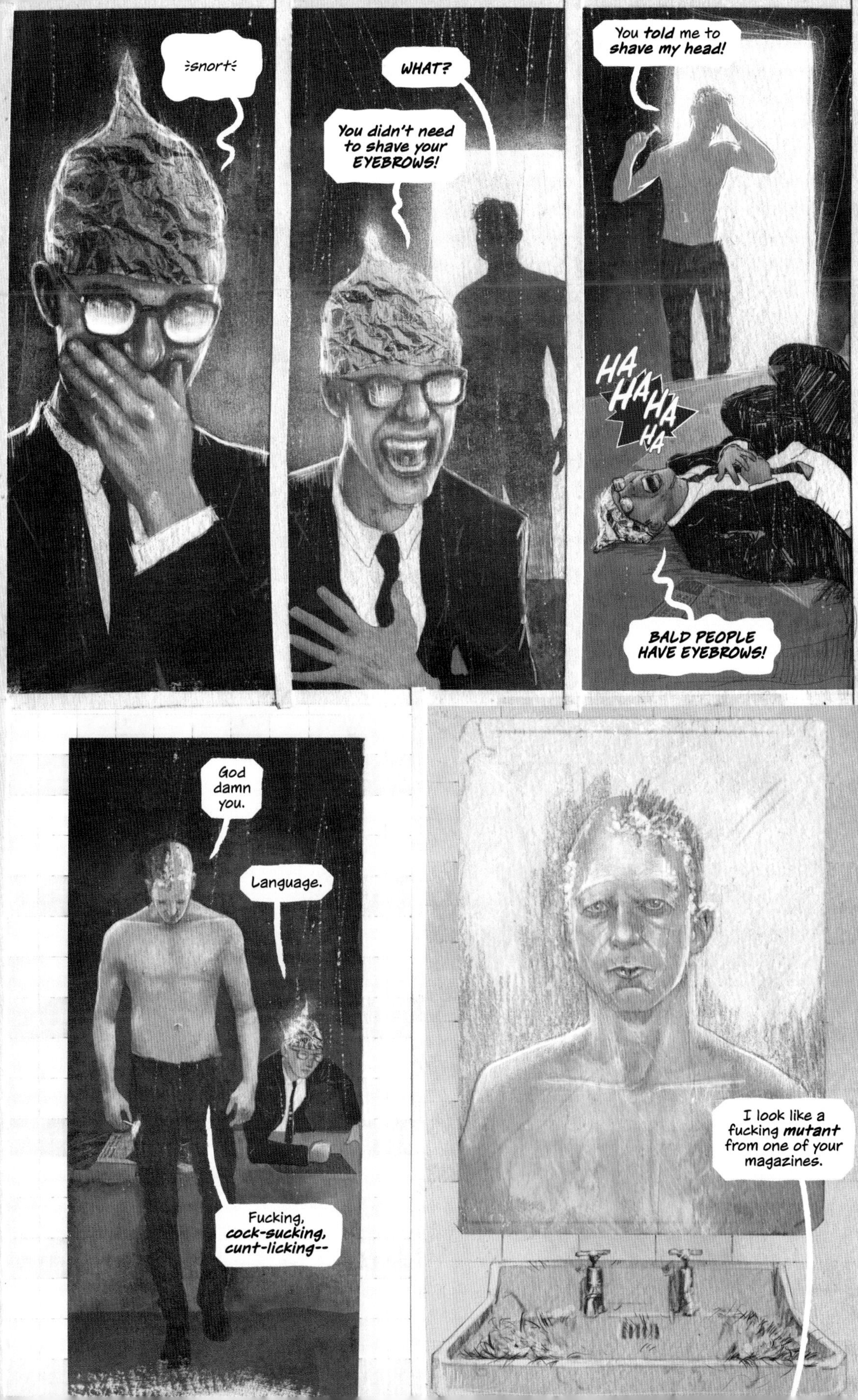

:snort:
WHAT?
You didn't need to shave your EYEBROWS!
You told me to shave my head!
HA HA HA HA HA
BALD PEOPLE HAVE EYEBROWS!
God damn you.
Language.
Fucking, cock-sucking, cunt-licking--
I look like a fucking mutant from one of your magazines.

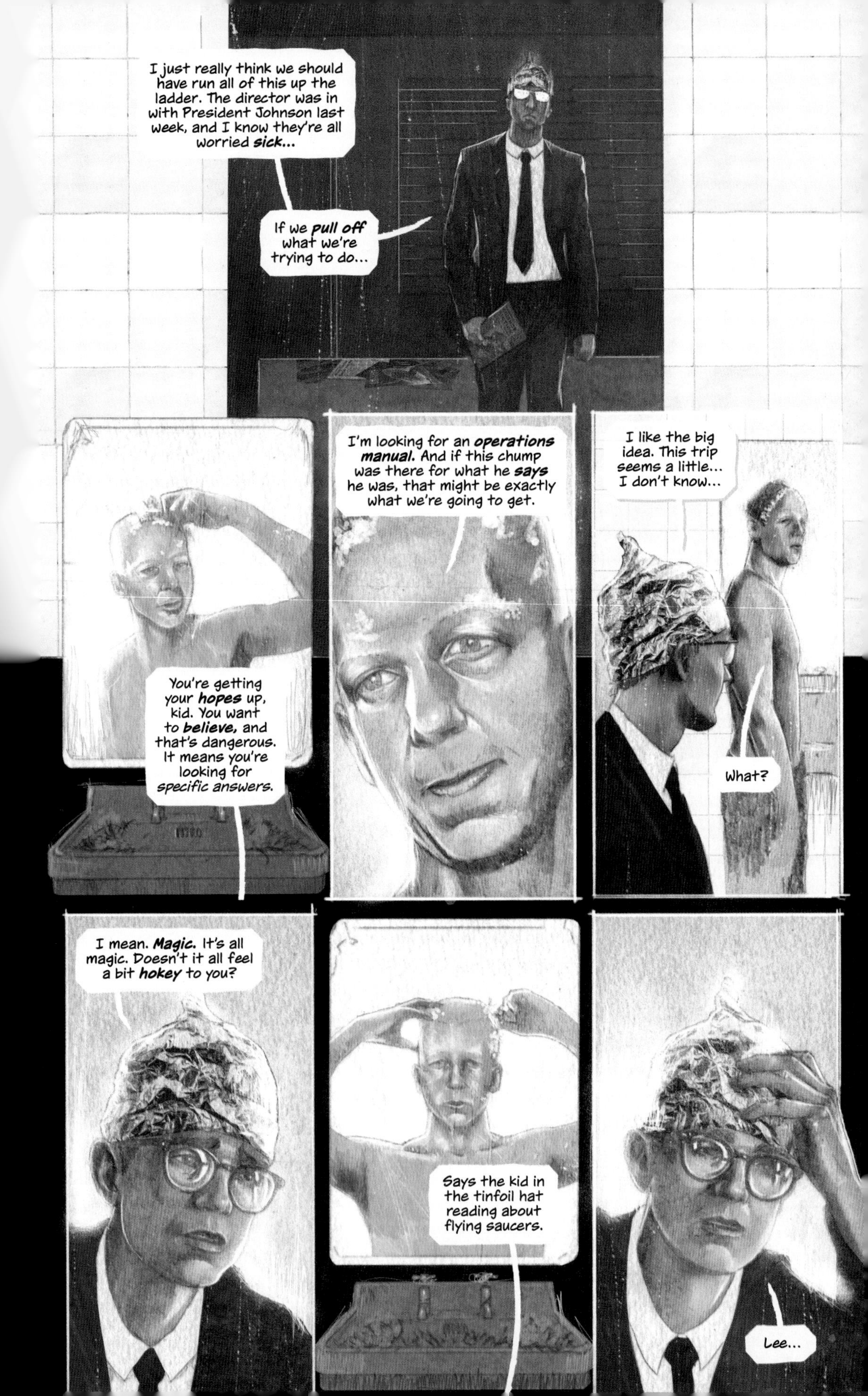
I just really think we should have run all of this up the ladder. The director was in with President Johnson last week, and I know they're all worried **sick...**
If we **pull off** what we're trying to do...
You're getting your **hopes** up, kid. You want to **believe,** and that's dangerous. It means you're looking for specific answers.
I'm looking for an **operations manual.** And if this chump was there for what he **says** he was, that might be exactly what we're going to get.
I like the big idea. This trip seems a little... I don't know...
What?
I mean. **Magic.** It's all magic. Doesn't it all feel a bit **hokey** to you?
Says the kid in the tinfoil hat reading about flying saucers.
Lee...

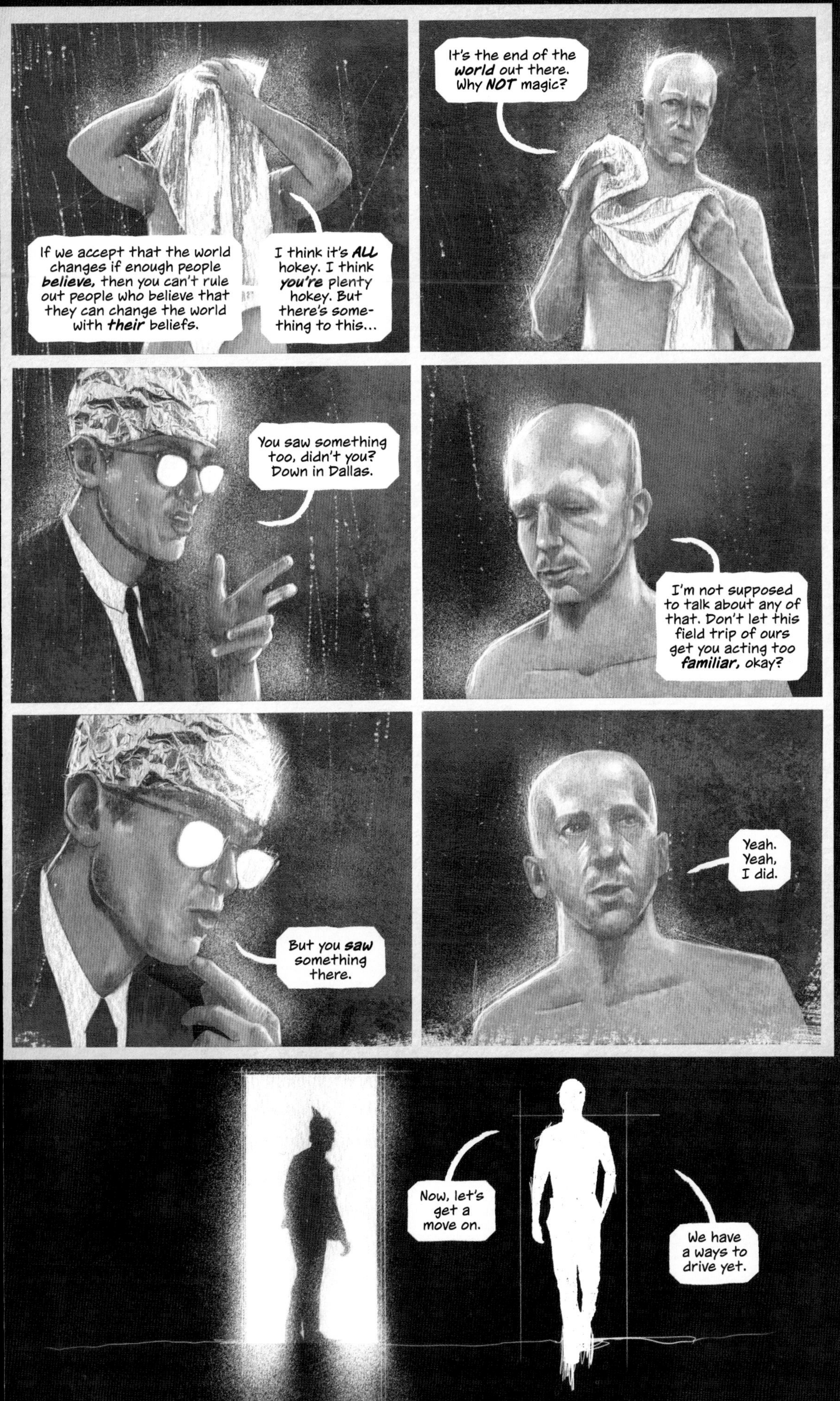
If we accept that the world changes if enough people **believe,** then you can't rule out people who believe that they can change the world with **their** beliefs.
I think it's **ALL** hokey. I think **you're** plenty hokey. But there's something to this...
It's the end of the **world** out there. Why **NOT** magic?
You saw something too, didn't you? Down in Dallas.
I'm not supposed to talk about any of that. Don't let this field trip of ours get you acting too **familiar,** okay?
But you **saw** something there.
Yeah. Yeah, I did.
Now, let's get a move on.
We have a ways to drive yet.

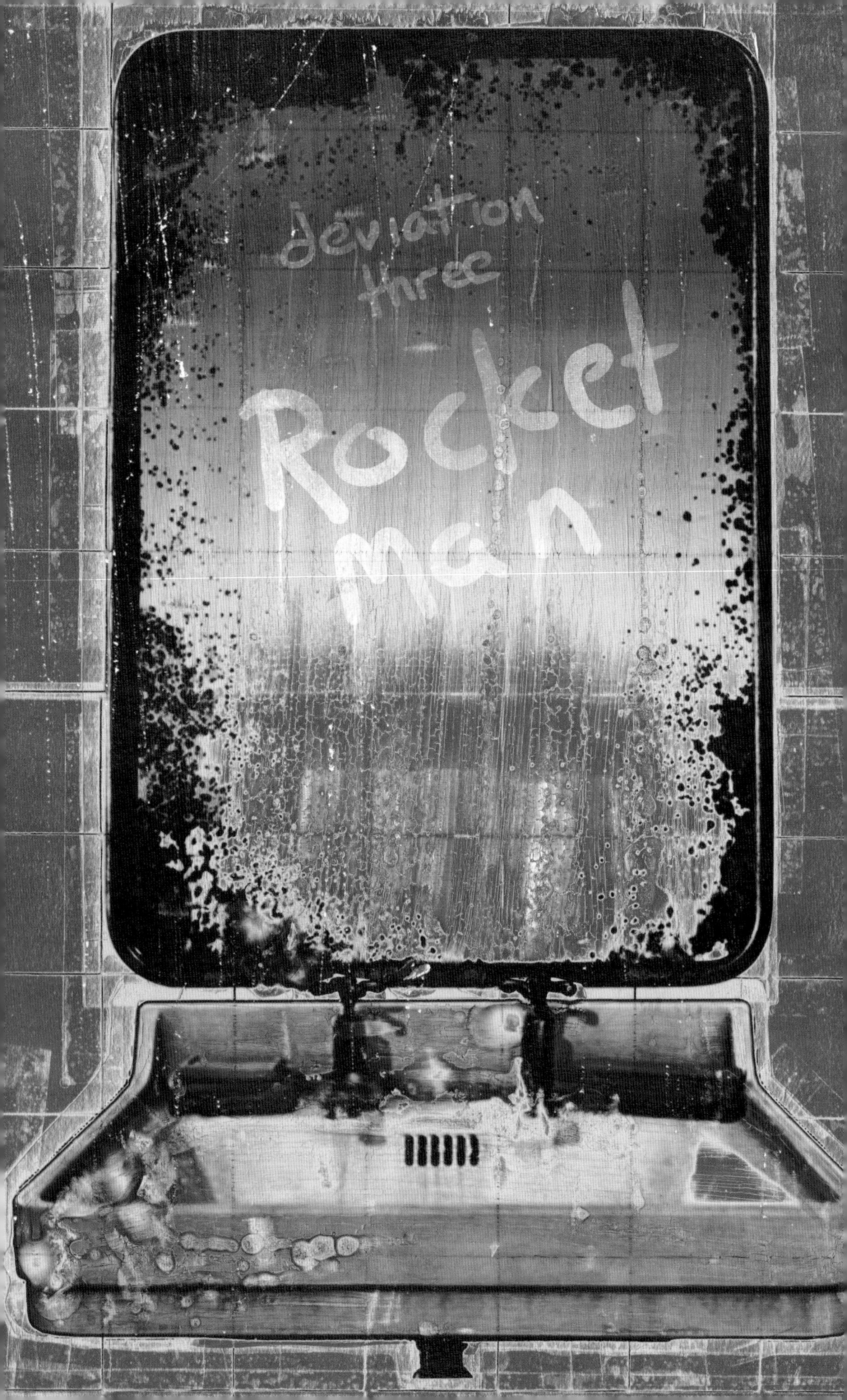
deviation three
Rocket man

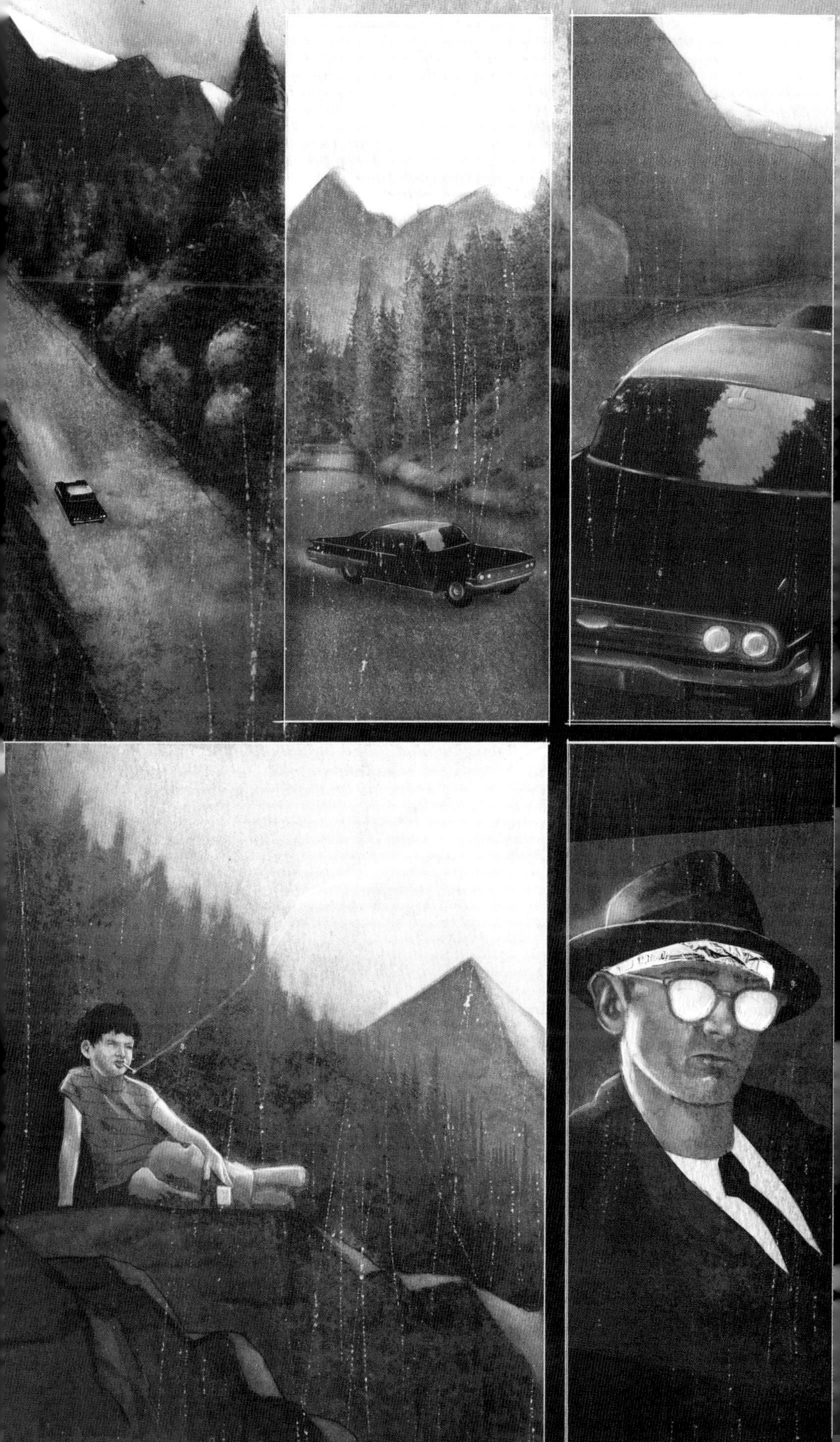

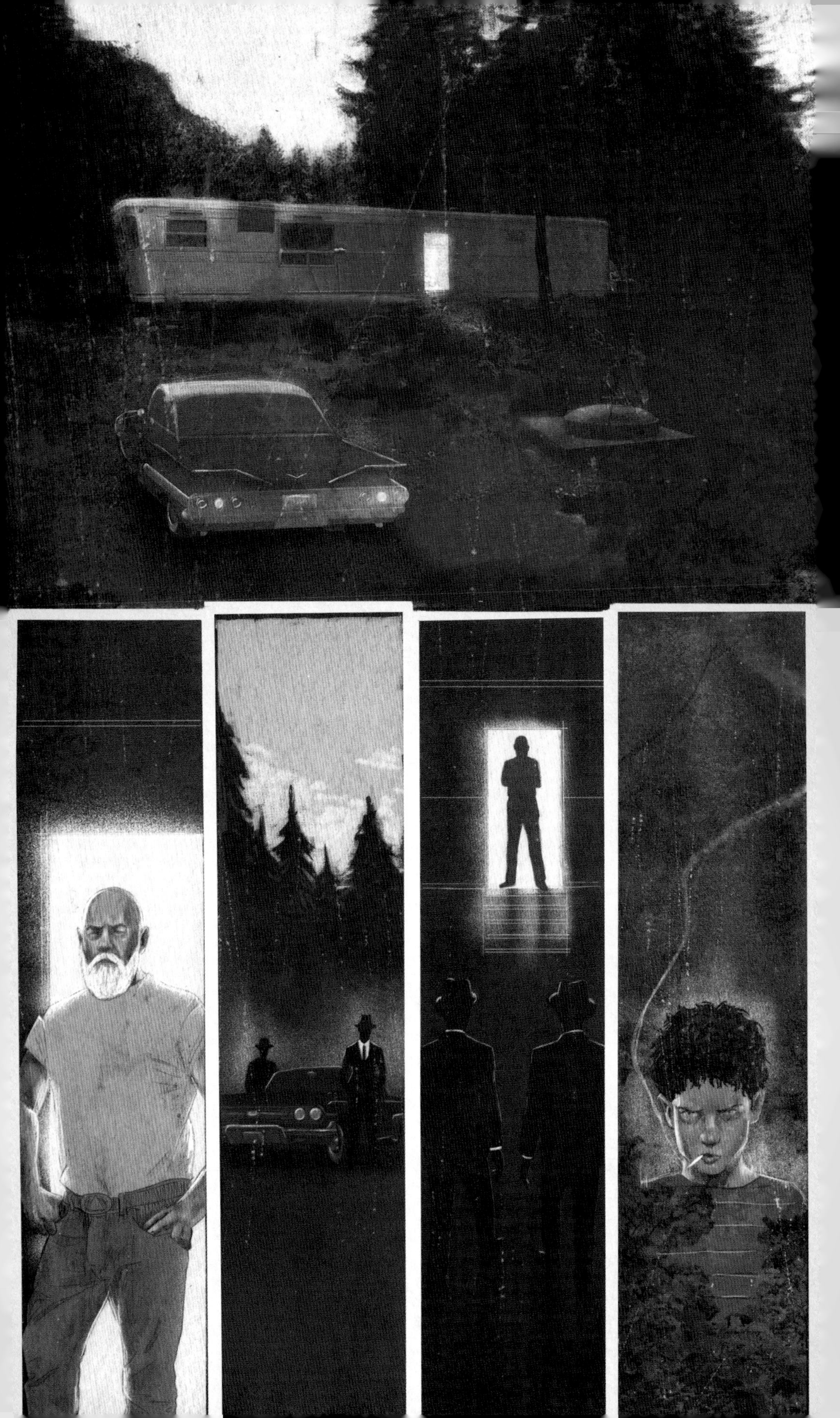

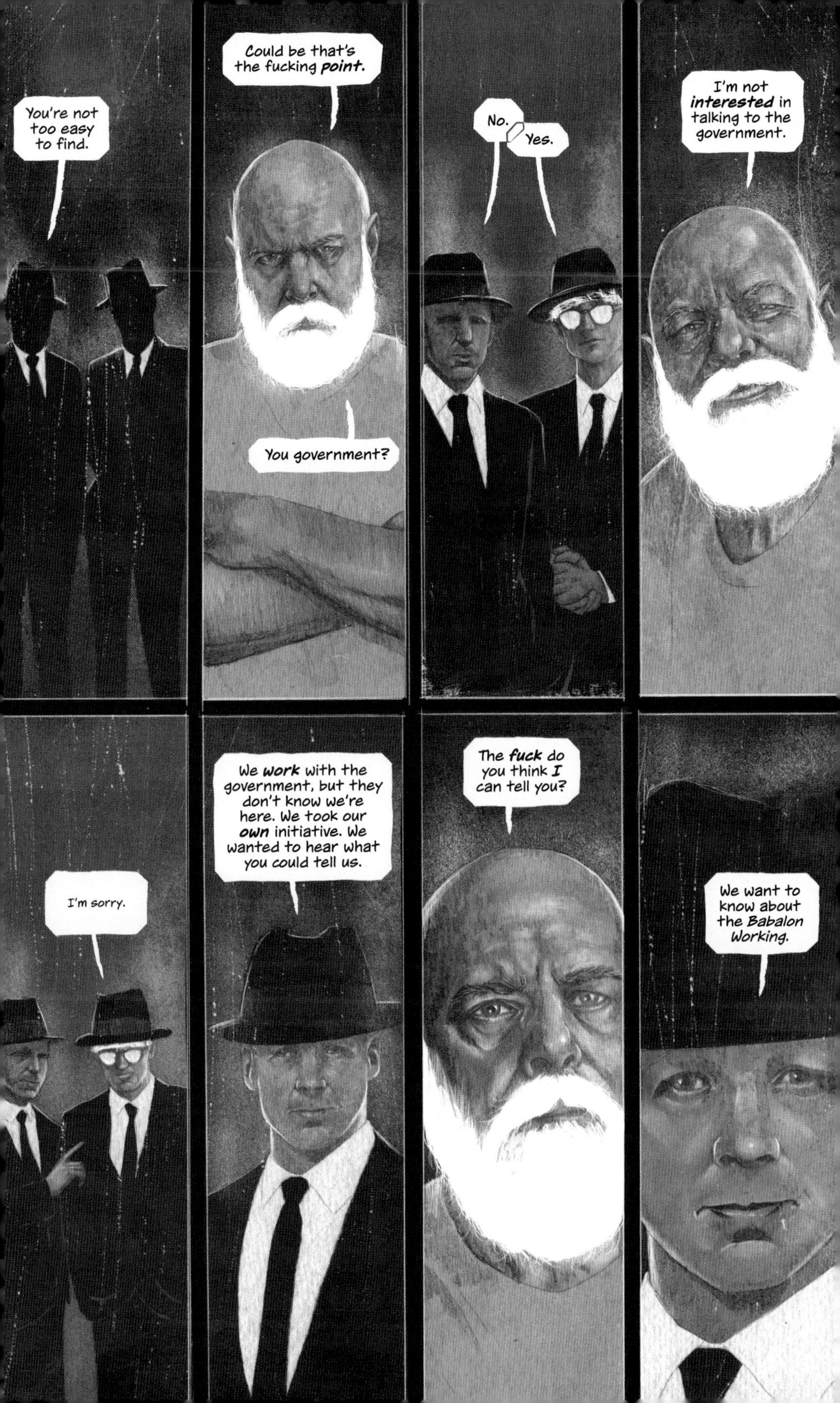

You're not too easy to find.
Could be that's the fucking **point**.
You government?
No.
Yes.
I'm not **interested** in talking to the government.
I'm sorry.
We **work** with the government, but they don't know we're here. We took our **own** initiative. We wanted to hear what you could tell us.
The **fuck** do you think **I** can tell you?
We want to know about the *Babalon Working*.

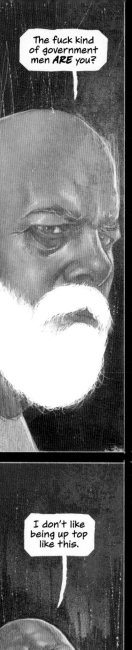
The fuck kind of government men **ARE** you?

The kind that's curious about all the weird shit happening in the shadows, all over the country. The ones who see it happening and are trying to figure out why.

Your hat's got silver bits coming out of it...

That's...that's *my* business, alright?

Yeah.

I don't like being up top like this.

BOY! We're going down.

Suit your fucking self!

Cute kid.

Yeah.

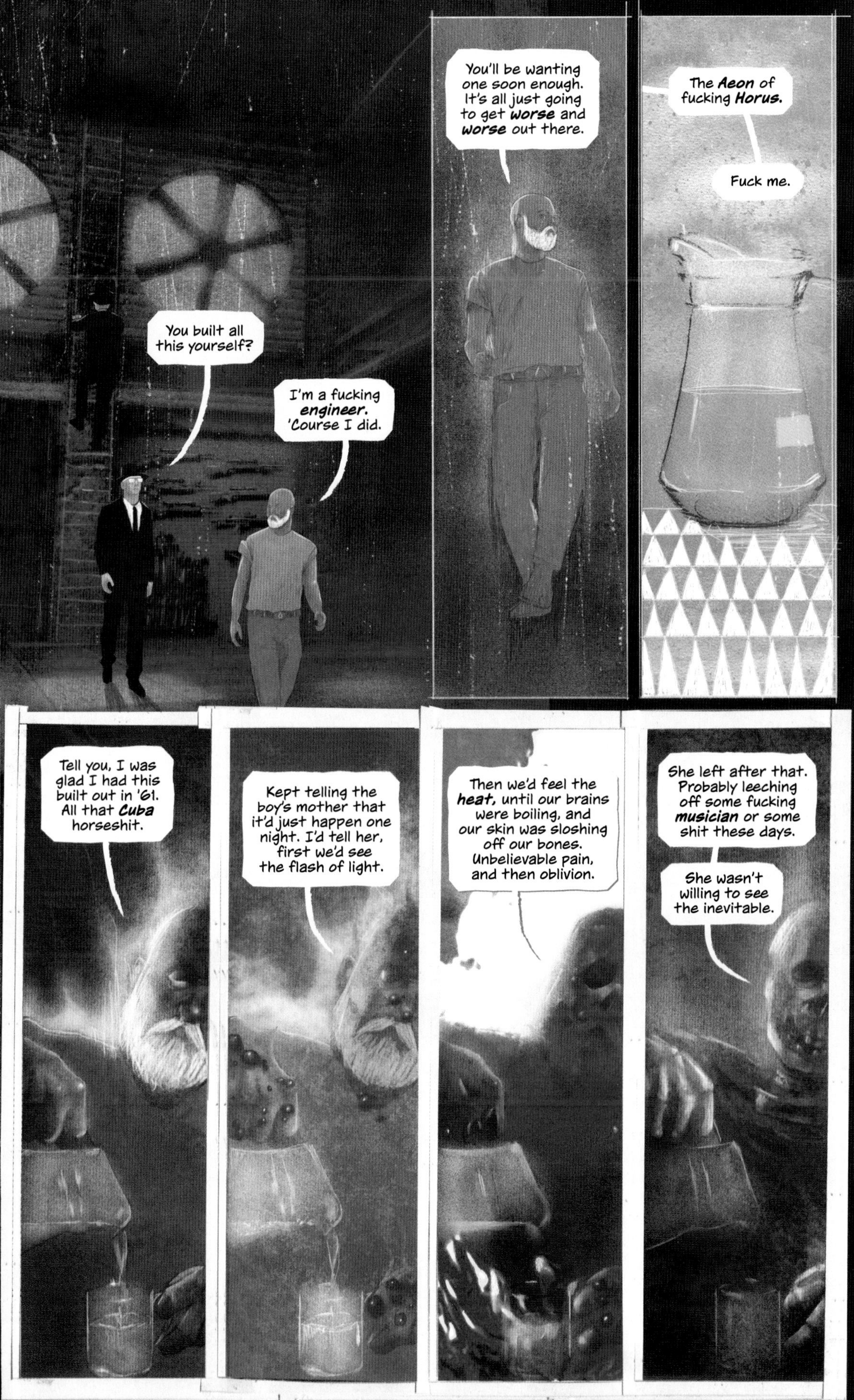
You built all this yourself?
I'm a fucking engineer. 'Course I did.
You'll be wanting one soon enough. It's all just going to get worse and worse out there.
The Aeon of fucking Horus.
Fuck me.
Tell you, I was glad I had this built out in '61. All that Cuba horseshit.
Kept telling the boy's mother that it'd just happen one night. I'd tell her, first we'd see the flash of light.
Then we'd feel the heat, until our brains were boiling, and our skin was sloshing off our bones. Unbelievable pain, and then oblivion.
She left after that. Probably leeching off some fucking musician or some shit these days.
She wasn't willing to see the inevitable.

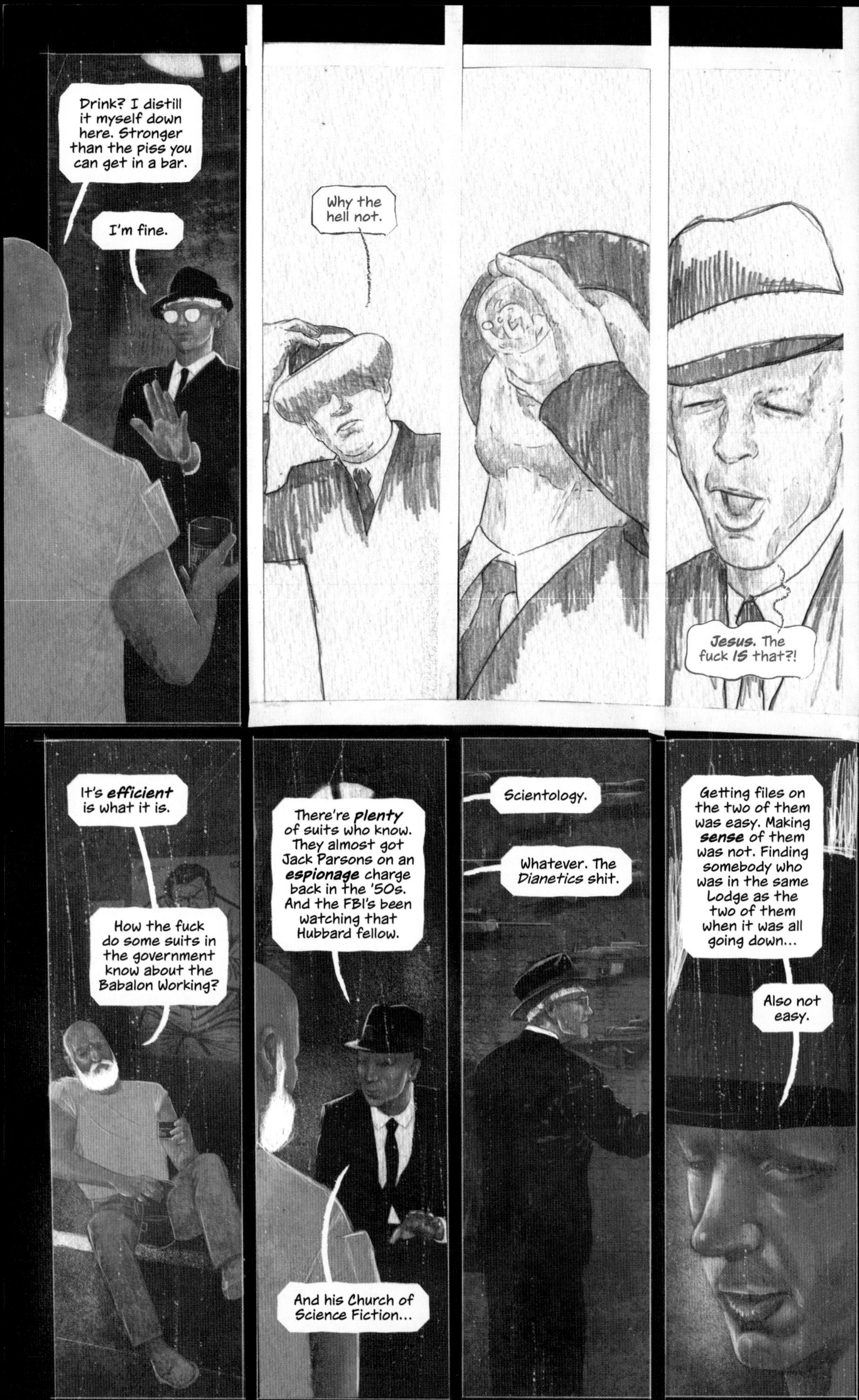

Drink? I distill it myself down here. Stronger than the piss you can get in a bar.
I'm fine.
Why the hell not.
Jesus. The fuck IS that?!
It's efficient is what it is.
How the fuck do some suits in the government know about the Babalon Working?
There're plenty of suits who know. They almost got Jack Parsons on an espionage charge back in the '50s. And the FBI's been watching that Hubbard fellow.
And his Church of Science Fiction...
Scientology.
Whatever. The Dianetics shit.
Getting files on the two of them was easy. Making sense of them was not. Finding somebody who was in the same Lodge as the two of them when it was all going down...
Also not easy.

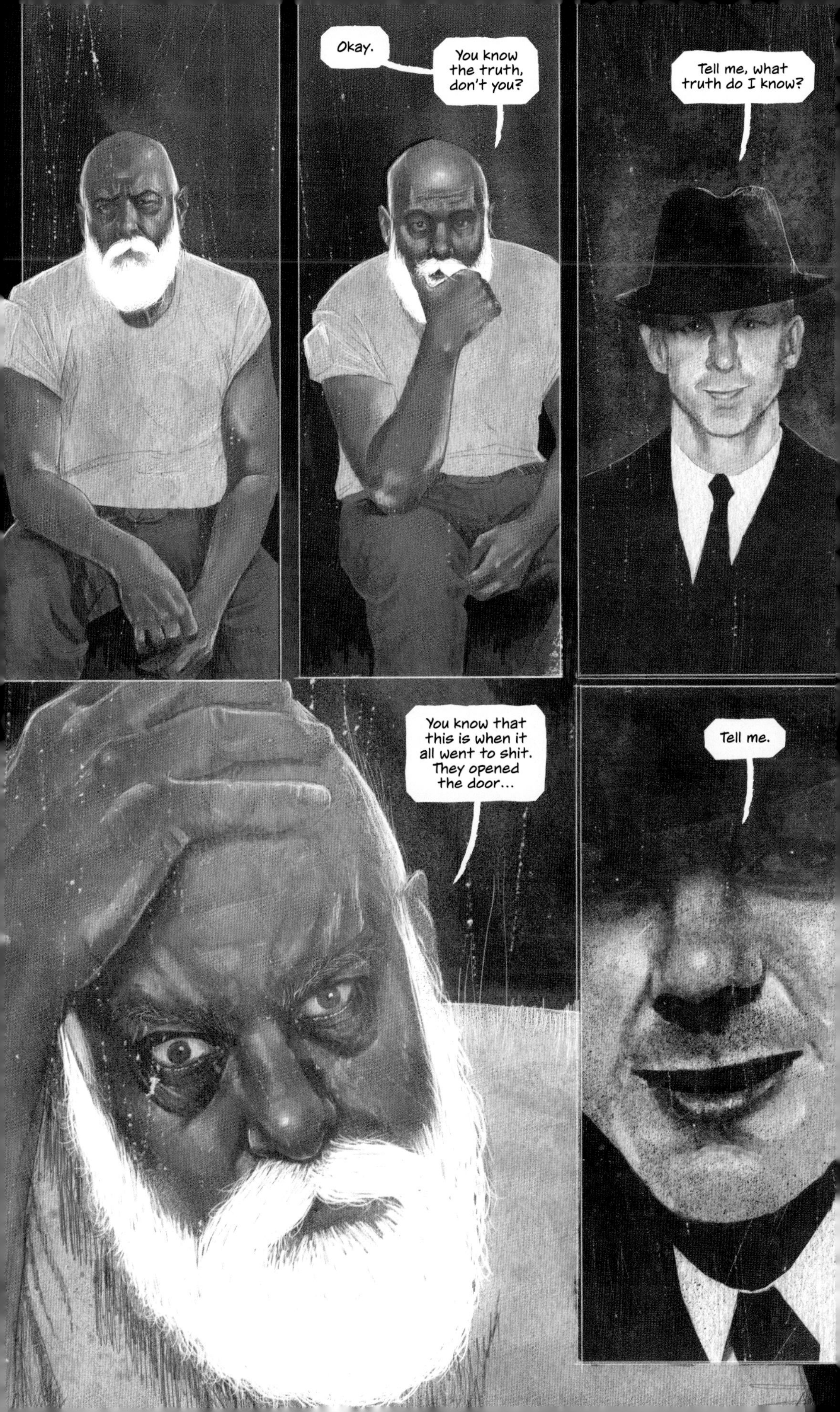
Okay.
You know the truth, don't you?
Tell me, what truth do I know?
You know that this is when it all went to shit. They opened the door...
Tell me.

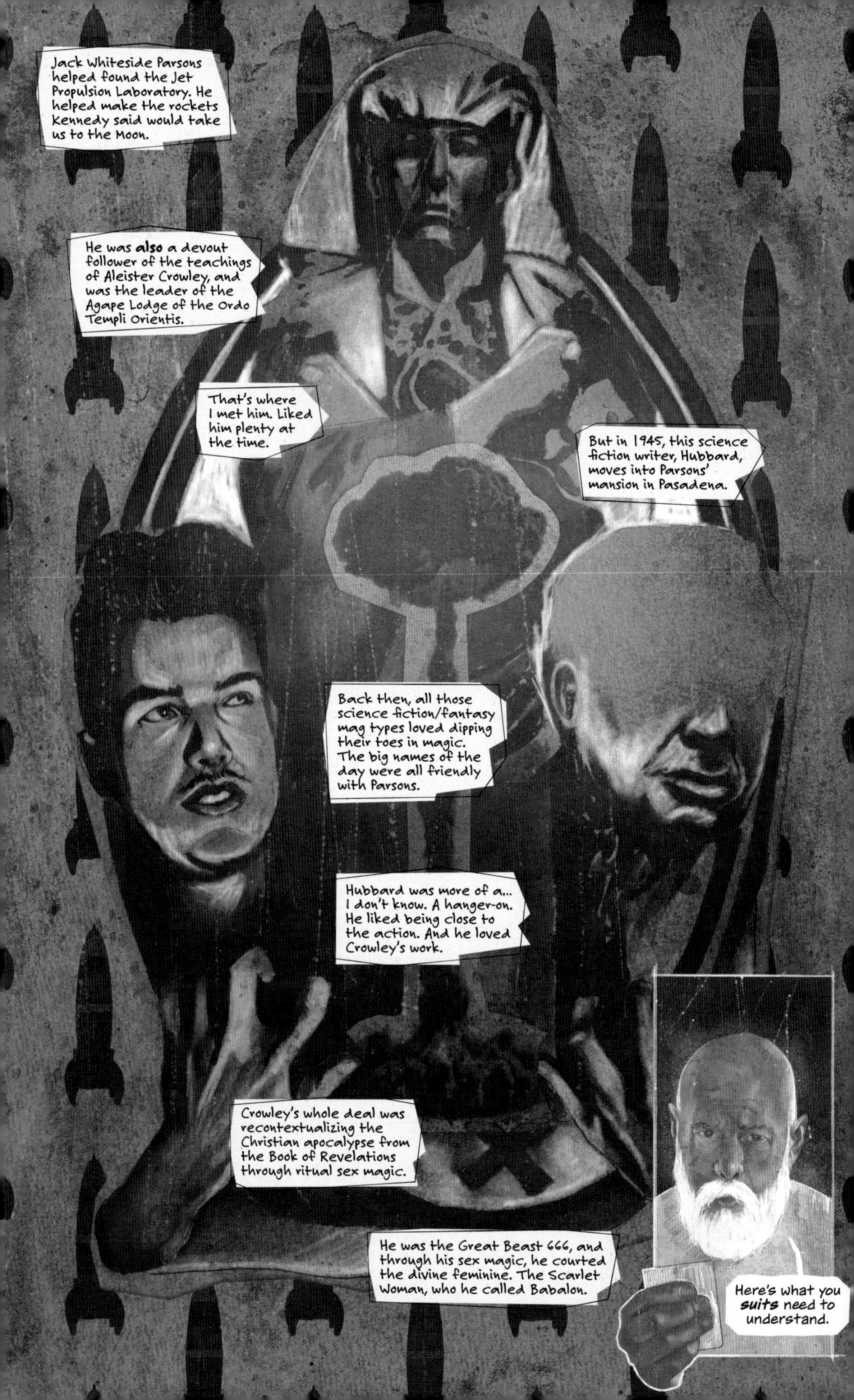
Jack Whiteside Parsons helped found the Jet Propulsion Laboratory. He helped make the rockets Kennedy said would take us to the Moon.
He was **also** a devout follower of the teachings of Aleister Crowley, and was the leader of the Agape Lodge of the Ordo Templi Orientis.
That's where I met him. Liked him plenty at the time.
But in 1945, this science fiction writer, Hubbard, moves into Parsons' mansion in Pasadena.
Back then, all those science fiction/fantasy mag types loved dipping their toes in magic. The big names of the day were all friendly with Parsons.
Hubbard was more of a... I don't know. A hanger-on. He liked being close to the action. And he loved Crowley's work.
Crowley's whole deal was recontextualizing the Christian apocalypse from the Book of Revelations through ritual sex magic.
He was the Great Beast 666, and through his sex magic, he courted the divine feminine. The Scarlet Woman, who he called Babalon.
Here's what you ***suits*** need to understand.

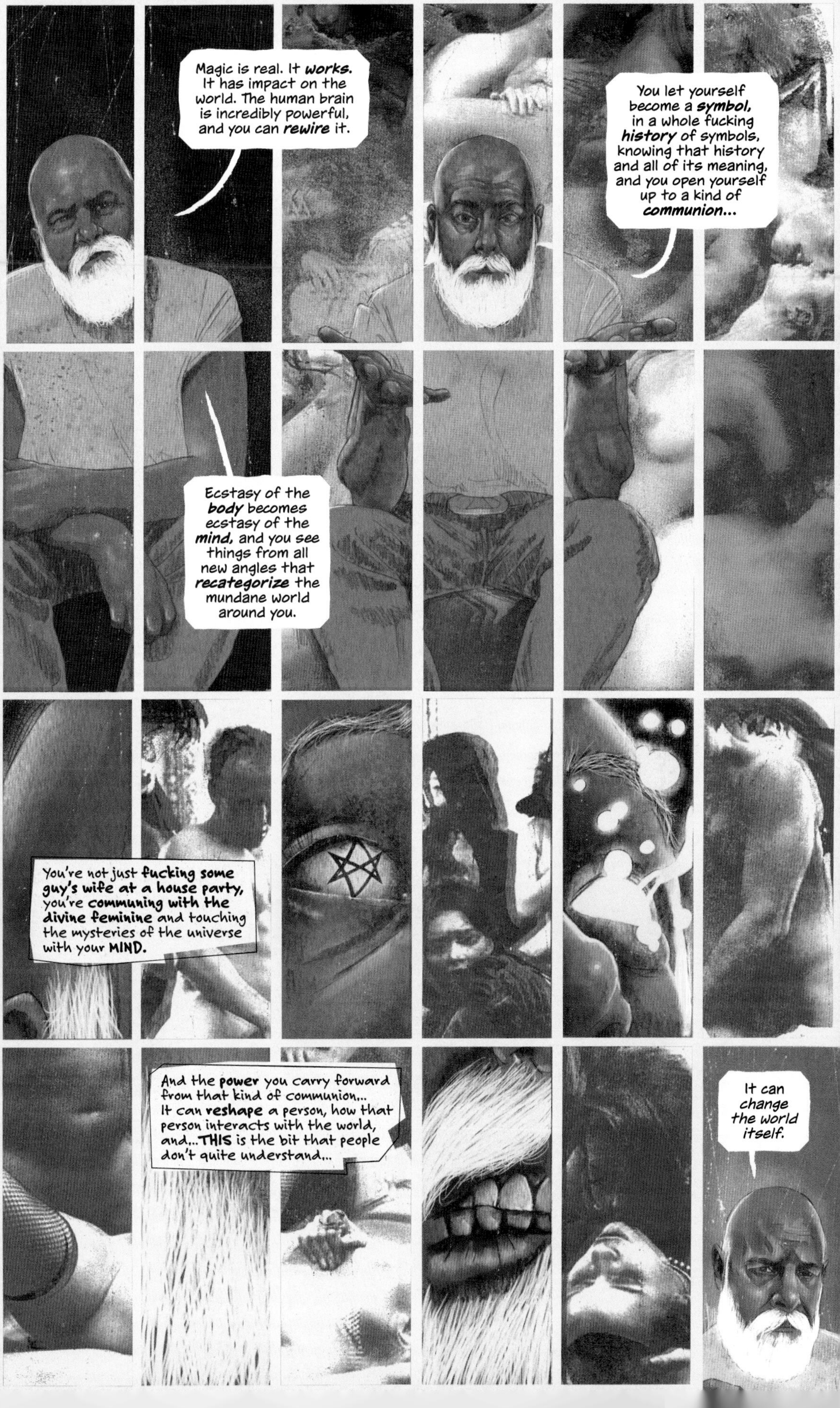
Magic is real. It works. It has impact on the world. The human brain is incredibly powerful, and you can rewire it.
You let yourself become a symbol, in a whole fucking history of symbols, knowing that history and all of its meaning, and you open yourself up to a kind of communion...
Ecstasy of the body becomes ecstasy of the mind, and you see things from all new angles that recategorize the mundane world around you.
You're not just fucking some guy's wife at a house party, you're communing with the divine feminine and touching the mysteries of the universe with your MIND.
And the power you carry forward from that kind of communion... It can reshape a person, how that person interacts with the world, and...THIS is the bit that people don't quite understand...
It can change the world itself.

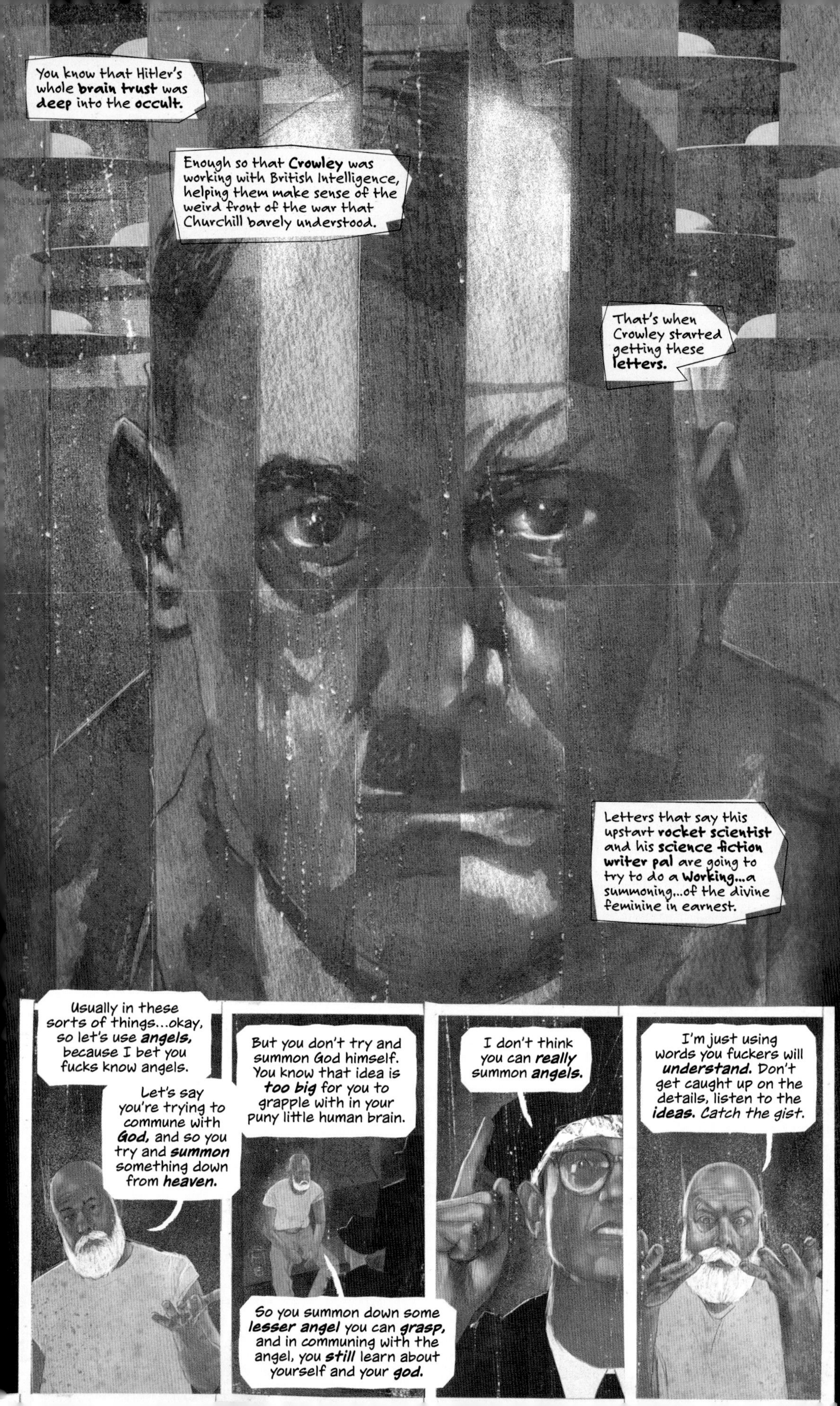

You know that Hitler's whole **brain trust** was **deep** into the **occult.**
Enough so that **Crowley** was working with British Intelligence, helping them make sense of the weird front of the war that Churchill barely understood.
That's when Crowley started getting these **letters.**
Letters that say this upstart **rocket scientist** and his **science fiction writer pal** are going to try to do a **Working...**a summoning...of the divine feminine in earnest.
Usually in these sorts of things...okay, so let's use ***angels,*** because I bet you fucks know angels.
Let's say you're trying to commune with ***God,*** and so you try and ***summon*** something down from ***heaven.***
But you don't try and summon God himself. You know that idea is ***too big*** for you to grapple with in your puny little human brain.
So you summon down some ***lesser angel*** you can ***grasp,*** and in communing with the angel, you ***still*** learn about yourself and your ***god.***
I don't think you can ***really*** summon ***angels.***
I'm just using words you fuckers will ***understand.*** Don't get caught up on the details, listen to the ***ideas.*** *Catch the gist.*

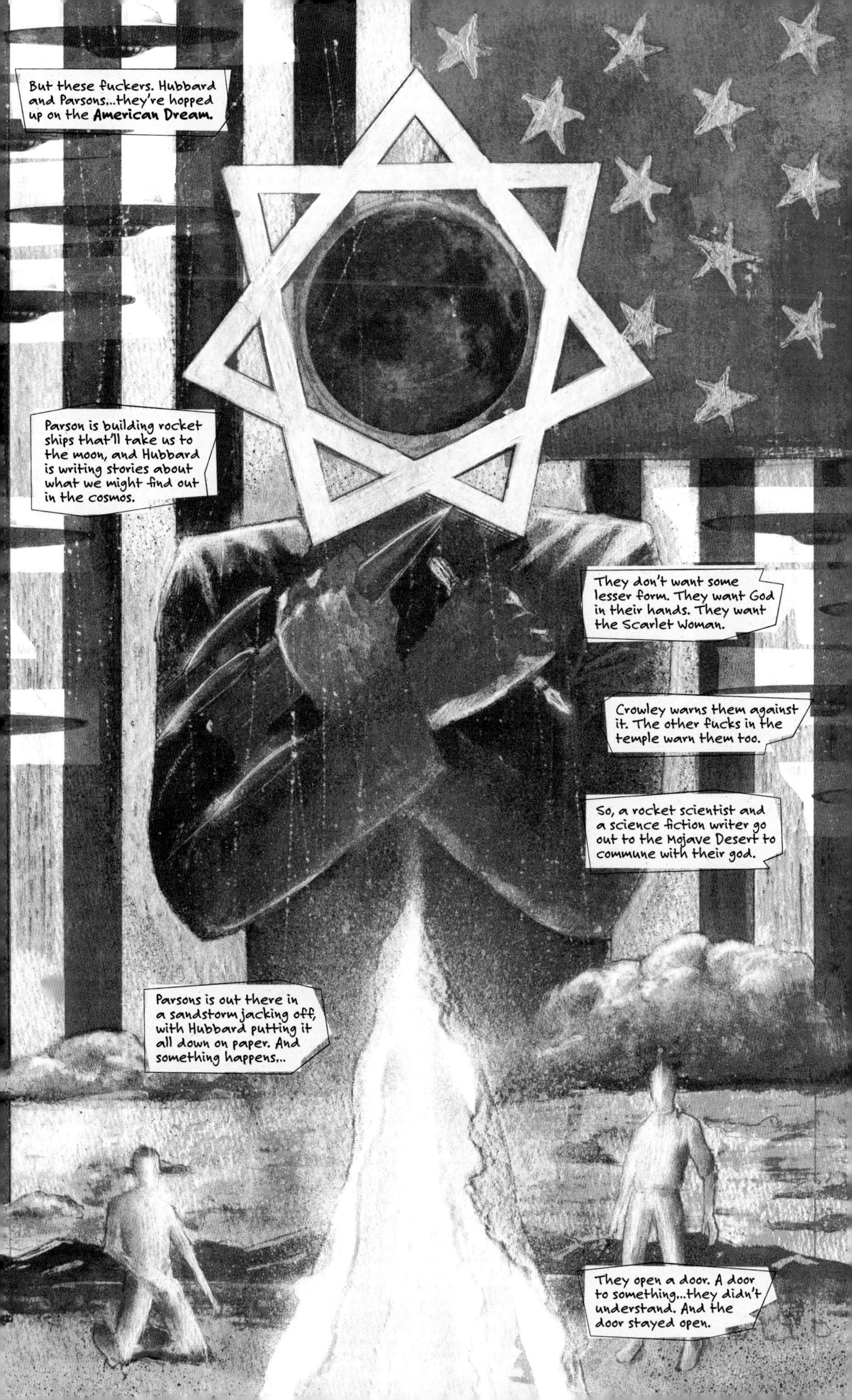
But these fuckers. Hubbard and Parsons...they're hopped up on the **American Dream.**
Parson is building rocket ships that'll take us to the moon, and Hubbard is writing stories about what we might find out in the cosmos.
They don't want some lesser form. They want God in their hands. They want the Scarlet Woman.
Crowley warns them against it. The other fucks in the temple warn them too.
So, a rocket scientist and a science fiction writer go out to the Mojave Desert to commune with their god.
Parsons is out there in a sandstorm jacking off, with Hubbard putting it all down on paper. And something happens...
They open a door. A door to something...they didn't understand. And the door stayed open.

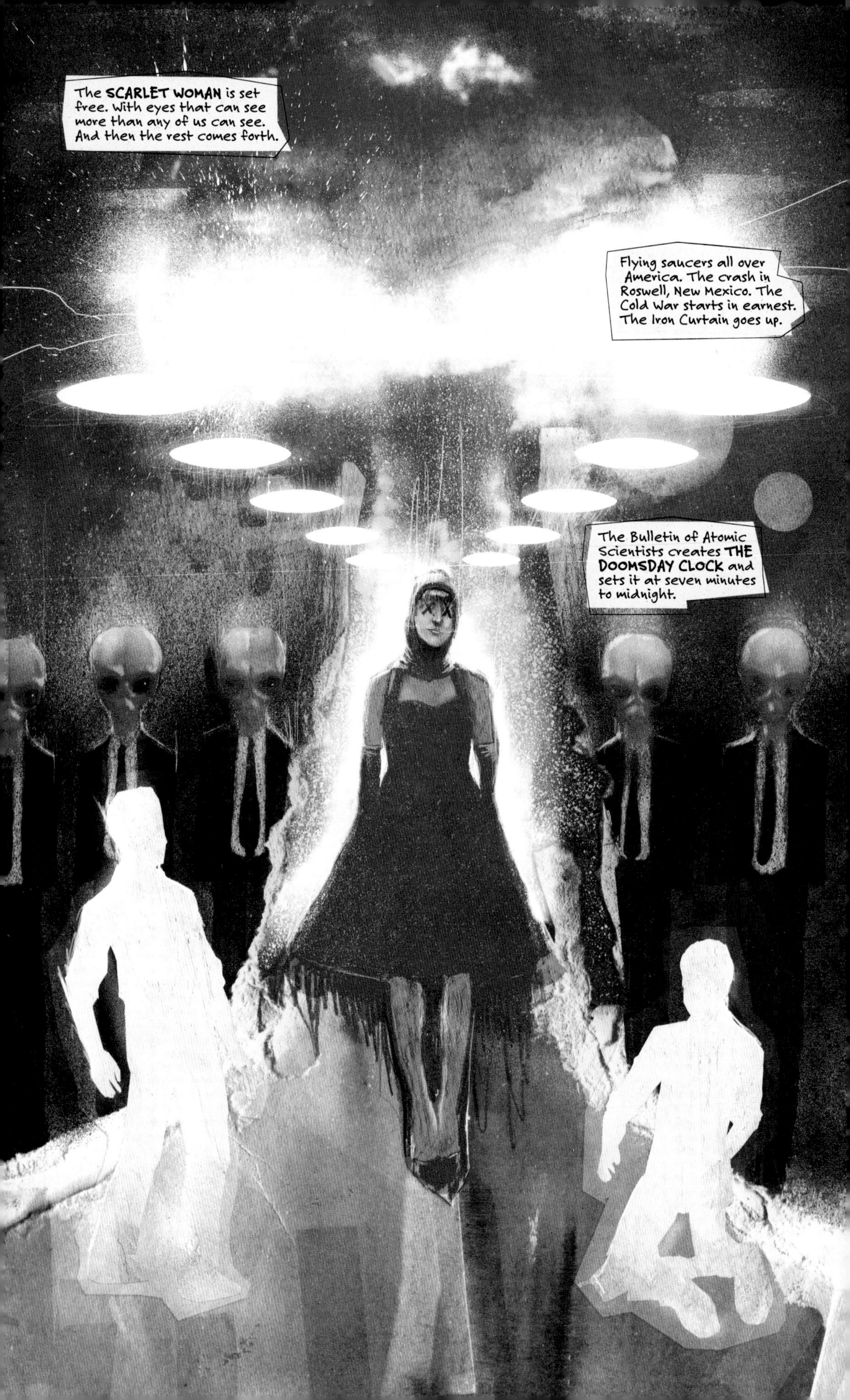

The SCARLET WOMAN is set free. With eyes that can see more than any of us can see. And then the rest comes forth.
Flying saucers all over America. The crash in Roswell, New Mexico. The Cold War starts in earnest. The Iron Curtain goes up.
The Bulletin of Atomic Scientists creates THE DOOMSDAY CLOCK and sets it at seven minutes to midnight.

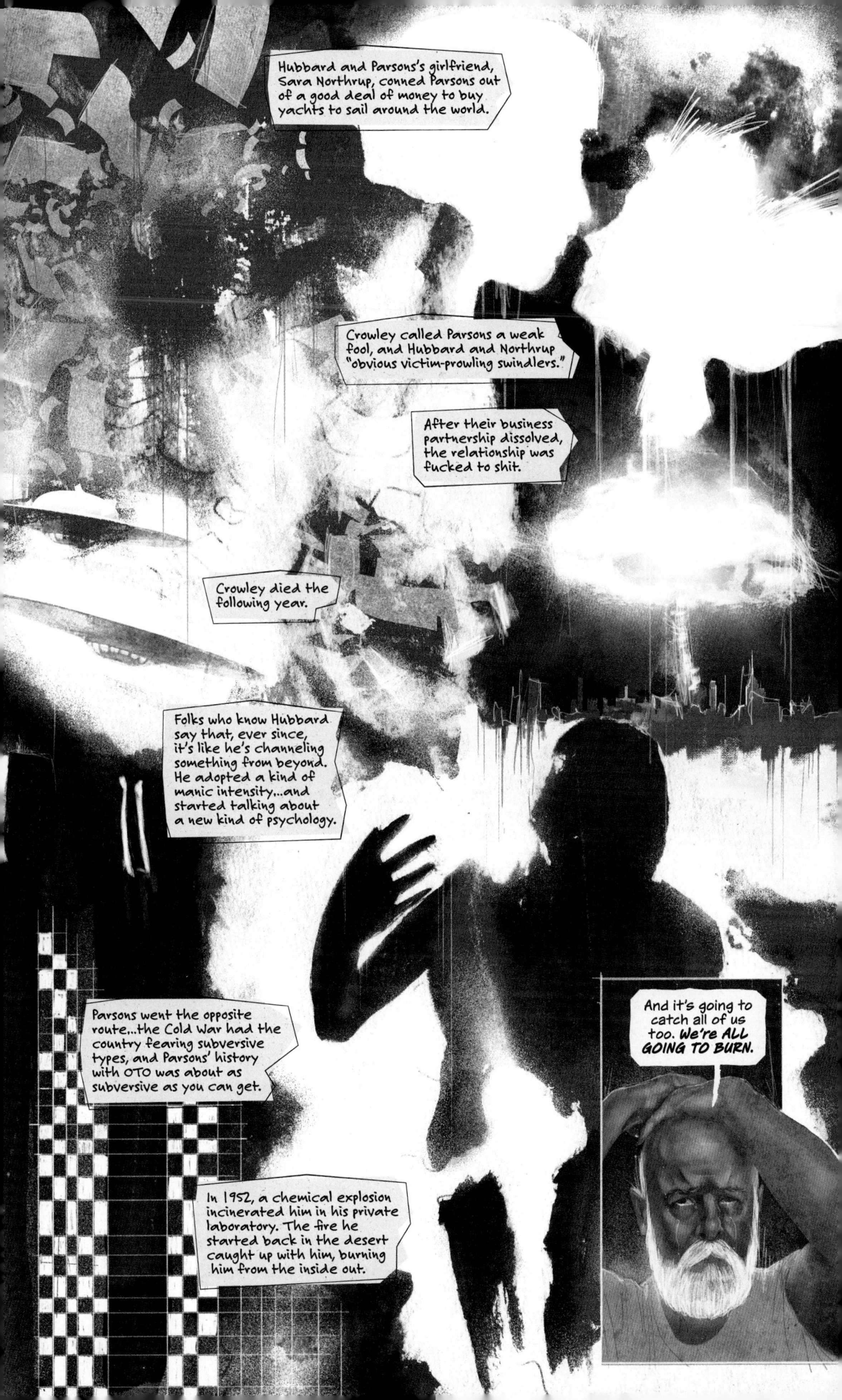
Hubbard and Parsons's girlfriend, Sara Northrup, conned Parsons out of a good deal of money to buy yachts to sail around the world.
Crowley called Parsons a weak fool, and Hubbard and Northrup "obvious victim-prowling swindlers."
After their business partnership dissolved, the relationship was fucked to shit.
Crowley died the following year.
Folks who know Hubbard say that, ever since, it's like he's channeling something from beyond. He adopted a kind of manic intensity...and started talking about a new kind of psychology.
Parsons went the opposite route...the Cold War had the country fearing subversive types, and Parsons' history with OTO was about as subversive as you can get.
In 1952, a chemical explosion incinerated him in his private laboratory. The fire he started back in the desert caught up with him, burning him from the inside out.
And it's going to catch all of us too. We're ALL GOING TO BURN.

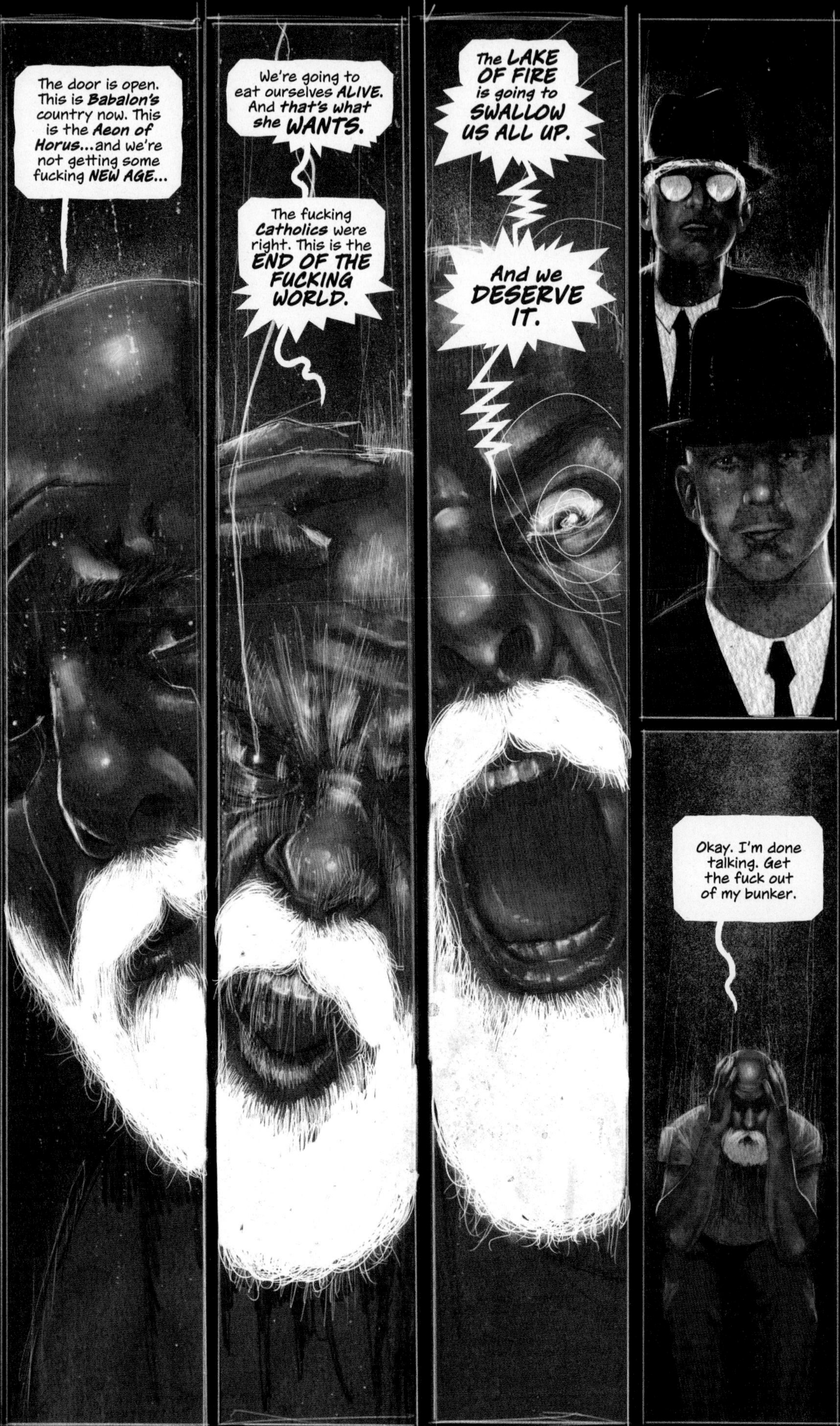
The door is open. This is **Babalon's** country now. This is the **Aeon of Horus...**and we're not getting some fucking **NEW AGE...**
We're going to eat ourselves **ALIVE.** And **that's what** she **WANTS.**
The fucking **Catholics** were right. This is the **END OF THE FUCKING WORLD.**
The **LAKE OF FIRE** is going to **SWALLOW US ALL UP.**
And we DESERVE IT.
Okay. I'm done talking. Get the fuck out of my bunker.

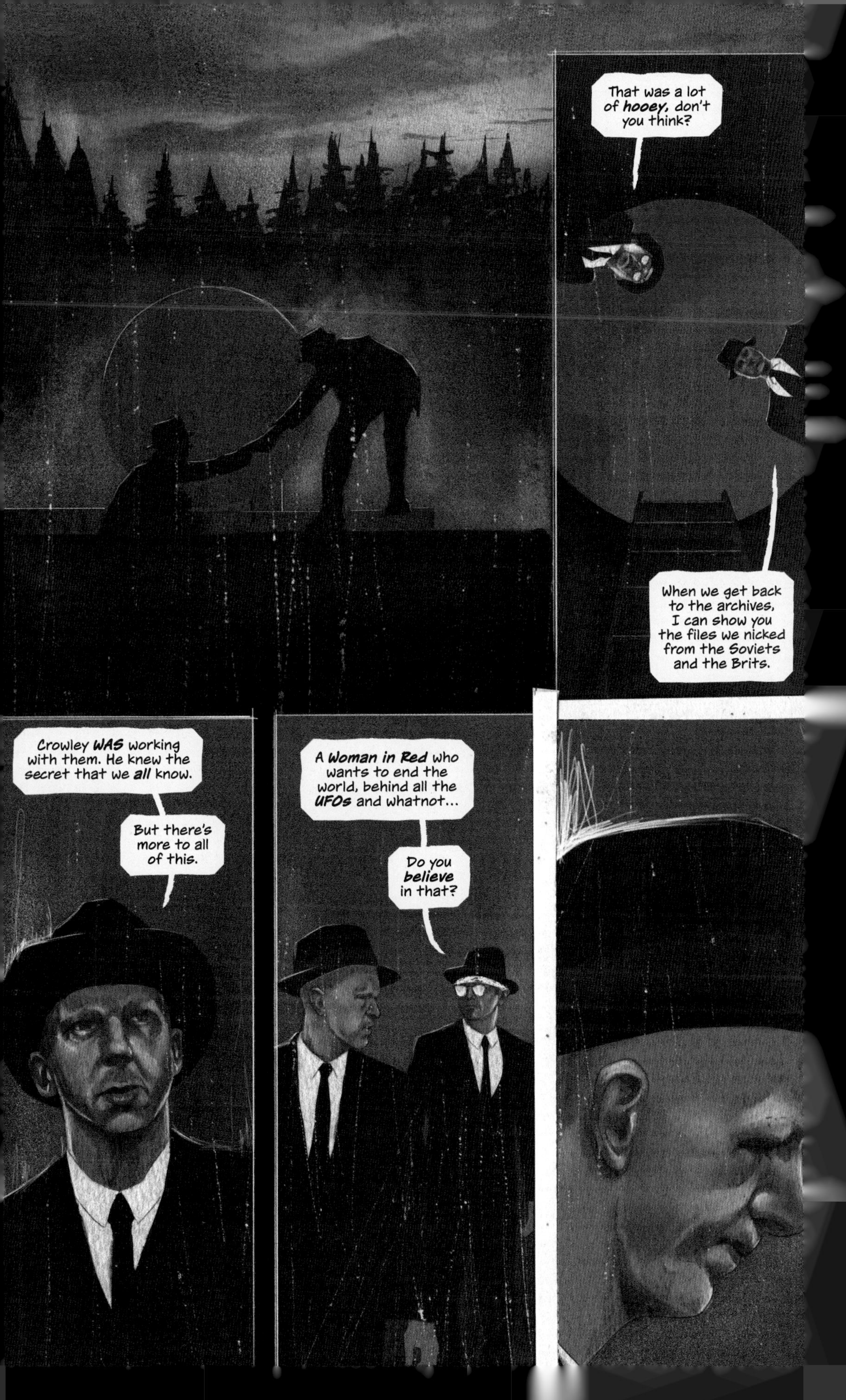
That was a lot of hooey, don't you think?
When we get back to the archives, I can show you the files we nicked from the Soviets and the Brits.
Crowley WAS working with them. He knew the secret that we all know.
But there's more to all of this.
A Woman in Red who wants to end the world, behind all the UFOs and whatnot...
Do you believe in that?

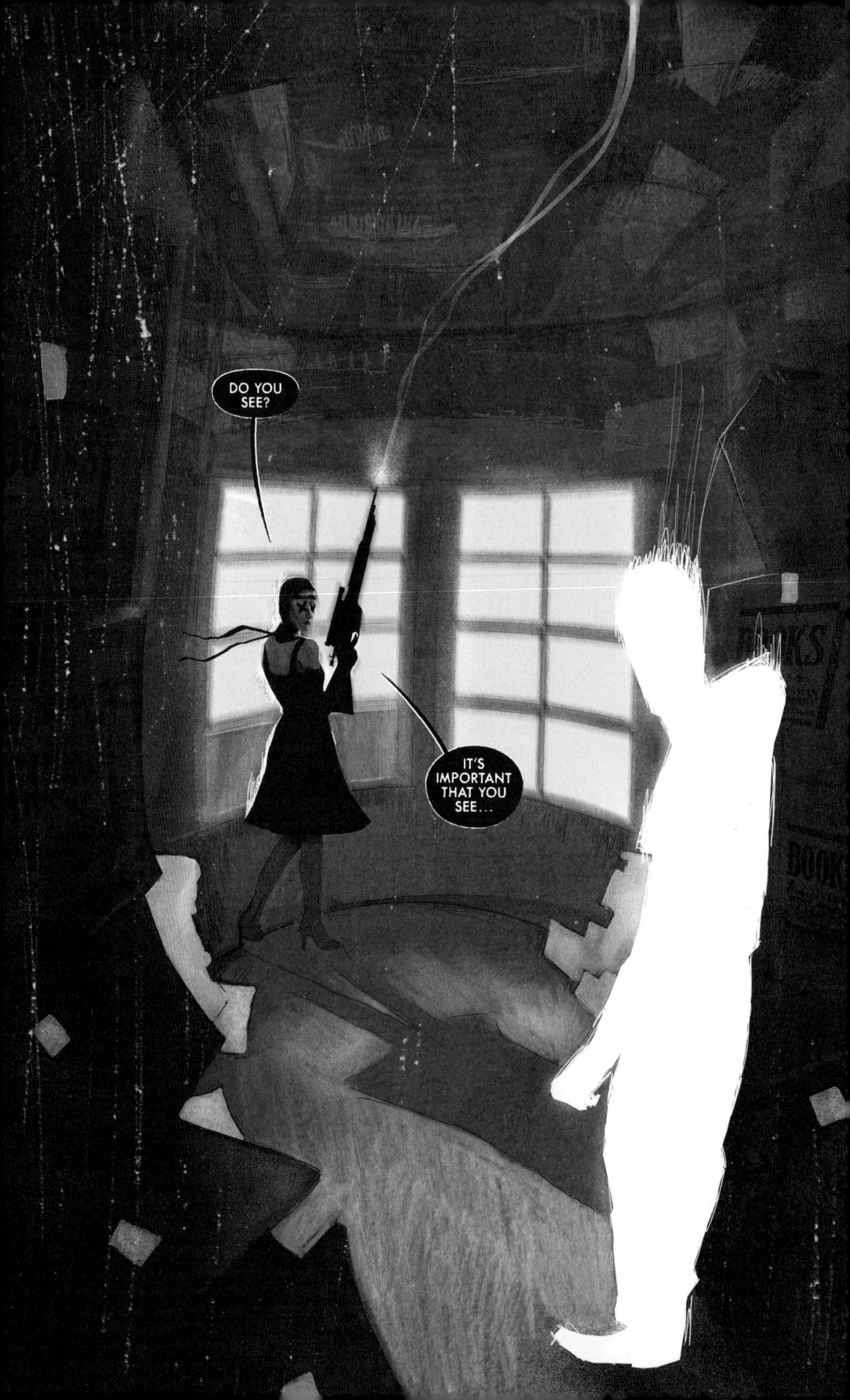
DO YOU SEE?
IT'S IMPORTANT THAT YOU SEE...

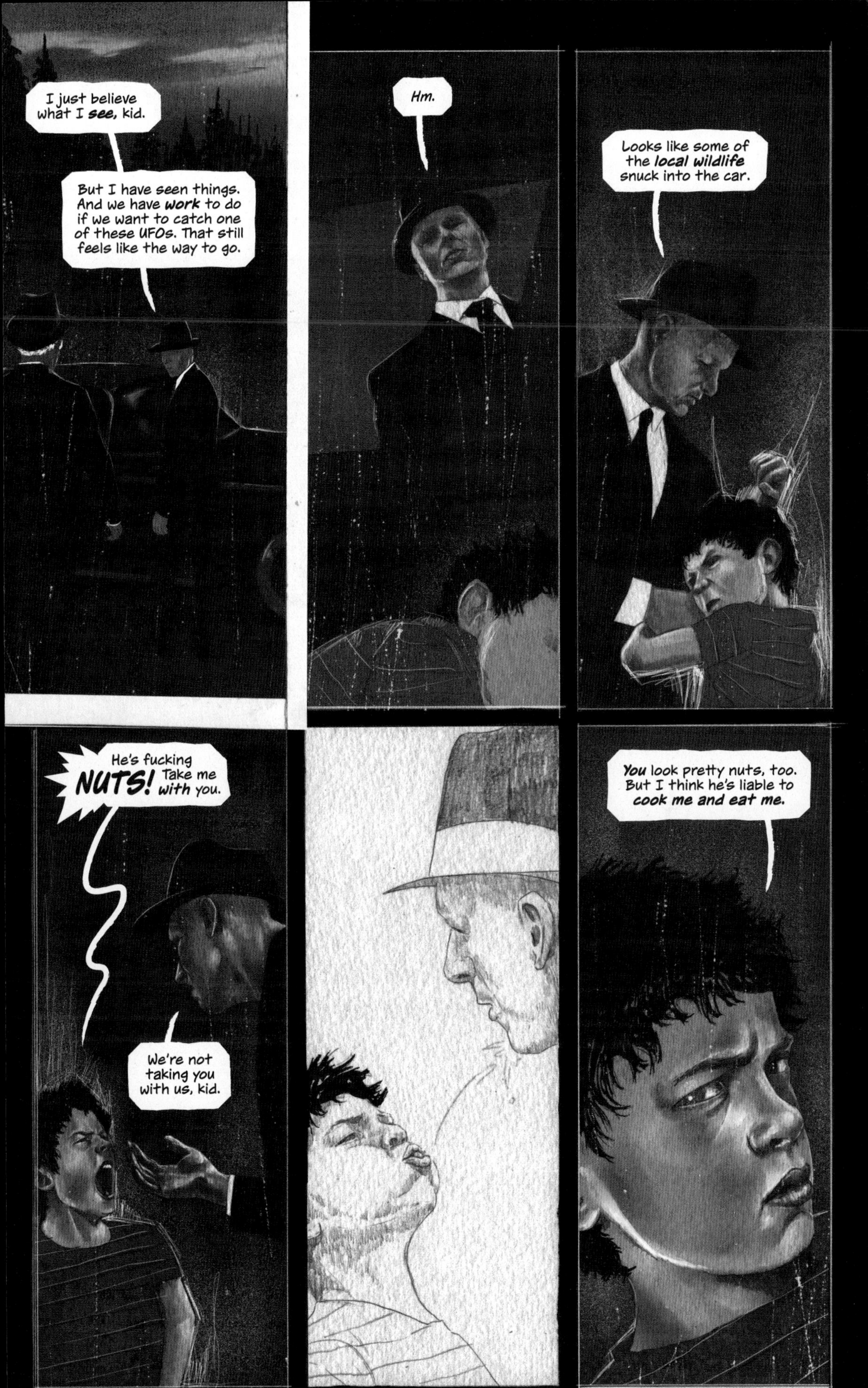
I just believe what I *see*, kid.
But I have seen things. And we have *work* to do if we want to catch one of these UFOs. That still feels like the way to go.
Hm.
Looks like some of the *local wildlife* snuck into the car.
He's fucking NUTS! Take me *with* you.
We're not taking you with us, kid.
You look pretty nuts, too. But I think he's liable to *cook me and eat me.*

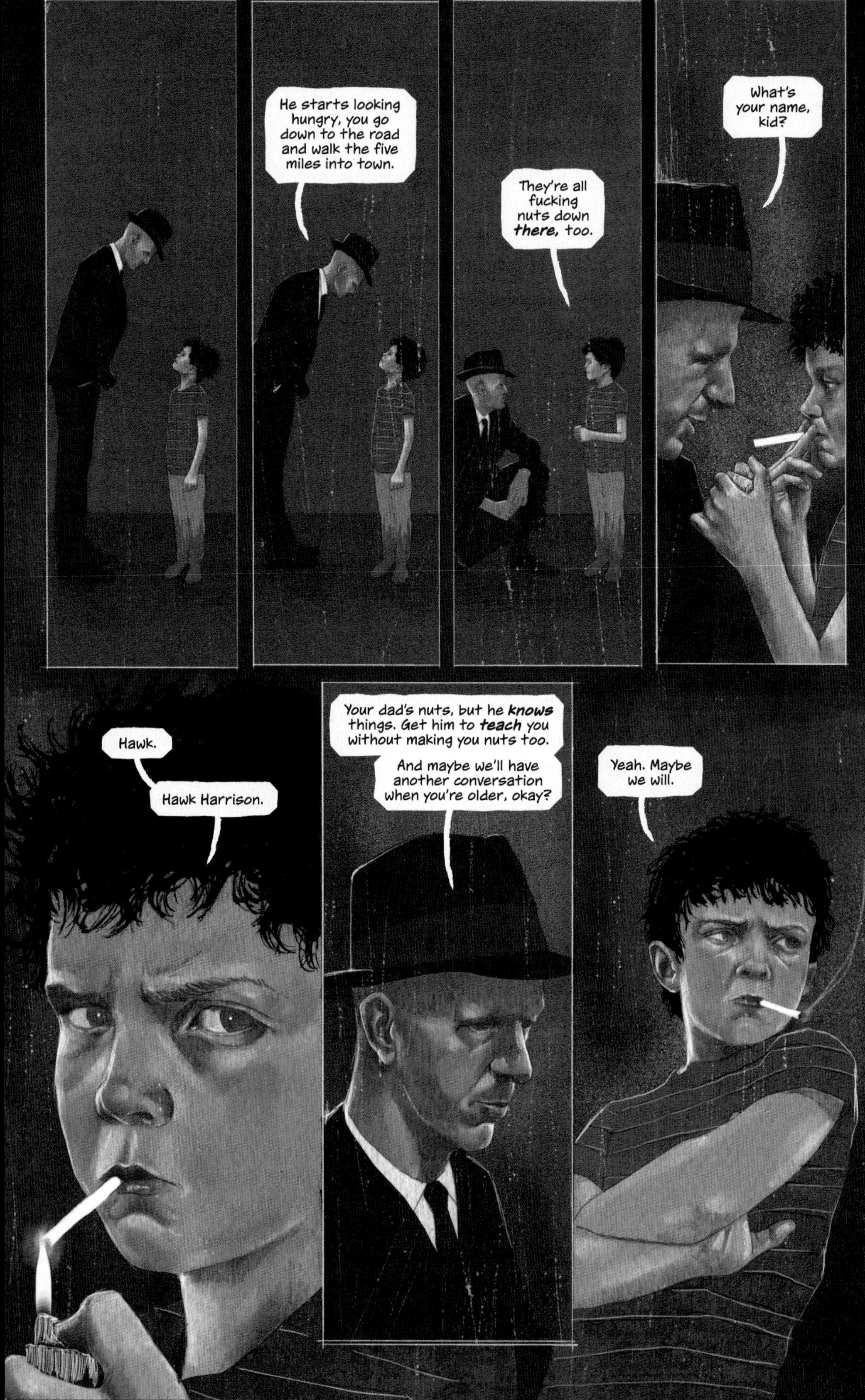
He starts looking hungry, you go down to the road and walk the five miles into town.
They're all fucking nuts down *there,* too.
What's your name, kid?
Hawk.
Hawk Harrison.
Your dad's nuts, but he *knows* things. Get him to *teach* you without making you nuts too.
And maybe we'll have another conversation when you're older, okay?
Yeah. Maybe we will.

DEPARTMEN

UNITED STATE

DEVIATION 4 /

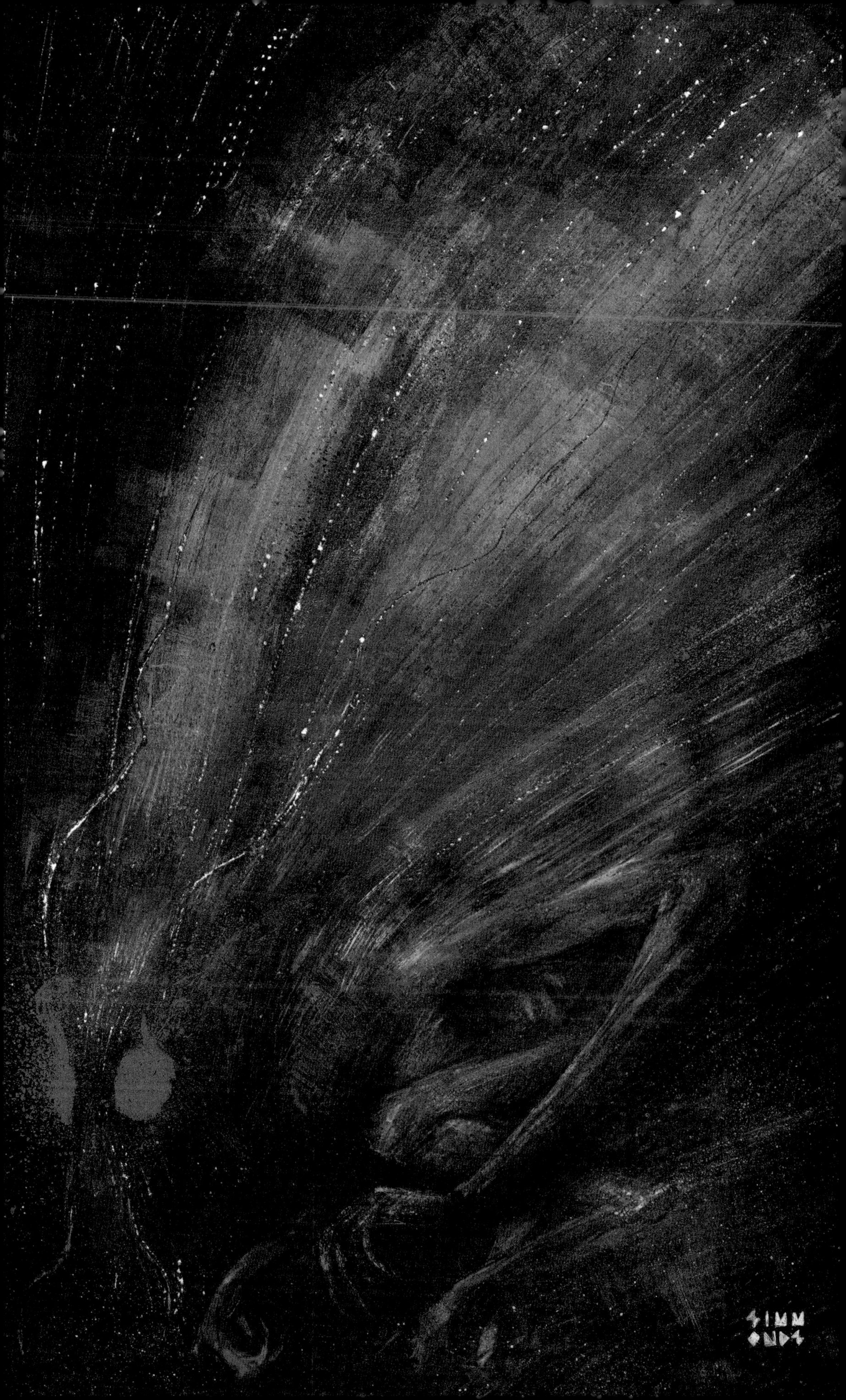
SIMM
ONDS

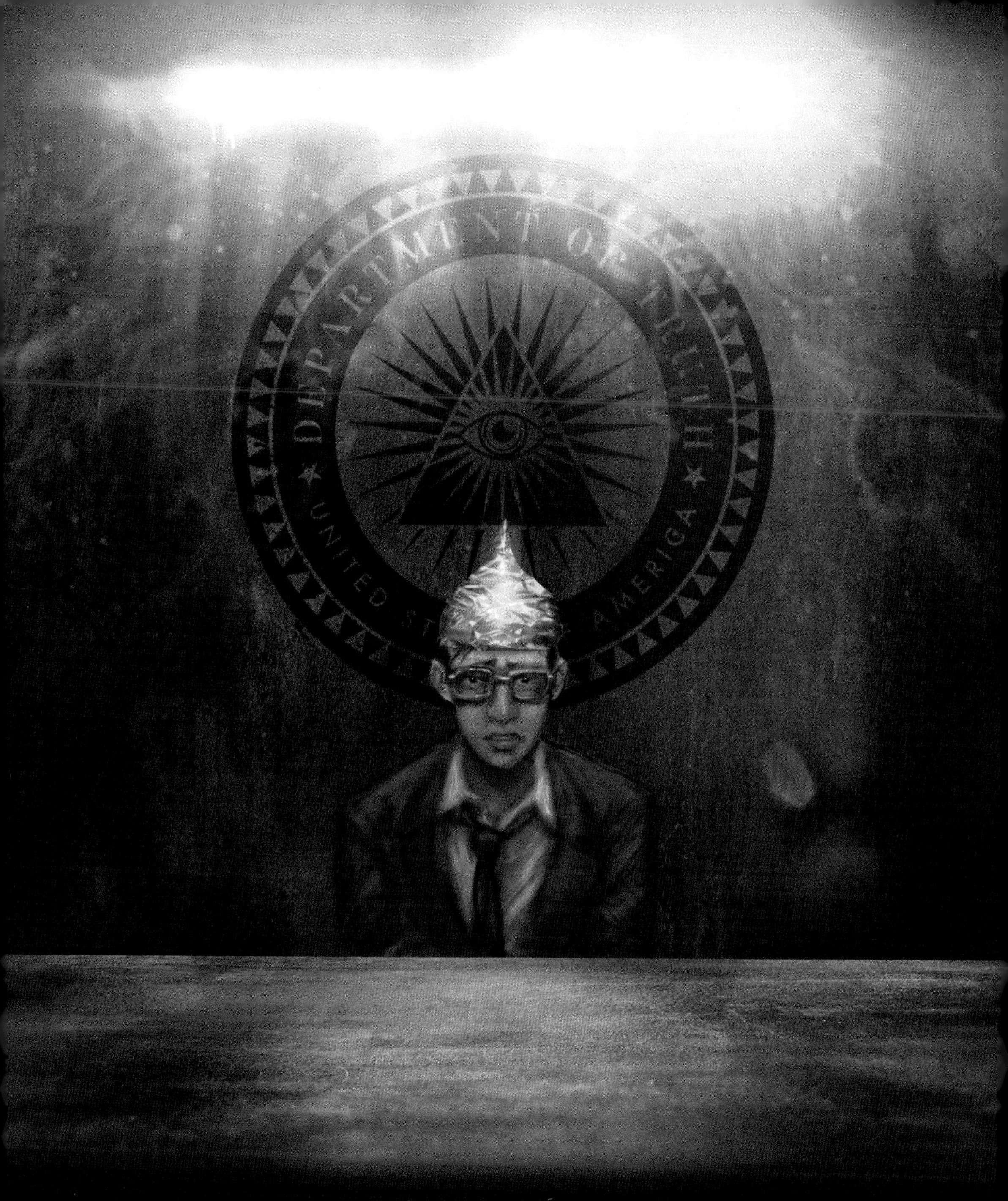
DEPARTMENT OF TRUTH
UNITED ST
AMERICA

DEVIATION FOUR:
Point Pleasant

Interview Transcript
Subject: DALTON HYNES
Internal Use Only
Ref.: [redacted]

[redacted]: State your name for the record.

HYNES: Oh, um... Dalton Hynes. I... uh... I go by "Doc."

HYNES: Junior Archivist, Department of Truth.

Point Pleasant, W. Va.

Strange Flying Objects' Reported in W. Va.

POINT PLEASANT, W. Va. - sightings clogged up the interstate

the volunteer fire department was called to assist near the roads

descriptions of the objects can be attributed to that of geese migration

[redacted]: You can relax, son.

HYNES: Oh, sure.

[redacted]: Do you feel like you can relax?

HYNES: It's just my own... I'm not good at relaxing in the best of times. And this isn't exactly, well... It's not ideal. I don't like being in trouble. I never got in trouble in school.

[redacted]: This isn't school.

HYNES: I know that, sir. I sure as heck know that now.

[redacted]: So, where did all of this start?

HYNES: It started with a theory, I guess. Since you founded this Department, it's been focused on messaging. We know there is a tipping point of belief that can materially change the world, so we make sure the majority is focused on believing in the America we want them to believe in. But if you take that idea to its extreme... If you start asking yourself, what if enough people believed in something strange? Could they manifest that strange fiction in the world? Lee wondered if that was already happening. If these UFOs were manifestations...

[redacted]: Can you define what you mean by manifestations?

HYNES: Unreal things made real by collective belief. Wild Fictions.

[redacted]: So, that was your theory.

HYNES: Our theory was that if we could get enough people to believe in something, we could force the balance into tipping deliberately. Create one of these Wild Fictions ourselves. And capture it.

[redacted]: You wanted to catch a UFO.

HYNES: Lee did. Yes.

[redacted]: How did you go about doing that?

HYNES: Inelegantly. First, we used the Department plants in newspapers all over the country to spread stories of "strange flying objects." That's the phrase we used. And for a while it seemed to work. There were mass sightings of UFOs all over the country in 1966, and we noticed the stories were catching in West Virginia in particular. Right along the Ohio River Valley. So we tried to focus our efforts there. Tried to narrow it down enough. The trouble was, our language... It wasn't specific enough.

[redacted]: Not specific enough?

HYNES: "Strange flying objects." We realized it when the first reports started coming in.

001 | As soon as our lights hit It, it was gone. It spread its wings a little and went straight up
002 | into the air. When we got to the armory it was flying over our car. We were going between
003 | 100 and 105 mph down that straight stretch and that thing was just gliding back and forth
004 | over the back end of the car. As we got there in front of the lights by the resort it dived
005 | at our car and went away.
006 |
007 | I could hear the wings flapping as if to get more speed as it went up. We were all terrified
008 | and kept yelling for Roger to go faster. As we came into that straight stretch by C. C.
009 | Lewis' [farm] the thing was over our car again. Then it disappeared as we came into the
010 | lights by C. C. Lewis' gates. We went on downtown and stopped at Dairyland and tried to
011 | decide what to do. We just sat there and looked at each other. 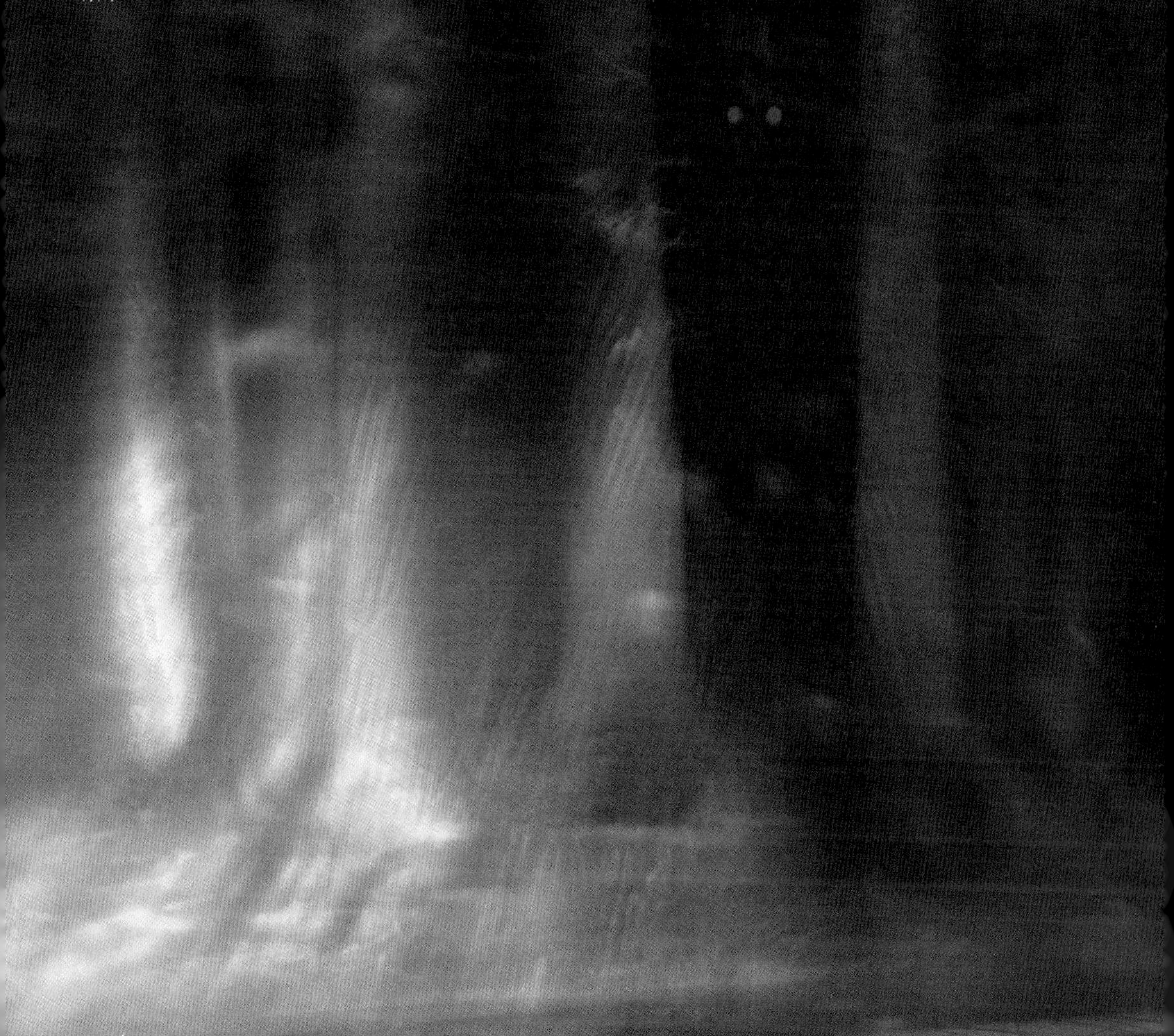
012 |

013 | I wanted to go to the police but Steve and Roger kept saying they'd just laugh at us.
014 | We talked about it awhile and Roger and Steve wanted to go back up the road. Mary and
015 | I kept trying to talk them out of it and finally when we go to C. C. Lewis' gate they decided
016 | they didn't want to go back up so we turned around.
017 |
018 | As we were turning we saw a big dead dog laying along the road. When we were almost
019 | turned around this thing jumped and leaped over our car and went through the field on
020 | the other side of the road. We decided to go to the police then and went down and around
021 | Tiny's Drive-In looking for them. Gary was outside the Drive-In getting ready to take a
022 | couple boys home so we told him about seeing this thing and asked him to call the police.
023 |

After the police came we went back up the road in our car with Gary and the police about 1/2 mile behind us. I saw it then in a pasture field with its wings out a little walking towards the car then it went up in the air and came at the car. As Gary's car lights came over the rise in the road and the lights shined on it, it disappeared. We went up and down the road looking for it but didn't see anymore. We went back down to the Drive-In and got in Gary's car and went back up. We finally found Millard Halstead and got with him and went to the powerhouse building.

We sat there with our lights out for about 15 or 20 minutes when I heard that squeaking sound like a mouse only a lot stronger. A shadow went across the building over on the hill across from us. Mary and I saw the red eyes then and told Millard. He shined the lights right on them without being told where they were. We saw dust coming from the ground or somewhere as Millard moved the spotlight around. We finally left and came to the trailer.

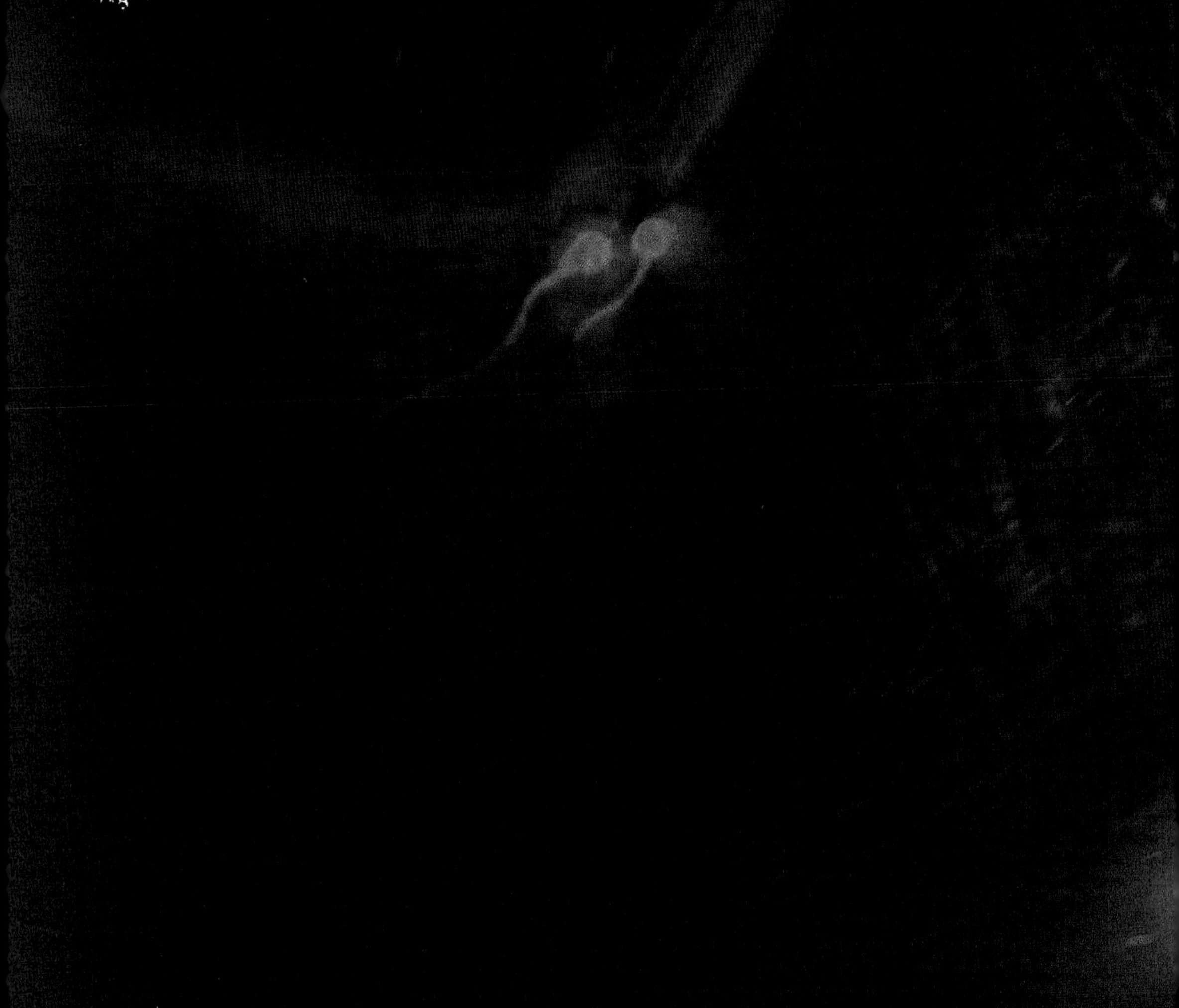

[The Mallettes] were afraid to go to their apartment so we decided to stay together but we didn't go to bed. We just turned on all the lights and stayed up. Wednesday we went up again to the building and found these off tracks around the building. Steve was around the boilers by himself and suddenly he came running out white as a sheet yelling for someone. He said he saw it in the boiler.

That night it was seen at Thomas's so we went up there and Mary and I stayed in the house while Steve and Roger and a few others [bystanders] went looking for it. On the way up I saw it from the highway above the trees gliding back and forth. They searched the area around Thomas's house but didn't find anything. We started home around 12:30 and I saw it in one of the maintenance buildings. Mary and I started crying and Roger took off. I kept thinking about that thing following us again but it didn't.

We went to my mother's and I went all to pieces. Roger and my dad took me down to the hospital. I finally got back home and we all stayed together that night again but didn't go to bed till 3 or 4 o'clock. We were still afraid to go to sleep. The next day Thursday we went back up with reporters and we all heard a clanging noise from inside the building. Roger and Steve and the reporters went back in and found the boiler door open that Steve had shut when he left a few minutes before that. That night we went back up and Mary Hyre and I saw the eyes inside the fenced off place beside the powerhouse building.

On the way home I saw its eyes back in some trees from the road as the car went past and looked back and could see its form. That is the last time I have seen it. To me it just looks like a man with wings. (It was a dirty gray color.) It has a body shape form with wings on its back that come around it. It has muscular legs like a man and fiery-red eyes that glow when the lights hit it. There was no glowing about it until the lights hit it. I couldn't see its head or arms. I don't know if the eyes are even in a head. When we came down the straight stretch by the armory it didn't even seem like it had any trouble keeping up with us. It must have had very powerful wings.

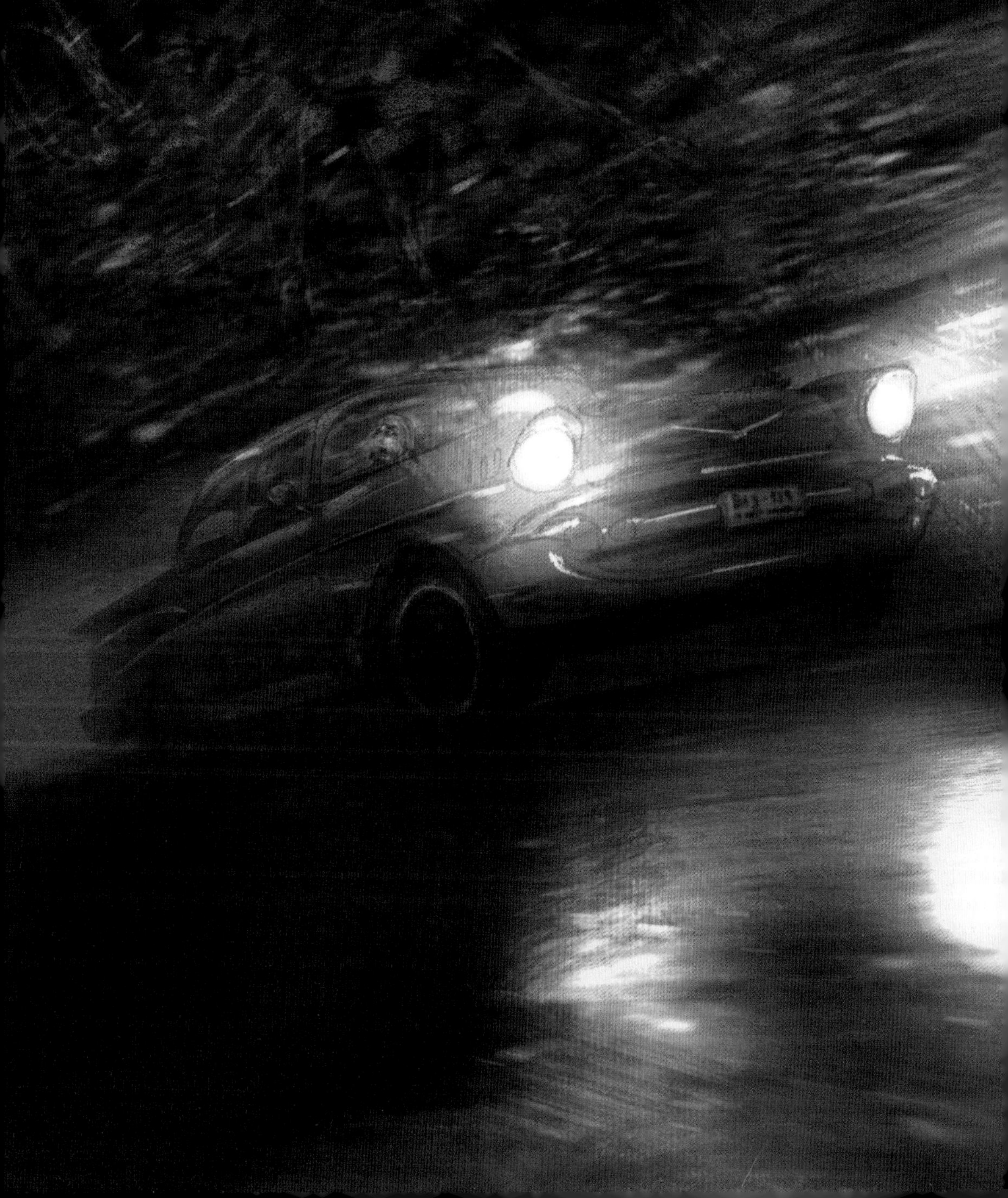

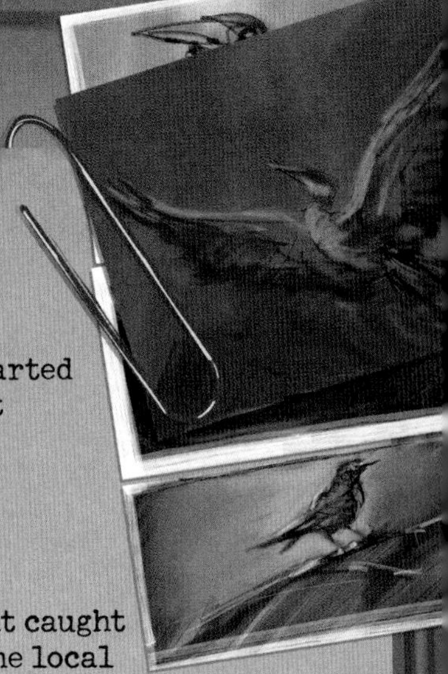

HYNES: It didn't actually start with the Mothman... It started with these strange sightings of giant birds. But it evolved quickly.

[redacted]: Strange flying objects.

HYNES: Yeah. Exactly. Strange flying objects. There were commonalities in the sightings. Weird details that caught in the public's imagination and spread through the local papers. Bright red eyes... Coming out of the thing's torso. Like it didn't have a proper head. And when it would fly, it usually wouldn't flap its wings. It would just raise into the air eerily and silently.

[redacted]: And what? You're telling me that you and Lee designed this creature?

HYNES: No... The people designed it. In their own way. I think... I think they all must have latched onto the same details, and then the news stories kept echoing those details, making it more defined in their heads.

[redacted]: Why do they call it Mothman? I've read the description. It doesn't sound like any moth I've seen.

HYNES: Well... It was a play on Batman. From the TV show and the comic books. It was a man-shaped thing with wings.

[redacted]: This Batman has wings?

HYNES: No sir. But people... They get caught on a fun idea. I think the papers like to try to get the name that sticks in the public's mind.

[redacted]: I see.

HYNES: Anyways... Once the details set, people kept seeing it out in the wild.

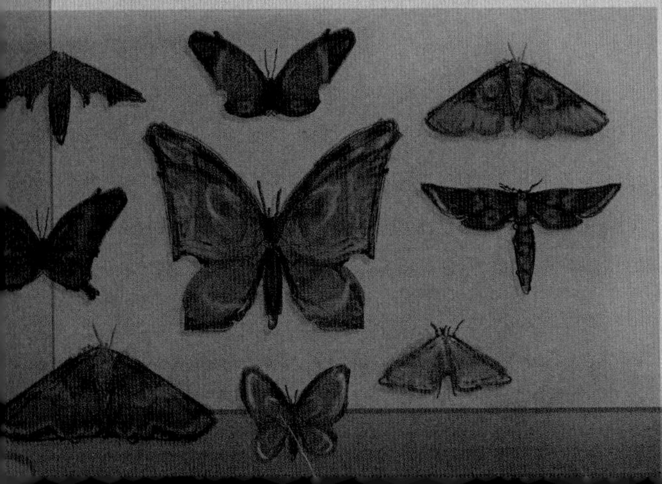

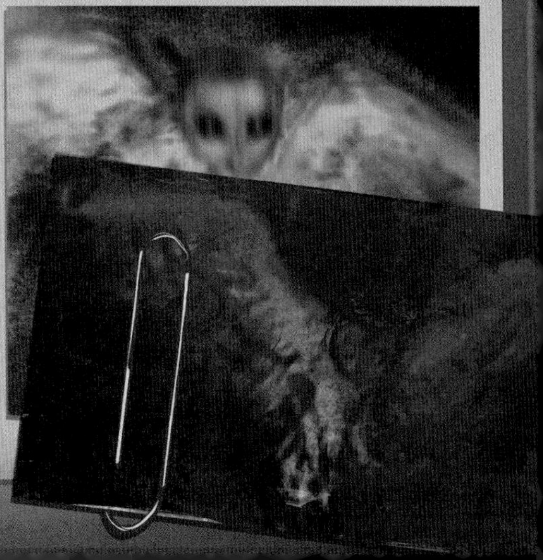

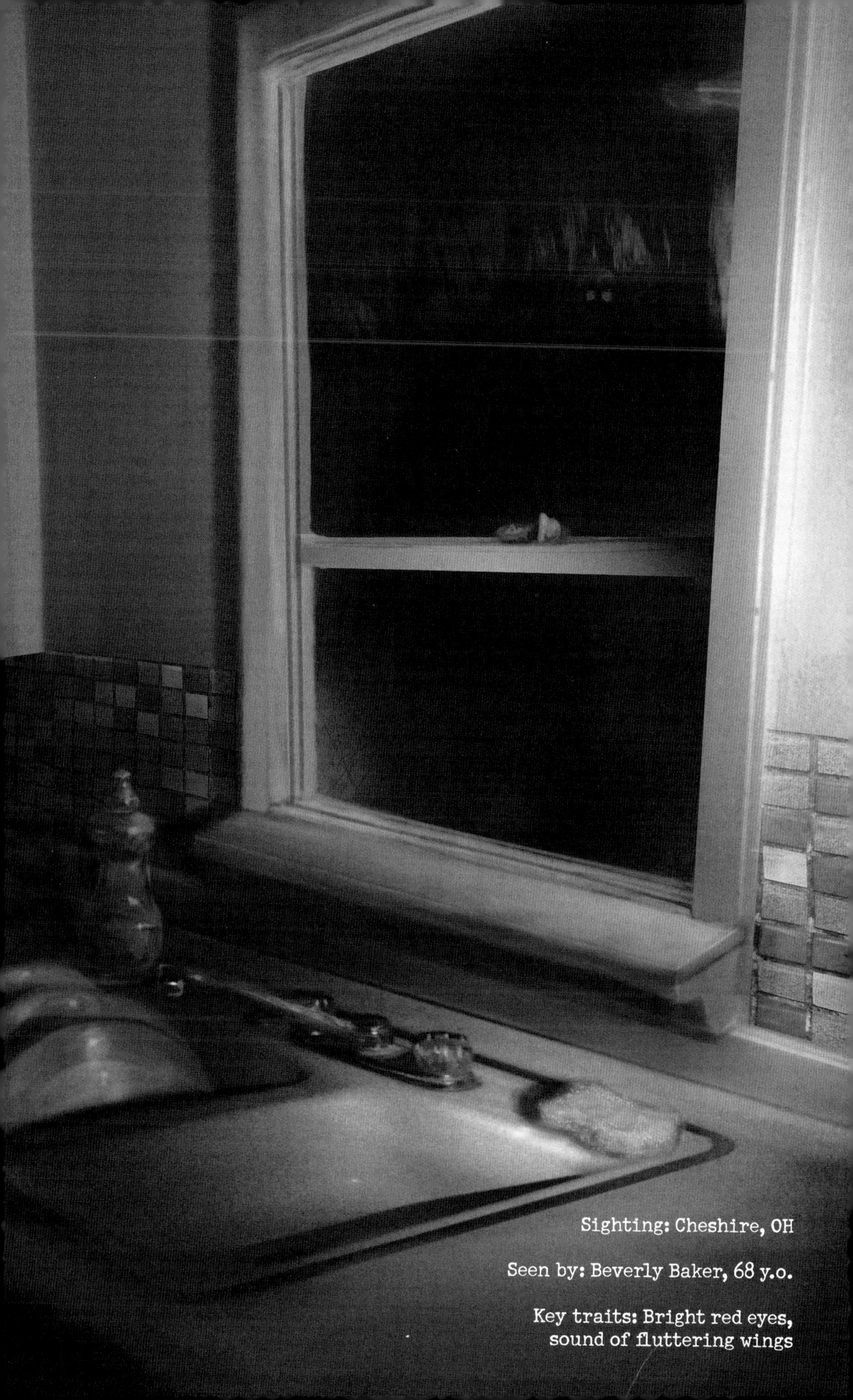

Sighting: Cheshire, OH

Seen by: Beverly Baker, 68 y.o.

Key traits: Bright red eyes, sound of fluttering wings

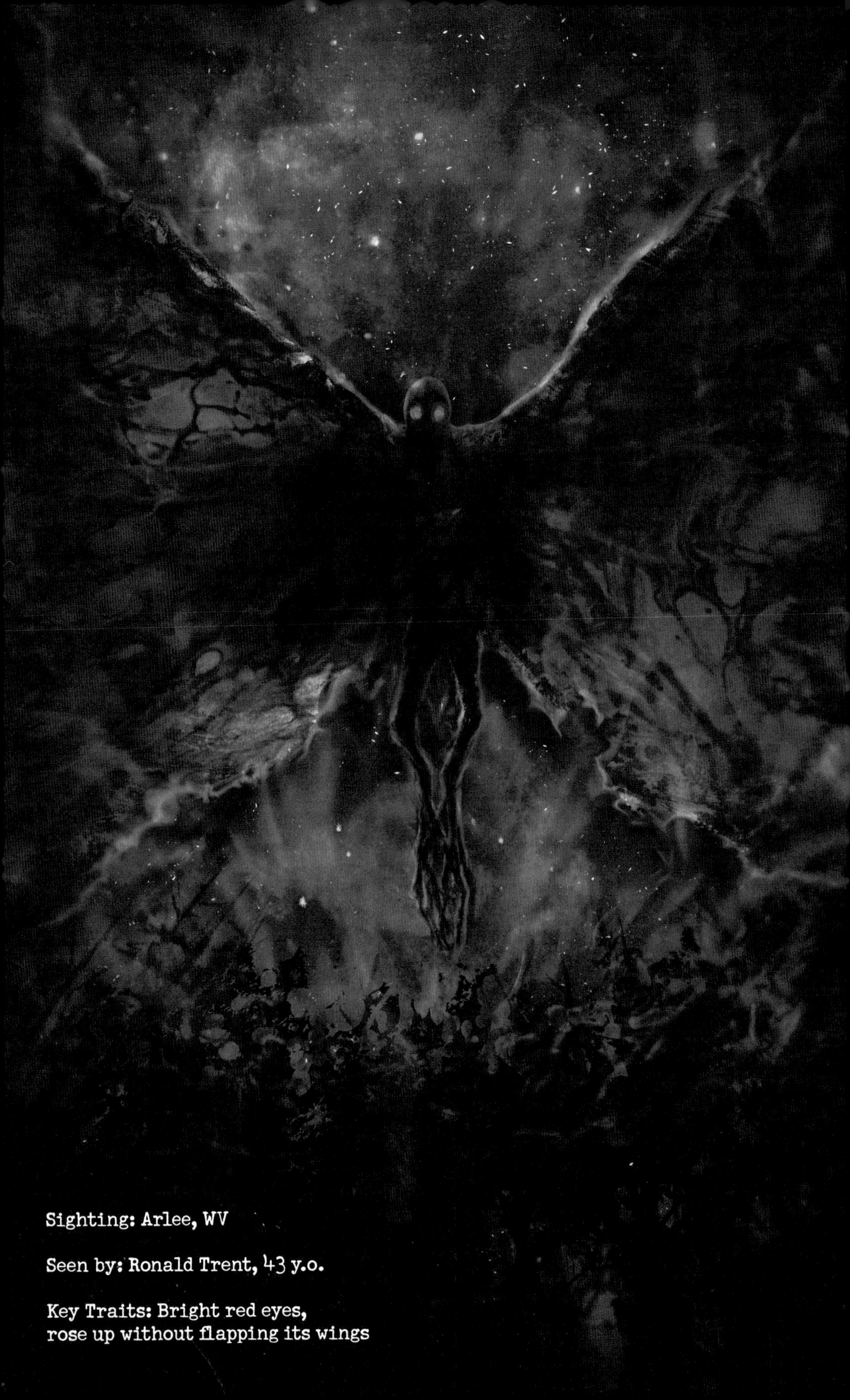

Sighting: Arlee, WV

Seen by: Ronald Trent, 43 y.o.

Key Traits: Bright red eyes,
rose up without flapping its wings

HYNES: I think... I'm developing some of my own theories here, so I'm sorry if they're a little unwieldy. But I think in our line of work... strangeness begets strangeness.

[redacted]: Explain how you mean.

HYNES: I think people out there... They have a sense of how the world works, and they're all comfortable with that sense. But once they see something that breaks the rules as they understand them... It breaks ALL of the rules. Then, the expectation of strangeness creates MORE strangeness. Weird things happen when people expect weird things to happen. The world, it starts to distort. And when it distorts, I think it... I think it catches the attention of these... Well, these figures.

[redacted]: Figures.

HYNES: I don't have a catchy name for them. They're not like the Wild Fictions. They don't feel like they are just here because people expected them to be here. I don't know, this all makes me sound crazy.

[redacted]: I've become very generous in what I'm willing and able to believe, Doc, but I need to you spell this out for me.

HYNES: So, I think... I think there are things like UFOs. And Mothman. And Dragons, the myths of old... They are more of an expression of people, you know? They don't have intent. They just have the intent that people want them to have.

[redacted]: Wild Fictions.

HYNES: Exactly. That's what I've been calling them. But then there are these strange figures, and they DO have intent.

[redacted]: Did Lee tell you about what he saw in Dallas back in 1963?

HYNES: He told me about [redacted]

[redacted]: And do you suspect that SHE is one of these figures with intent?

HYNES: Based on what I've heard... I do. But she isn't the one I was talking about.

[redacted]: You're talking about Indrid Cold.

HYNES: Yes. Indrid Cold.

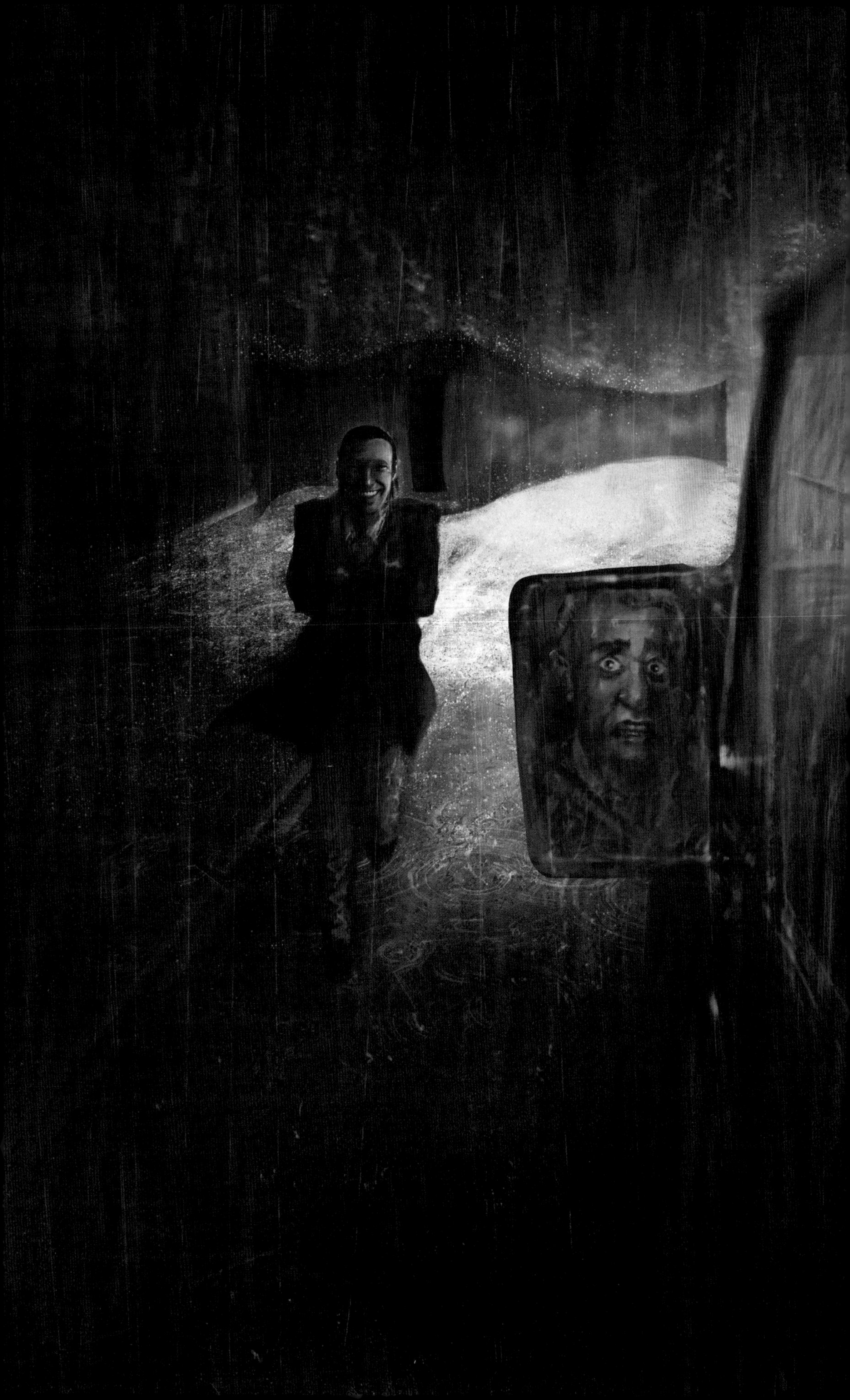

"INDRID COLD"
Derenberger Sighting
Summary of Direct Account
Mineral Wells, WV
November 1966

While driving his truck on Interstate 7, Woodrow "Woody" Derenberger noticed a strange vehicle following him that he presumed to be a police car. It was 7 p.m., on a rainy day. He was startled when the vehicle moved in front of his truck, at which point he noticed it was shaped like a kerosene lamp chimney and floating in the air. The vehicle blocked the road and a door opened in its side.

A man exited the ship. He wore a dark topcoat over what appeared to be a strange green, metallic garment that shimmered in the light of Derenberger's car. His skin was tan, his hair slicked back, and his smile wide. As he moved away from the ship, it rose fifty feet in the air above the road.

Derenberger did not hear the man but could feel the man's intent in his mind. He wanted Derenberger to roll down his window. The strange smiling man communicated directly with Derenberger's mind. He informed Derenberger that he meant him no harm. That he came from a country much less powerful than his. He informed Derenberger that his name was Cold. That he slept, breathed, and bled just as Derenberger did.

Cold inquired about the nearby city of Parkersburg. Derenberger did his best to explain the idea of a city to Cold. Cold informed Derenberger that on his world, these places were called "Gatherings." Cold told Derenberger to report the encounter to the authorities, and that he would confirm the report to the authorities at a later date. He then told Derenberger he would see him again soon.

The vehicle lowered into the road, allowing Cold to enter, and then it rose quickly and quietly until it disappeared out of sight.

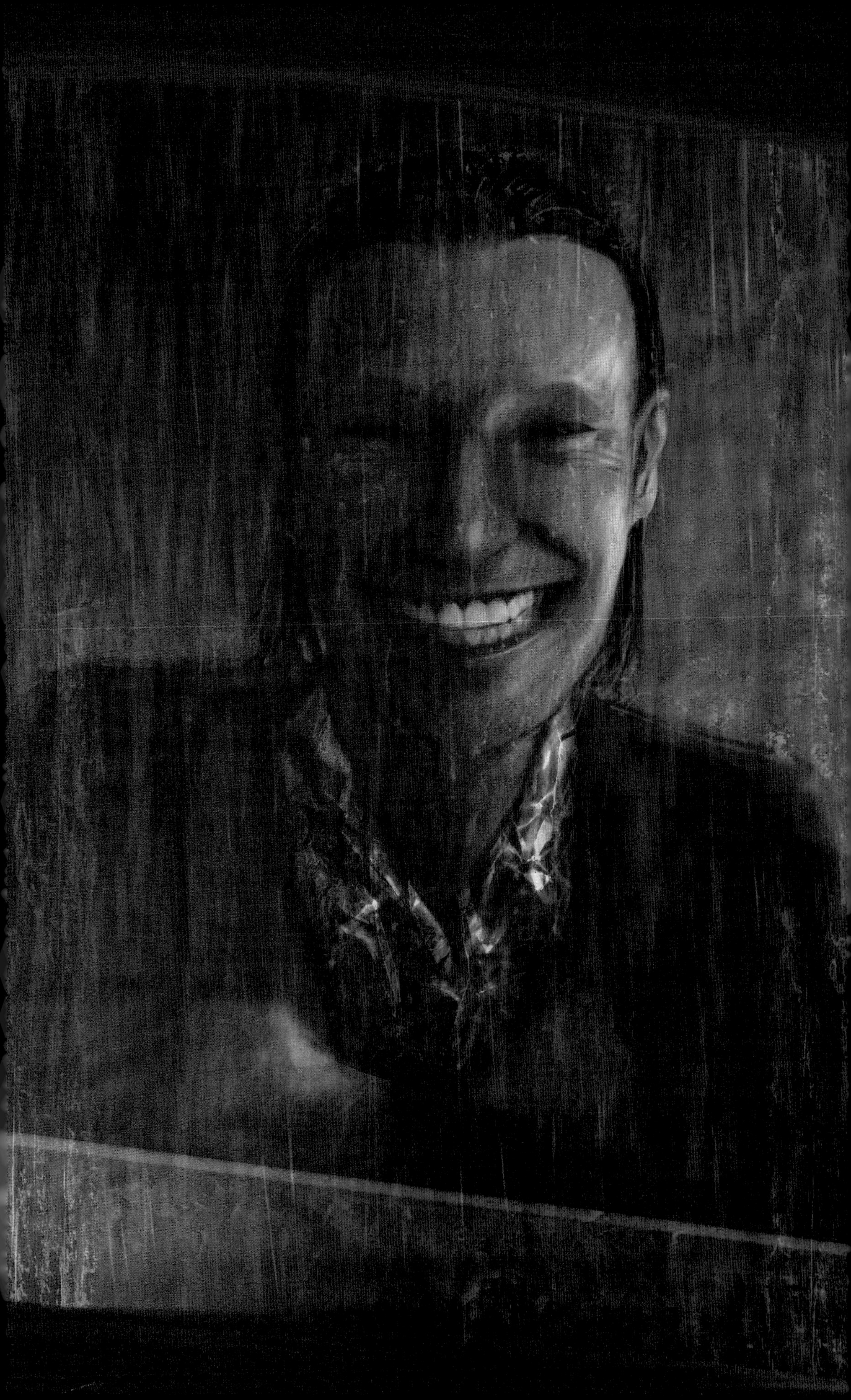

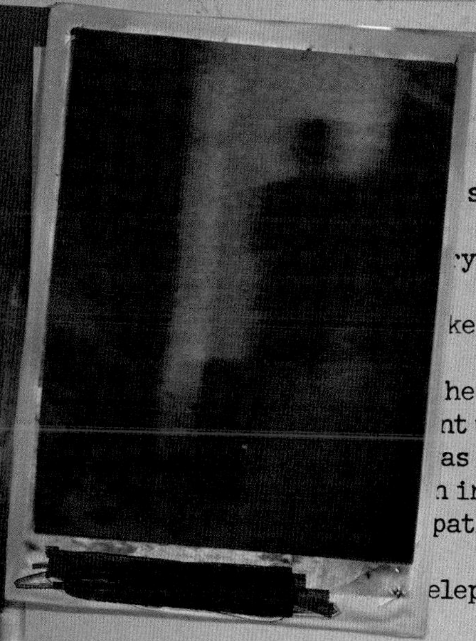

scares you, doesn't he?

y much so.

ke to know why.

he Department... After I was interviewed
nt that first time in the diner by my
as visited by this figure. This...
n in Black. And it warned me with these
pathic visions.

elepathic.

HYNES: It spoke directly into my brain. It showed me pictures. The only way I could make it stop was by putting on the tin foil. But there was something to him... There was intent.

[redacted]: Do you think the figure you spoke with could be this Indrid Cold?

HYNES: (unintelligible)

[redacted]: Speak up, son.

HYNES: Yes. I do think it could have been Indrid Cold. Or... I don't know. I think they could all be connected somehow. Maybe all the Men in Black are connected to him somehow.

[redacted]: You don't think this Derenberger could have made it all up?

HYNES: I... No I don't. We'll get to why, that all happened at the end, but I don't think he did. And either way, after that encounter, reports of strange men in black suits started spreading.

[redacted]: That's when you informed the home office of what you and Lee had been doing. How you had defied orders to run this operation. How you had misappropriated Department of Truth resources.

HYNES: Yes, sir. I was scared. I felt that strangeness begets strangeness, and it was all getting stranger. Lee was furious with me, but I knew things were getting out of hand. A few notable ufologists were starting to poke around. Gray Barker and John Keel. I could see where it was all heading.

[redacted]: And then you tried to scare some people off, didn't you?

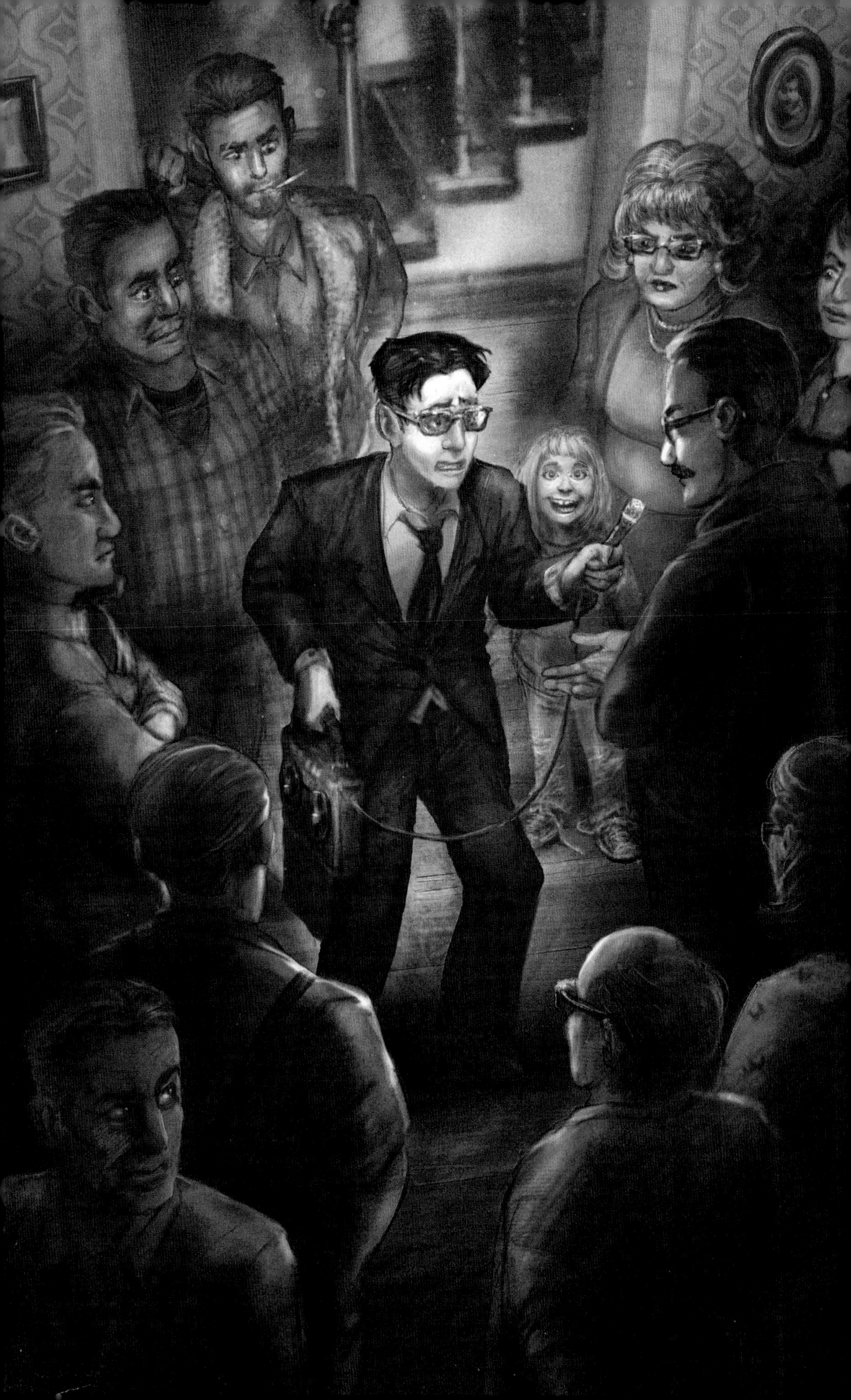

HYNES: I... Yes. We did. Or rather, I did. We thought Lee was too much of a risk. It's honestly kind of funny...

██████: Funny?

HYNES: Well... Lee made me take off my tin foil before I went to this meeting of people in Point Pleasant who had seen UFOs. I was supposed to act like a kid ufologist, because in a lot of ways, that's still exactly what I was. But taking off the tin foil had me so anxious that I must have come across very strange. I was trying to convince people not to talk to Keel or Barker, to keep everything contained. A few months later there were stories about the young Man in Black, acting bizarrely at the party, asking strange questions.

██████: You became one of your own Men in Black.

HYNES: Yes. And it just... Well, it just made everything worse. The panic was dialing up and up, and the less funny part is the implication of what happens when the public notices us in some ways. The idea that there are mysterious men in dark suits who know more about the UFOs and the Mothmen. It's one thing when they are telling stories about these Wild Fictions, but it's another thing when they are telling stories about us. When they have truth on their side, it feels like what they believe about us could have a measurable effect on who we are and what we do. So I was getting more and more nervous, and Lee was getting more and more desperate. He wanted to capture the UFO he had set out to capture. He didn't want to stop all of the stories spreading in the press. He wanted to lean into Point Pleasant and see if we could really drive it to manifest there. And it did.

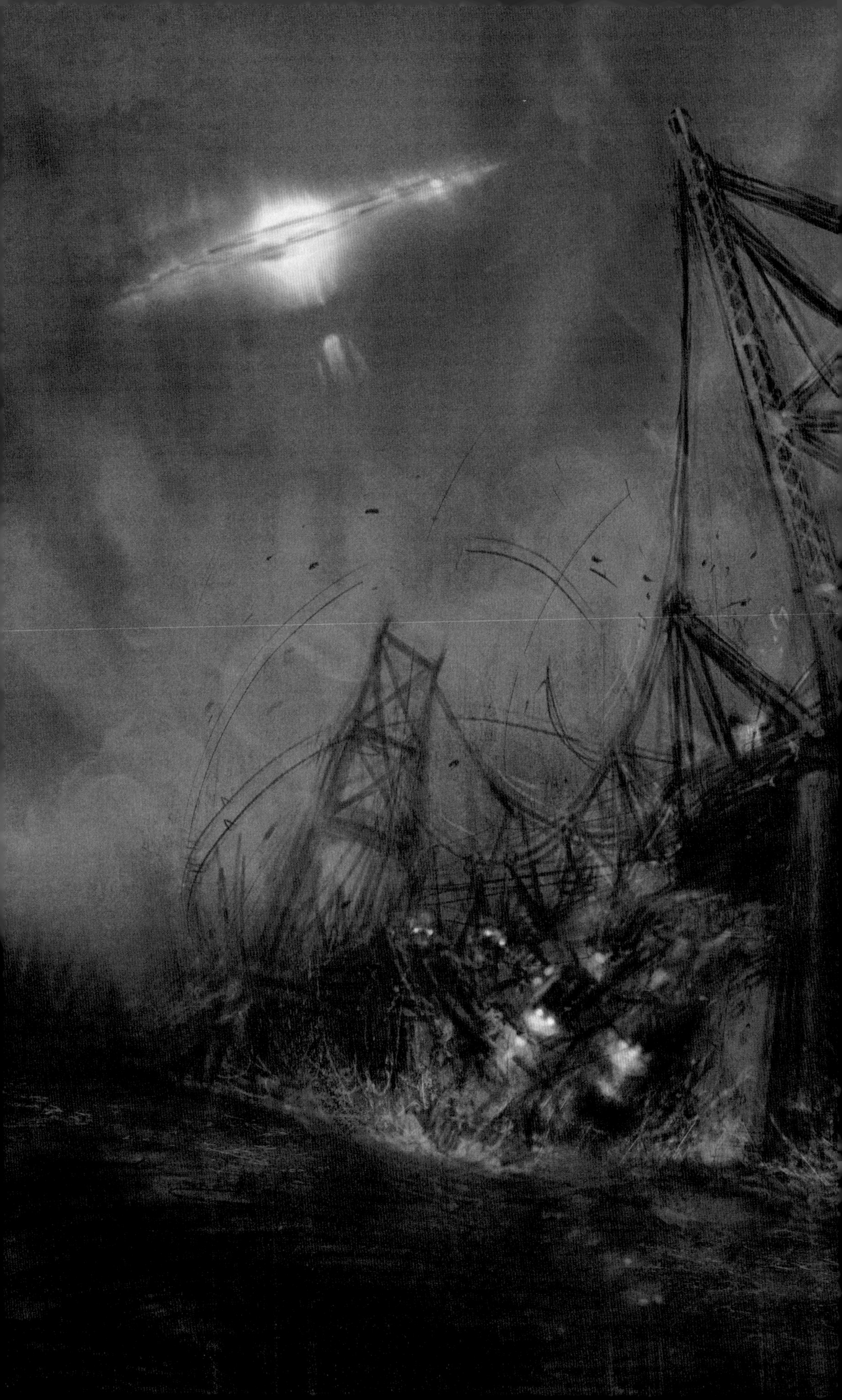

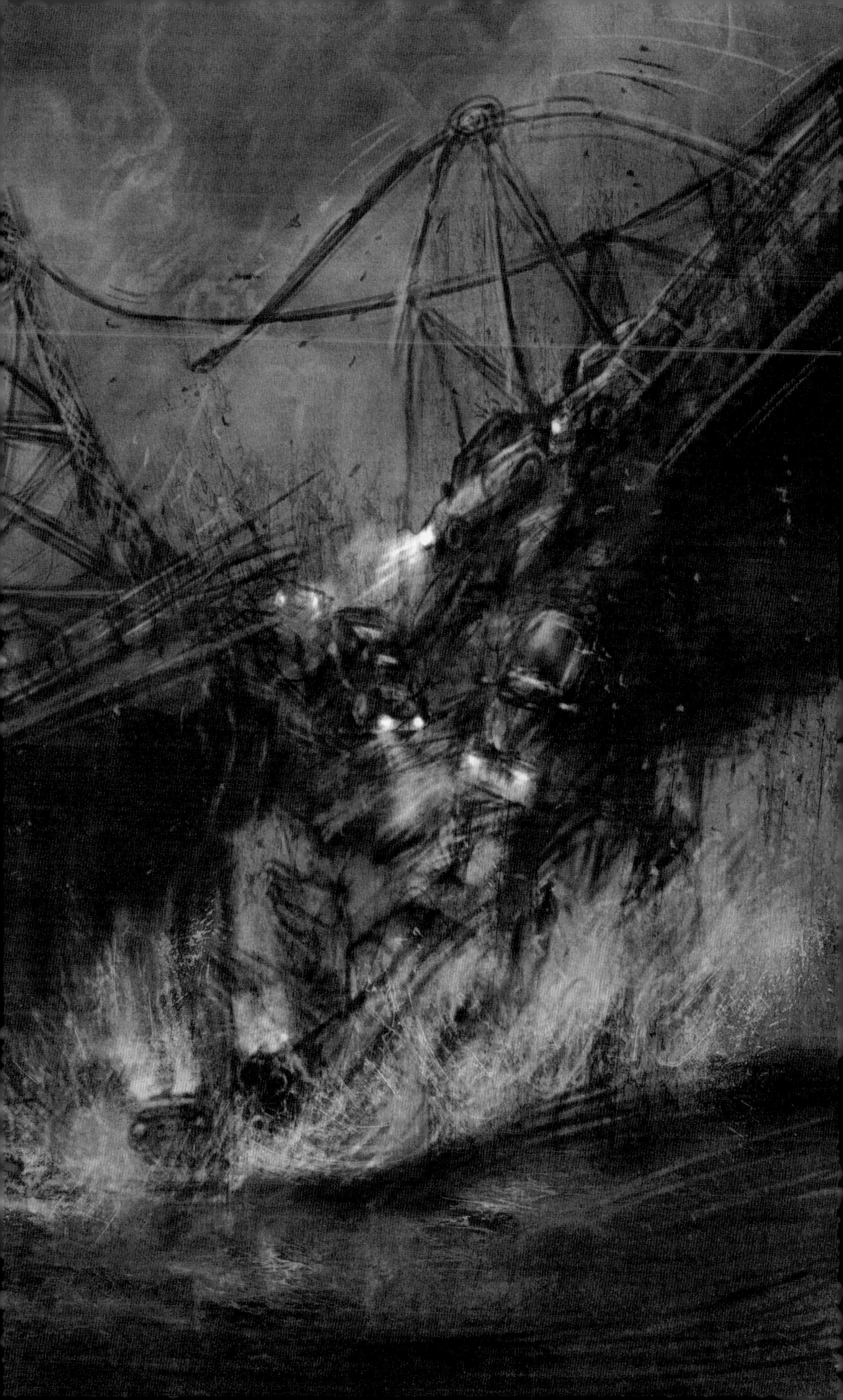

HYNES: The Silver Bridge ran across the Ohio River. It was about
5 p.m. when drivers saw something bright in the sky
overhead. And then the bridge began to collapse. There
were 32 vehicles that sank into the river that day.
40 people died.

████████: And you think the UFO did it?

HYNES: I think enough people began to believe that all of these
sightings were a message of some kind. An omen of
something terrible that might happen on the horizon.
And that belief, spread and focused, made something
happen. I told Lee that I wanted to stop. But he had
another idea. He had called in a ranger from out west.
They'd been tracking the Mothman, and he had sprung
a trap for it. He wanted to get SOMETHING.

████████: And that upset you.

HYNES: It upset me that the bridge didn't seem to bother him at
all. That all of those dead... They didn't shake his focus
at all. If anything, I think it made him feel like he was
more right. Like the bridge somehow proved that all of
this was worth it. And he wanted his trophy. At this
point I just wanted to get it all over with, so I followed
him into the woods.

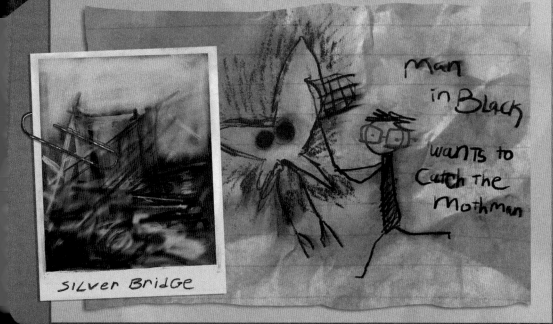

Man in Black wants to Catch The Mothman

Silver Bridge

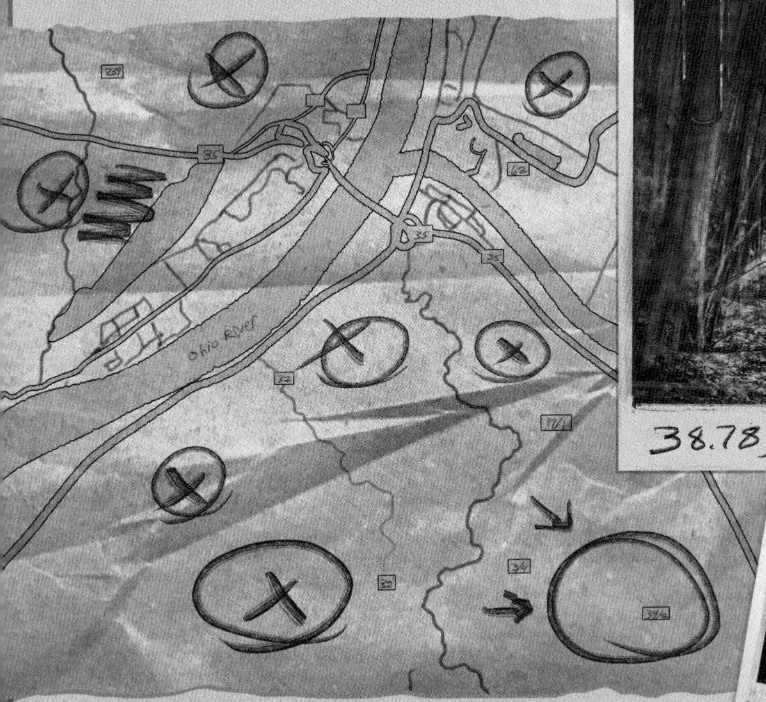
Ohio River
35
62

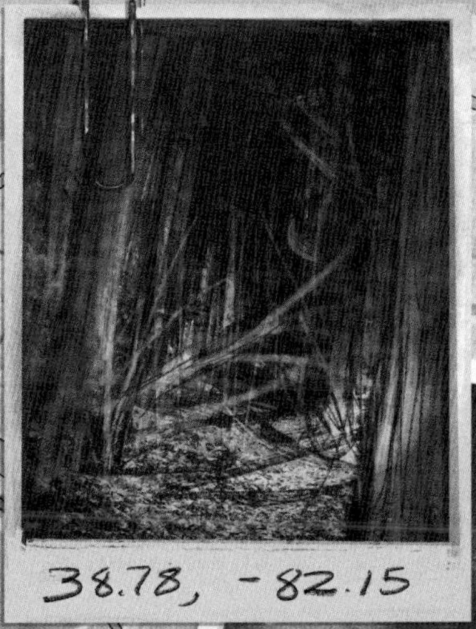
38.78, -82.15

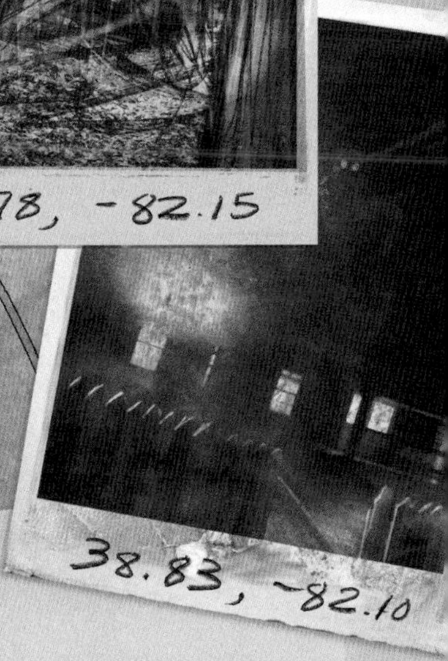
38.83, -82.10

[redacted]: And that's when you saw it?

HYNES: The smell was awful. Beyond awful. It was this strange thing in our sights and the sight and smell of it just made my head ache. I think my foil hat worked against me there.

[redacted]: In what way?

HYNES: We were staring at an impossible creature that hadn't existed longer than a year. Something totally fictional. Entirely invented. That means it's not quite real. That it's still, in some very real ways, made out of imagination. A kind of... Psychic impression on reality. But there was a part of it that was living and breathing because people believed it was real. I think that's why the elephant tranquilizers worked. People believing it was real meant that on some level it followed the rules of other living things.

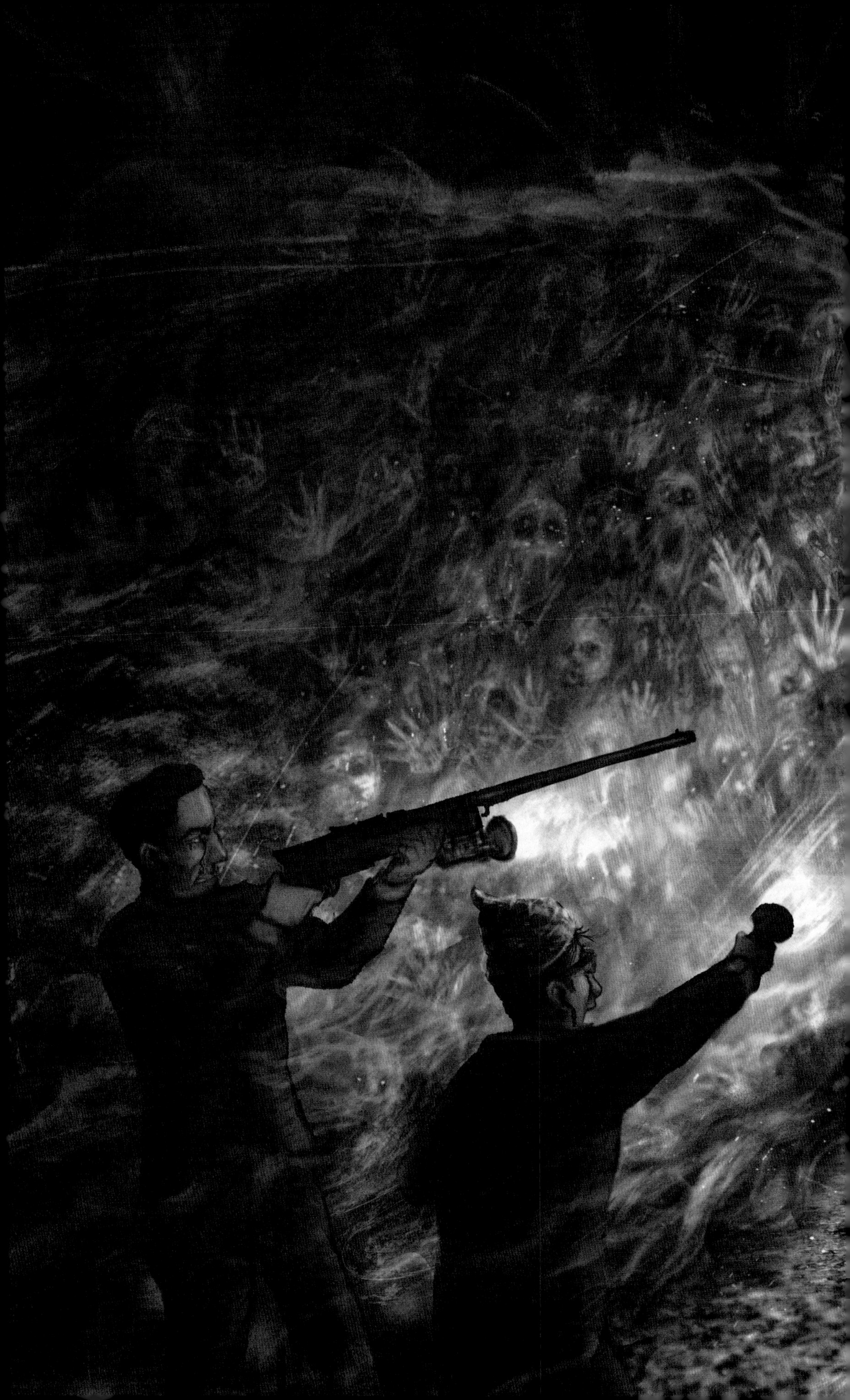

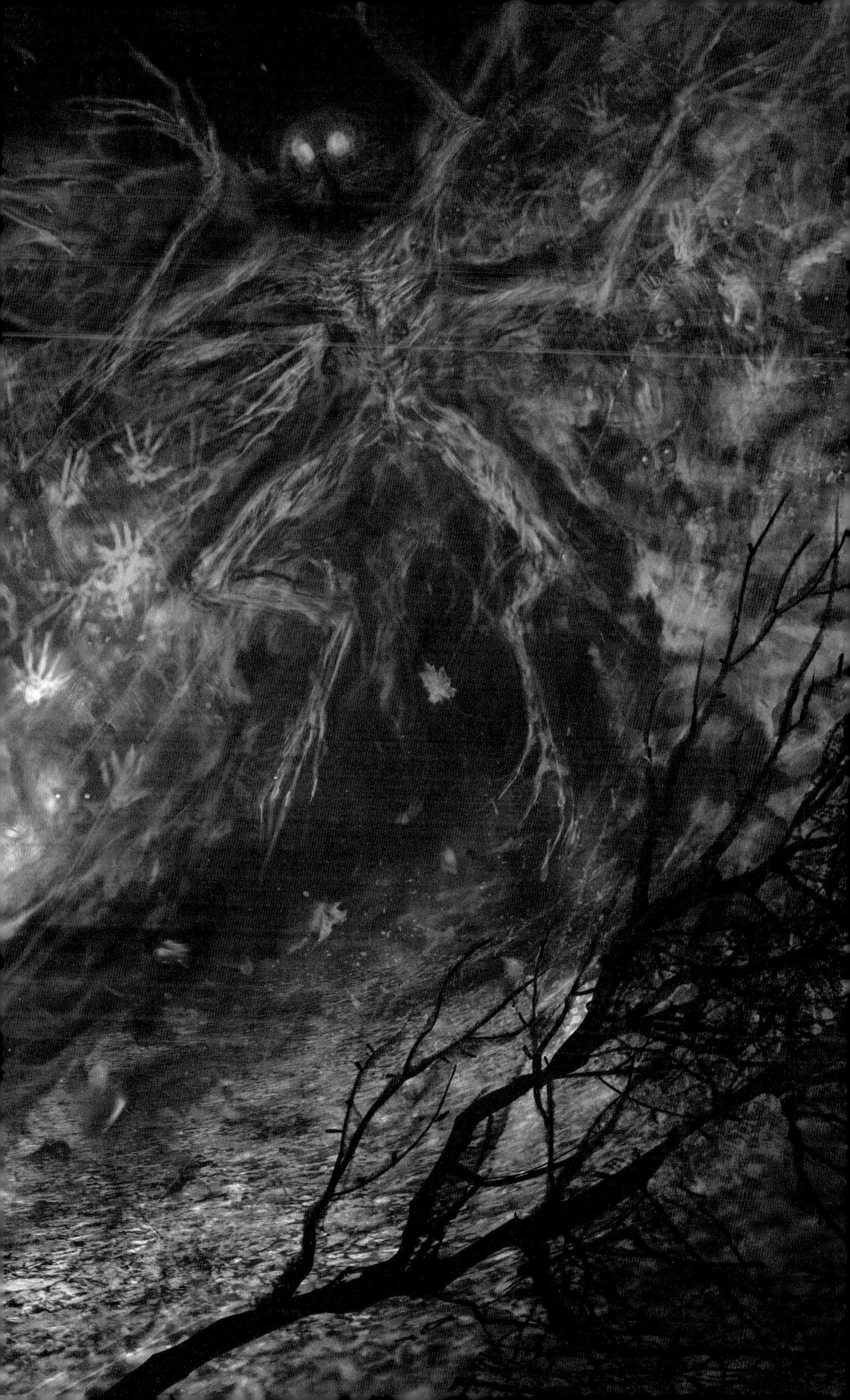

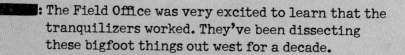

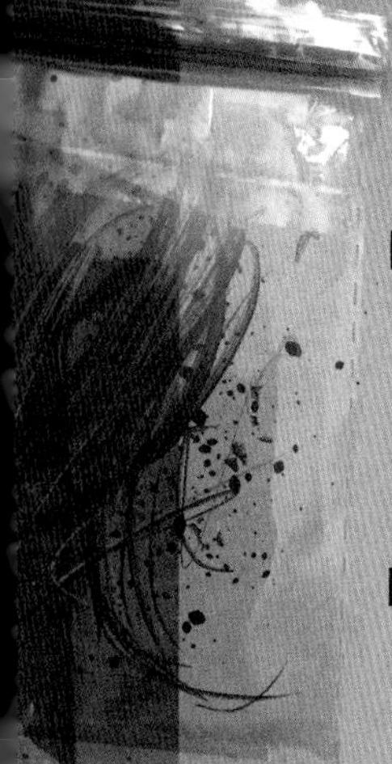

[redacted]: The Field Office was very excited to learn that the tranquilizers worked. They've been dissecting these bigfoot things out west for a decade.

HYNES: I'm glad our work wasn't a total loss.

[redacted]: Son, I know you're spooked, but we've never taken a thing like this alive. I don't know anybody that has. Particularly one of these... Fictions. The Soviets haven't done this. The Nazis tried, but they never succeeded. I don't want to encourage behavior like this behind my back, but we haven't had the stomach to look the strangest things in the face. And it's a limit to us, a limit we need to move beyond.

HYNES: Thank you, sir.

[redacted]: But what happened next. This is the part I don't quite grasp. I need you to help me with it. This is why you're afraid, isn't it?

HYNES: Yes, sir.

[redacted]: You had your own encounter with this Indrid Cold?

HYNES: It started with the ship landing in the clearing. Lee was shouting, cheerful. He thought maybe we could bag a UFO and a Mothman all at once. But then the door opened and Cold walked out. And Lee went silent, and white as a sheet.

[redacted]: He said something? Was it this... Telepathy? Could you hear what was said?

HYNES: I didn't... I just... I just bore witness to it all. The Mothman had made me feel sick, but Cold's arrival was like a knife directly in my brain. But he wasn't talking to me. He wasn't interested in me. He wanted LEE.

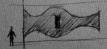

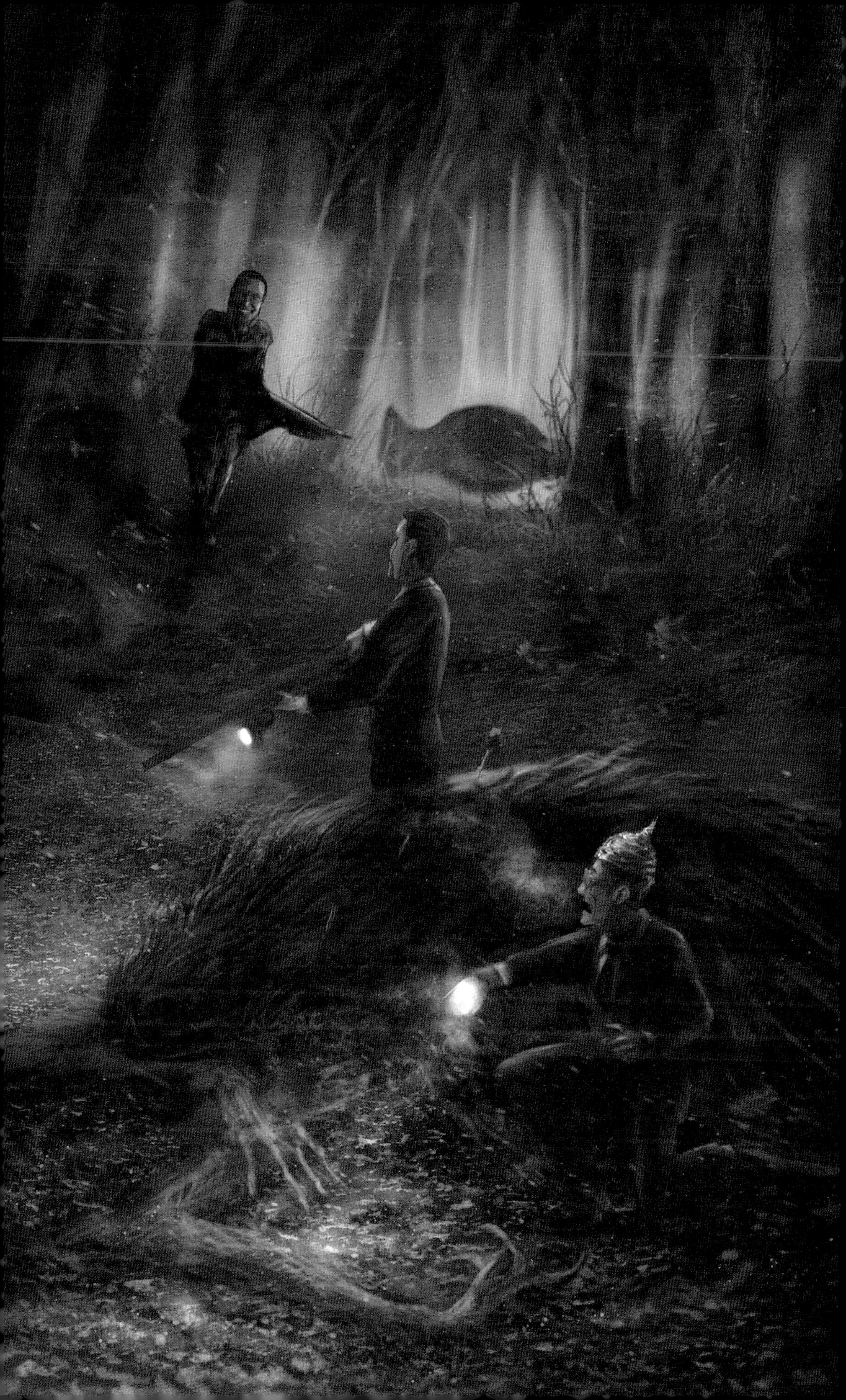

HYNES: It only lasted a few minutes, but Lee... He looked terrified. He looked like something had shaken him to his core. I tried to get him to talk about it, but he refused. And that just scared me more.

[redacted]: What do you think that this Cold fellow... This strange alien man... What would he have to say to Lee?

HYNES: That's the question, isn't it? I mean, part of it could just be intent. If this Cold person, if he understands in some metaphysical way how the world really works, then maybe he could see that it was Lee's idea that had set all this in motion, ending with us standing over the unconscious Mothman. Maybe he's just an observer, and he told Lee what he observed.

[redacted]: But that's not what scares you.

HYNES: No, sir. It's not.

[redacted]: Explain yourself.

HYNES: Before I do... I just want it on the record that I don't want to do any more field work. I'd rather stay in the archives. I think I'm more comfortable with the theory of it all instead of the practice. I want to understand what our impact on the world is.

[redacted]: You know, I tried to get Lee to grapple with that same question. But you seem like you might actually be up to the task. I'll grant your wish, if you tell me why you're scared.

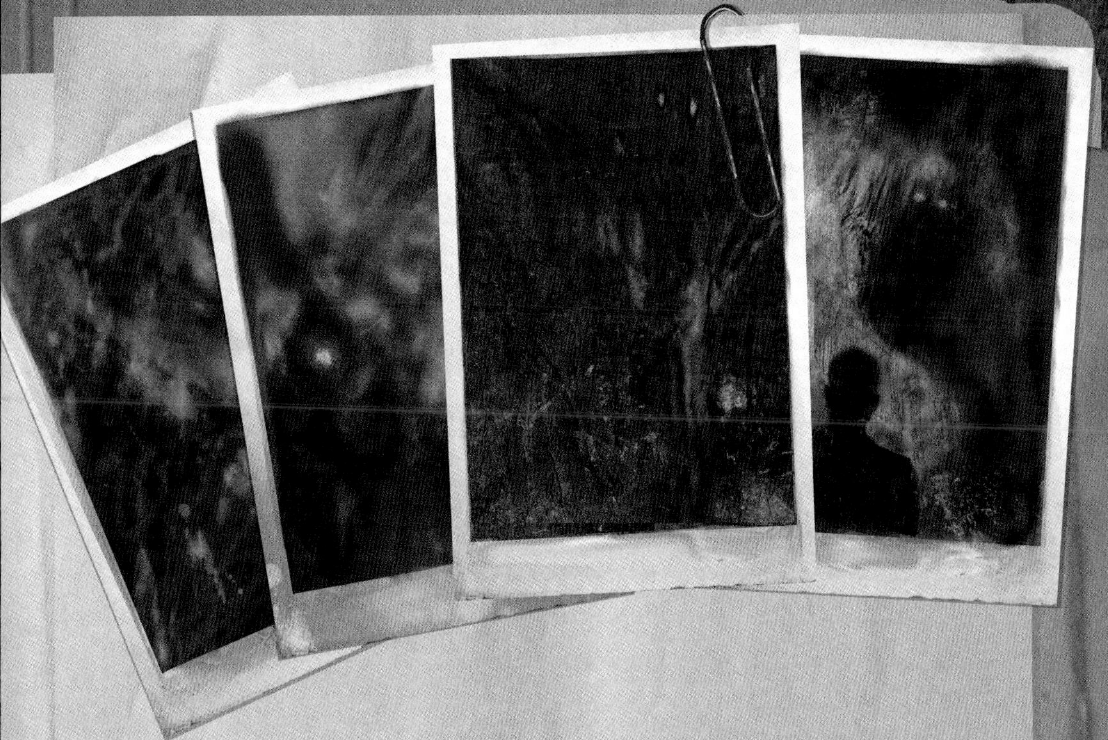

HYNES: I think... I think there's something WRONG with Lee. There was a way he was looking at the Mothman all the way back to Washington. And when we set it up in the basement, he sat alone with it for hours. And I had this thought. This dark thought.

[redacted]: What was it?

HYNES: I was thinking that I was looking at two of the strangest monsters of the decade. Two American Monsters, just alike each other. Things made of secrets that the world just speculates on, to try and make sense of their little lives. The thought was that the two of them were more the same than different.

[redacted]: And that's the last time you saw Lee Harvey Oswald? Before his disappearance?

HYNES: Yes sir. I haven't seen him since.

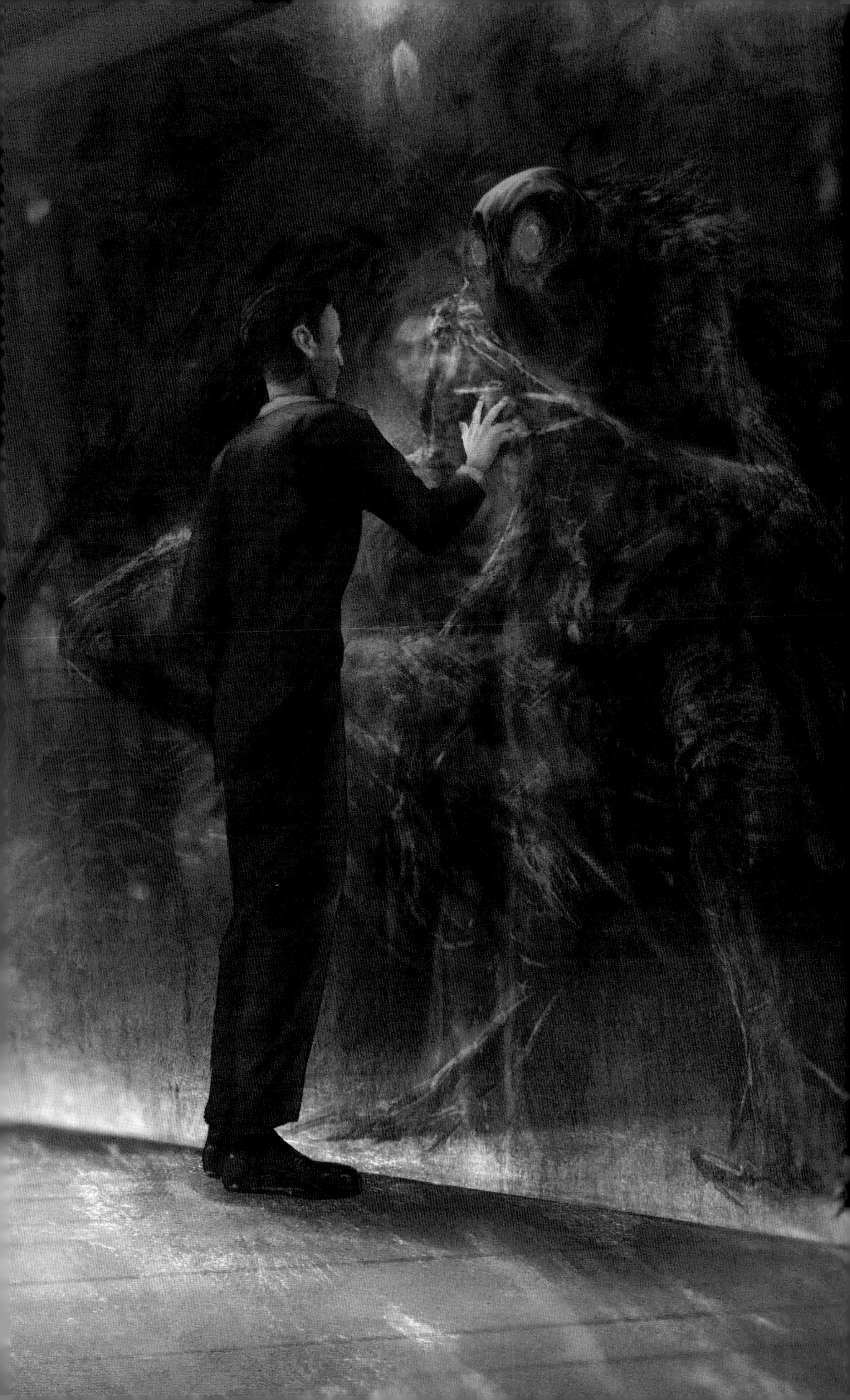

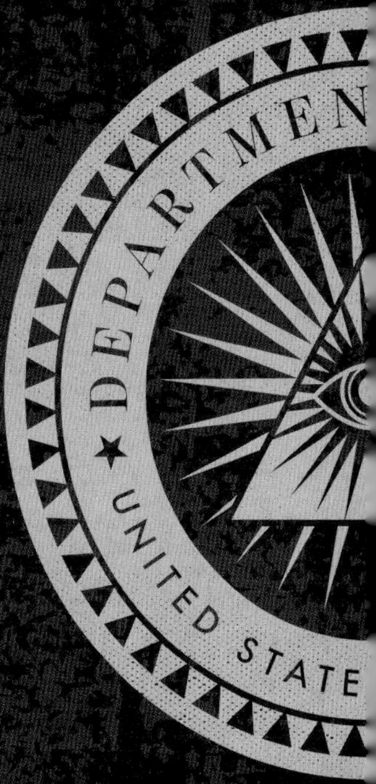
DEPARTMEN
UNITED STATE

DEVIATION 5

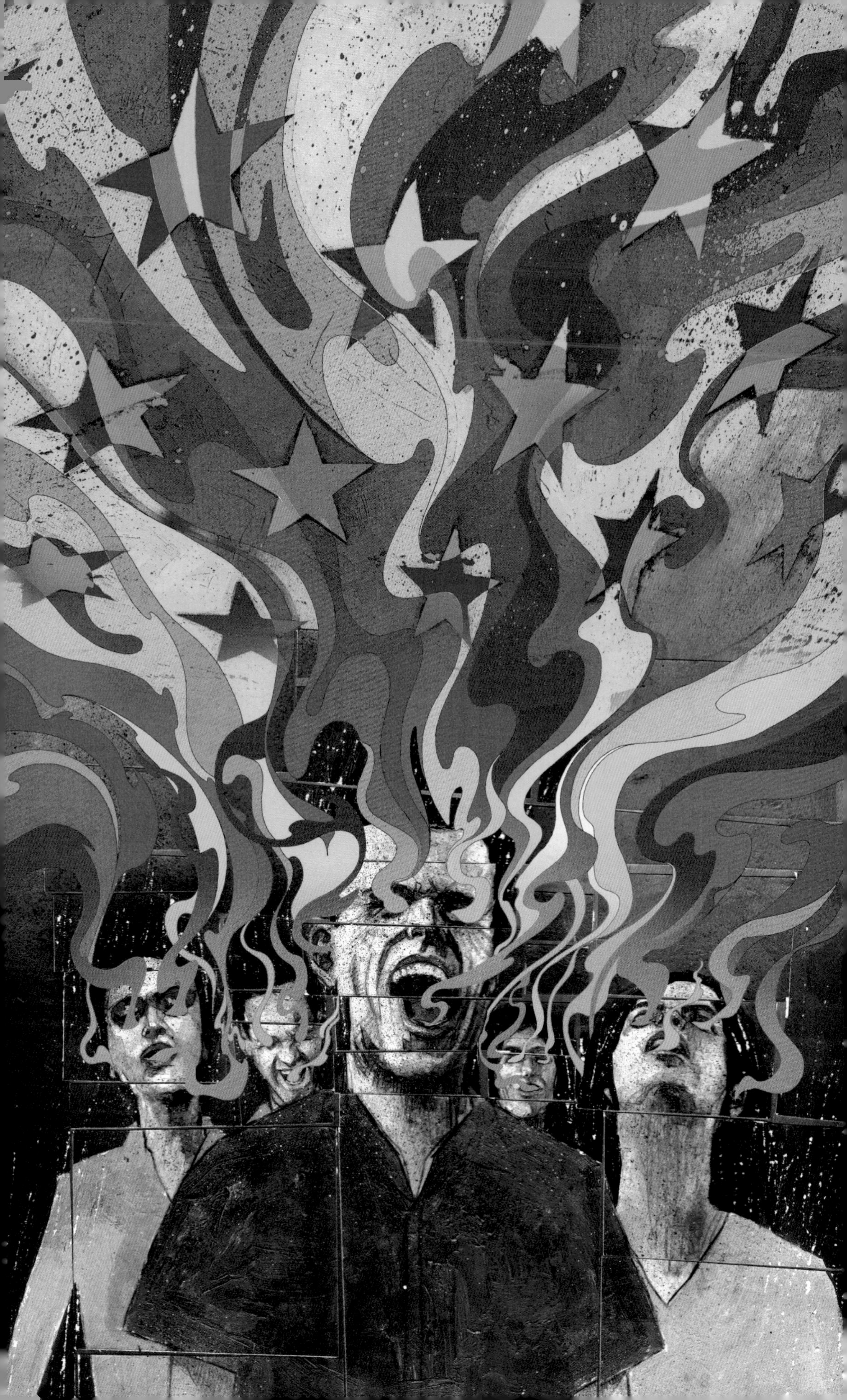

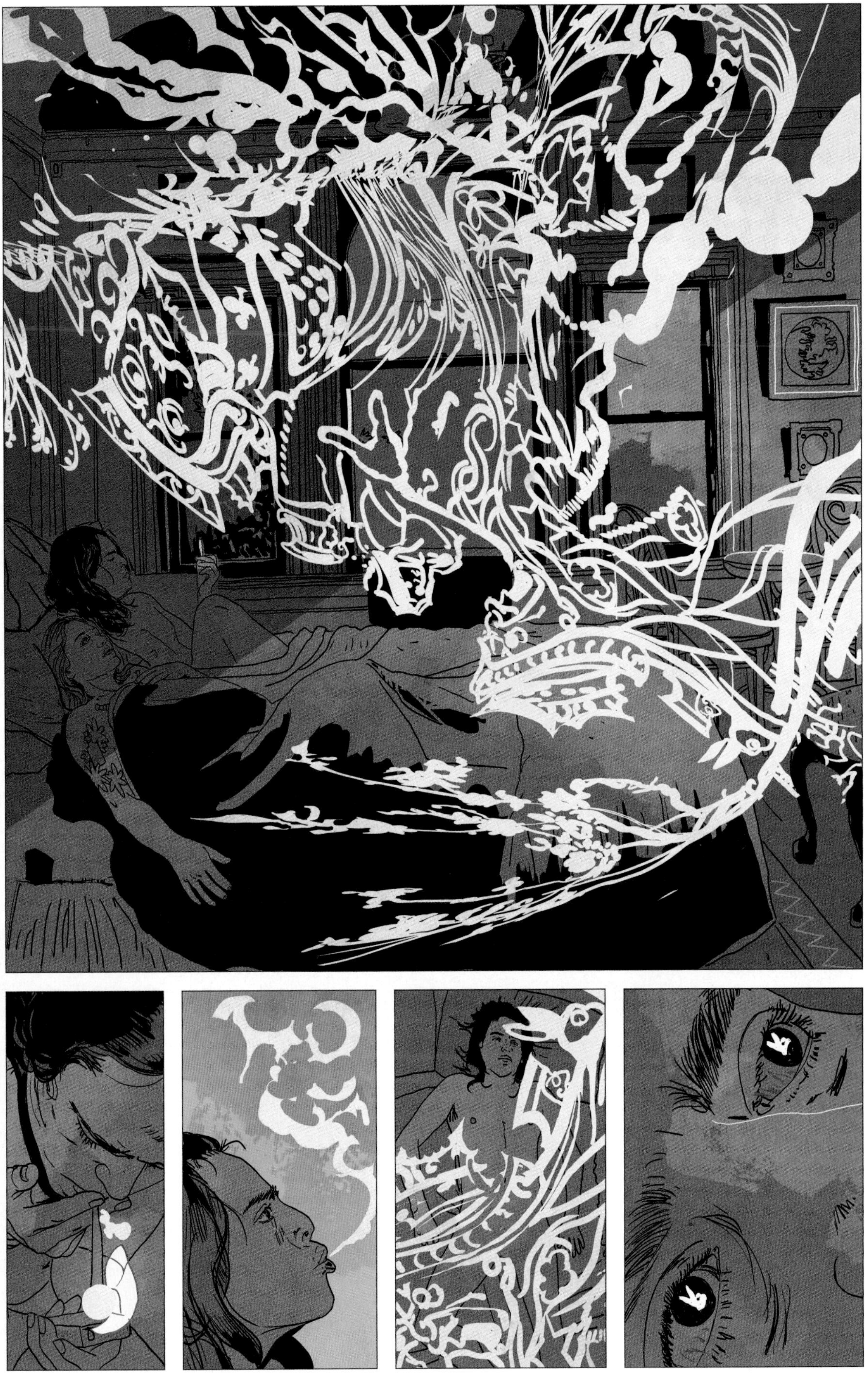

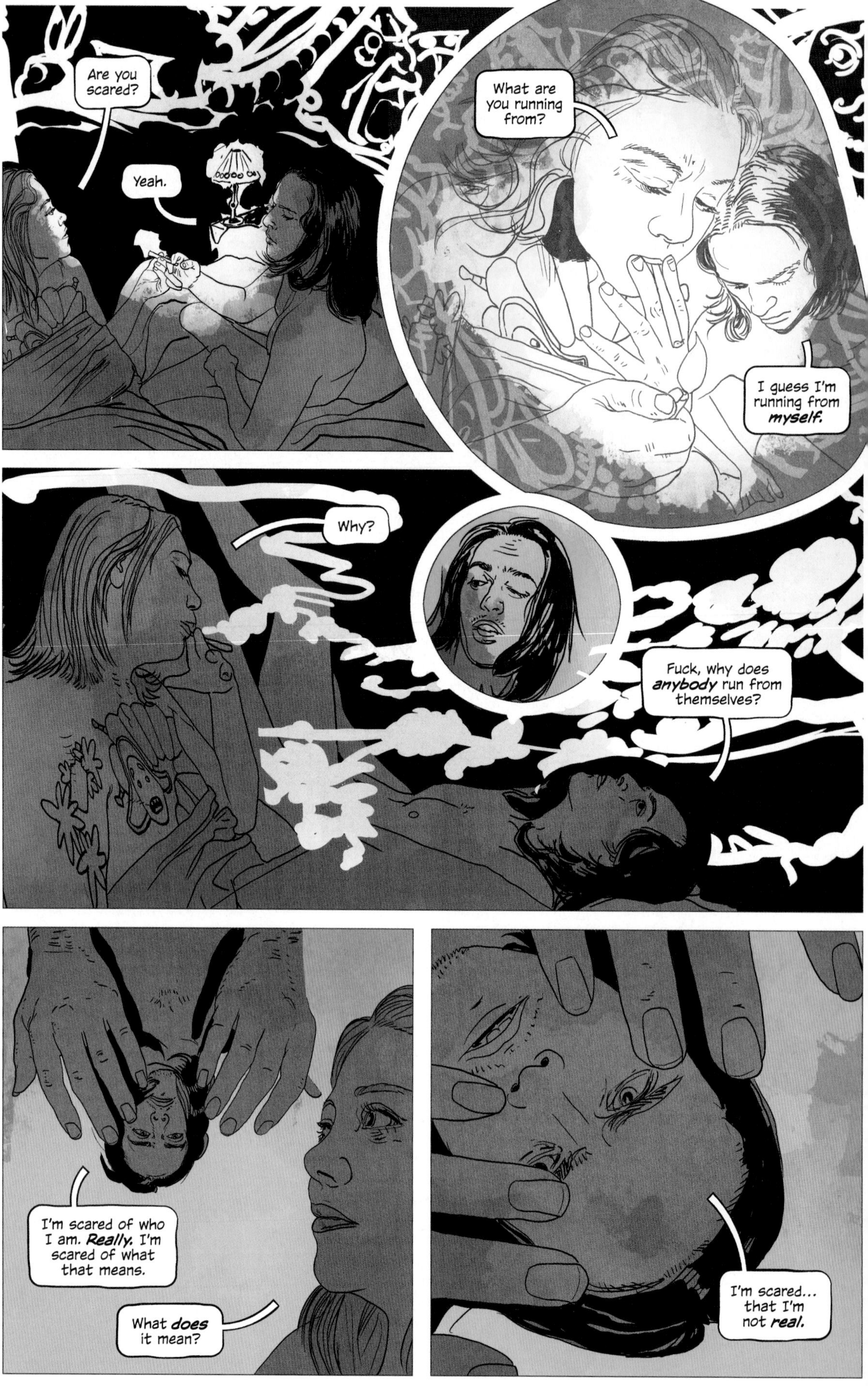
Are you scared?
Yeah.
What are you running from?
I guess I'm running from *myself.*
Why?
Fuck, why does *anybody* run from themselves?
I'm scared of who I am. *Really.* I'm scared of what that means.
What *does* it mean?
I'm scared... that I'm not *real.*

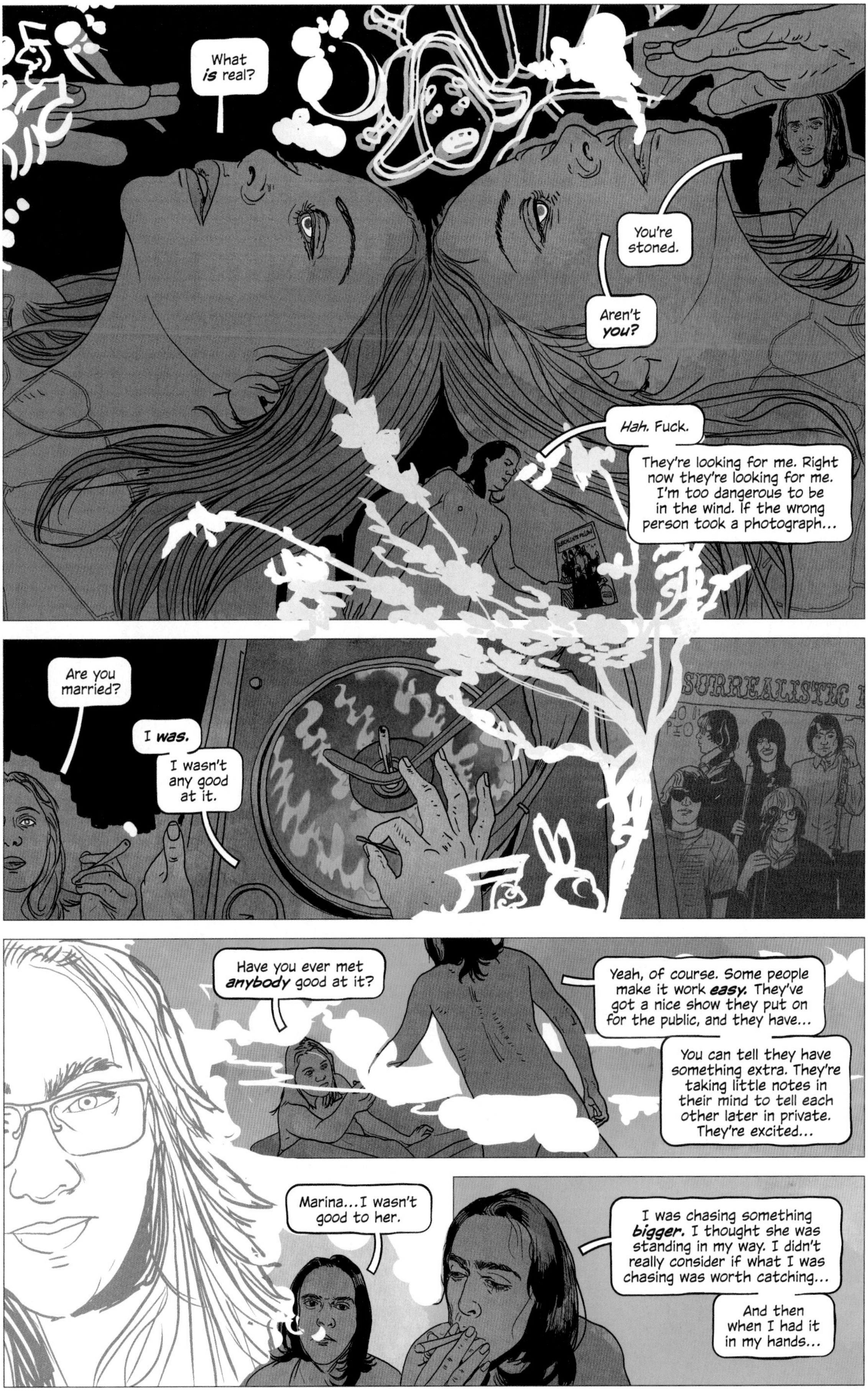

What *is* real?
You're stoned.
Aren't *you?*
Hah. Fuck.
They're looking for me. Right now they're looking for me. I'm too dangerous to be in the wind. If the wrong person took a photograph...
Are you married?
I *was.*
I wasn't any good at it.
SURREALISTIC
Have you ever met *anybody* good at it?
Yeah, of course. Some people make it work *easy.* They've got a nice show they put on for the public, and they have...
You can tell they have something extra. They're taking little notes in their mind to tell each other later in private. They're excited...
Marina...I wasn't good to her.
I was chasing something *bigger.* I thought she was standing in my way. I didn't really consider if what I was chasing was worth catching...
And then when I had it in my hands...

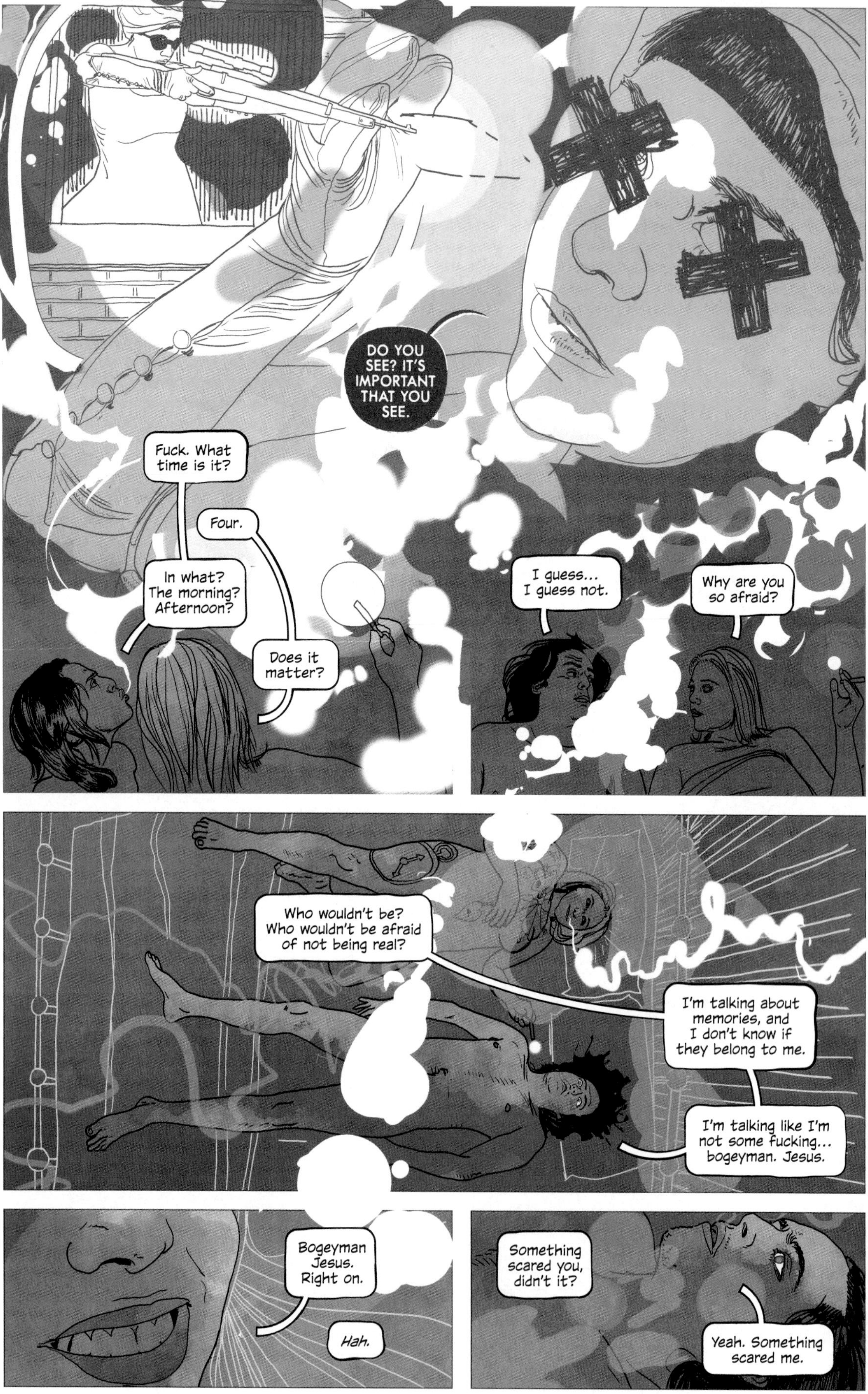
DO YOU SEE? IT'S IMPORTANT THAT YOU SEE.
Fuck. What time is it?
Four.
In what? The morning? Afternoon?
Does it matter?
I guess... I guess not.
Why are you so afraid?
Who wouldn't be? Who wouldn't be afraid of not being real?
I'm talking about memories, and I don't know if they belong to me.
I'm talking like I'm not some fucking... bogeyman. Jesus.
Bogeyman Jesus. Right on.
Hah.
Something scared you, didn't it?
Yeah. Something scared me.

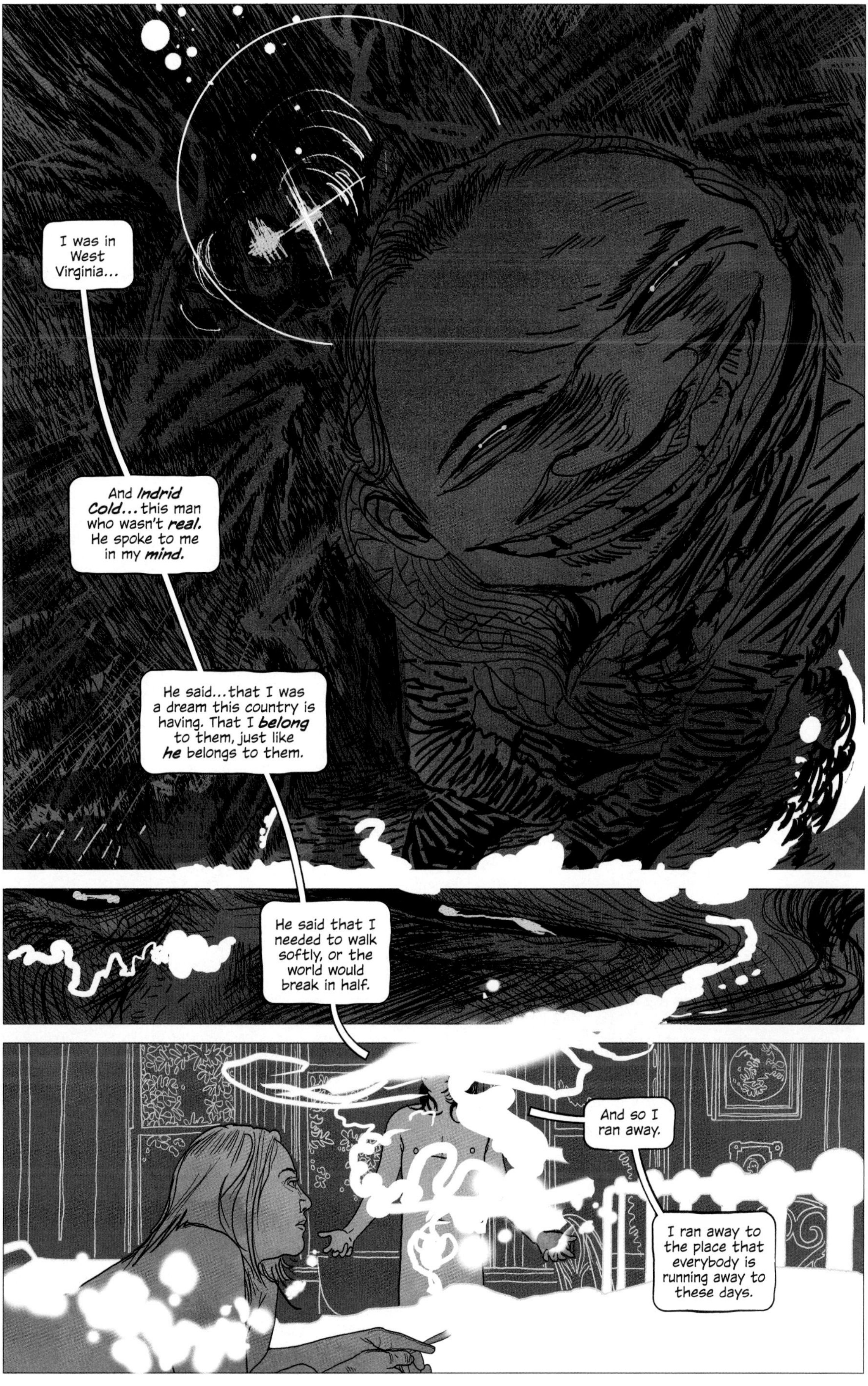
I was in West Virginia...
And *Indrid Cold...* this man who wasn't ***real.*** He spoke to me in my ***mind.***
He said...that I was a dream this country is having. That I ***belong*** to them, just like ***he*** belongs to them.
He said that I needed to walk softly, or the world would break in half.
And so I ran away.
I ran away to the place that everybody is running away to these days.

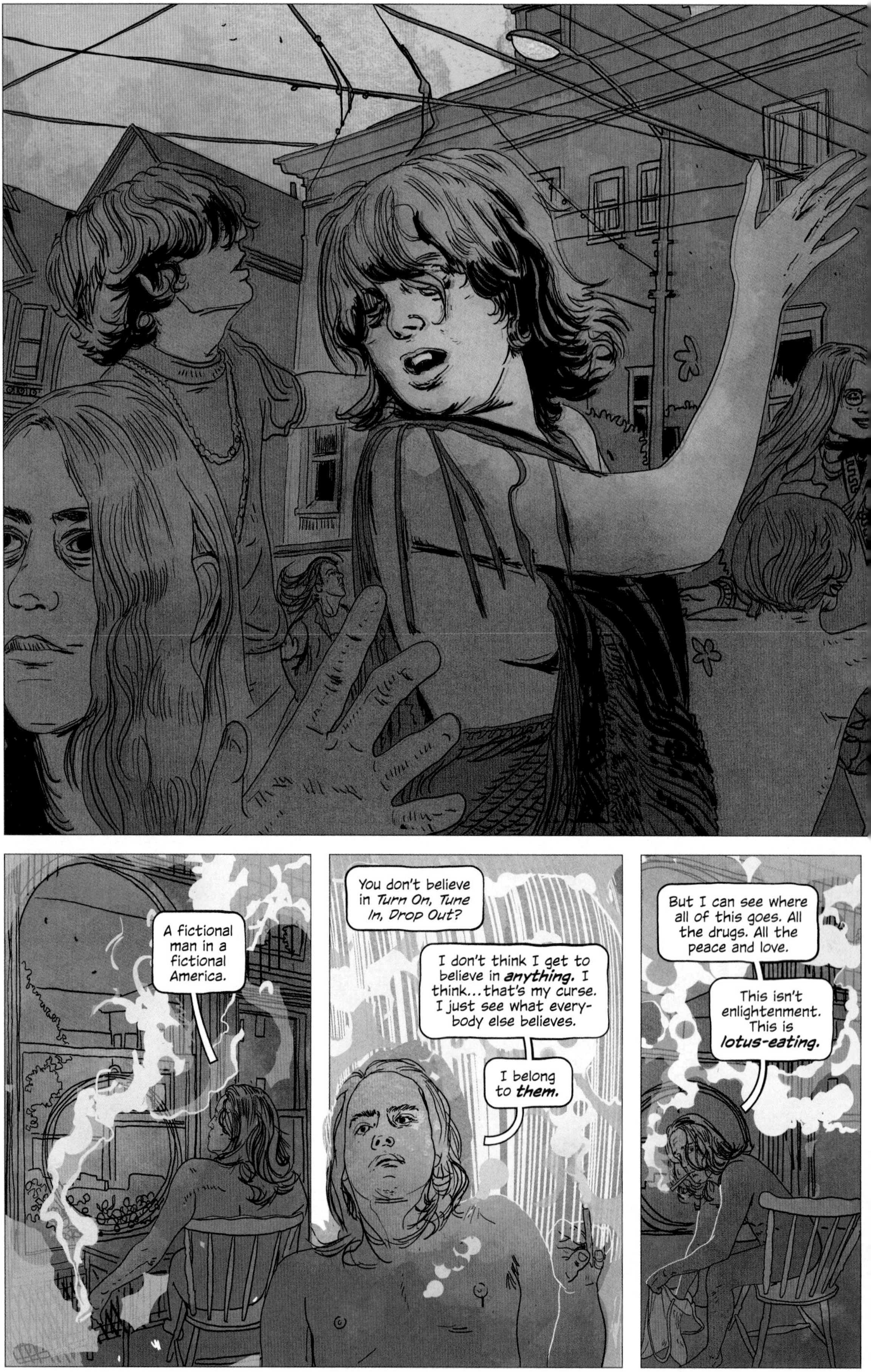
A fictional man in a fictional America.
You don't believe in *Turn On, Tune In, Drop Out?*
I don't think I get to believe in ***anything.*** I think...that's my curse. I just see what everybody else believes.
I belong to ***them.***
But I can see where all of this goes. All the drugs. All the peace and love.
This isn't enlightenment. This is ***lotus-eating.***

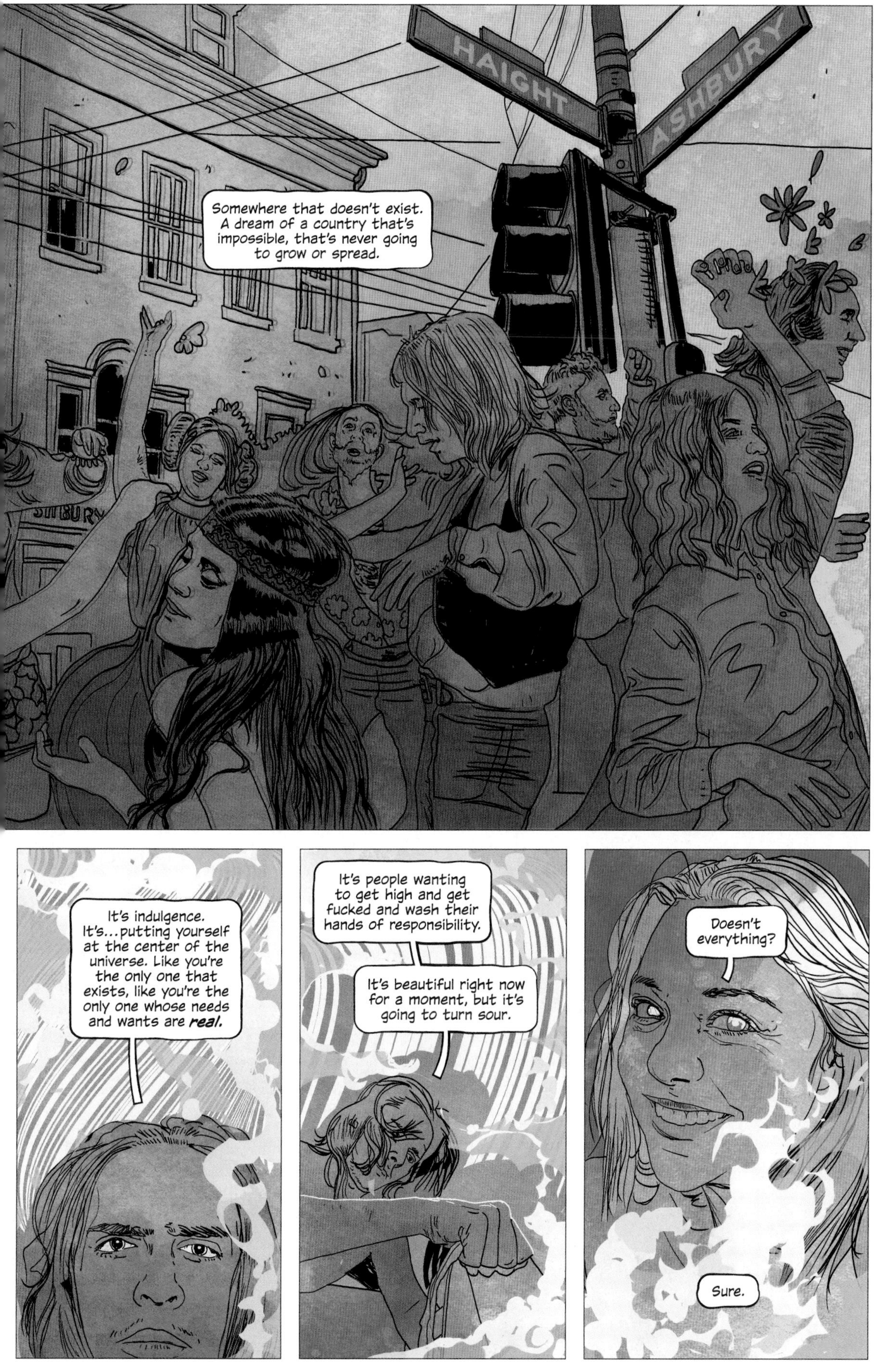
HAIGHT
ASHBURY
Somewhere that doesn't exist. A dream of a country that's impossible, that's never going to grow or spread.
It's indulgence. It's...putting yourself at the center of the universe. Like you're the only one that exists, like you're the only one whose needs and wants are *real.*
It's people wanting to get high and get fucked and wash their hands of responsibility.
It's beautiful right now for a moment, but it's going to turn sour.
Doesn't everything?
Sure.

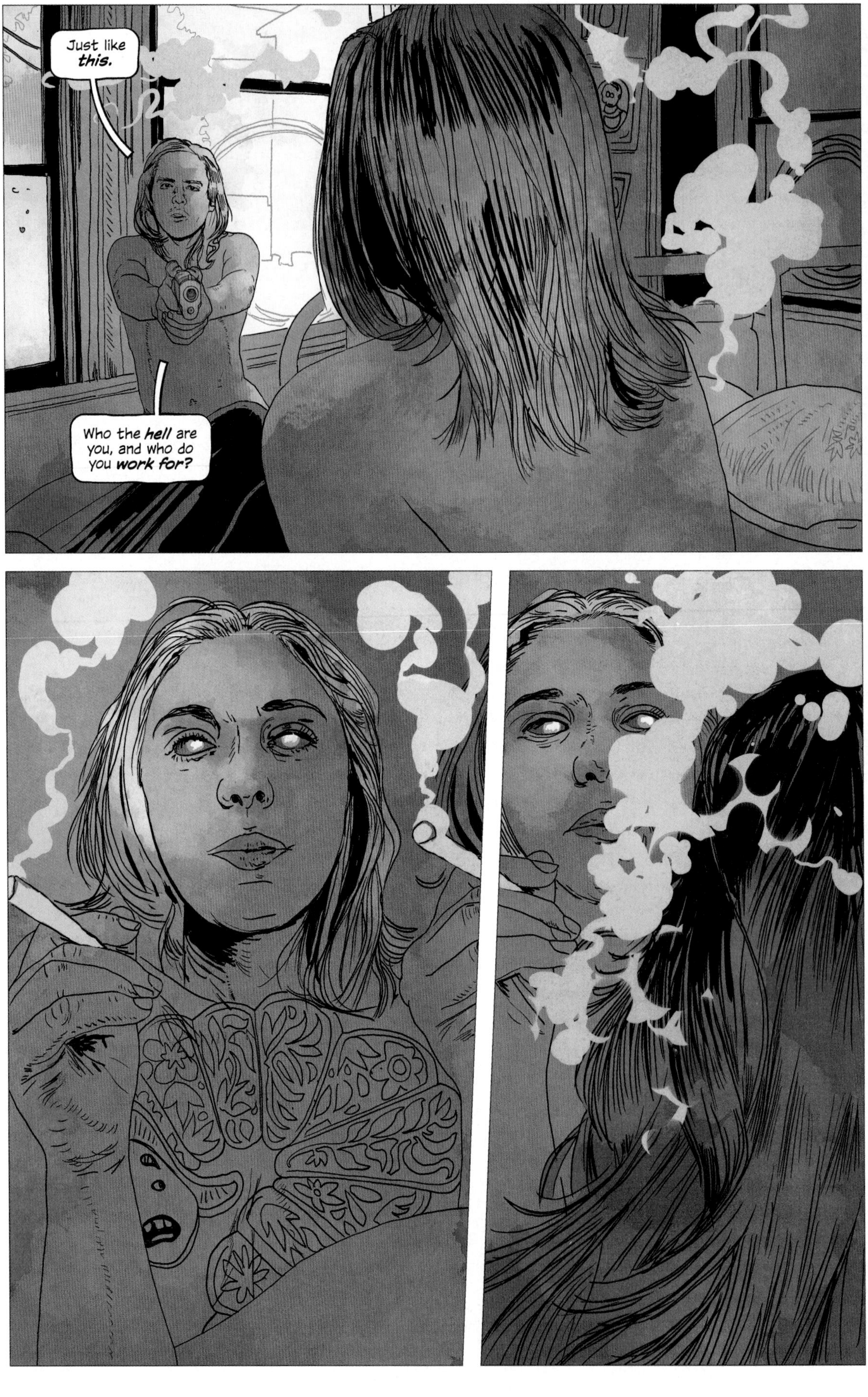
Just like this.
Who the hell are you, and who do you work for?

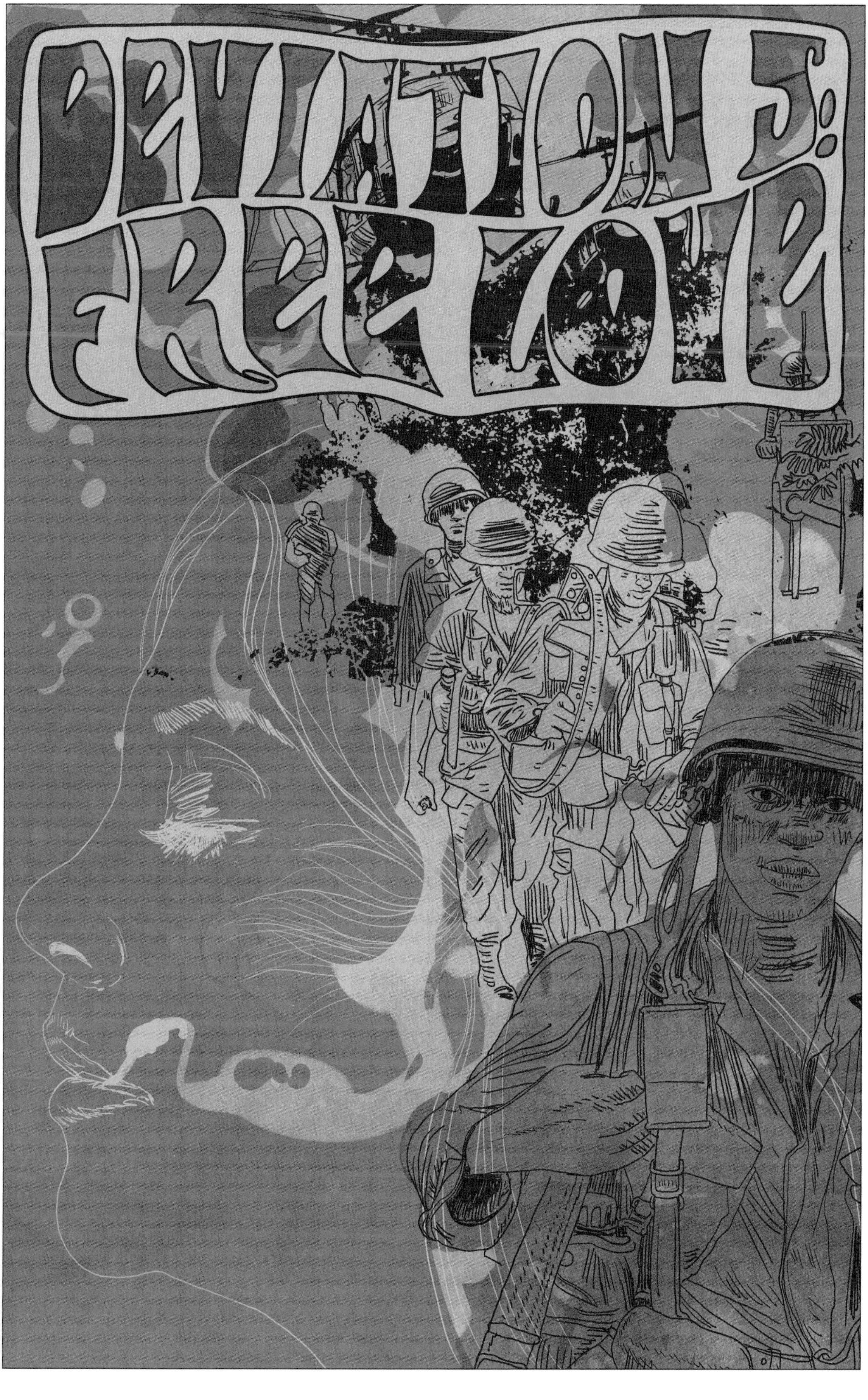
DEVIATION 5:
FREE LOVE

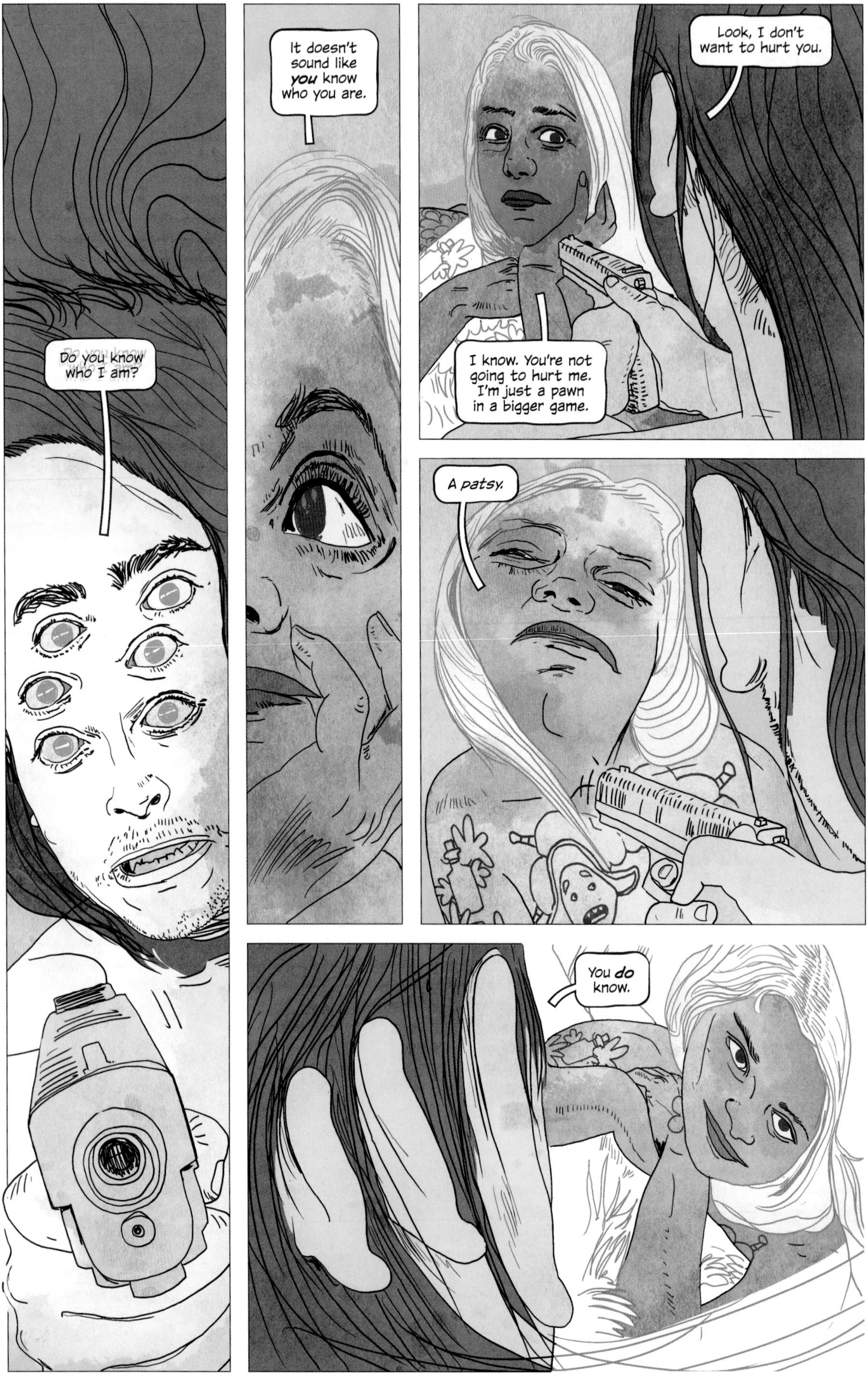
Do you know who I am?
It doesn't sound like *you* know who you are.
Look, I don't want to hurt you.
I know. You're not going to hurt me. I'm just a pawn in a bigger game.
A *patsy.*
You *do* know.

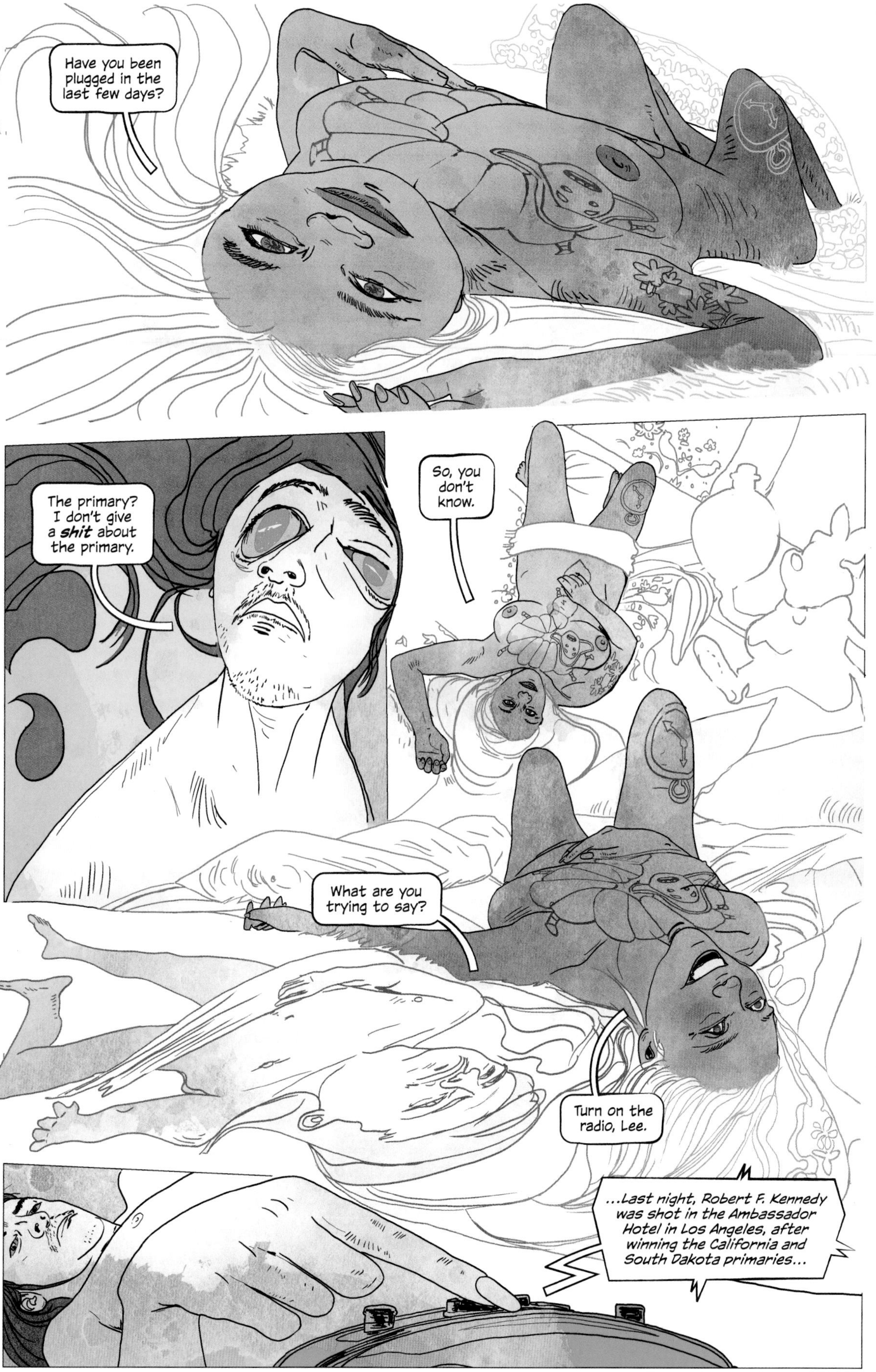

Have you been plugged in the last few days?
The primary? I don't give a ***shit*** about the primary.
So, you don't know.
What are you trying to say?
Turn on the radio, Lee.
...Last night, Robert F. Kennedy was shot in the Ambassador Hotel in Los Angeles, after winning the California and South Dakota primaries...

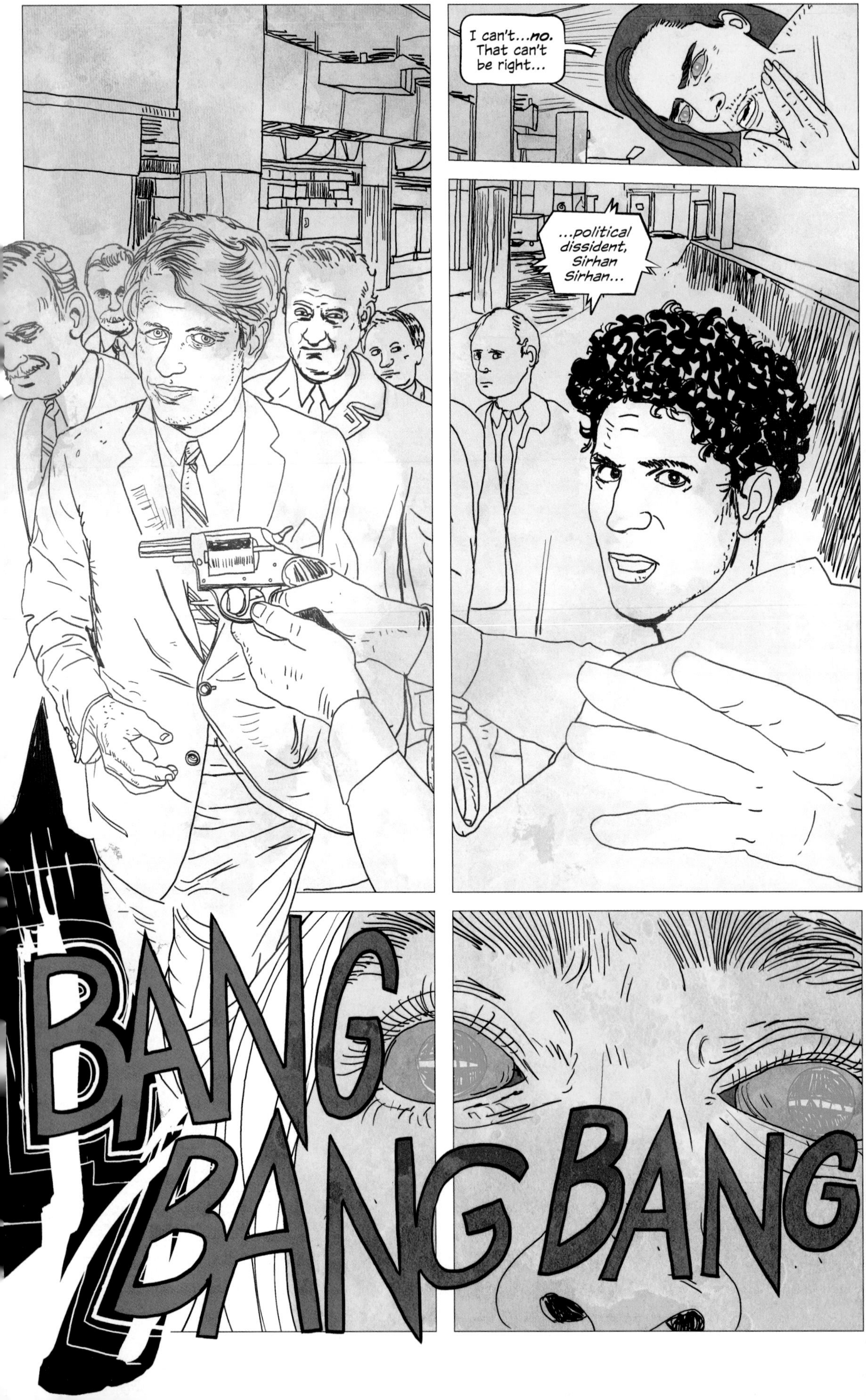

I can't...**no.** That can't be right...
...political dissident, Sirhan Sirhan...
BANG
BANG
BANG
BANG

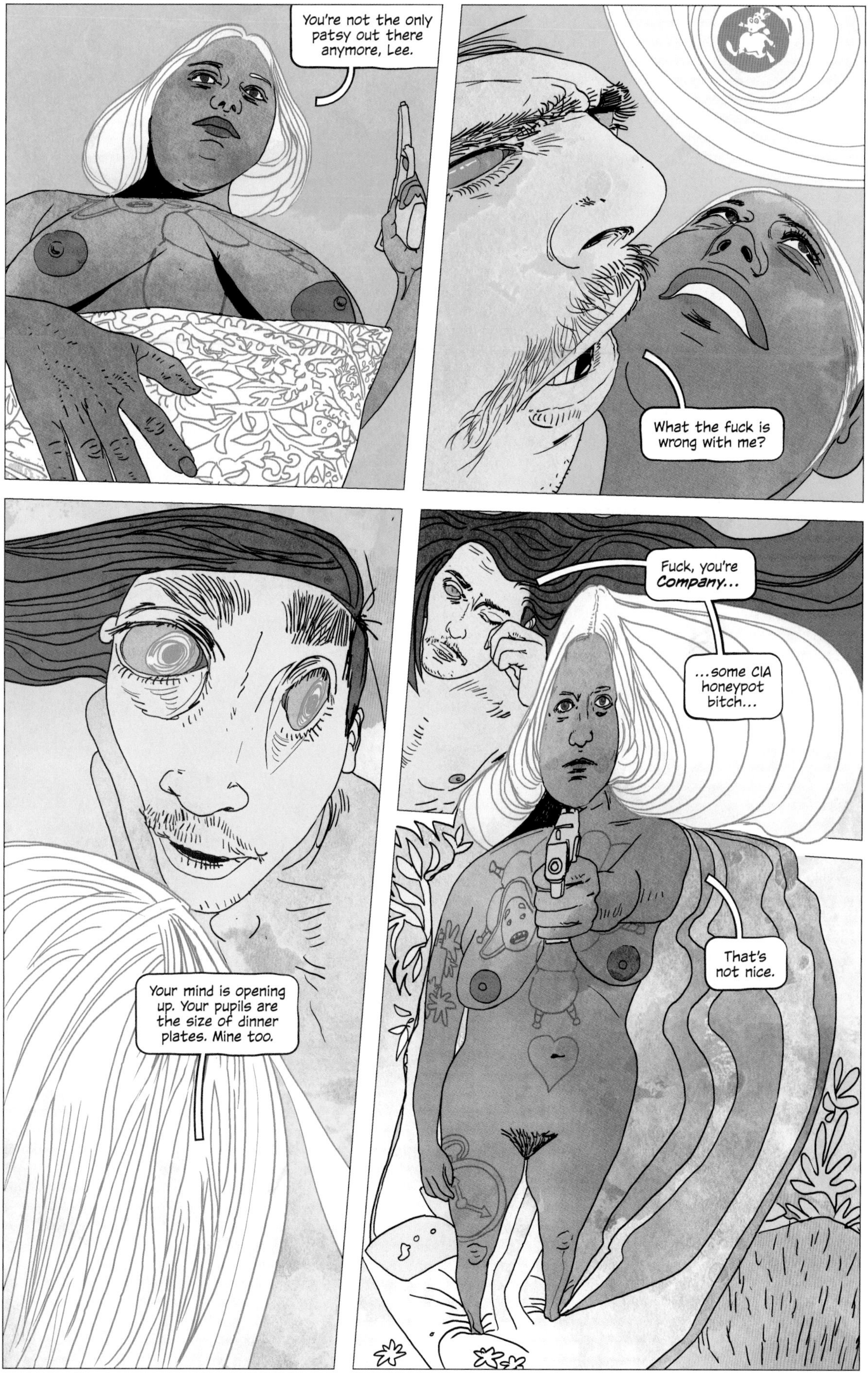
You're not the only patsy out there anymore, Lee.
What the fuck is wrong with me?
Your mind is opening up. Your pupils are the size of dinner plates. Mine too.
Fuck, you're *Company*...
...some CIA honeypot bitch...
That's not nice.

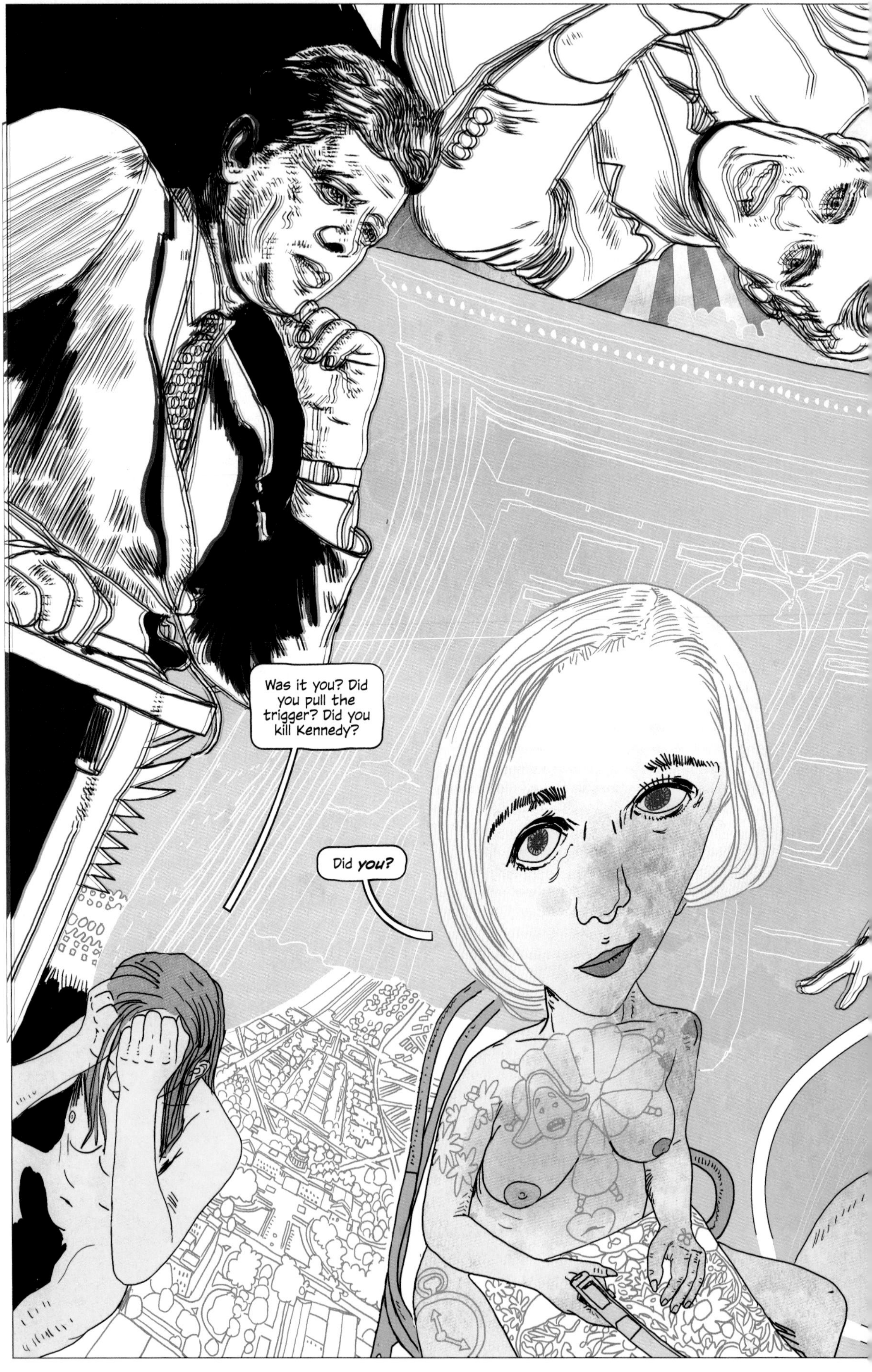
Was it you? Did you pull the trigger? Did you kill Kennedy?
Did *you?*

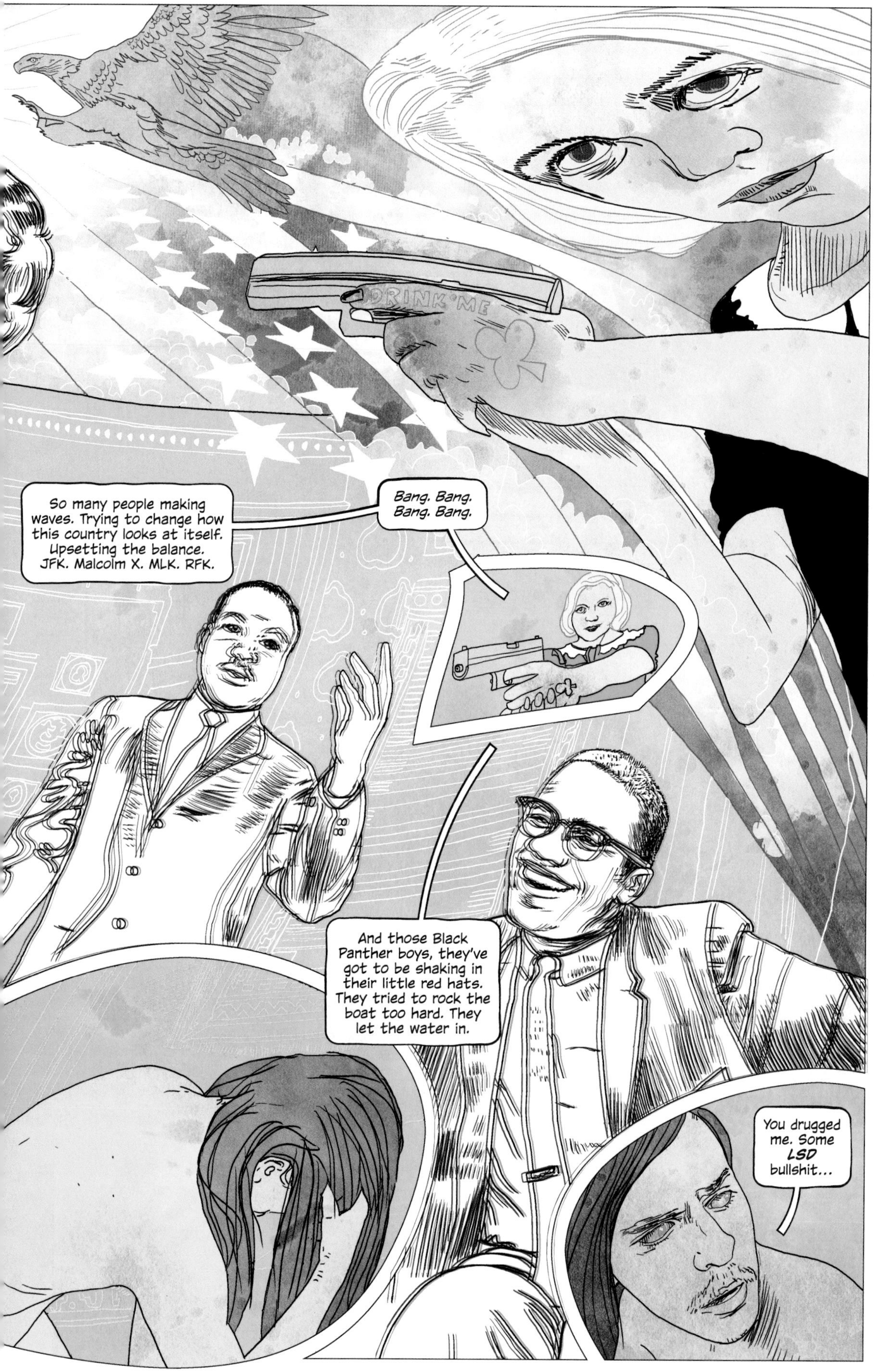
DRINK ME
So many people making waves. Trying to change how this country looks at itself. Upsetting the balance. JFK. Malcolm X. MLK. RFK.
Bang. Bang. Bang. Bang.
And those Black Panther boys, they've got to be shaking in their little red hats. They tried to rock the boat too hard. They let the water in.
You drugged me. Some LSD bullshit...

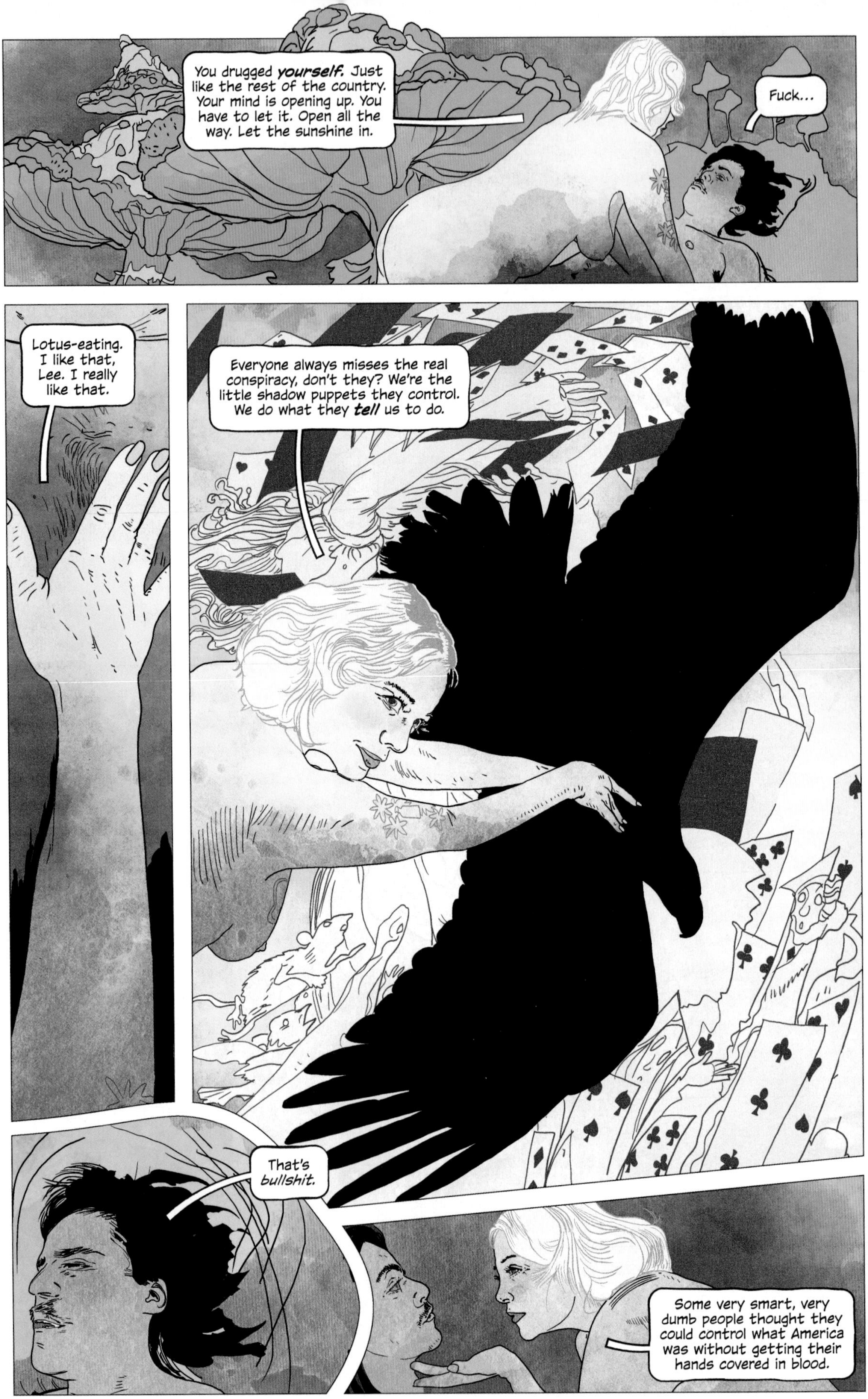
You drugged *yourself.* Just like the rest of the country. Your mind is opening up. You have to let it. Open all the way. Let the sunshine in.
Fuck...
Lotus-eating. I like that, Lee. I really like that.
Everyone always misses the real conspiracy, don't they? We're the little shadow puppets they control. We do what they *tell* us to do.
That's *bullshit.*
Some very smart, very dumb people thought they could control what America was without getting their hands covered in blood.

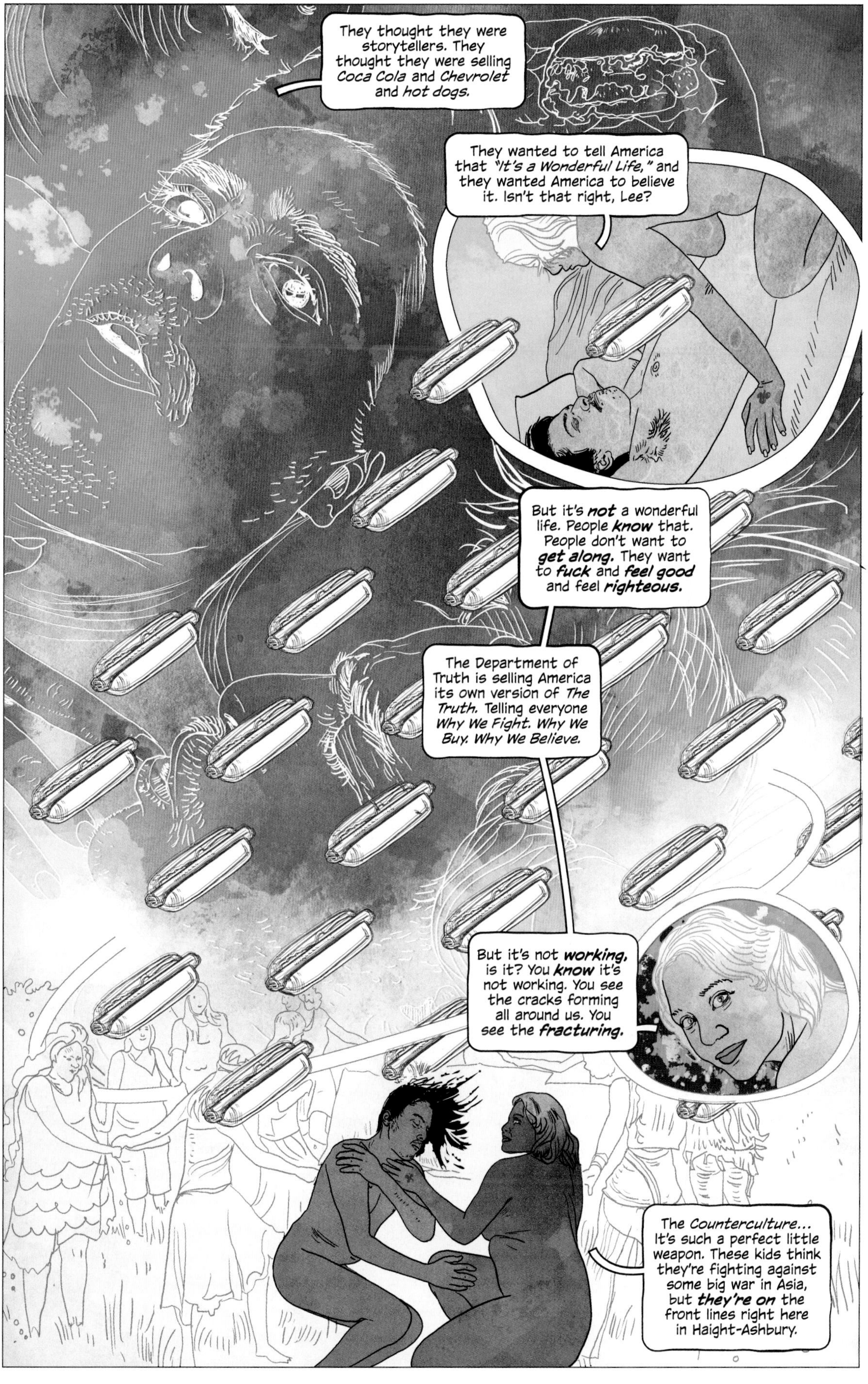
They thought they were storytellers. They thought they were selling *Coca Cola* and *Chevrolet* and *hot dogs.*
They wanted to tell America that *"It's a Wonderful Life,"* and they wanted America to believe it. Isn't that right, Lee?
But it's ***not*** a wonderful life. People ***know*** that. People don't want to ***get along.*** They want to ***fuck*** and ***feel good*** and feel ***righteous.***
The Department of Truth is selling America its own version of *The Truth.* Telling everyone *Why We Fight. Why We Buy. Why We Believe.*
But it's not ***working,*** is it? You ***know*** it's not working. You see the cracks forming all around us. You see the ***fracturing.***
The *Counterculture...* It's such a perfect little weapon. These kids think they're fighting against some big war in Asia, but ***they're on*** the front lines right here in Haight-Ashbury.

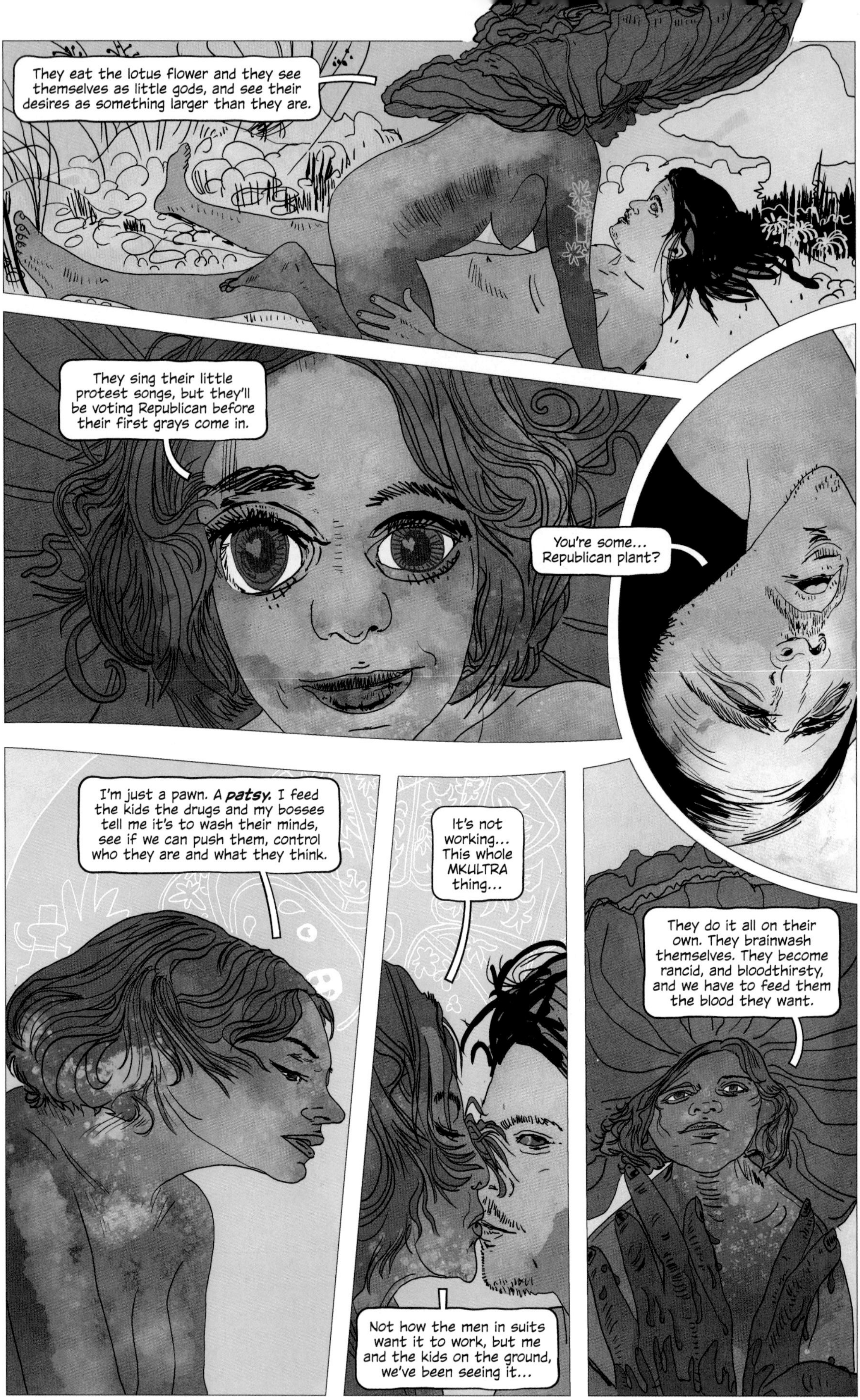
They eat the lotus flower and they see themselves as little gods, and see their desires as something larger than they are.
They sing their little protest songs, but they'll be voting Republican before their first grays come in.
You're some... Republican plant?
I'm just a pawn. A **patsy.** I feed the kids the drugs and my bosses tell me it's to wash their minds, see if we can push them, control who they are and what they think.
It's not working... This whole MKULTRA thing...
Not how the men in suits want it to work, but me and the kids on the ground, we've been seeing it...
They do it all on their own. They brainwash themselves. They become rancid, and bloodthirsty, and we have to feed them the blood they want.

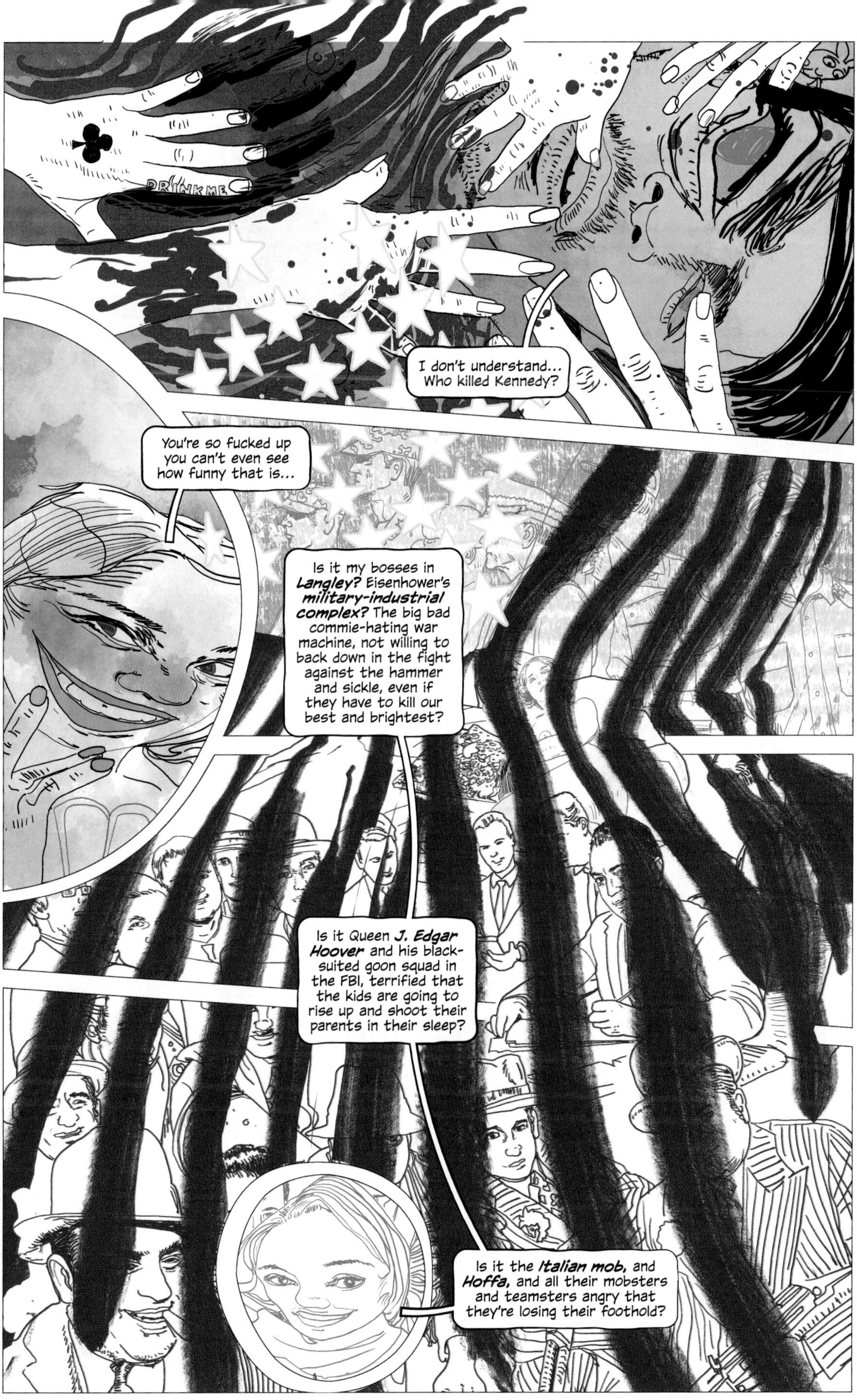
DRINK ME
I don't understand... Who killed Kennedy?
You're so fucked up you can't even see how funny that is...
Is it my bosses in ***Langley?*** Eisenhower's ***military-industrial complex?*** The big bad commie-hating war machine, not willing to back down in the fight against the hammer and sickle, even if they have to kill our best and brightest?
Is it Queen ***J. Edgar Hoover*** and his black-suited goon squad in the FBI, terrified that the kids are going to rise up and shoot their parents in their sleep?
Is it the ***Italian mob,*** and ***Hoffa,*** and all their mobsters and teamsters angry that they're losing their foothold?

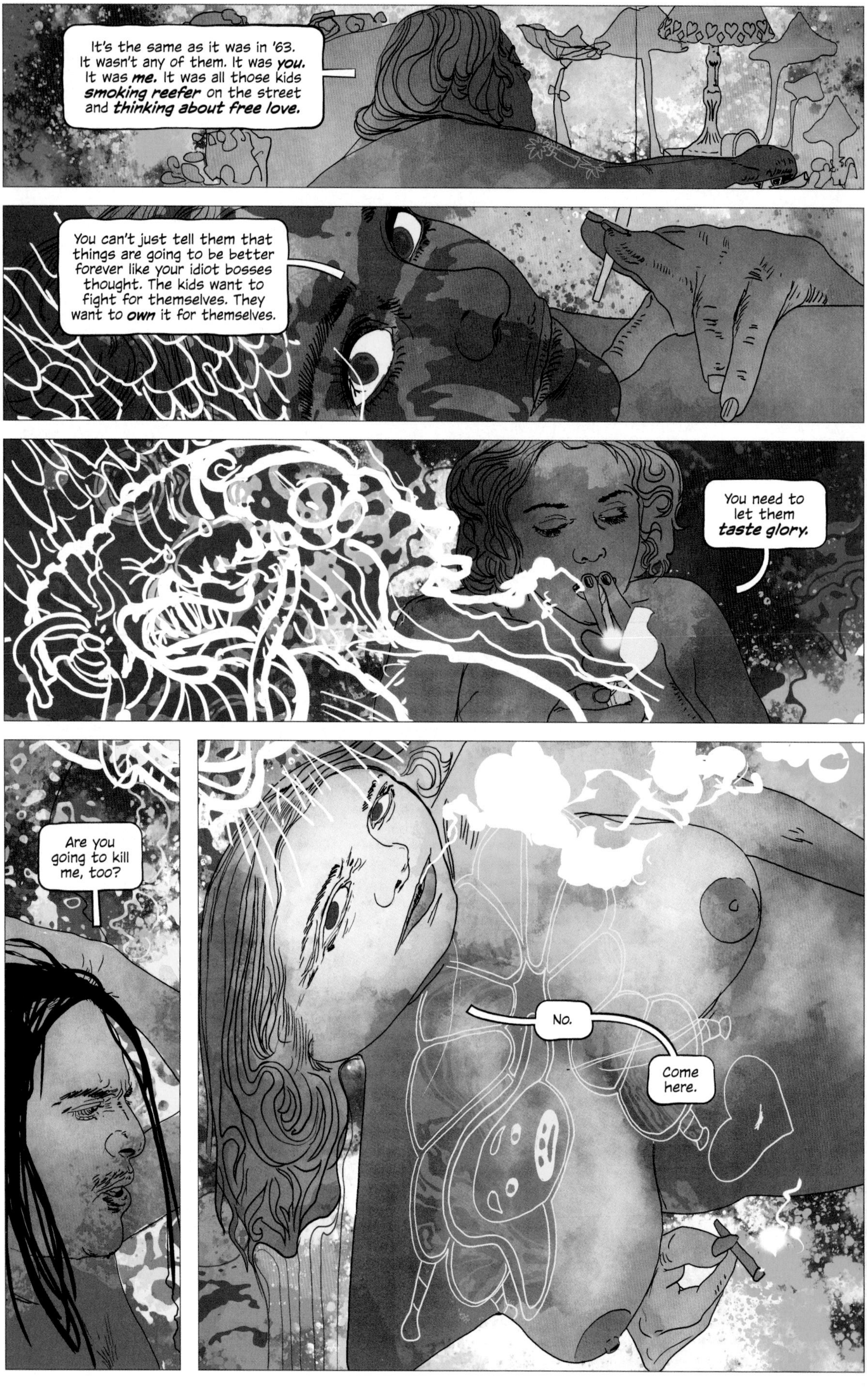

It's the same as it was in '63. It wasn't any of them. It was *you.* It was *me.* It was all those kids ***smoking reefer*** on the street and ***thinking about free love.***
You can't just tell them that things are going to be better forever like your idiot bosses thought. The kids want to fight for themselves. They want to ***own*** it for themselves.
You need to let them ***taste glory.***
Are you going to kill me, too?
No.
Come here.

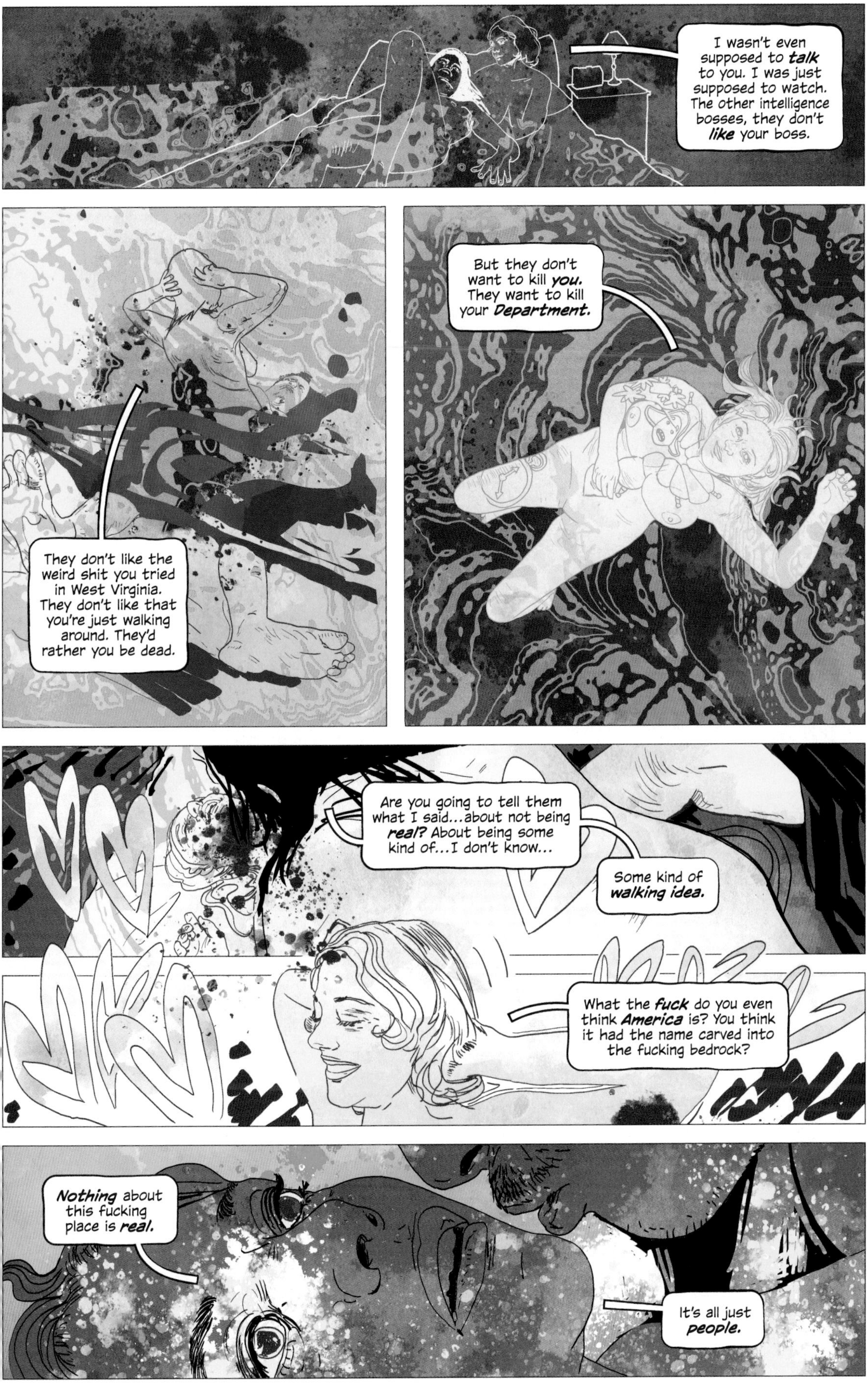

I wasn't even supposed to *talk* to you. I was just supposed to watch. The other intelligence bosses, they don't *like* your boss.
They don't like the weird shit you tried in West Virginia. They don't like that you're just walking around. They'd rather you be dead.
But they don't want to kill *you.* They want to kill your *Department.*
Are you going to tell them what I said...about not being *real?* About being some kind of...I don't know...
Some kind of *walking idea.*
What the *fuck* do you even think *America* is? You think it had the name carved into the fucking bedrock?
Nothing about this fucking place is *real.*
It's all just *people.*

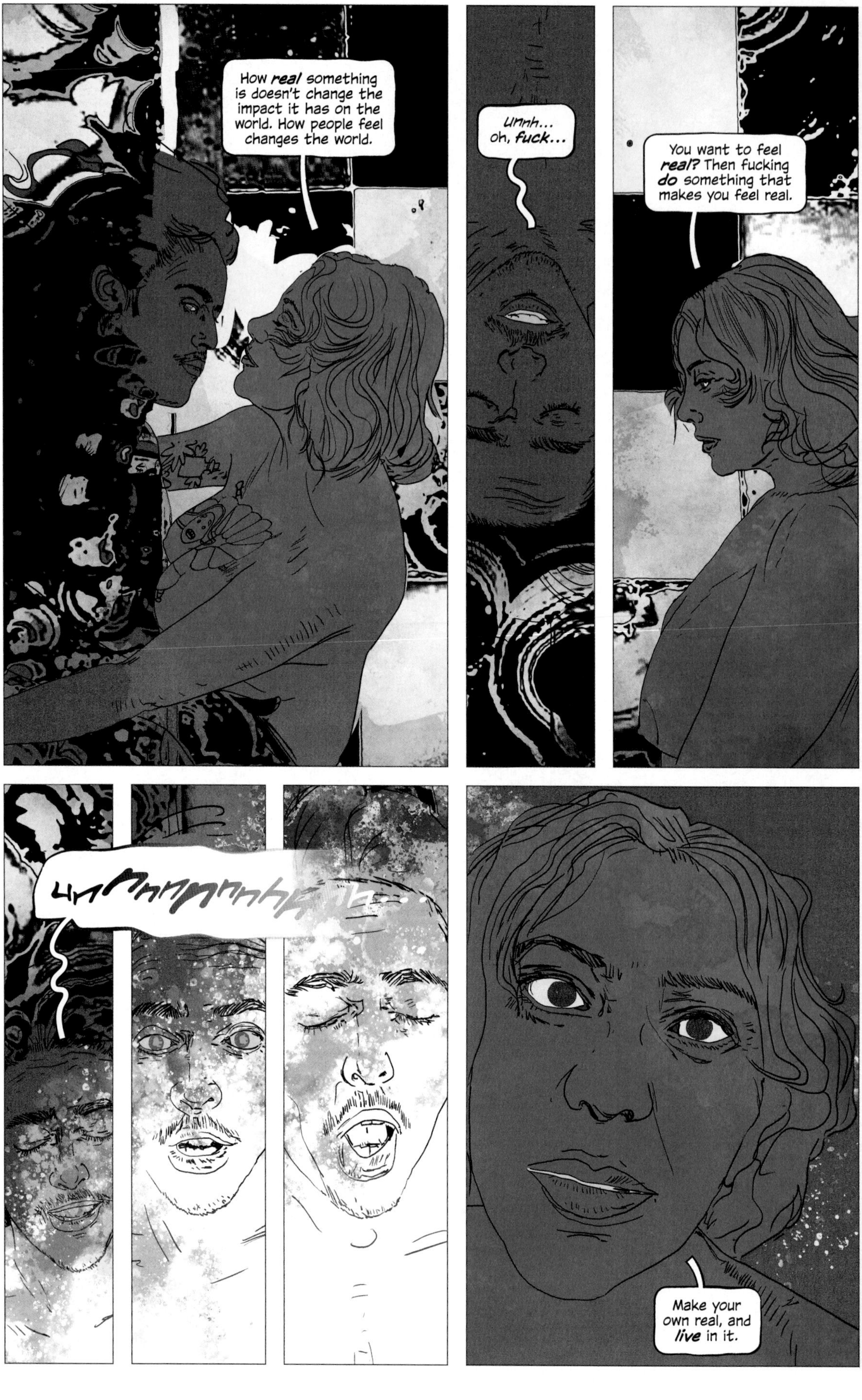
How *real* something is doesn't change the impact it has on the world. How people feel changes the world.
unnh... oh, *fuck*...
You want to feel *real?* Then fucking *do* something that makes you feel real.
unnnnnnnnnhhhh...
Make your own real, and *live* in it.

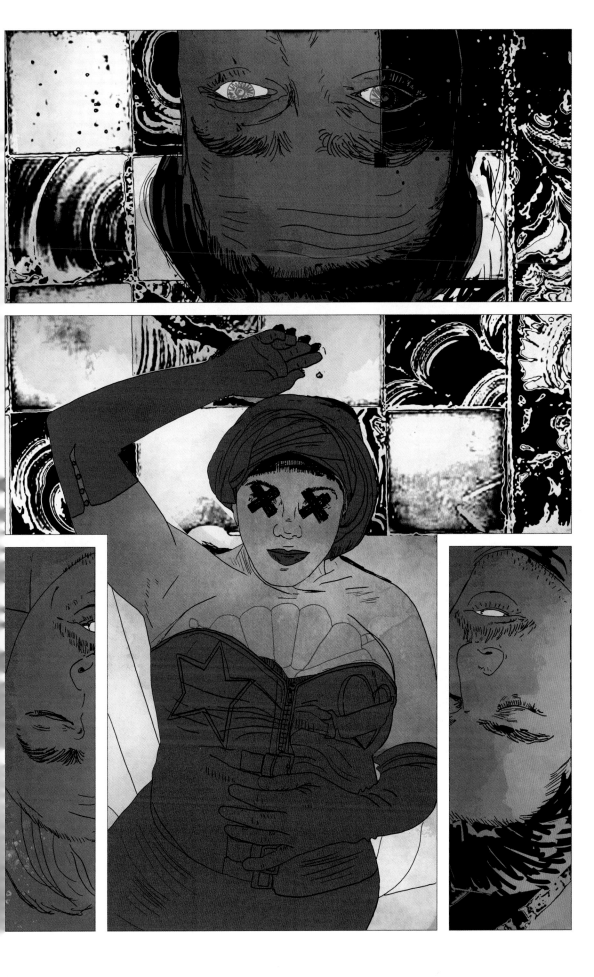

1968

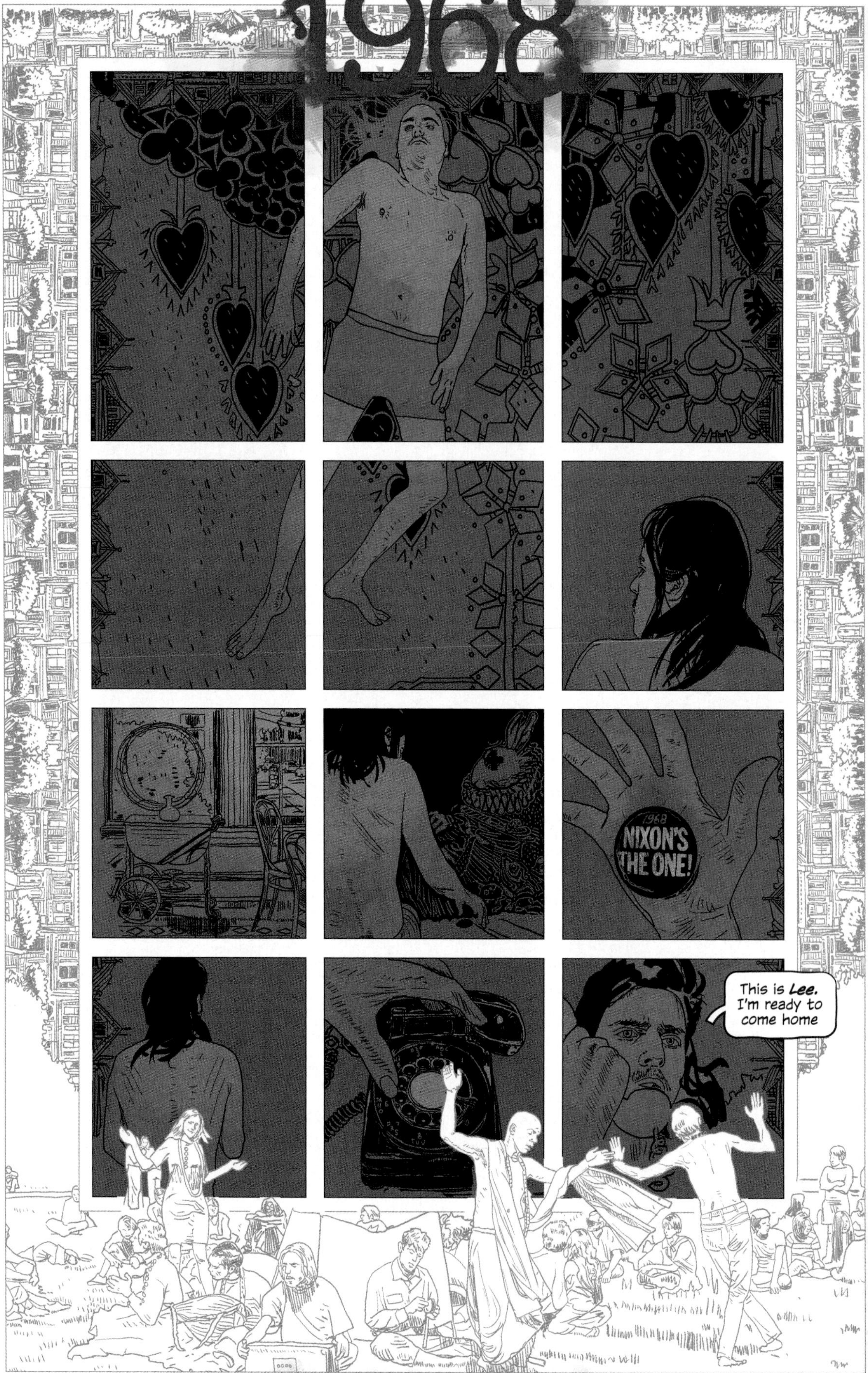
1968
NIXON'S THE ONE!
This is *Lee.* I'm ready to come home

Feed Your Head

DEPARTMEN

★ UNITED STATE

DEVIATION 6 /

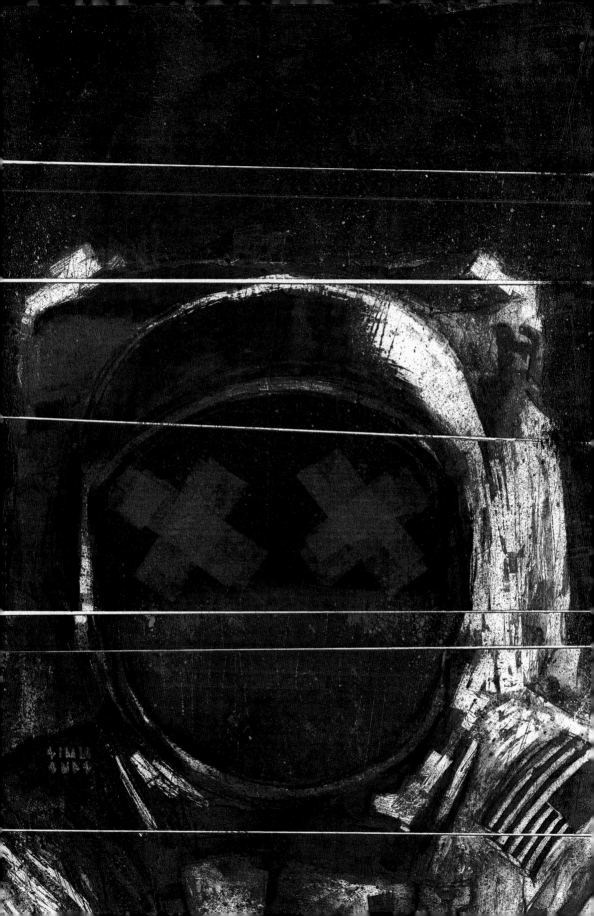

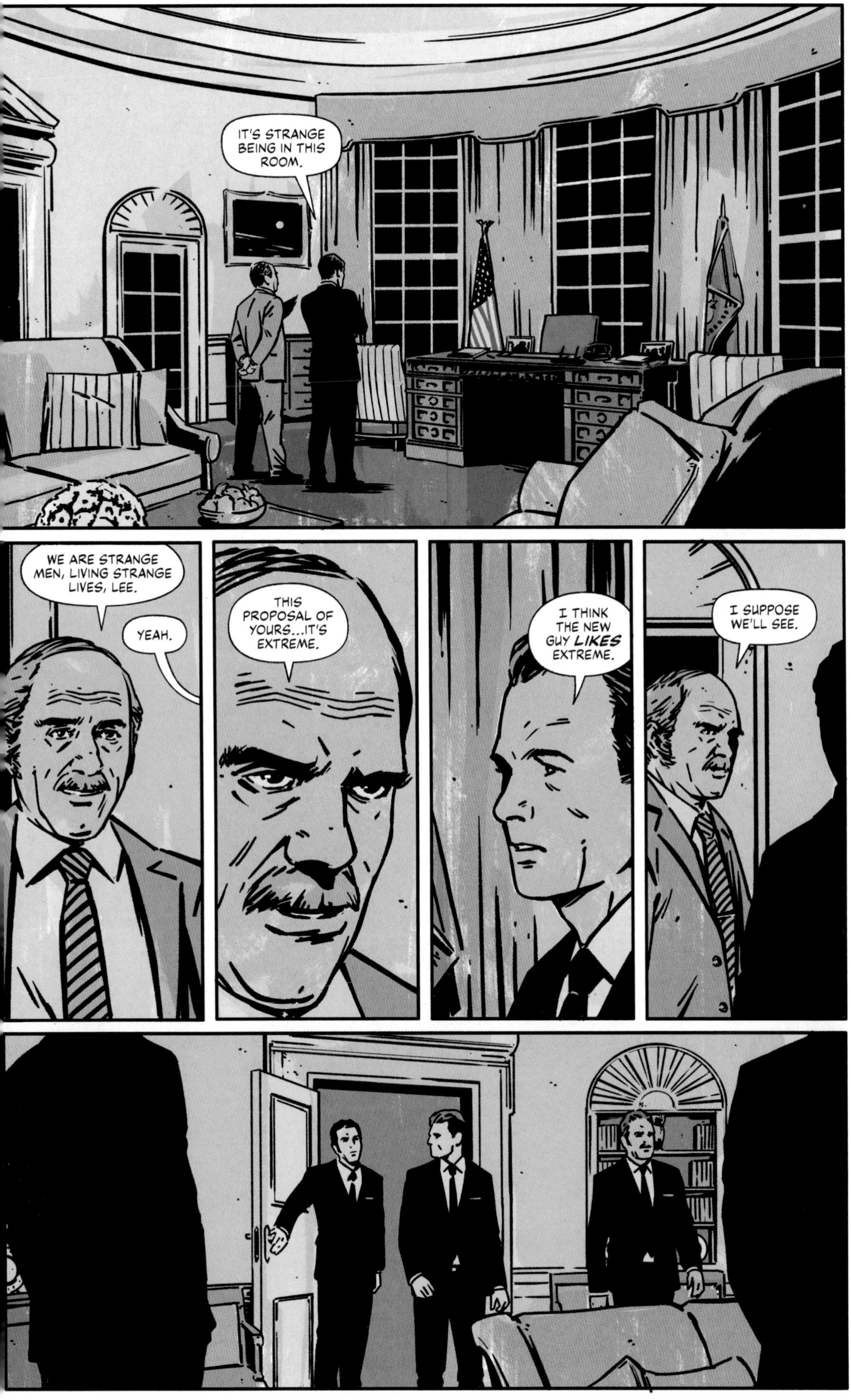
IT'S STRANGE BEING IN THIS ROOM.
WE ARE STRANGE MEN, LIVING STRANGE LIVES, LEE.
YEAH.
THIS PROPOSAL OF YOURS...IT'S EXTREME.
I THINK THE NEW GUY LIKES EXTREME.
I SUPPOSE WE'LL SEE.

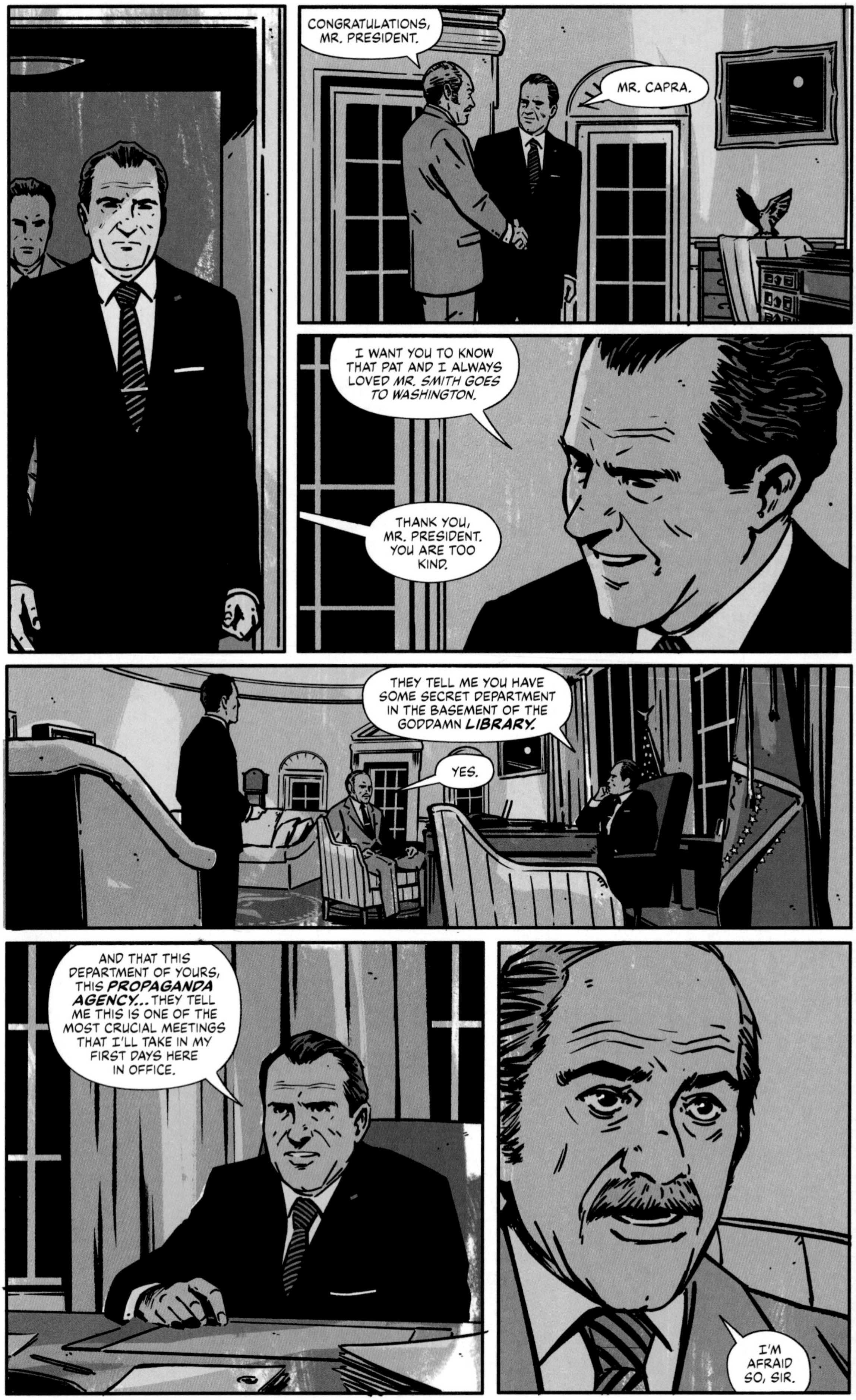
CONGRATULATIONS, MR. PRESIDENT.
MR. CAPRA.
I WANT YOU TO KNOW THAT PAT AND I ALWAYS LOVED *MR. SMITH GOES TO WASHINGTON.*
THANK YOU, MR. PRESIDENT. YOU ARE TOO KIND.
THEY TELL ME YOU HAVE SOME SECRET DEPARTMENT IN THE BASEMENT OF THE GODDAMN ***LIBRARY.***
YES.
AND THAT THIS DEPARTMENT OF YOURS, THIS ***PROPAGANDA AGENCY...*** THEY TELL ME THIS IS ONE OF THE MOST CRUCIAL MEETINGS THAT I'LL TAKE IN MY FIRST DAYS HERE IN OFFICE.
I'M AFRAID SO, SIR.

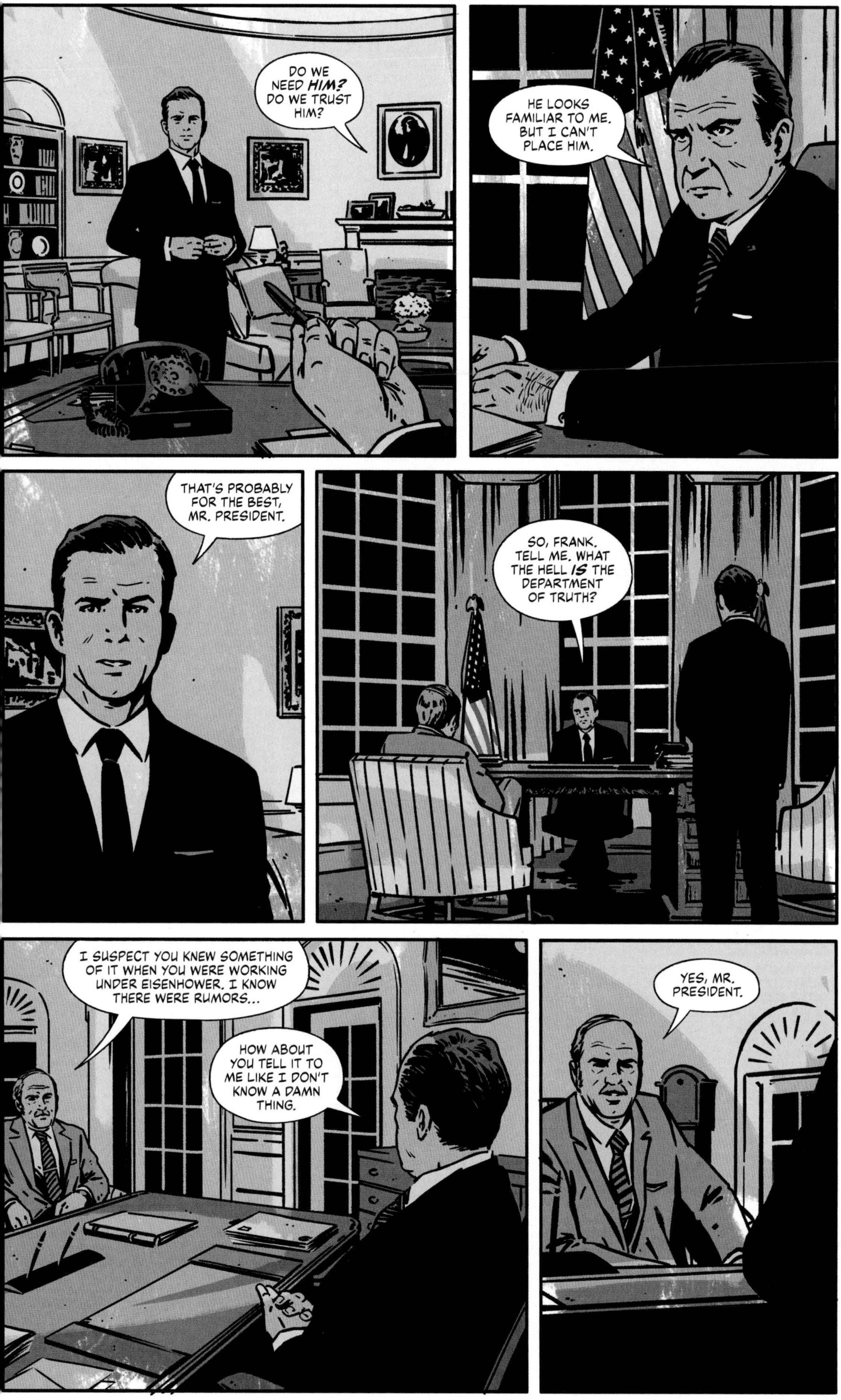
DO WE NEED HIM? DO WE TRUST HIM?
HE LOOKS FAMILIAR TO ME. BUT I CAN'T PLACE HIM.
THAT'S PROBABLY FOR THE BEST, MR. PRESIDENT.
SO, FRANK. TELL ME. WHAT THE HELL IS THE DEPARTMENT OF TRUTH?
I SUSPECT YOU KNEW SOMETHING OF IT WHEN YOU WERE WORKING UNDER EISENHOWER. I KNOW THERE WERE RUMORS...
HOW ABOUT YOU TELL IT TO ME LIKE I DON'T KNOW A DAMN THING.
YES, MR. PRESIDENT.

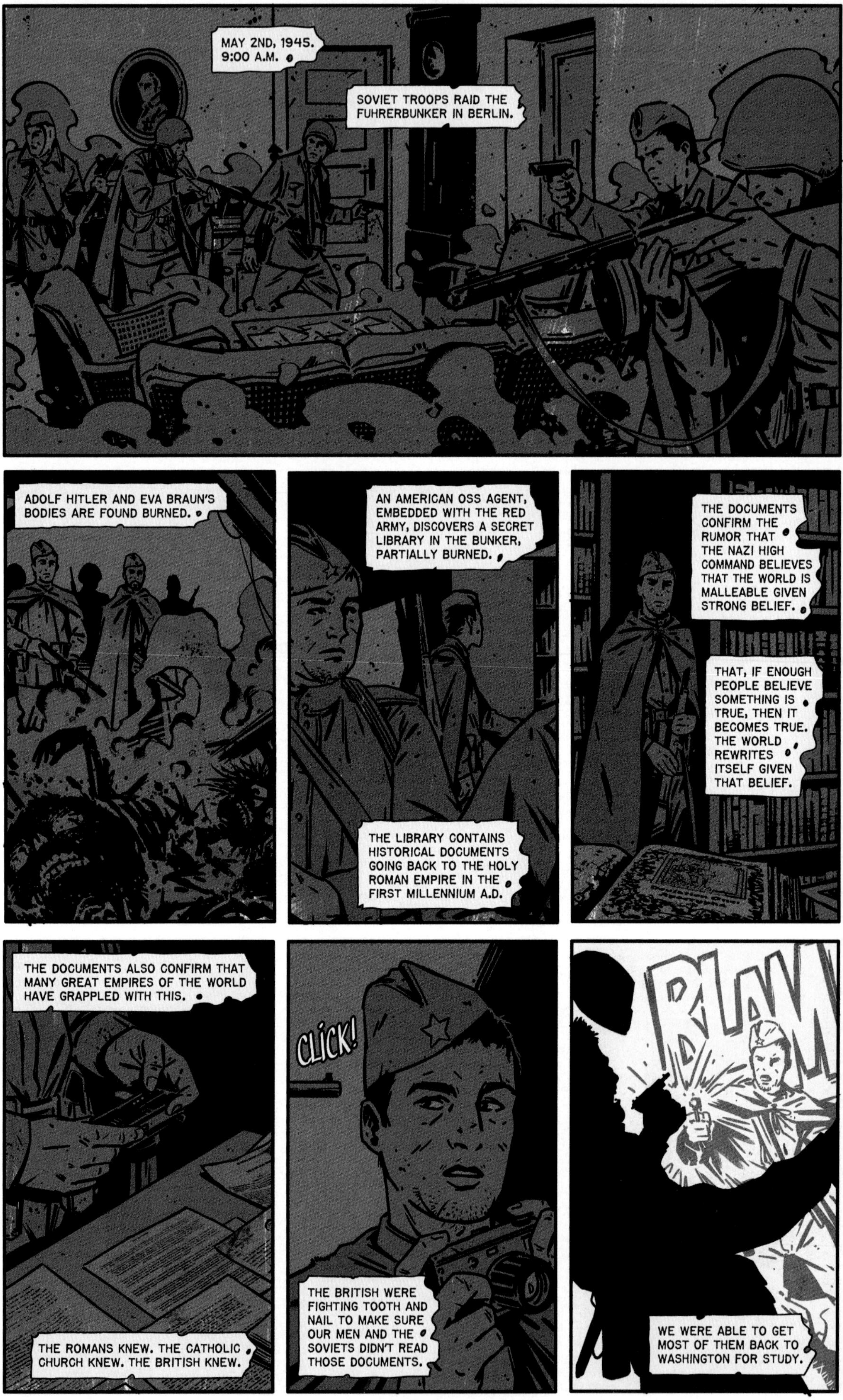
MAY 2ND, 1945.
9:00 A.M.
SOVIET TROOPS RAID THE FUHRERBUNKER IN BERLIN.
ADOLF HITLER AND EVA BRAUN'S BODIES ARE FOUND BURNED.
AN AMERICAN OSS AGENT, EMBEDDED WITH THE RED ARMY, DISCOVERS A SECRET LIBRARY IN THE BUNKER, PARTIALLY BURNED.
THE LIBRARY CONTAINS HISTORICAL DOCUMENTS GOING BACK TO THE HOLY ROMAN EMPIRE IN THE FIRST MILLENNIUM A.D.
THE DOCUMENTS CONFIRM THE RUMOR THAT THE NAZI HIGH COMMAND BELIEVES THAT THE WORLD IS MALLEABLE GIVEN STRONG BELIEF.
THAT, IF ENOUGH PEOPLE BELIEVE SOMETHING IS TRUE, THEN IT BECOMES TRUE. THE WORLD REWRITES ITSELF GIVEN THAT BELIEF.
THE DOCUMENTS ALSO CONFIRM THAT MANY GREAT EMPIRES OF THE WORLD HAVE GRAPPLED WITH THIS.
THE ROMANS KNEW. THE CATHOLIC CHURCH KNEW. THE BRITISH KNEW.
CLICK!
THE BRITISH WERE FIGHTING TOOTH AND NAIL TO MAKE SURE OUR MEN AND THE SOVIETS DIDN'T READ THOSE DOCUMENTS.
BLAM
WE WERE ABLE TO GET MOST OF THEM BACK TO WASHINGTON FOR STUDY.

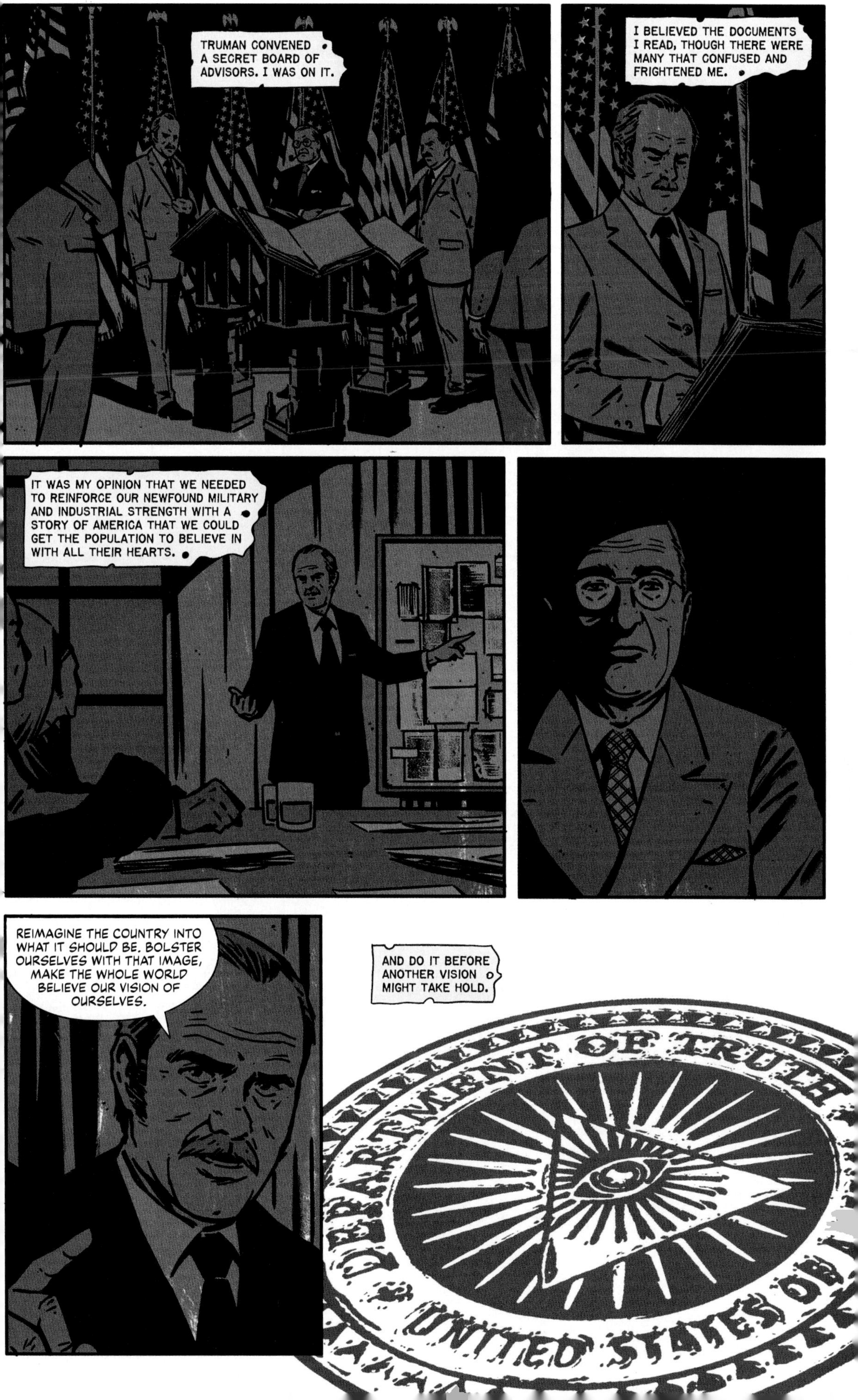
TRUMAN CONVENED A SECRET BOARD OF ADVISORS. I WAS ON IT.
I BELIEVED THE DOCUMENTS I READ, THOUGH THERE WERE MANY THAT CONFUSED AND FRIGHTENED ME.
IT WAS MY OPINION THAT WE NEEDED TO REINFORCE OUR NEWFOUND MILITARY AND INDUSTRIAL STRENGTH WITH A STORY OF AMERICA THAT WE COULD GET THE POPULATION TO BELIEVE IN WITH ALL THEIR HEARTS.
REIMAGINE THE COUNTRY INTO WHAT IT SHOULD BE. BOLSTER OURSELVES WITH THAT IMAGE, MAKE THE WHOLE WORLD BELIEVE OUR VISION OF OURSELVES.
AND DO IT BEFORE ANOTHER VISION MIGHT TAKE HOLD.
DEPARTMENT OF TRUTH
UNITED STATES OF A

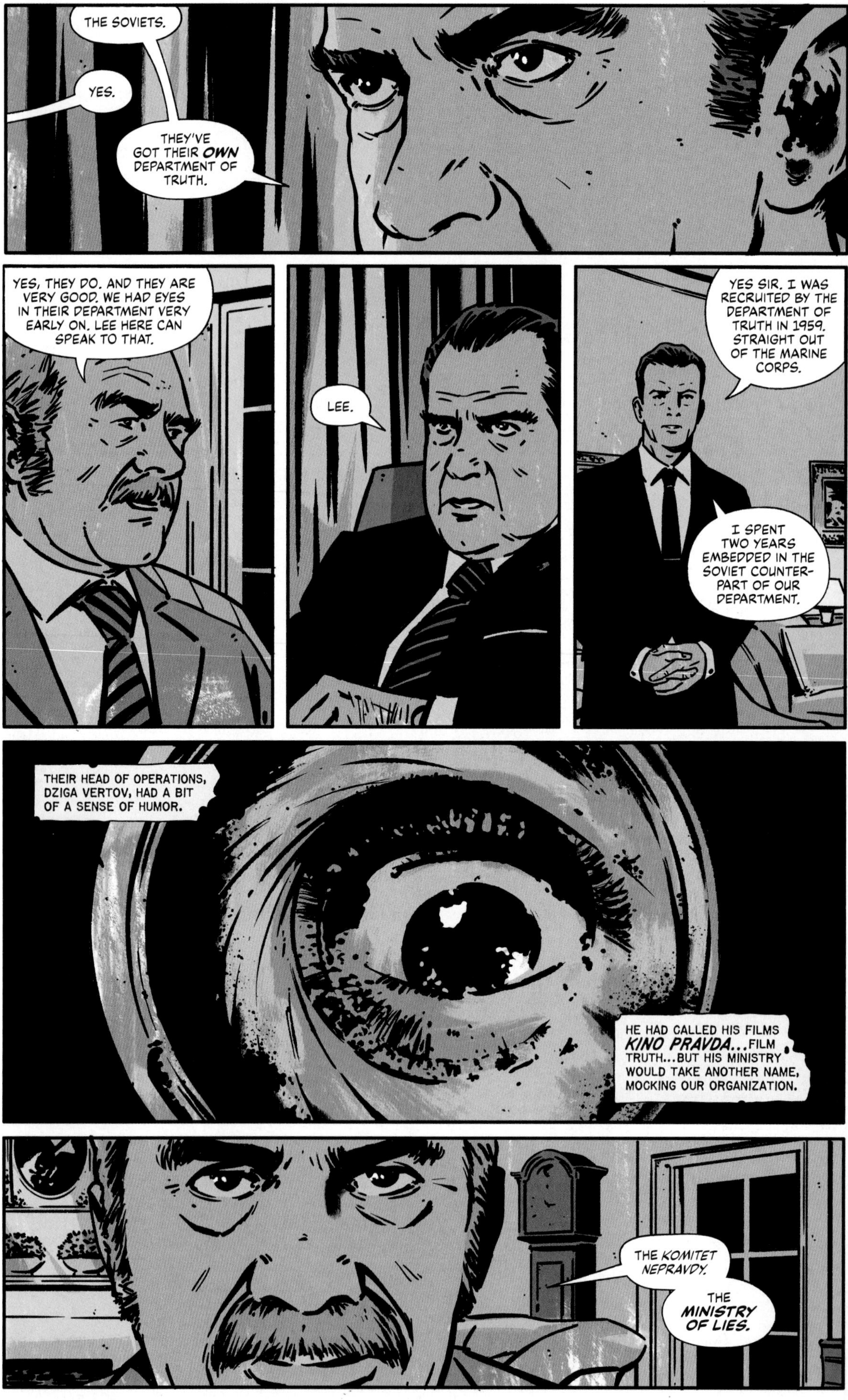
THE SOVIETS.
YES.
THEY'VE GOT THEIR OWN DEPARTMENT OF TRUTH.
YES, THEY DO. AND THEY ARE VERY GOOD. WE HAD EYES IN THEIR DEPARTMENT VERY EARLY ON. LEE HERE CAN SPEAK TO THAT.
LEE.
YES SIR. I WAS RECRUITED BY THE DEPARTMENT OF TRUTH IN 1959. STRAIGHT OUT OF THE MARINE CORPS.
I SPENT TWO YEARS EMBEDDED IN THE SOVIET COUNTER-PART OF OUR DEPARTMENT.
THEIR HEAD OF OPERATIONS, DZIGA VERTOV, HAD A BIT OF A SENSE OF HUMOR.
HE HAD CALLED HIS FILMS KINO PRAVDA...FILM TRUTH...BUT HIS MINISTRY WOULD TAKE ANOTHER NAME, MOCKING OUR ORGANIZATION.
THE KOMITET NEPRAVDY.
THE MINISTRY OF LIES.

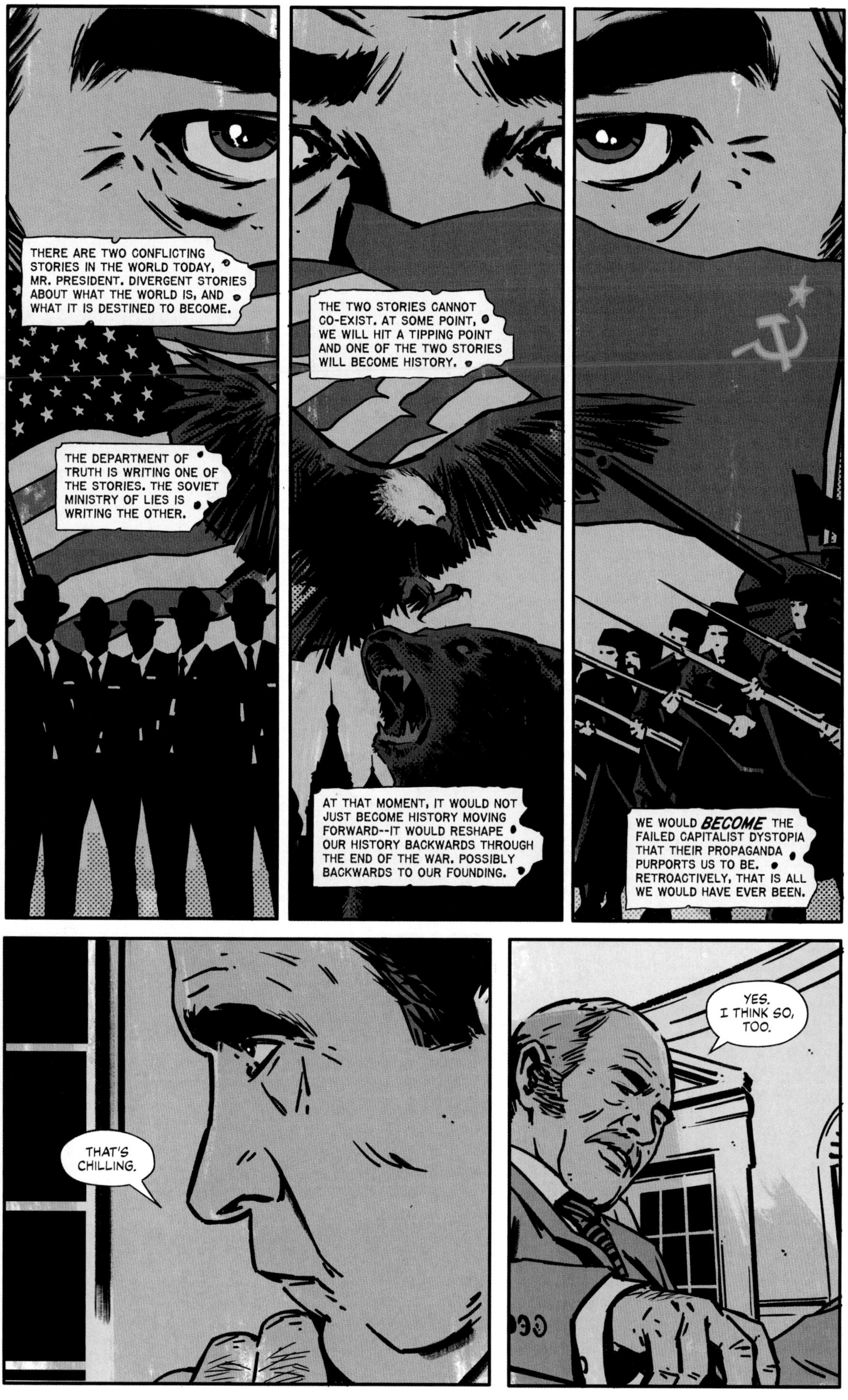
THERE ARE TWO CONFLICTING STORIES IN THE WORLD TODAY, MR. PRESIDENT. DIVERGENT STORIES ABOUT WHAT THE WORLD IS, AND WHAT IT IS DESTINED TO BECOME.
THE DEPARTMENT OF TRUTH IS WRITING ONE OF THE STORIES. THE SOVIET MINISTRY OF LIES IS WRITING THE OTHER.
THE TWO STORIES CANNOT CO-EXIST. AT SOME POINT, WE WILL HIT A TIPPING POINT AND ONE OF THE TWO STORIES WILL BECOME HISTORY.
AT THAT MOMENT, IT WOULD NOT JUST BECOME HISTORY MOVING FORWARD--IT WOULD RESHAPE OUR HISTORY BACKWARDS THROUGH THE END OF THE WAR. POSSIBLY BACKWARDS TO OUR FOUNDING.
WE WOULD *BECOME* THE FAILED CAPITALIST DYSTOPIA THAT THEIR PROPAGANDA PURPORTS US TO BE. RETROACTIVELY, THAT IS ALL WE WOULD HAVE EVER BEEN.
THAT'S CHILLING.
YES. I THINK SO, TOO.

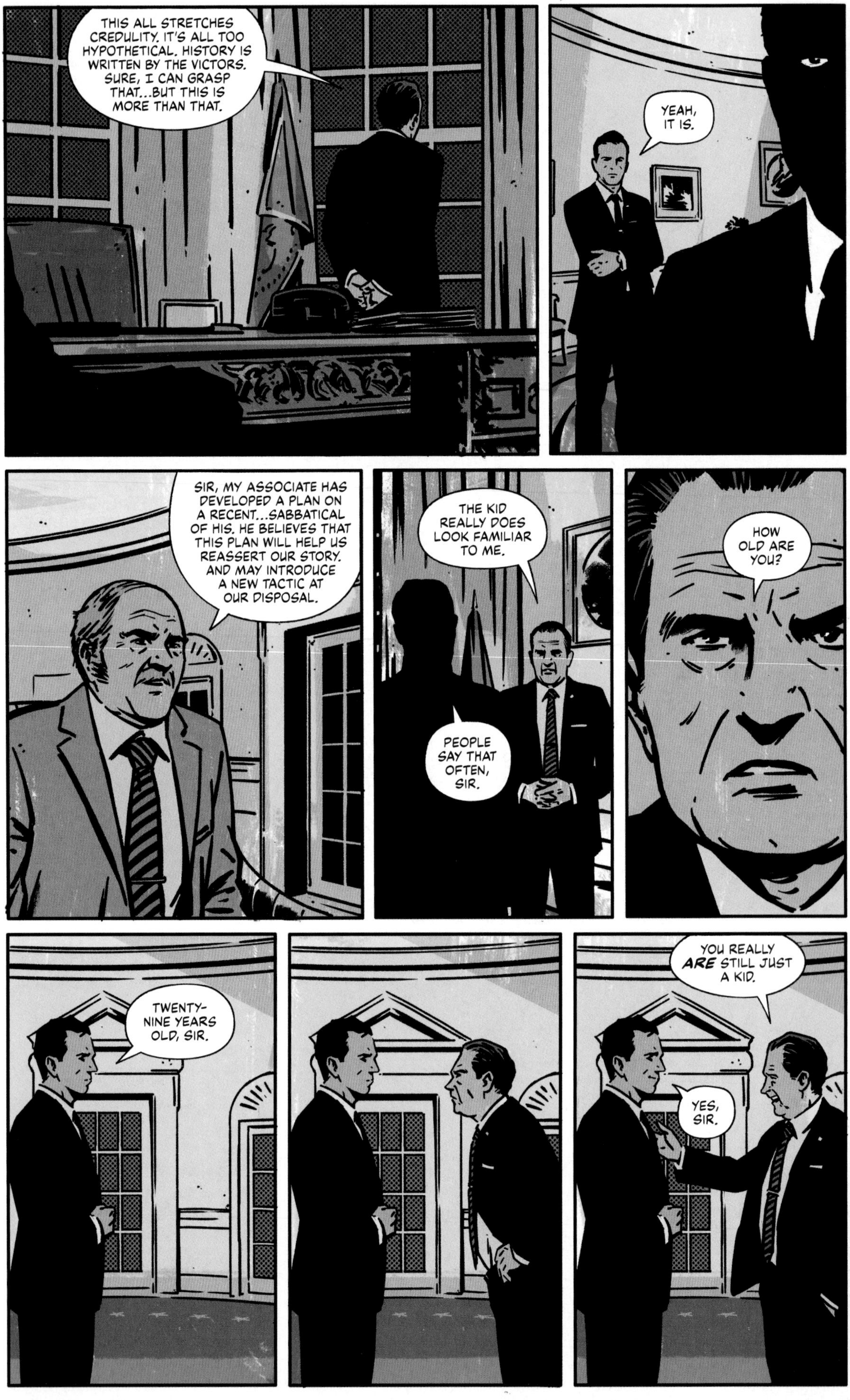
THIS ALL STRETCHES CREDULITY. IT'S ALL TOO HYPOTHETICAL. HISTORY IS WRITTEN BY THE VICTORS. SURE, I CAN GRASP THAT...BUT THIS IS MORE THAN THAT.
YEAH, IT IS.
SIR, MY ASSOCIATE HAS DEVELOPED A PLAN ON A RECENT...SABBATICAL OF HIS. HE BELIEVES THAT THIS PLAN WILL HELP US REASSERT OUR STORY. AND MAY INTRODUCE A NEW TACTIC AT OUR DISPOSAL.
THE KID REALLY DOES LOOK FAMILIAR TO ME.
PEOPLE SAY THAT OFTEN, SIR.
HOW OLD ARE YOU?
TWENTY-NINE YEARS OLD, SIR.
YOU REALLY ***ARE*** STILL JUST A KID.
YES, SIR.

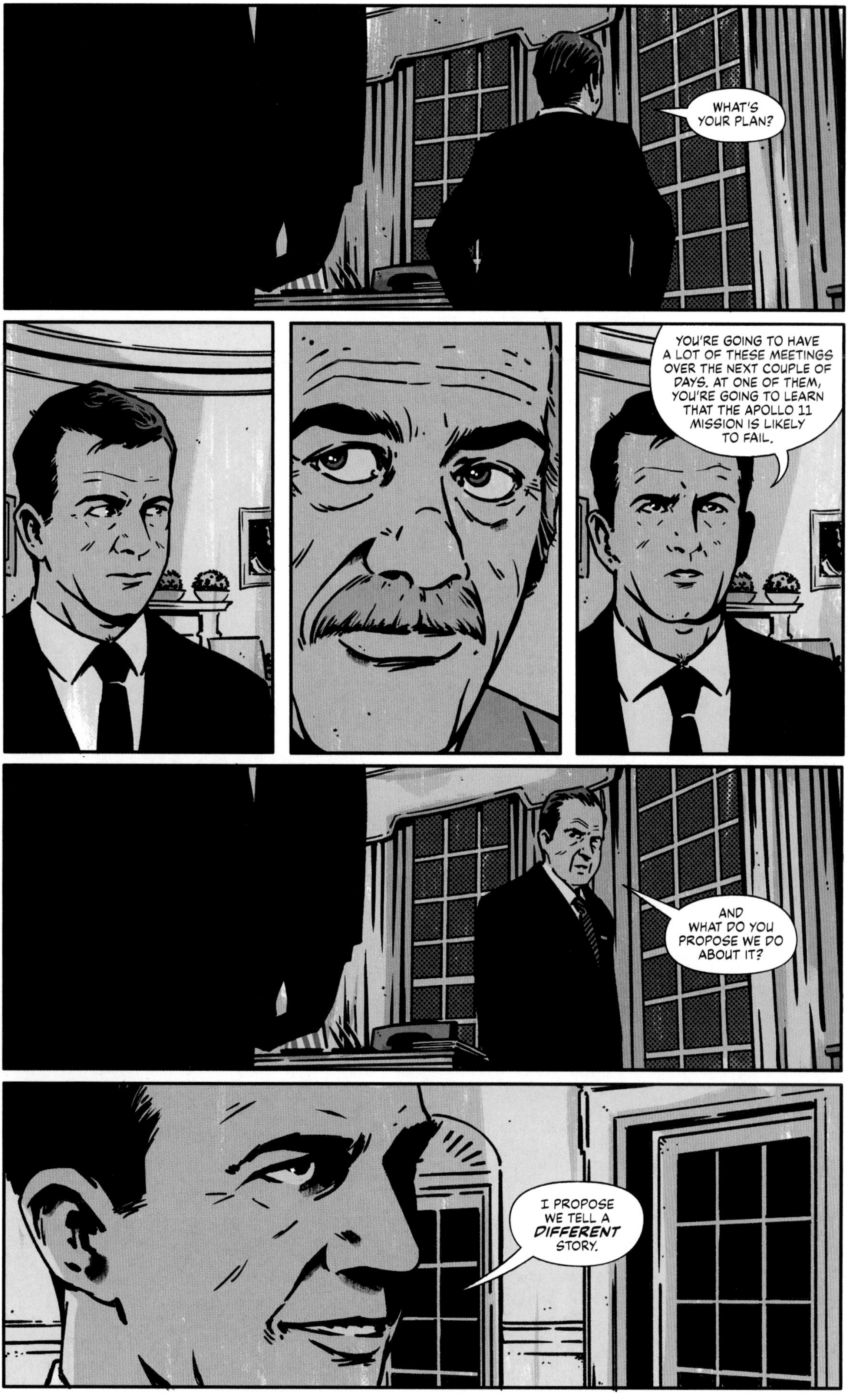
WHAT'S YOUR PLAN?
YOU'RE GOING TO HAVE A LOT OF THESE MEETINGS OVER THE NEXT COUPLE OF DAYS. AT ONE OF THEM, YOU'RE GOING TO LEARN THAT THE APOLLO 11 MISSION IS LIKELY TO FAIL.
AND WHAT DO YOU PROPOSE WE DO ABOUT IT?
I PROPOSE WE TELL A *DIFFERENT* STORY.

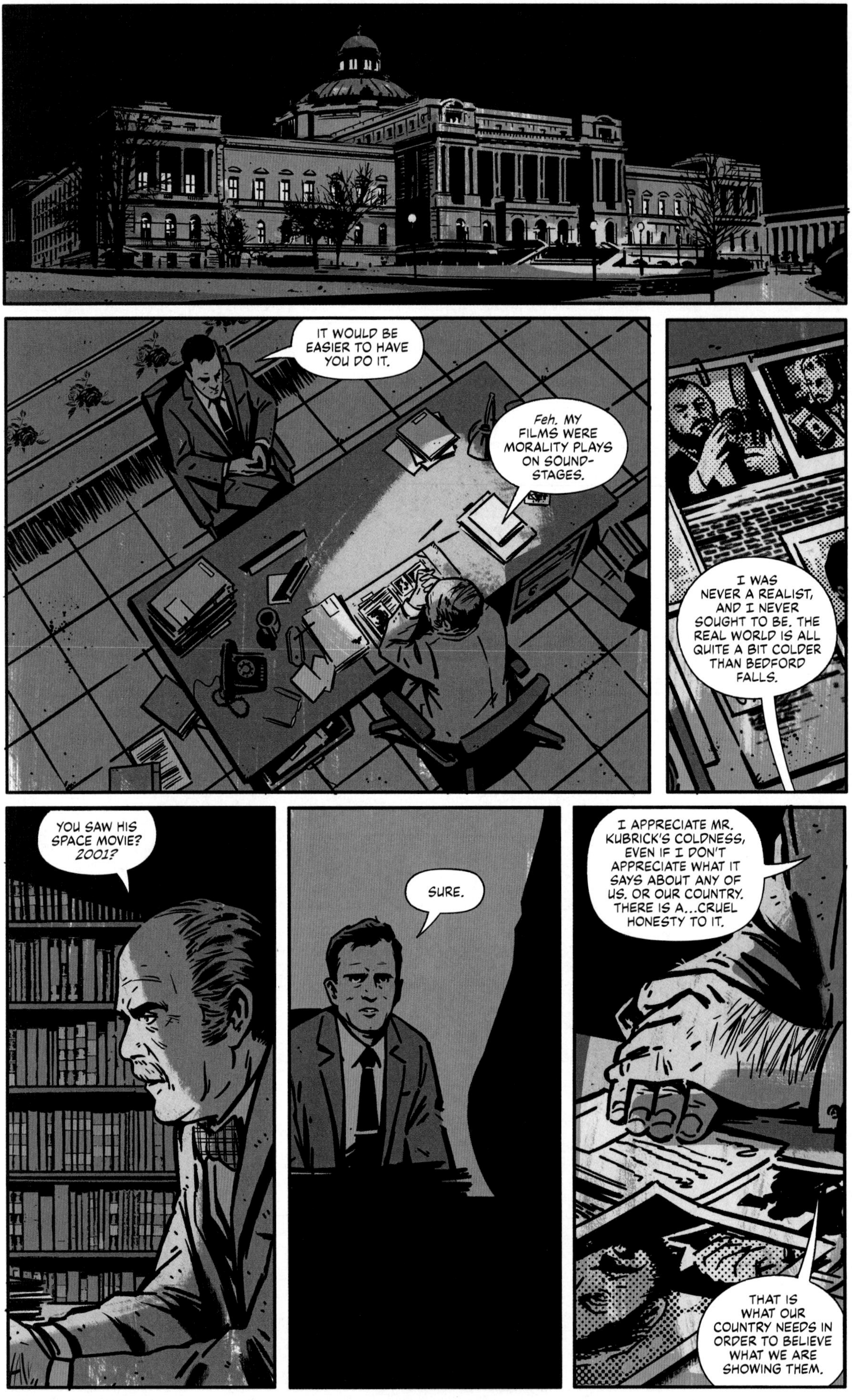
IT WOULD BE EASIER TO HAVE YOU DO IT.
Feh. MY FILMS WERE MORALITY PLAYS ON SOUND-STAGES.
I WAS NEVER A REALIST, AND I NEVER SOUGHT TO BE. THE REAL WORLD IS ALL QUITE A BIT COLDER THAN BEDFORD FALLS.
YOU SAW HIS SPACE MOVIE? *2001?*
SURE.
I APPRECIATE MR. KUBRICK'S COLDNESS, EVEN IF I DON'T APPRECIATE WHAT IT SAYS ABOUT ANY OF US. OR OUR COUNTRY. THERE IS A...CRUEL HONESTY TO IT.
THAT IS WHAT OUR COUNTRY NEEDS IN ORDER TO BELIEVE WHAT WE ARE SHOWING THEM.

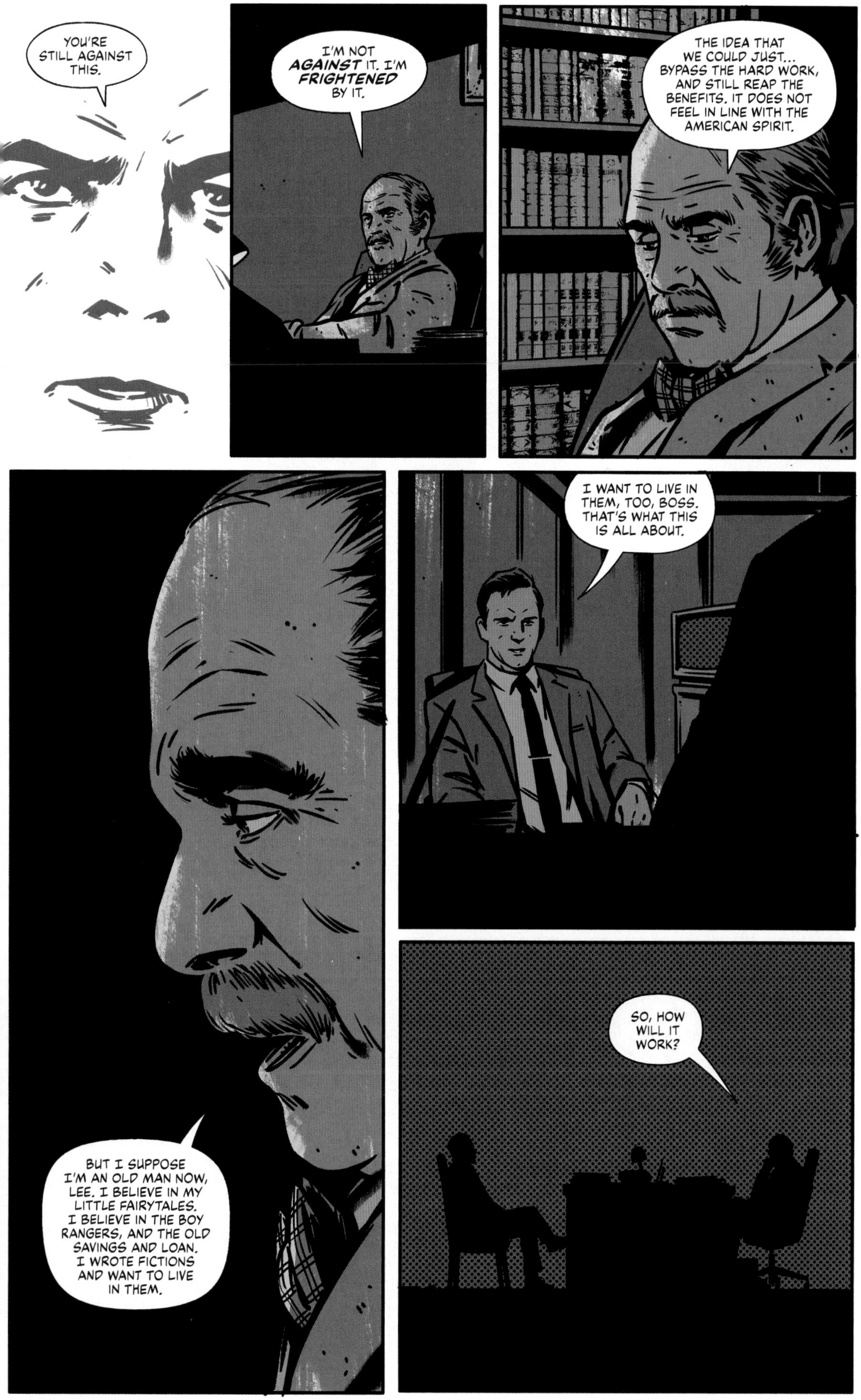
YOU'RE STILL AGAINST THIS.
I'M NOT *AGAINST* IT. I'M *FRIGHTENED* BY IT.
THE IDEA THAT WE COULD JUST... BYPASS THE HARD WORK, AND STILL REAP THE BENEFITS. IT DOES NOT FEEL IN LINE WITH THE AMERICAN SPIRIT.
BUT I SUPPOSE I'M AN OLD MAN NOW, LEE. I BELIEVE IN MY LITTLE FAIRYTALES. I BELIEVE IN THE BOY RANGERS, AND THE OLD SAVINGS AND LOAN. I WROTE FICTIONS AND WANT TO LIVE IN THEM.
I WANT TO LIVE IN THEM, TOO, BOSS. THAT'S WHAT THIS IS ALL ABOUT.
SO, HOW WILL IT WORK?

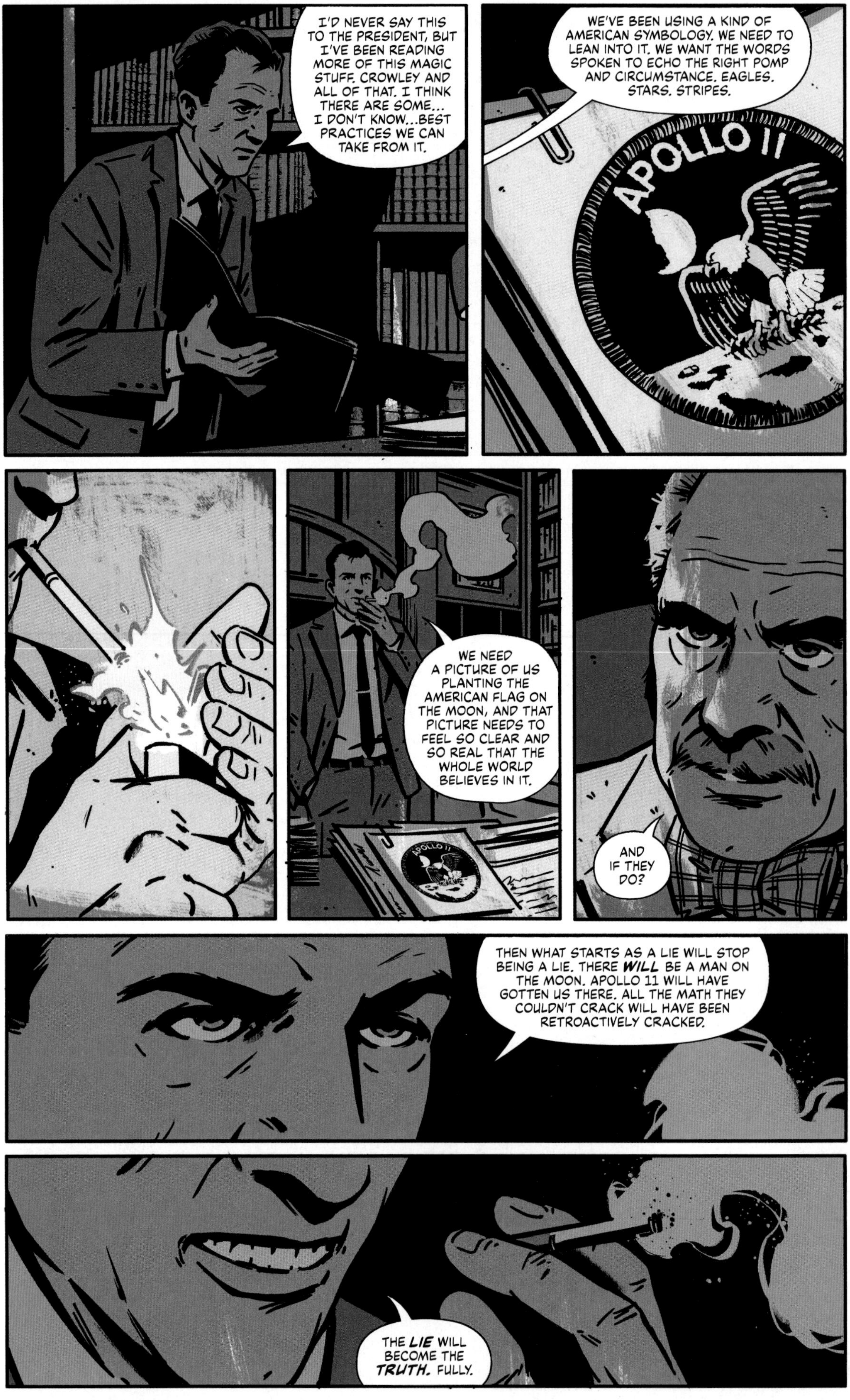
I'D NEVER SAY THIS TO THE PRESIDENT, BUT I'VE BEEN READING MORE OF THIS MAGIC STUFF. CROWLEY AND ALL OF THAT. I THINK THERE ARE SOME... I DON'T KNOW...BEST PRACTICES WE CAN TAKE FROM IT.
WE'VE BEEN USING A KIND OF AMERICAN SYMBOLOGY. WE NEED TO LEAN INTO IT. WE WANT THE WORDS SPOKEN TO ECHO THE RIGHT POMP AND CIRCUMSTANCE. EAGLES. STARS. STRIPES.
APOLLO 11
WE NEED A PICTURE OF US PLANTING THE AMERICAN FLAG ON THE MOON, AND THAT PICTURE NEEDS TO FEEL SO CLEAR AND SO REAL THAT THE WHOLE WORLD BELIEVES IN IT.
AND IF THEY DO?
THEN WHAT STARTS AS A LIE WILL STOP BEING A LIE. THERE WILL BE A MAN ON THE MOON. APOLLO 11 WILL HAVE GOTTEN US THERE. ALL THE MATH THEY COULDN'T CRACK WILL HAVE BEEN RETROACTIVELY CRACKED.
THE LIE WILL BECOME THE TRUTH. FULLY.

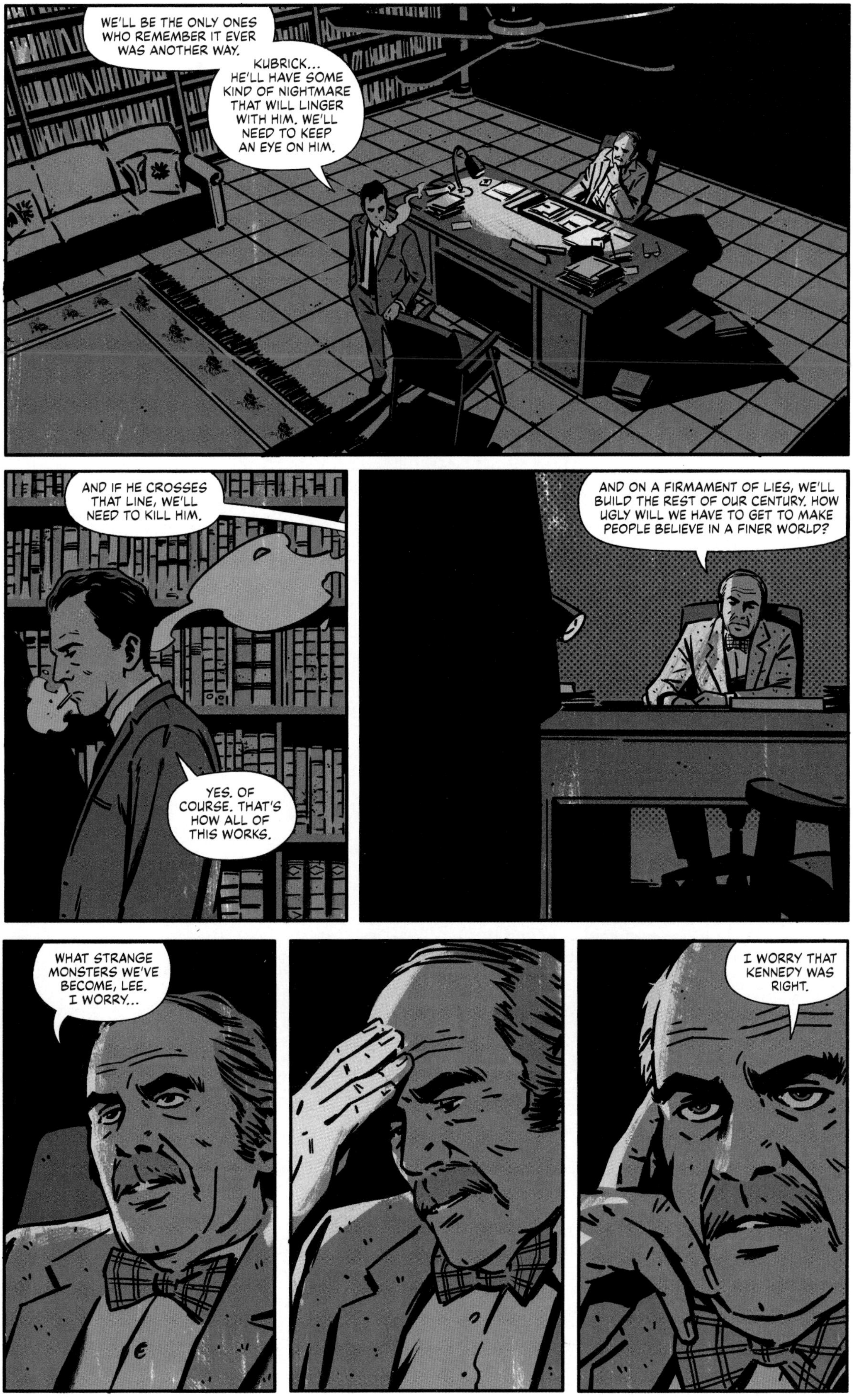
WE'LL BE THE ONLY ONES WHO REMEMBER IT EVER WAS ANOTHER WAY.
KUBRICK... HE'LL HAVE SOME KIND OF NIGHTMARE THAT WILL LINGER WITH HIM. WE'LL NEED TO KEEP AN EYE ON HIM.
AND IF HE CROSSES THAT LINE, WE'LL NEED TO KILL HIM.
YES. OF COURSE. THAT'S HOW ALL OF THIS WORKS.
AND ON A FIRMAMENT OF LIES, WE'LL BUILD THE REST OF OUR CENTURY. HOW UGLY WILL WE HAVE TO GET TO MAKE PEOPLE BELIEVE IN A FINER WORLD?
WHAT STRANGE MONSTERS WE'VE BECOME, LEE. I WORRY...
I WORRY THAT KENNEDY WAS RIGHT.

WE SPENT TWO DECADES TRYING TO CRAFT A STORY ABOUT A PERFECT AMERICA, BUT WE COULDN'T MAKE IT STICK.

IT STARTED COMING APART IN OUR HANDS, AND WE BLAMED THE WRONG PEOPLE.

IN THE END, IT WASN'T US WHO PULLED THE TRIGGER.

WE PUT THE GUN IN THE WINDOW. WE AS GOOD AS DID THE JOB OURSELVES. AND WHAT ANSWERS DO WE HAVE? I PUT YOU IN THE ARCHIVES TO TRY TO SOLVE A RIDDLE...

WHO IS THIS...FICTIONAL WOMAN? WHY DID SHE PULL THE TRIGGER? WHY IS SHE THERE EVERY TIME THE WORLD CHANGES? WHY TAKE AN ACTIVE ROLE...

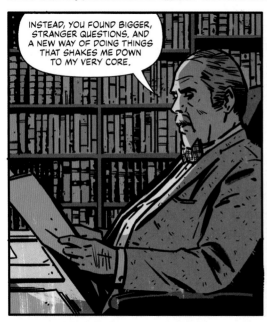

INSTEAD, YOU FOUND BIGGER, STRANGER QUESTIONS. AND A NEW WAY OF DOING THINGS THAT SHAKES ME DOWN TO MY VERY CORE.

MAYBE THE CATHOLICS WERE RIGHT. MAYBE SHE IS THE DEVIL. A PRINCESS OF LIES, PULLING US ALL TOWARD DAMNATION AND SORROW.

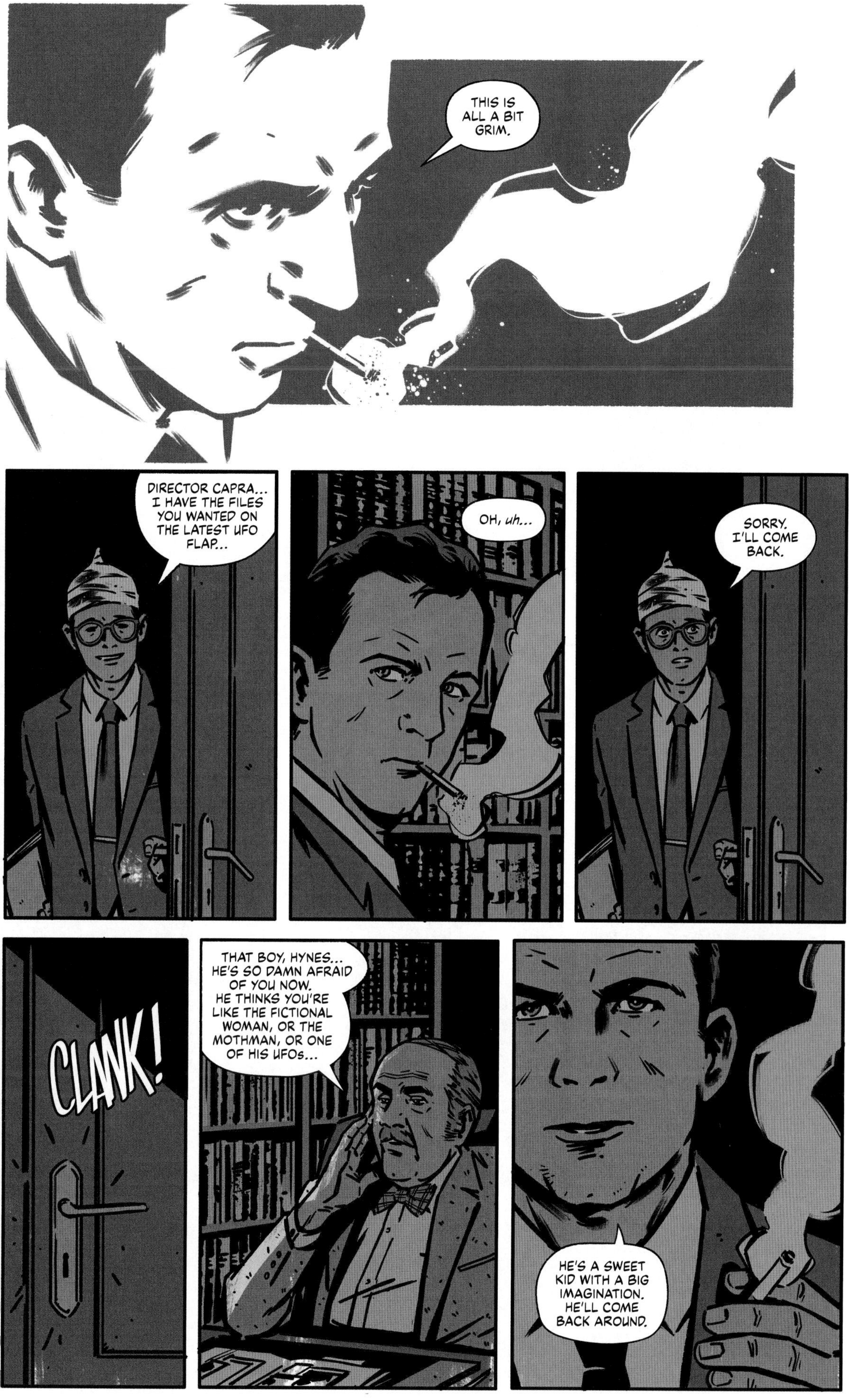
THIS IS ALL A BIT GRIM.
DIRECTOR CAPRA... I HAVE THE FILES YOU WANTED ON THE LATEST UFO FLAP...
OH, uh...
SORRY. I'LL COME BACK.
CLANK!
THAT BOY, HYNES... HE'S SO DAMN AFRAID OF YOU NOW. HE THINKS YOU'RE LIKE THE FICTIONAL WOMAN, OR THE MOTHMAN, OR ONE OF HIS UFOs...
HE'S A SWEET KID WITH A BIG IMAGINATION. HE'LL COME BACK AROUND.

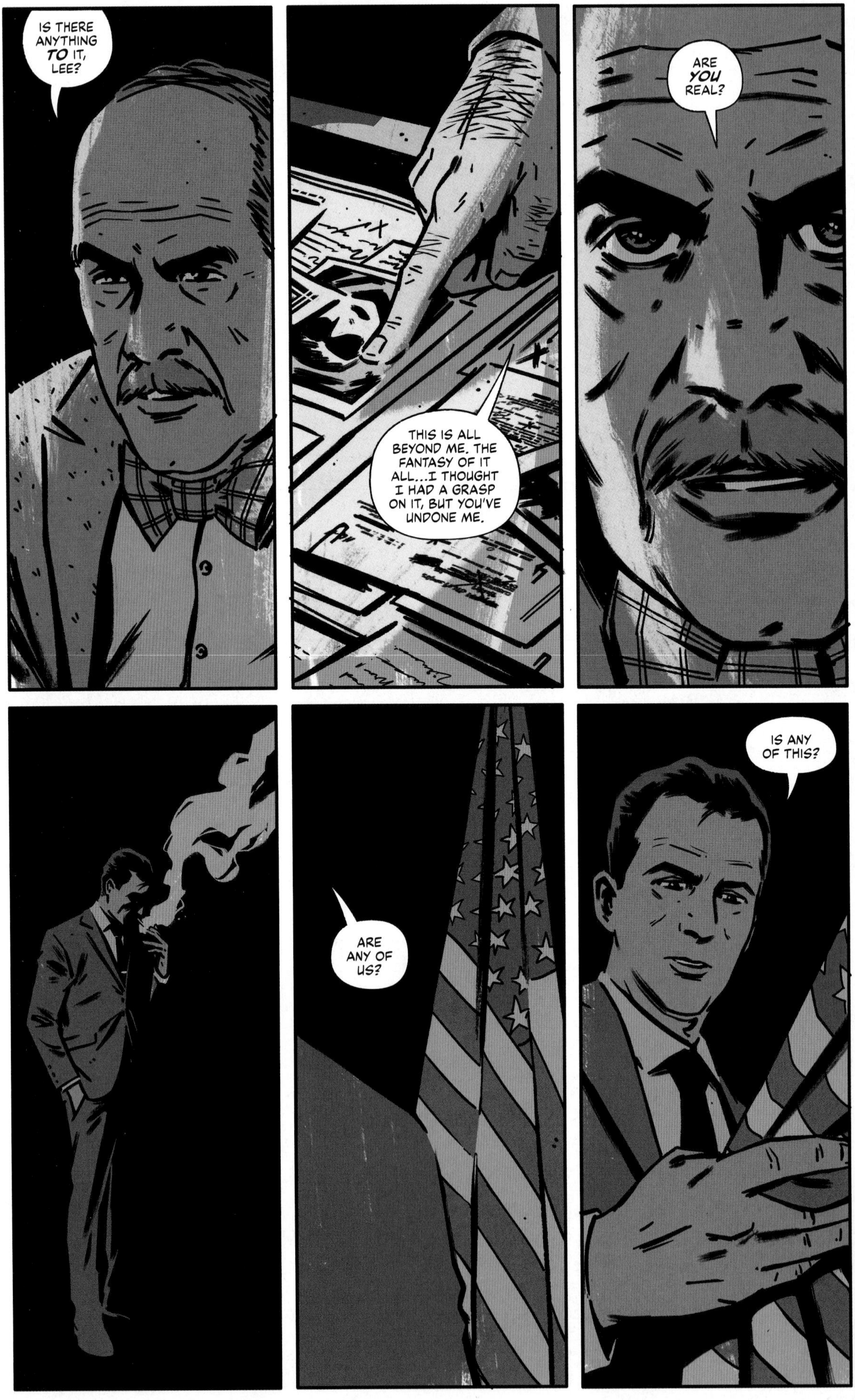
IS THERE ANYTHING TO IT, LEE?
THIS IS ALL BEYOND ME. THE FANTASY OF IT ALL...I THOUGHT I HAD A GRASP ON IT, BUT YOU'VE UNDONE ME.
ARE YOU REAL?
ARE ANY OF US?
IS ANY OF THIS?

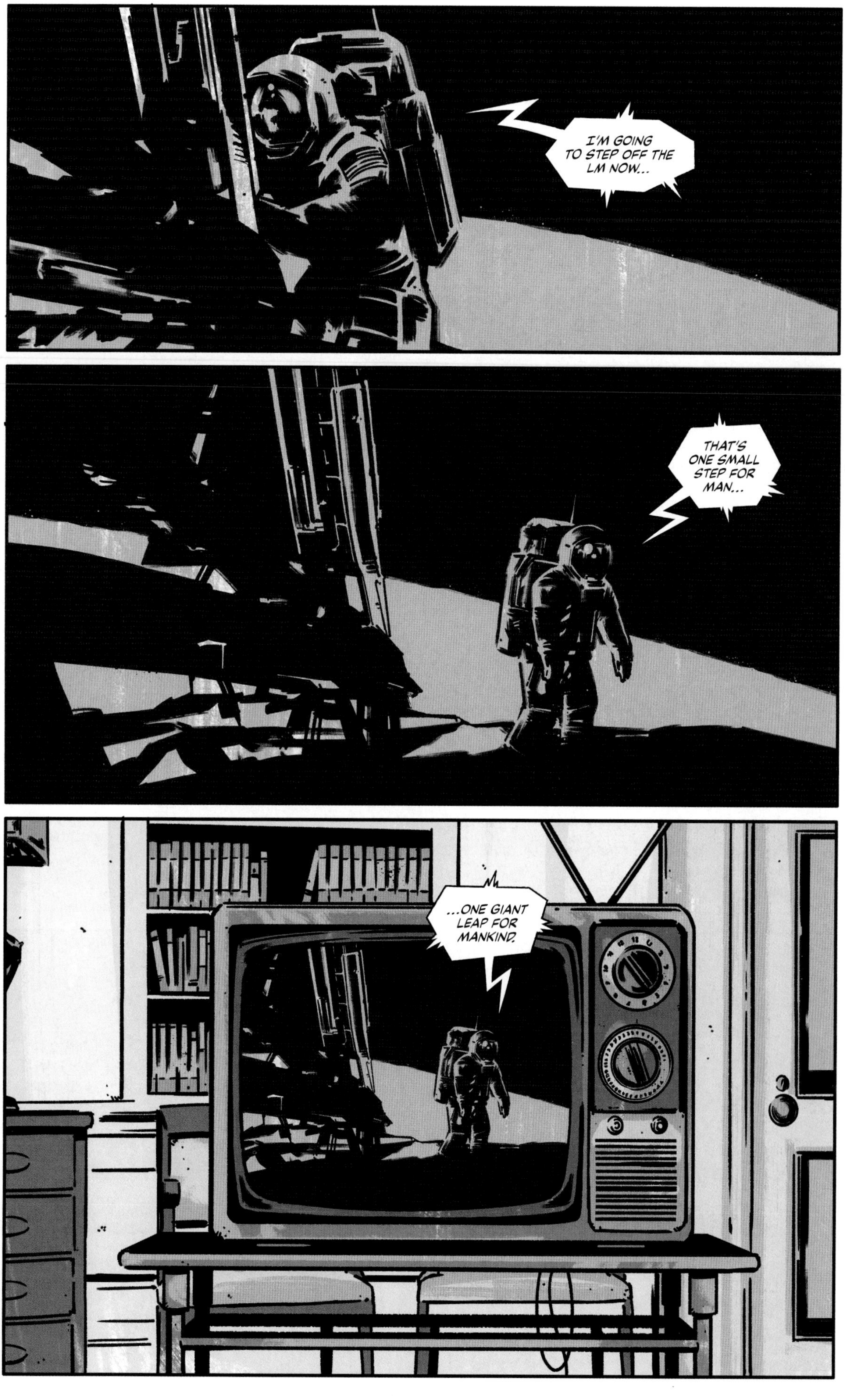
I'M GOING TO STEP OFF THE LM NOW...
THAT'S ONE SMALL STEP FOR MAN...
...ONE GIANT LEAP FOR MANKIND.

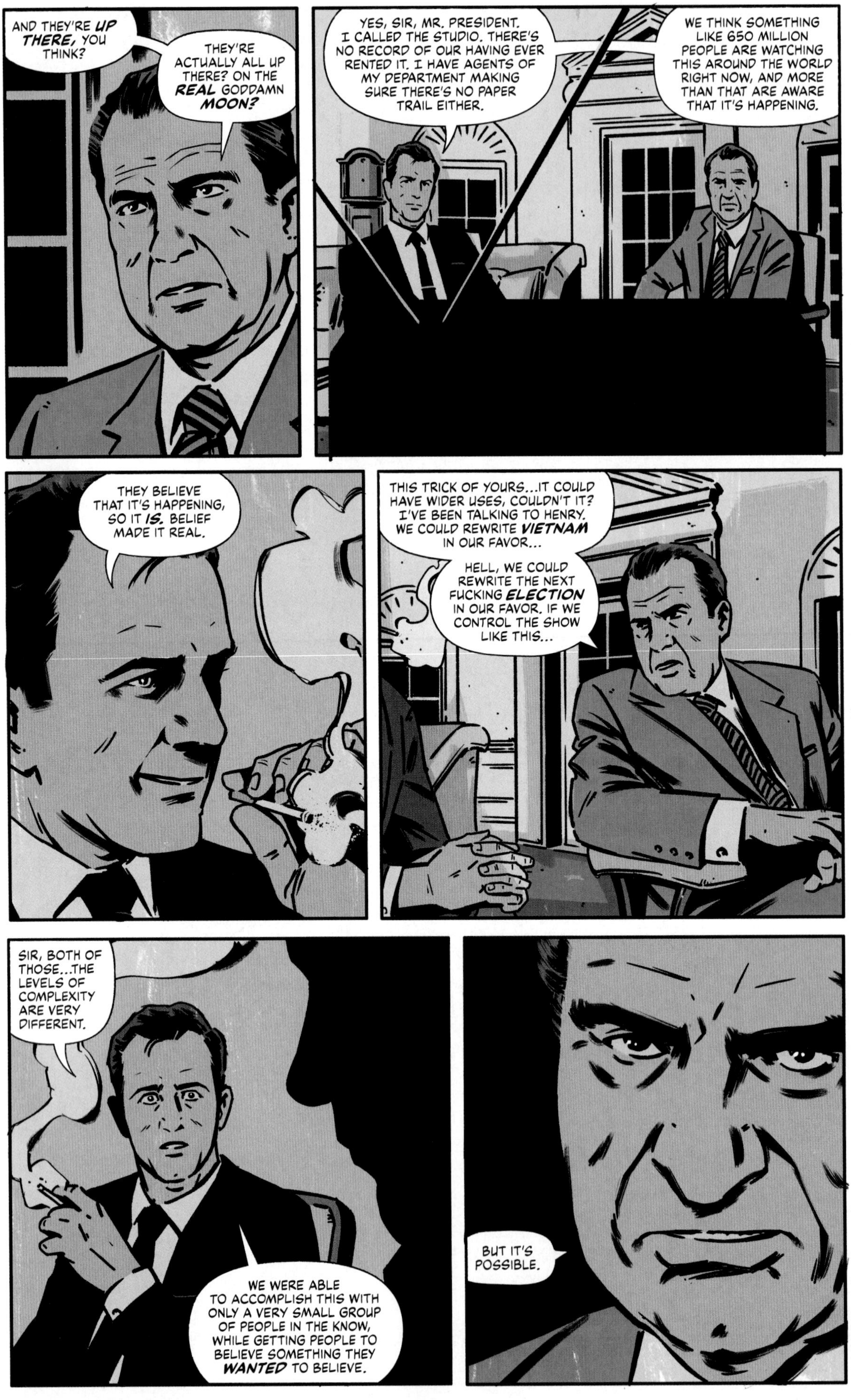
AND THEY'RE UP THERE, YOU THINK?
THEY'RE ACTUALLY ALL UP THERE? ON THE REAL GODDAMN MOON?
YES, SIR, MR. PRESIDENT. I CALLED THE STUDIO. THERE'S NO RECORD OF OUR HAVING EVER RENTED IT. I HAVE AGENTS OF MY DEPARTMENT MAKING SURE THERE'S NO PAPER TRAIL EITHER.
WE THINK SOMETHING LIKE 650 MILLION PEOPLE ARE WATCHING THIS AROUND THE WORLD RIGHT NOW, AND MORE THAN THAT ARE AWARE THAT IT'S HAPPENING.
THEY BELIEVE THAT IT'S HAPPENING, SO IT IS. BELIEF MADE IT REAL.
THIS TRICK OF YOURS...IT COULD HAVE WIDER USES, COULDN'T IT? I'VE BEEN TALKING TO HENRY. WE COULD REWRITE VIETNAM IN OUR FAVOR...
HELL, WE COULD REWRITE THE NEXT FUCKING ELECTION IN OUR FAVOR. IF WE CONTROL THE SHOW LIKE THIS...
SIR, BOTH OF THOSE...THE LEVELS OF COMPLEXITY ARE VERY DIFFERENT.
WE WERE ABLE TO ACCOMPLISH THIS WITH ONLY A VERY SMALL GROUP OF PEOPLE IN THE KNOW, WHILE GETTING PEOPLE TO BELIEVE SOMETHING THEY WANTED TO BELIEVE.
BUT IT'S POSSIBLE.

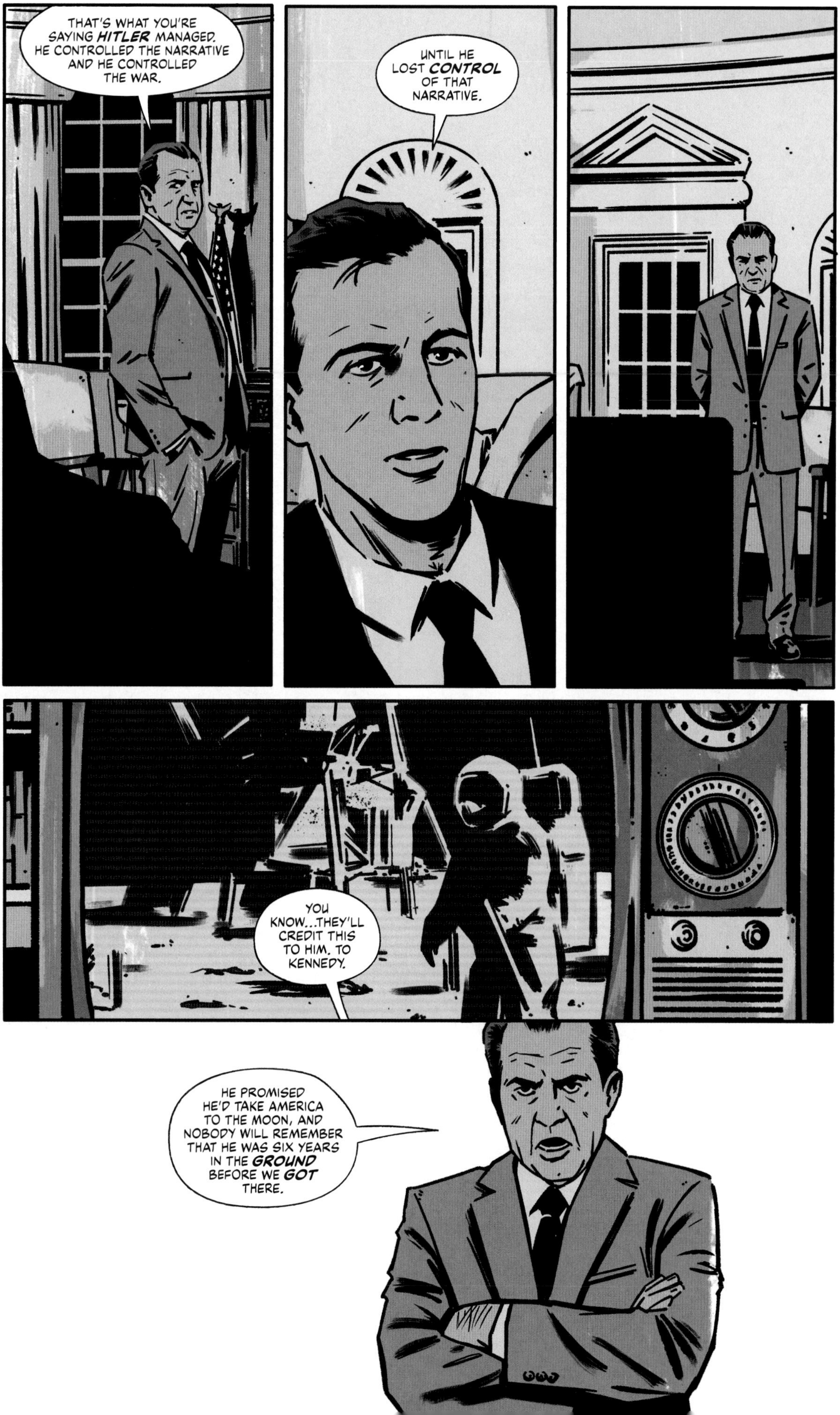
THAT'S WHAT YOU'RE SAYING HITLER MANAGED. HE CONTROLLED THE NARRATIVE AND HE CONTROLLED THE WAR.
UNTIL HE LOST CONTROL OF THAT NARRATIVE.
YOU KNOW...THEY'LL CREDIT THIS TO HIM. TO KENNEDY.
HE PROMISED HE'D TAKE AMERICA TO THE MOON, AND NOBODY WILL REMEMBER THAT HE WAS SIX YEARS IN THE GROUND BEFORE WE GOT THERE.

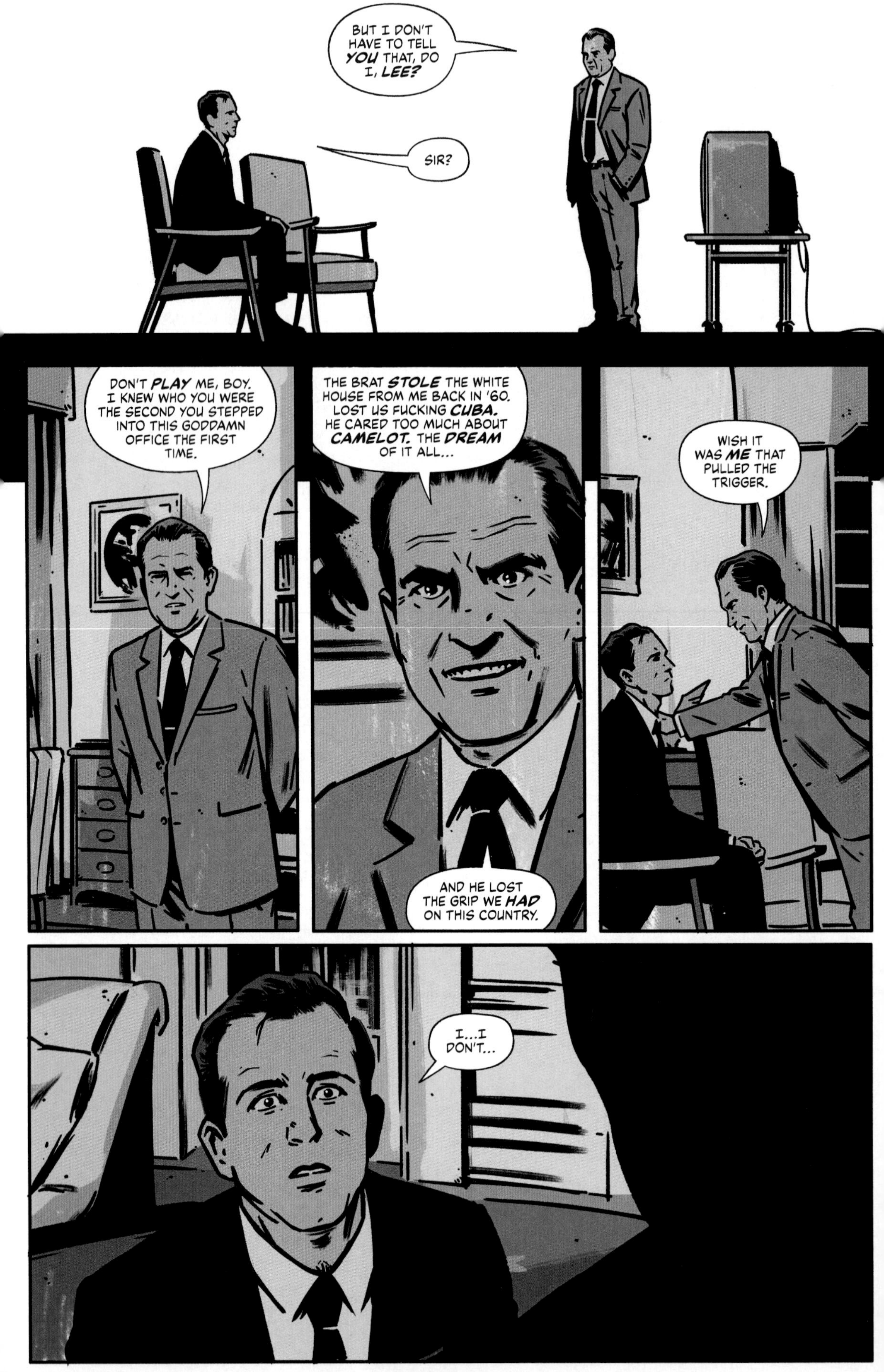
BUT I DON'T HAVE TO TELL YOU THAT, DO I, LEE?
SIR?
DON'T PLAY ME, BOY. I KNEW WHO YOU WERE THE SECOND YOU STEPPED INTO THIS GODDAMN OFFICE THE FIRST TIME.
THE BRAT STOLE THE WHITE HOUSE FROM ME BACK IN '60. LOST US FUCKING CUBA. HE CARED TOO MUCH ABOUT CAMELOT. THE DREAM OF IT ALL...
AND HE LOST THE GRIP WE HAD ON THIS COUNTRY.
WISH IT WAS ME THAT PULLED THE TRIGGER.
I...I DON'T...

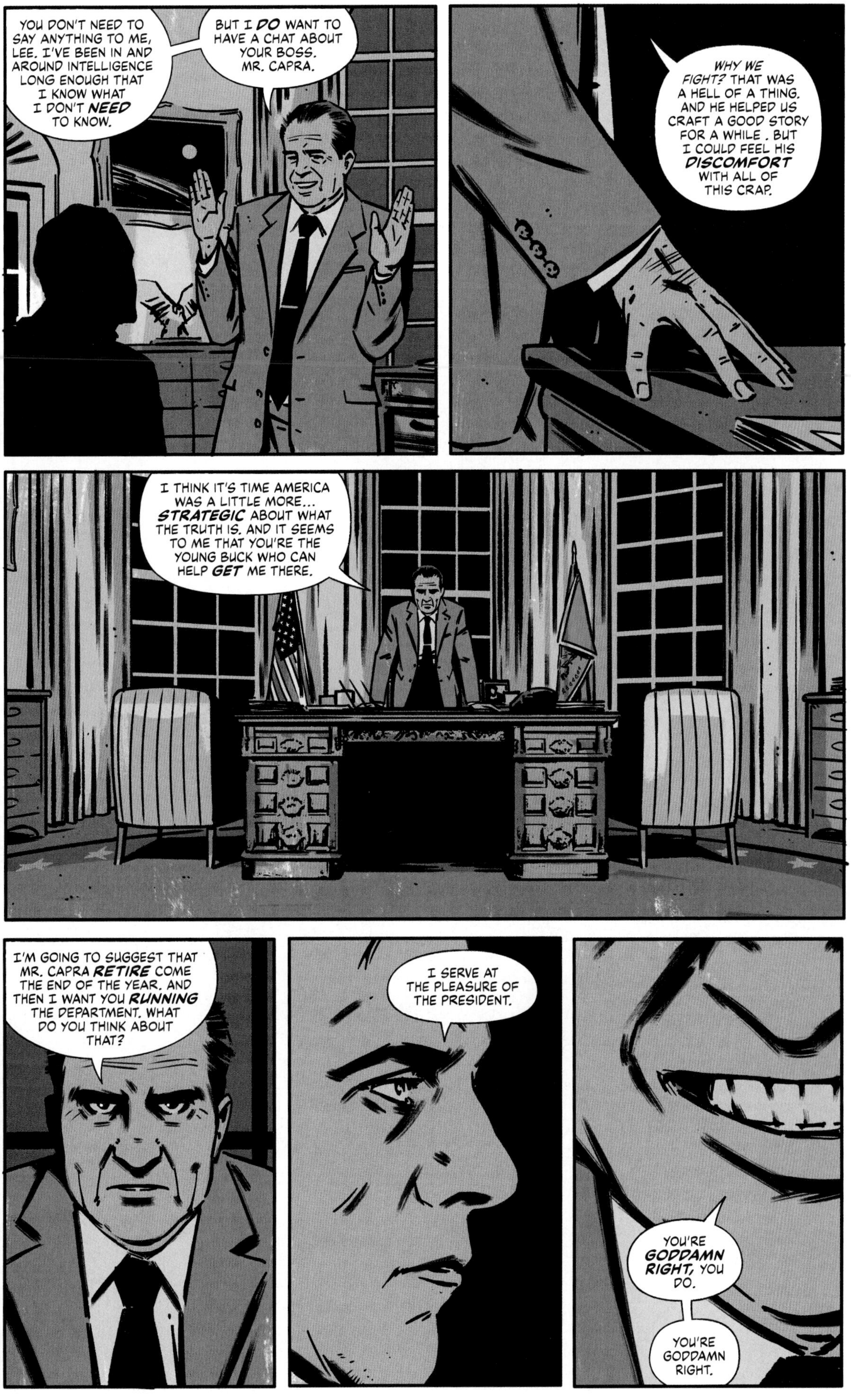
YOU DON'T NEED TO SAY ANYTHING TO ME, LEE. I'VE BEEN IN AND AROUND INTELLIGENCE LONG ENOUGH THAT I KNOW WHAT I DON'T NEED TO KNOW.
BUT I DO WANT TO HAVE A CHAT ABOUT YOUR BOSS. MR. CAPRA.
WHY WE FIGHT? THAT WAS A HELL OF A THING. AND HE HELPED US CRAFT A GOOD STORY FOR A WHILE . BUT I COULD FEEL HIS DISCOMFORT WITH ALL OF THIS CRAP.
I THINK IT'S TIME AMERICA WAS A LITTLE MORE... STRATEGIC ABOUT WHAT THE TRUTH IS. AND IT SEEMS TO ME THAT YOU'RE THE YOUNG BUCK WHO CAN HELP GET ME THERE.
I'M GOING TO SUGGEST THAT MR. CAPRA RETIRE COME THE END OF THE YEAR. AND THEN I WANT YOU RUNNING THE DEPARTMENT. WHAT DO YOU THINK ABOUT THAT?
I SERVE AT THE PLEASURE OF THE PRESIDENT.
YOU'RE GODDAMN RIGHT, YOU DO.
YOU'RE GODDAMN RIGHT.

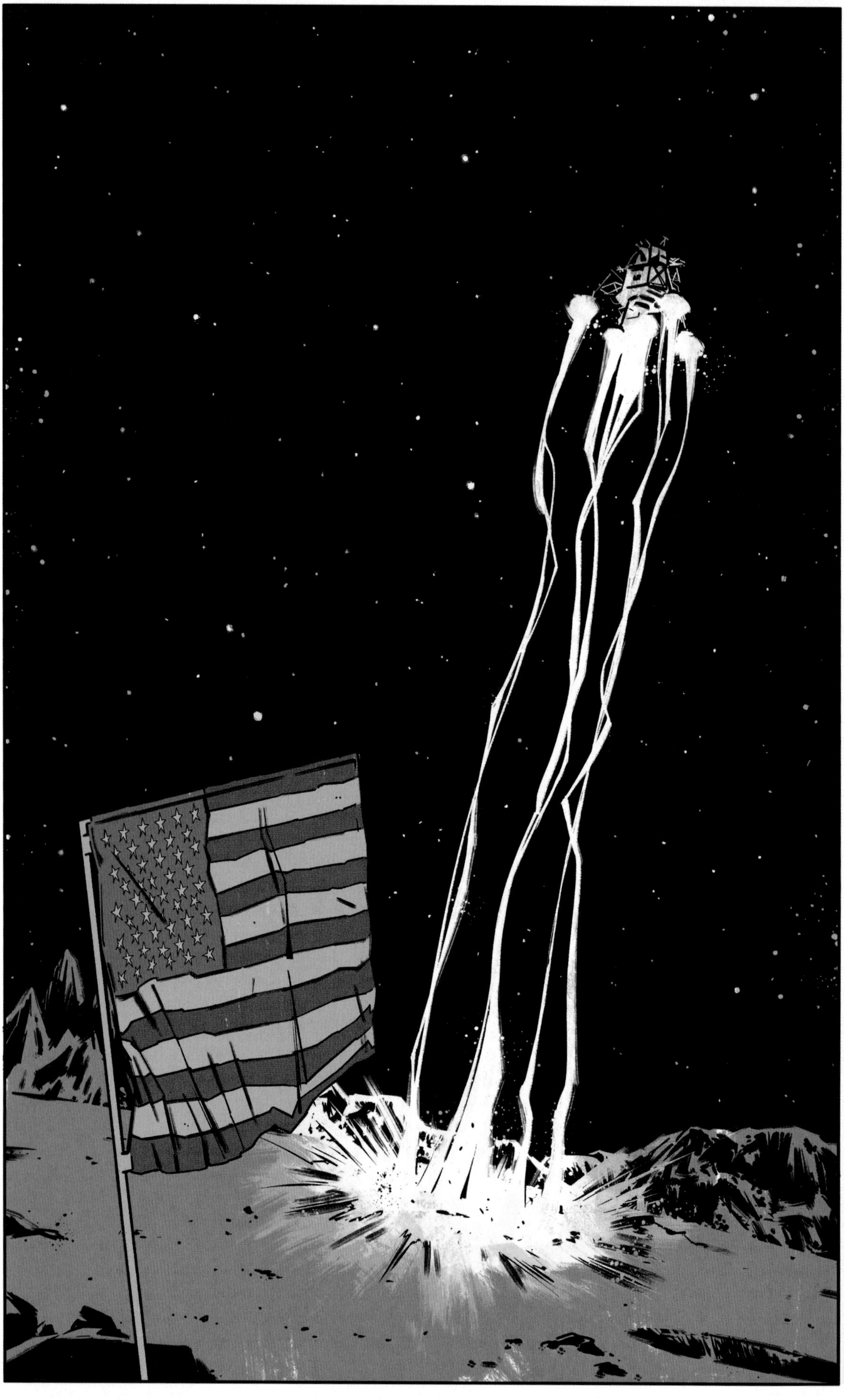

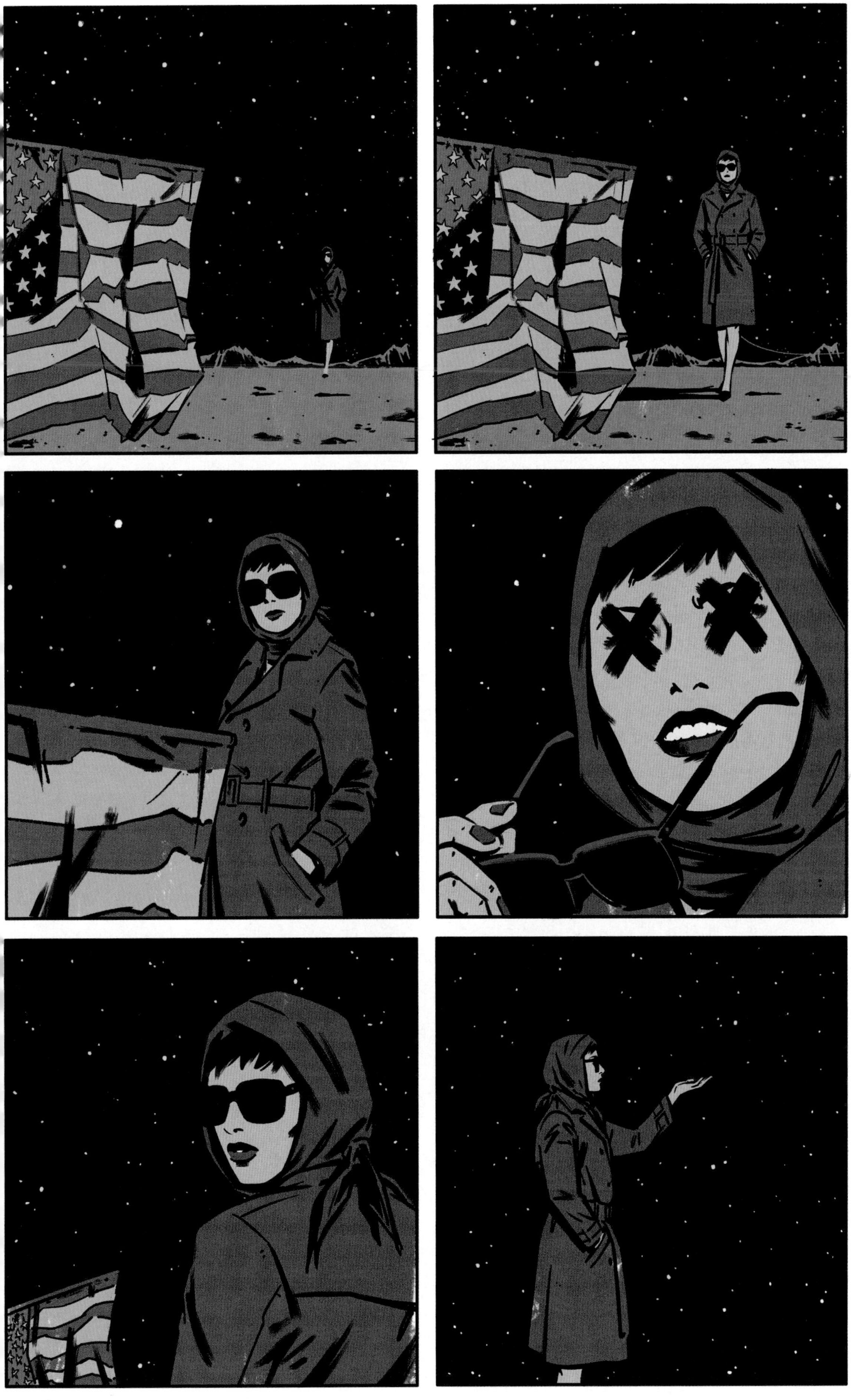

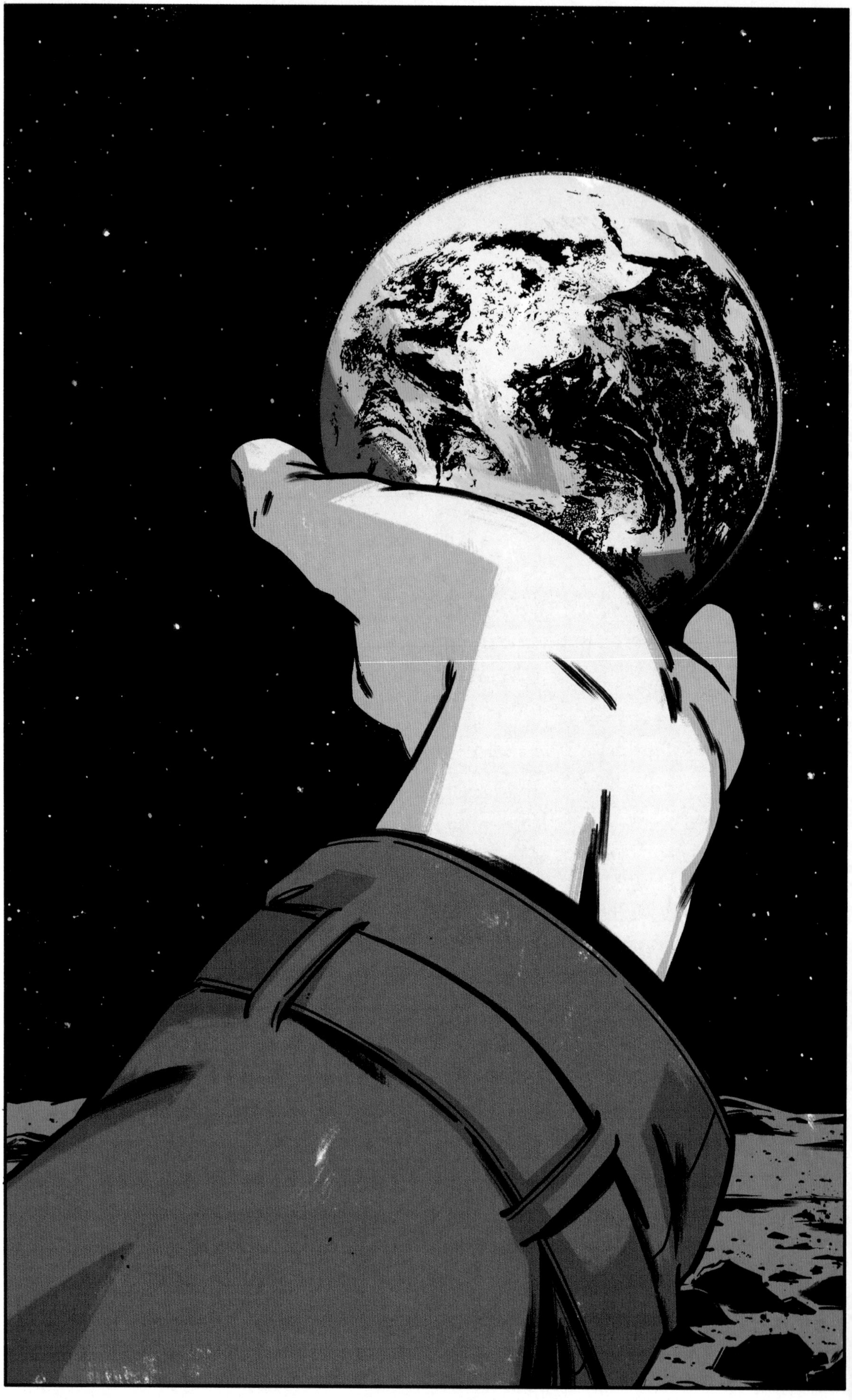

DEPARTMENT OF TRUTH

UNITED STATES OF AMERICA

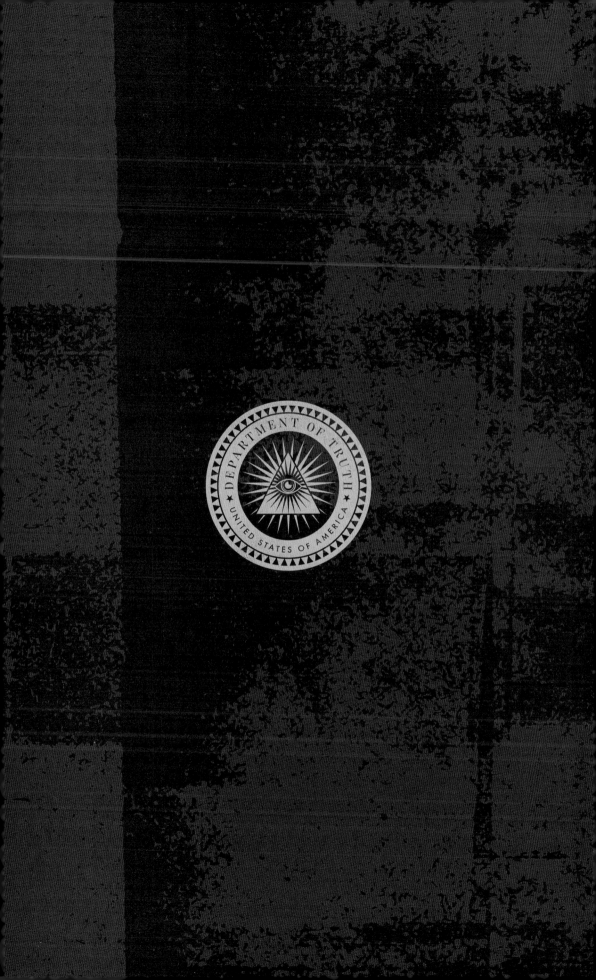

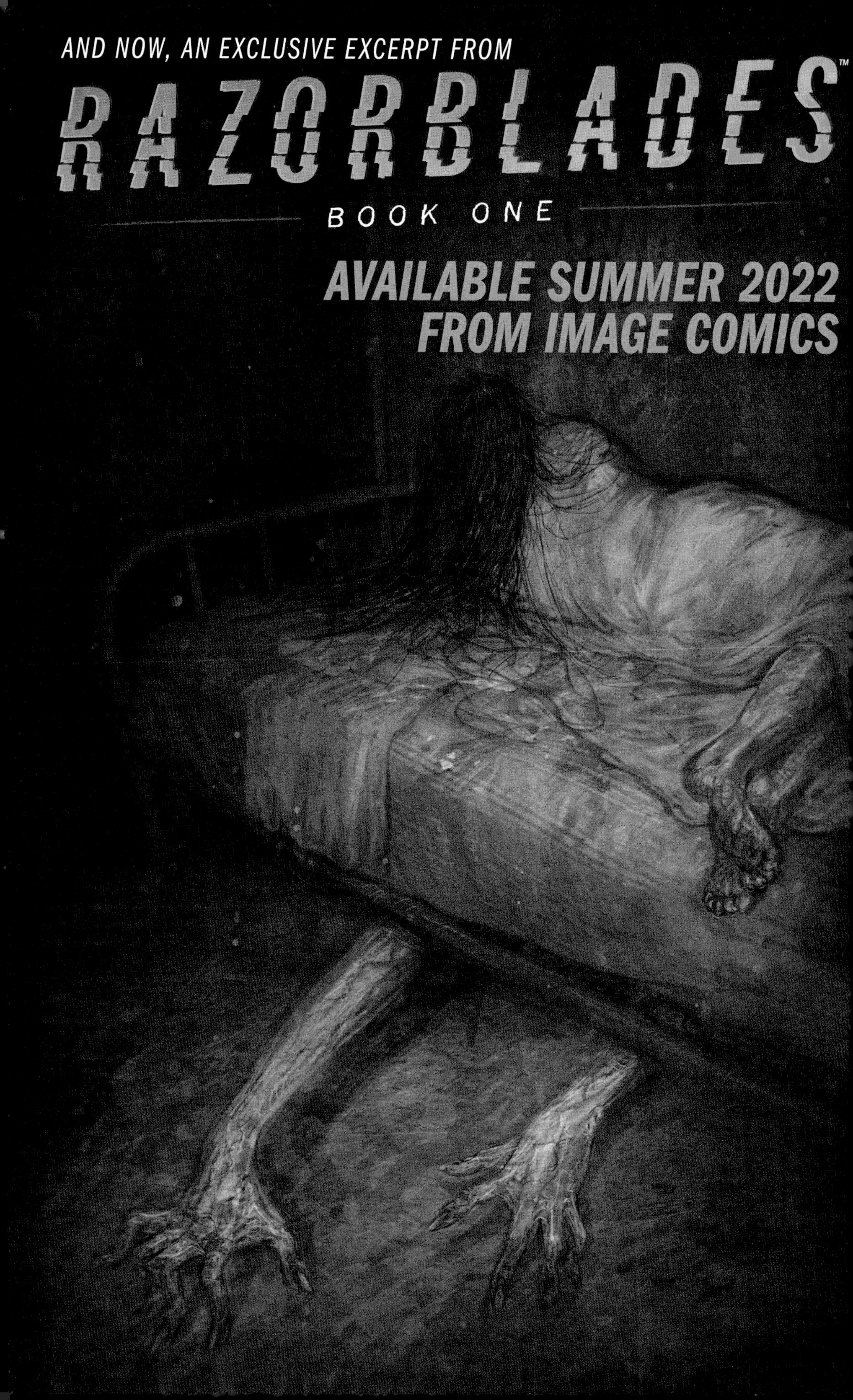
AND NOW, AN EXCLUSIVE EXCERPT FROM
RAZORBLADES™
BOOK ONE
AVAILABLE SUMMER 2022
FROM IMAGE COMICS

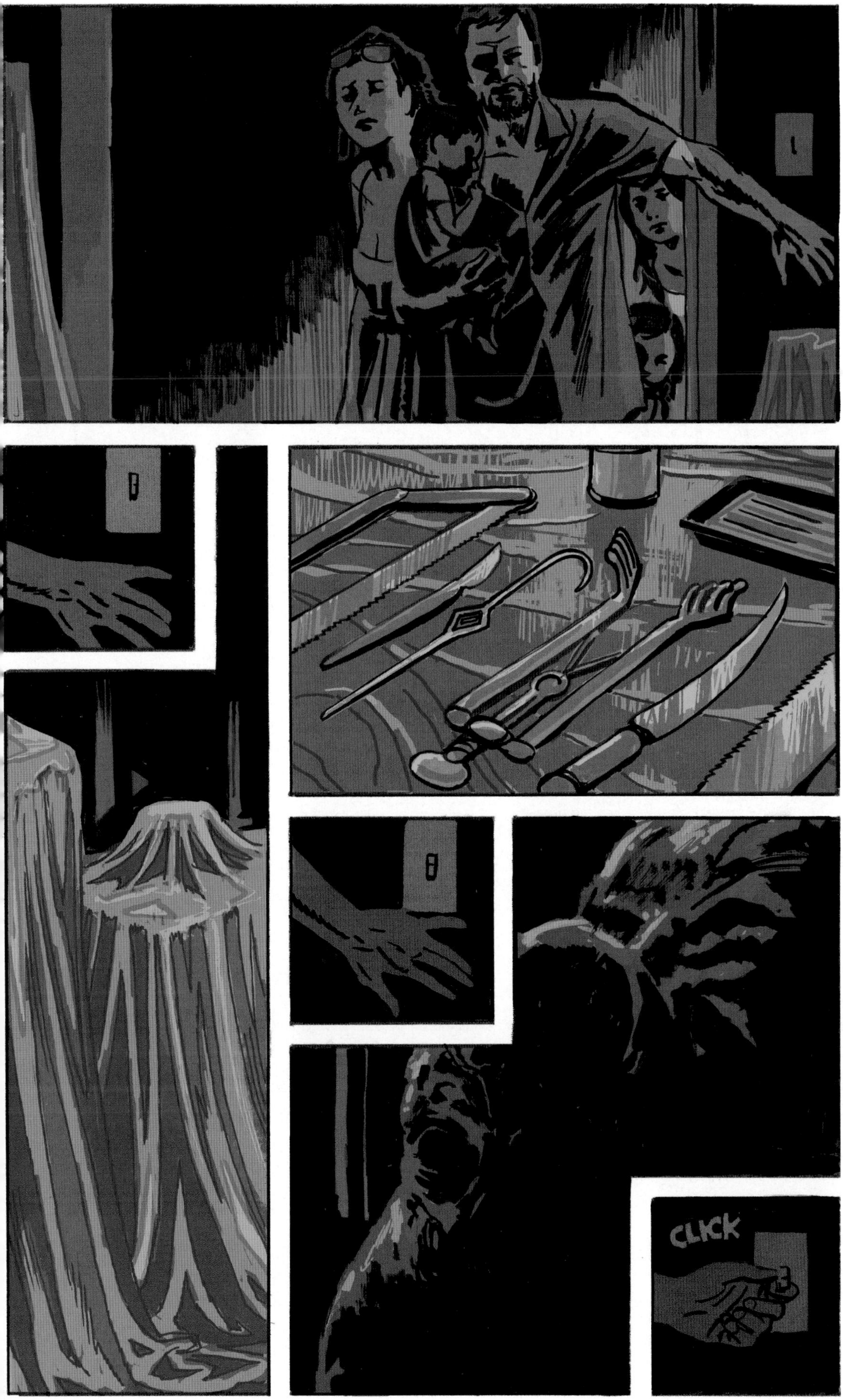
CLICK

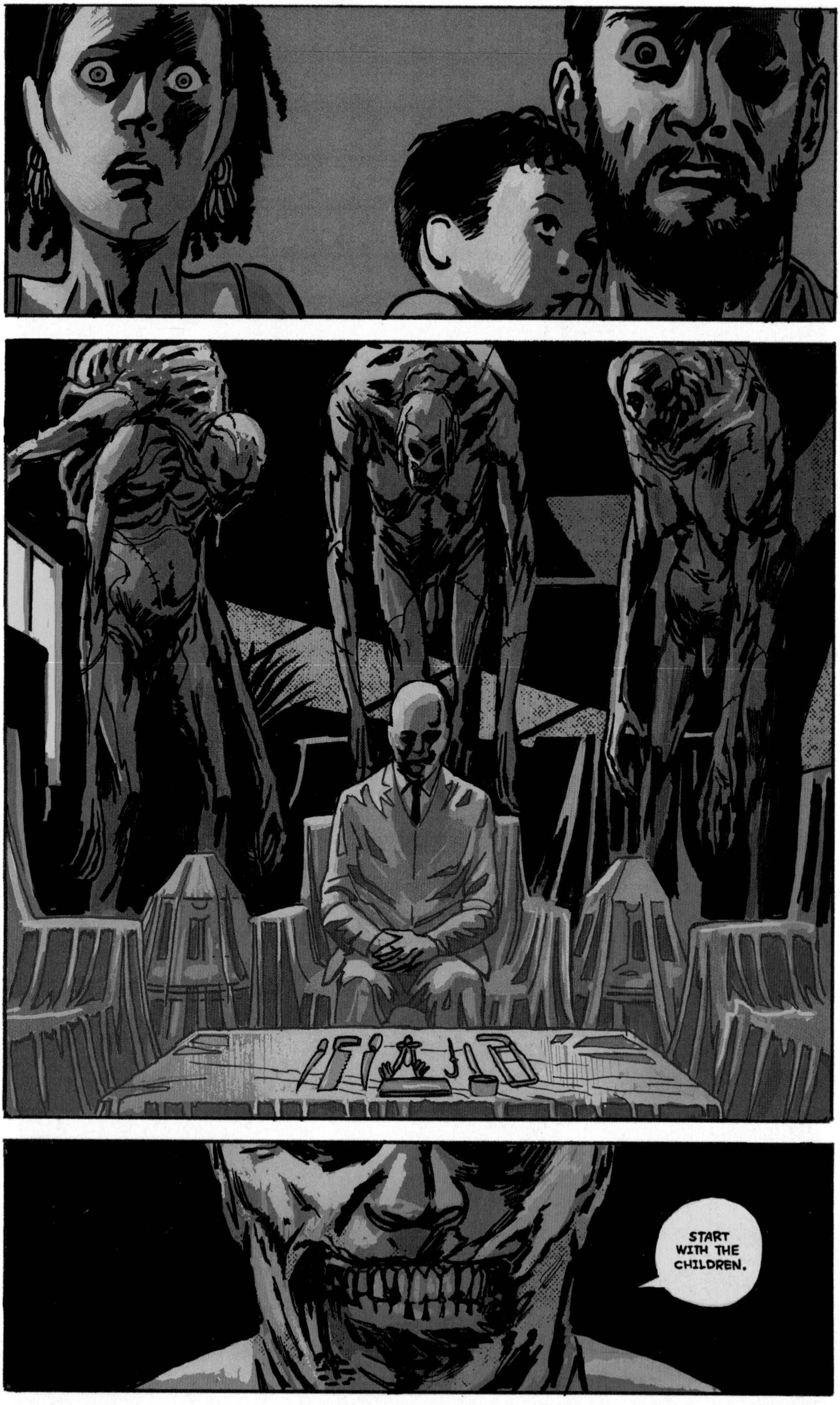
START WITH THE CHILDREN.